CISCO TCP/IP ROUTING PROFESSIONAL REFERENCE

THE McGRAW-HILL SERIES ON COMPUTER COMMUNICATIONS (SELECTED TITLES)

0-07-005147-X Bates *Voice and Data Communications Handbook*
0-07-005669-2 Benner *Fibre Channel: Gigabit Communications and I/O Computer Networks*
0-07-005560-2 Black *TCP/IP and Related Protocols,* 2/e
0-07-005590-4 Black *Frame Relay Networks: Specifications & Implementation,* 2/e
0-07-011456-2 Chiong *SNA Interconnections: Bridging and Routing SNA in Hierarchical, Peer, and High-Speed Networks*
0-07-016769-9 Dhawan *Mobile Computing: A Systems Integrator's Handbook*
0-07-020359-8 Feit *SNMP: A Guide to Network Management*
0-07-021389-5 Feit *TCP/IP: Architecture, Protocols & Implementation with IPv6 and IP Security,* 2/e
0-07-024043-4 Goralski *Introduction to ATM Networking*
0-07-034249-0 Kessler *ISDN: Concepts, Facilities, and Services,* 3/e
0-07-035968-7 Kumar *Broadband Communications*
0-07-041051-8 Matusow *SNA, APPN, HPR and TCP/IP Integration*
0-07-060362-6 McDysan/Spohn *ATM: Theory and Applications*
0-07-044362-9 Muller *Network Planning Procurement and Management*
0-07-046380-8 Nemzow *The Ethernet Management Guide,* 3/e
0-07-051506-9 Ranade/Sacket *Introduction to SNA Networking,* 2/e
0-07-054991-5 Russell *Signaling System #7*
0-07-057199-6 Saunders *The McGraw-Hill High-Speed LANs Handbook*
0-07-057639-4 Simonds *Network Security: Data and Voice Communications*
0-07-069416-8 Summers *ISDN Implementor's Guide*
0-07-063263-4 Taylor *The McGraw-Hill Internetworking Handbook*
0-07-063301-0 Taylor *McGraw-Hill Internetworking Command Reference*
0-07-063639-7 Terplan *Effective Management of Local Area Networks,* 2/e
0-07-065766-1 Udupa *Network Management System Essentials*

Cisco TCP/IP Routing Professional Reference

Chris Lewis

McGraw-Hill, Inc.
New York · San Francisco · Washington, D.C.
Auckland · Bogotá · Caracas · Lisbon · London
Madrid · Mexico City · Milan · Montreal · New Delhi
San Juan · Singapore · Sydney · Tokyo · Toronto

Library of Congress Cataloging-in-Publication Data

Lewis, Chris (Christopher S.)
Cisco TCP/IP routing professional reference / Chris Lewis.
p. cm.
Includes index.
ISBN 0-07-041088-7
1. TCP/IP (Computer network protocol)—Handbooks, manuals, etc.
I. Title.
TK5105.585.L49 1997
004.6—dc21 97-23553
CIP

McGraw-Hill

A Division of The ***McGraw-Hill*** *Companies*

2 3 4 5 6 7 8 9 0 FGR/FGR 9 0 2 1 0 9 8 7

ISBN 0-07-041088-7

The sponsoring editor for this book was John Wyzalek, the editing supervisor was Sally Glover, and the production supervisor was Pamela Pelton. It was set in Vendome ICG by Kim Sheran of McGraw-Hill's Professional Book Group composition unit, Hightstown, N.J.

Printed and bound by Quebecor/Fairfield.

This book is printed on recycled, acid-free paper containing a minimum of 50% recycled, de-inked fiber.

CONTENTS

ACKNOWLEDGMENTS

First, I have to thank my wife Claudia, whose love and support were my greatest resources when writing this book. Next I have to thank Thomas Astuto and Deborah Curtis for doing a fine job of creating all the figures and for making all the changes I regularly requested. I also thank Mike Barnow and the rest of the Westchester Track Club for giving me something to do that was completely unrelated to TCP/IP during the last six months.

Throughout the text, I have referred to the Cisco published documentation to check the syntax of commands used. References to the Cisco documentation are used with the permission of Cisco Systems Inc., copyright ©1996, all rights reserved. The authorization I received gave me permission to use the materials "as is," with no expressed or implied warranties from Cisco, who disclaims all liability arising out of the authorized use of such material.

Contents

INTRODUCTION

This book differs from most other books on TCP/IP because it focuses on how to implement the TCP/IP protocols using the most prevalent TCP/IP routing device in use today, the Cisco router. The book provides detailed descriptions, examples, and configurations that can be used for building real-world internetworks. The text begins at a level appropriate for the TCP/IP and router novice, but advances to cover topics such as routing protocol optimization, security, implementing multiprotocol networks, and troubleshooting techniques that experienced router engineers will find useful.

The TCP/IP set of networking protocols rapidly is becoming the de facto standard for local and wide area networking. Its prominence is due in part to its openness. It is considered an open standard because no one commercial organization controls the standard. This allows all vendors an equal footing when developing TCP/IP products and gives devices from different vendors a better-than-even chance of working together properly.

In addition to being an open standard, the TCP/IP protocols have proved themselves durable in the largest network in the world, the Internet.

Fueling the current growth of the Internet are World Wide Web services, which make it easy for anyone who can operate a computer mouse to retrieve information from anywhere in the world. This technology is so attractive to organizations that most forward-thinking companies are building much of their information storage and retrieval systems around it on their own internal intranets. Intranets use the same TCP/IP network protocols as the public Internet but are implemented on the company's own private network.

To support this new computing paradigm, a TCP/IP network is required. To implement a TCP/IP network, you need routers. If you are involved in any way with network administration, design, or management, router technology either is or will become important to you.

This book is clearly not a novel, and I don't expect it to be read as one. Of course, you can start at Chapter 1 and read all chapters in sequence, but this is not how I use my technical books. I suspect that most people will read the chapters that are of particular interest to them

at different times. To support this type of use, there is some duplication of information across chapters when necessary.

Terminology

Throughout the book, I have used some terms that should be defined. First, let's discuss how we identify, in networking terms, computers that are grouped together. An *internetwork* is a collection of networks connected together. A *network* refers to all devices that belong to one network number. A *subnetwork,* or *subnet,* is a section of a network configured to act as if it were a separate network as far as other computers configured on the same network number are concerned.

Another potentially confusing term is that of *gateway.* In general networking terms, a gateway is an Application layer device, something that converts from one type of communications protocol to another. In TCP/IP language, a gateway is synonymous with a router.

Conventions

Outputs from Cisco router screen displays are presented in many figures and parts of the text. Any text or commands that are to be entered into the terminal attached to the router are in **`boldface`** type; the `nonbold` text represents what is displayed by the router. In these screen displays, I have had to indicate that at times, a shifting key and letter key must be depressed simultaneously to get the desired response. An example is <Ctrl-Z>, which means that you hold down the key labeled "Ctrl" while pressing the "Z" key.

TRADEMARKS

Many of the company names referred to in this text are claimed as trademarks by their respective organizations. The trademarks used in this text that I am aware of are: Cisco, the Cisco Systems logo, AT&T, Racal, Windows, Windows NT, Microsoft, Novell, NetWare, IBM, MCI, and Cabletron.

About the Author

Christopher S. Lewis (London, UK) is a vice-president at ILX Systems, a chartered engineer, a member of the Institution of Electrical Engineers and frequently publishes articles in leading networking journals.

CHAPTER 1

Router Basics

Objectives

The objectives of this chapter are as follows:

- Explain the role of a router in an internetwork.
- Discuss how a router is both similar to and different from other network computing devices.
- Introduce the Cisco router user interface.

Router Concepts

This section introduces router technology and its responsibility in an *internetwork,* an accepted networking industry term for a set of many interconnected networks. Each individual network will have its own network number that must be unique for that particular internetwork. If some of the terms used here are unfamiliar, don't worry; all the ideas presented in this overview are discussed in more detail and explained fully in later chapters.

Routers direct traffic through an internetwork, based on information learned from network protocols. Let's discuss some of the goals of these computer network protocols.

With an internetwork that has hundreds or even thousands of computers linked together, there has to be some agreed-upon way for those devices to address one another and communicate. As a network grows larger, it is not feasible for each computer to keep track of the individual address of every other computer on the internetwork. There must be some scheme for reducing the amount of information each computer has to hold locally in order to communicate with every other computer.

The scheme used involves splitting an internetwork into many discrete but connected networks, which may themselves be split into subnetworks (Fig. 1-1). The job of keeping track of these discrete networks is then given to specialized computers called *routers.* Using this method, the network computers need only keep track of the networks on the internetwork, rather than keeping track of every network computer.

The best analogy I can think of for describing how computers on an internetwork address each other is the postal service. When you address a letter, you provide an apartment number, street name and number, town, and state. In computer terms, messages are delivered by *application*

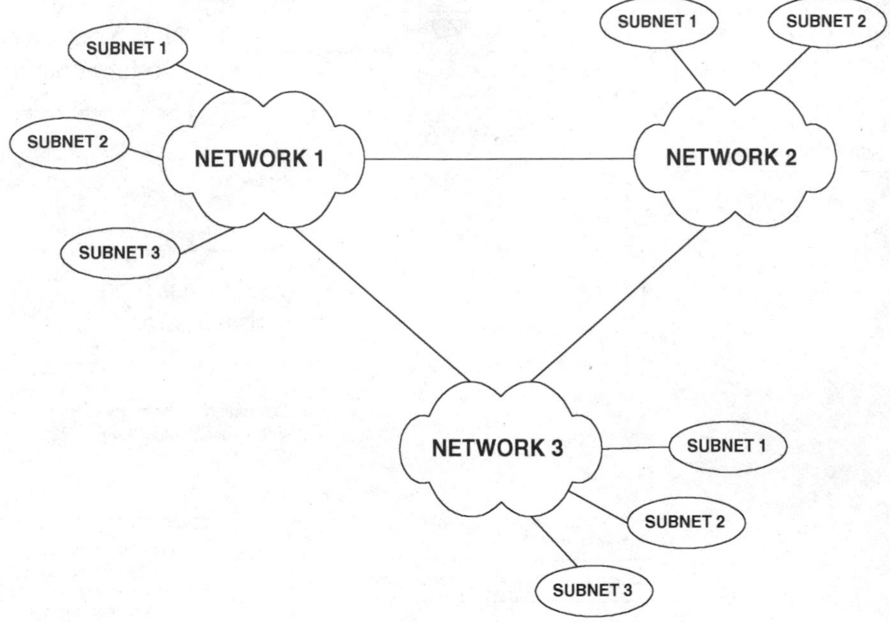

Figure 1-1 Interconnection of networks and subnetworks on an internetwork

port number, host number, subnet number, and *network number* (Fig. 1-2). These terms will be discussed fully in subsequent sections.

The key concept is that when the postal service receives a letter for delivery to another town, the first thing postal workers do is to send it to the distribution office in the destination town. From there the letter goes to the people that deliver for that particular street, and finally, the letter is delivered to its destination.

Computer networks follow a similar process. The message sent on the internetwork initially gets sent to a router that is connected to the destination network number. This router, in effect acting as a distribution center for this network, will send the message out on the destination subnet number, and finally the message is delivered to the destination port number in the destination machine.

Figure 1-3 shows a simple internetwork with routers connecting different network numbers. In this figure, networks 1, 2, 3, and 4 have hosts on them and networks 5, 6, and 7 do not. Networks 5, 6, and 7 are there purely to connect the routers over a local or wide area network. In this internetwork, hosts X and Z must be configured for the same network number (in this case, 2). In addition, the router interfaces that are connected to the same network (for example, interface 2 on router C and interface 1 on router A), must be configured for the same network number (in this case, 5).

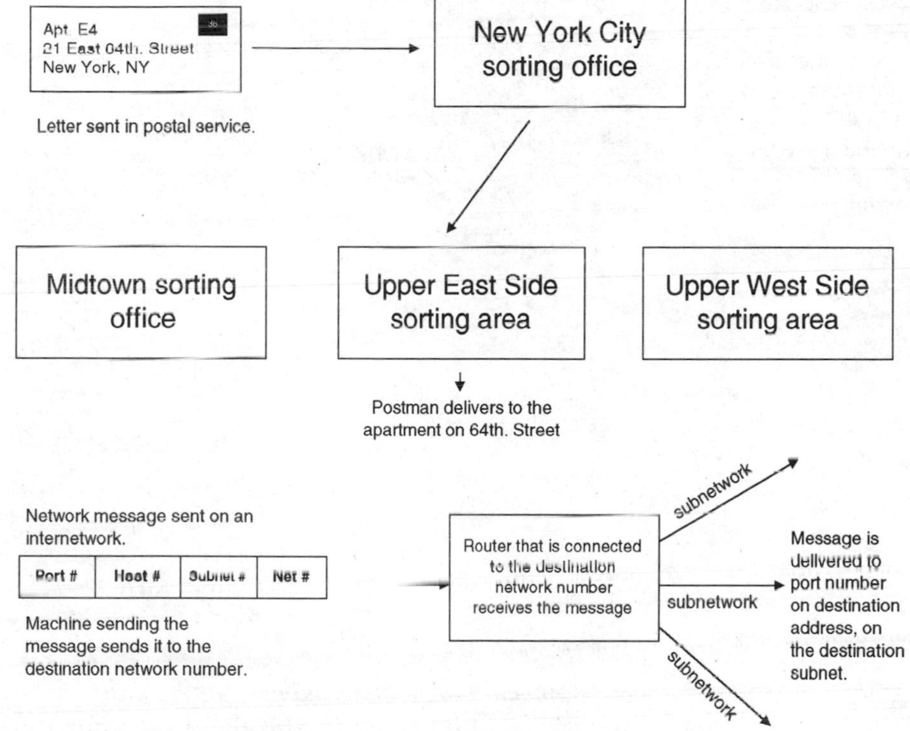

Figure 1-2 Comparing the Postal Service to an internetwork addressing scheme

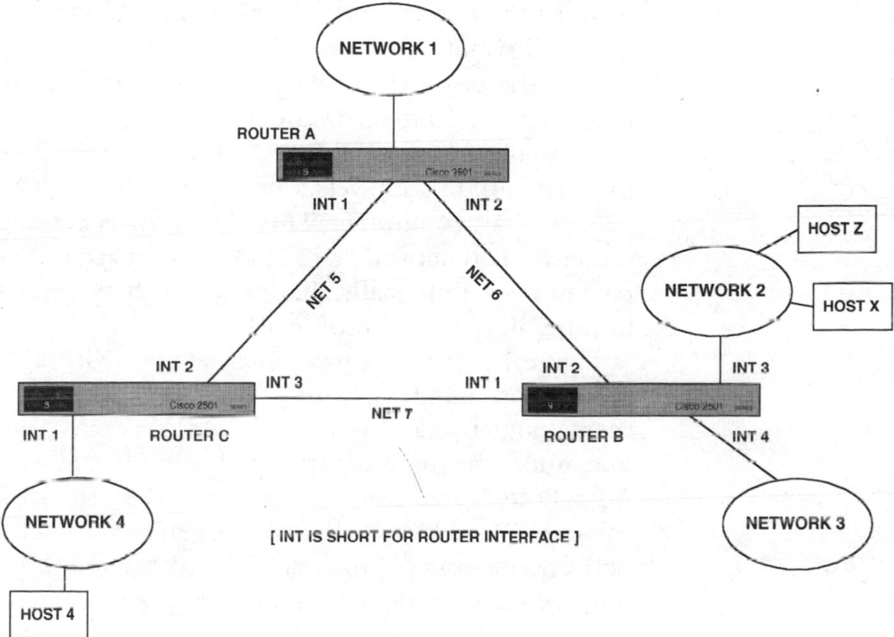

Figure 1-3 Simple internetwork connectivity

Using the postal service analogy again, routers that are connected to two networks can be thought of as houses that have entrances on two streets. In Fig. 1-4, we see a house that has two entrances, one on Subnet-1 Street and the other on Subnet-2 Street. Both the address on Subnet-1 Street and the address on Subnet-2 Street are good for purposes of delivering a letter to the house. This is analogous to a router being connected to two network numbers. In Fig. 1-3, the address for interface 1, interface 2, or interface 3 is good for delivering a message to router A.

Routers by their very nature seek to route packets from one network number to another. This statement has two immediate practical implications for us. First, you cannot configure the same network number on more than one interface on a router. (Much later we will cover the case in which subnet masks allow the same network number, but different subnet numbers, to be configured on different interfaces on the same router.) Second, because a broadcast has a destination network number, a router does not forward broadcasts by default. (Again, we will discuss later how a router can be configured to forward broadcast packets).

Routers Compared to Bridges

Routers typically are used to connect geographically dispersed networks together, and to make feasible connecting a large number of computers together. Before routers became popular, *bridges* often were used to achieve the same goals. Bridges were good for small networks, but had problems working in larger environments. Bridges keep track

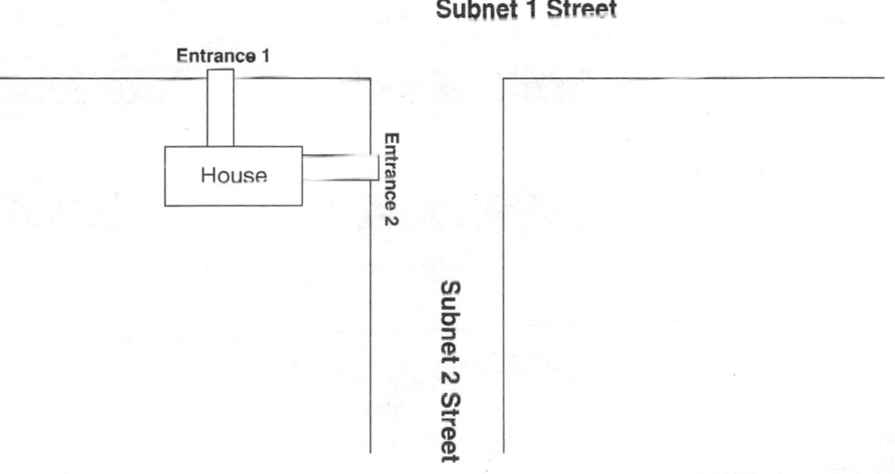

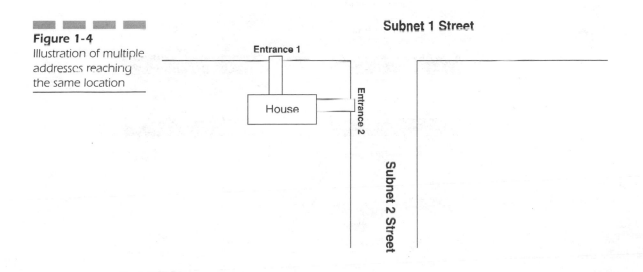

Figure 1-4
Illustration of multiple addresses reaching the same location

of all the individual computers on a network. The problem with using bridges to connect large numbers of computers together is that bridges do not understand network numbers, so any broadcast generated anywhere on the network gets sent everywhere. The difference between how routers and bridges handle broadcasts is illustrated in Fig. 1-5.

Many PC networking systems make extensive use of broadcasts, which leads to bridged networks having significant amounts of their usable bandwidth consumed by broadcasts.

At this point, it is worth contrasting the routing decisions made by routers and typical workstations or hosts on an internetwork.

Figure 1-5 Illustration of how routers and bridges handle broadcasts differently

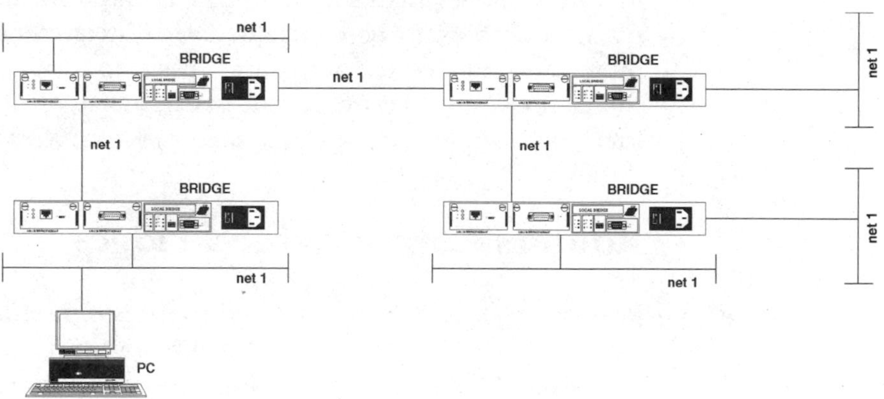

If PC sends broadcast, it will get sent to all segments by the bridges.

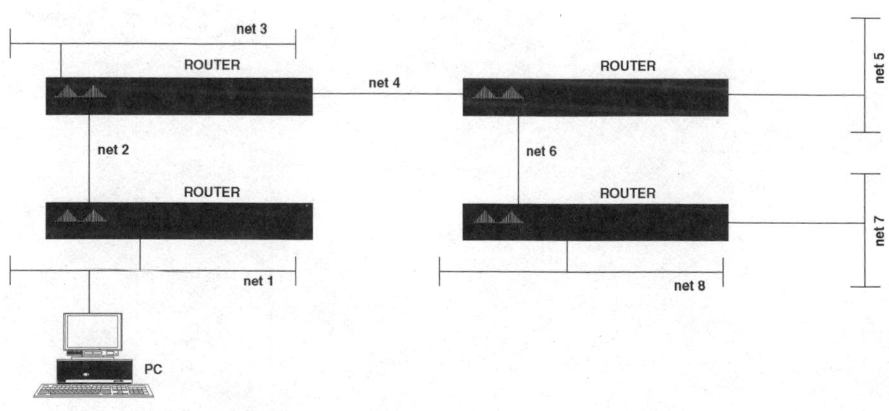

If PC sends broadcast onto net 1, it is not propagated any futher on the internetwork.

A typical workstation (a PC running a popular TCP/IP stack, for example) will require some manual configuration before it can operate on a TCP/IP network. At a minimum, you will have to configure an *IP address,* a *subnet mask,* and a *default gateway.*

The routing decisions of a workstation configured in this manner are simple. If the workstation has to send a packet to another machine that is on the same network number, the packet is sent directly to the destination machine. If the destination is on a different network number, the packet is forwarded to the default gateway for routing through the internetwork and on to the final destination.

Routers make more complex decisions. They must know how to get to all other network numbers on the internetwork and the best way to route the packets, and they need to keep track of an internetwork topology that is constantly changing due to equipment or other failures. To execute these responsibilities, a router maintains a *routing table,* which lists all the known network numbers and how to get to them. Routers also use routing protocols that keep the routing table accurate for a changing internetwork.

Routers Compared to Other Computers

Now let's look at how a Cisco router is similar to and different from other computers on an internetwork. A router is similar to other computers in that it has memory, an operating system, a configuration, and a user interface. (In Cisco routers, the operating system is called the *Internetwork Operating System,* or *IOS,* and is proprietary to Cisco.) A router also has a boot process similar to other computers in that bootstrap code is loaded from ROM, which enables the machine to load its operating system and configuration into memory.

What makes a router different from other computers is the user interface and the configuration of memory.

Router Memory Types. Typically a DOS or Unix system has one physical bank of memory chips that will be allocated by software to different functions. Routers have separate banks of memory, each dedicated to a different function. The function of these memory banks also differs between routers. An overview of the function of router memory types is presented in Table 1.1.

ROM. *Read-only memory* (ROM) contains a copy of the IOS that the router is using. The 7000-series routers have ROM chips on the route

TABLE 1.1

Summary of Router Memory Details

Type of Memory	7000	4000	2500
ROM	Upgradeable IOS	Upgradeable IOS	Non-upgradeable basic OS
RAM Shared	Storage Buffers	Storage Buffers	Storage Buffers
RAM Main	IOS loaded from Flash, plus route tables and other data structures	as 7000	Routing tables and other IOS data structures only
Flash	Contains IOS	Contains IOS	Contains IOS (Router runs IOS from flash)
NVRAM	Config files	Config files	Config files

Note: Because the 2500 series runs its IOS from flash memory, a 2500 might not have enough memory in it to have the IOS upgraded while the router is running. In the 7000 and 4000 series the IOS is running in main RAM; therefore flash can be upgraded while the router is running.

processor board. The 4000 has ROM chips on the motherboard. In the 7000 and the 4000, the ROM chips can be upgraded to contain new versions of IOS. In the 2500 router and 1000-series LAN extender, the ROM chips cannot be upgraded and contain a very limited operating system, just enough to make the router operational. The IOS for a 2500-series router is contained in what is known as *flash memory.*

If you are running a version of Cisco IOS earlier than version 11, you will see one unnerving feature of the 2500 series if you attach a terminal to the console port during boot-up. The ROM IOS checks the configuration file and will not recognize most of the commands. This results in many error messages being reported to the screen. This is normal operation. When the IOS in flash memory loads, normally no error messages are displayed.

RAM. *Random access memory* (RAM) is split by the IOS into *shared* and *main* memory. *Main memory* is used to store router configuration and IOS data structures relevant to the protocol being routed. For IP, main memory is used for such things as holding routing tables and ARP tables; for IPX, main memory holds SAP and other tables. (These terms are explained later.)

Shared memory buffers packets waiting to be processed. This type of memory is only used by 4000- and 2500-series routers. The 7000 routers have a switch processor that controls the flow of packets through the router.

Flash Memory. *Flash memory* holds the current version of IOS running on the router. Flash memory is erasable memory that can be overwritten with newer versions of the IOS—unlike ROM, which is located in physical chips that cannot have their contents overwritten.

NVRAM. *Nonvolatile RAM* (NVRAM) does not lose its contents when the router is switched off. NVRAM holds the router configuration.

Booting a Router. Routers boot up in a similar fashion to PCs; the procedure is as follows:

1. Load bootstrap program from ROM.
2. Load operating system (IOS, the Internetwork Operating System) from flash memory.
3. Find and load configuration file in NVRAM or on a prespecified network server. If no configuration file exists, the router enters setup mode.

Getting to Know Your Router

This section explains connecting a terminal to a router, understanding the Cisco user interface, and executing basic Cisco commands.

Connecting a Terminal to a Cisco Router

The discussion here uses connection to a Cisco 2500-series router as an example. Throughout this section, it is assumed that the router to which you are connecting has already received a basic configuration. A later section will cover configuring a router from scratch.

Figure 1-6 shows the connections that we need to make at the rear of a 2501. Each router will come with a console connection kit, which comprises a black RJ-45 cable and an array of connectors. To connect a Wyse or other standard ASCII terminal as the console, do the following:

1. Connect the RJ-45 cable to the console port on the back of the router.
2. Connect the 25-pin attachment labeled "terminal" to the other end of the RJ-45 cable.
3. Connect a male-to-male gender changer to this 25-pin connector.
4. Connect this 25-pin attachment to the Wyse port.

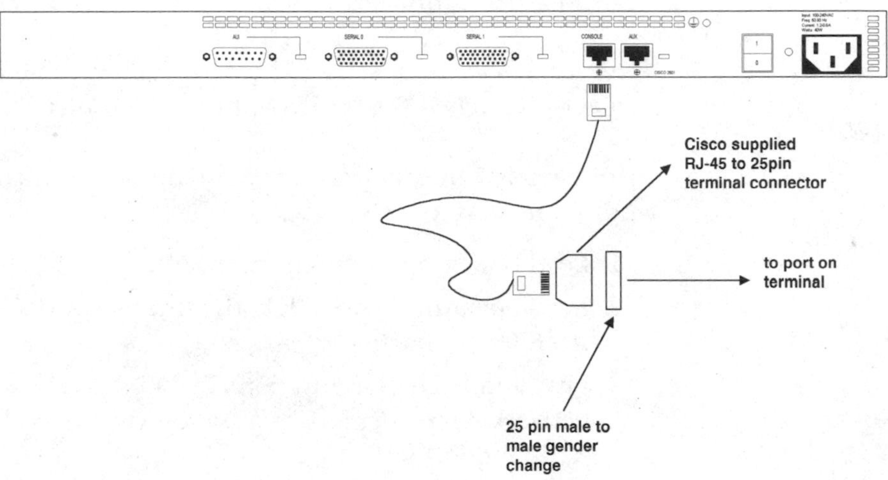

Figure 1-6
Router console port to ASCII terminal connections

A gender changer is needed because many ASCII terminal providers supply only female connectors on their terminals.

If you want to connect your router to a PC and run a terminal emulator of some kind, life is easier. Most PCs come with 9-pin serial port connectors, so just connect the 9-pin serial connector to the RJ-45 cable and link the router console port to the PC serial port. As long as you set your terminal emulation program to 9600 bps, with 8 data bits, no parity, and 1 stop bit, you should be okay.

The Cisco User Interface

A large part of this text will be devoted to entering configuration, reporting, or other commands, and viewing the router's responses. To do this efficiently in practice, it will help you to know how the Cisco user interface works. Think of this as similar to learning DOSKEY in the PC world or the *vi* editor in the Unix world. It's important to know at the beginning that you do not have to type in the entire command for the router to know what to do for you. As long as you type enough to identify a unique command, the router will accept it. Here's an example:

```
Hostname#wri t
```

This is the abbreviation for the command `write terminal`; the string `wri t` is enough information for the router to interpret the command correctly, and, as we shall see later, this command will cause the router to display its configuration to the screen.

Assuming you have connected a terminal to the console port of a previously configured router, you will be presented with a password or router prompt. After entering an appropriate password, if necessary, the display will look something like this:

```
Hostname>
```

At this stage, we can start to enter commands. In the Cisco user interface, there are two levels of access: *user* and *privileged*. The first level of access that allows you to view router status is known as *user EXEC mode*.

The privileged mode is known as *privileged EXEC mode*. This mode is needed to view router configuration, change configuration, and run debugging commands. Privileged EXEC mode often is referred to as *Enable mode* because, in order to get into privileged EXEC mode, you have to enter the `enable` command followed by an appropriate password. This is achieved as follows:

```
Hostname>enable   Press the Enter key
password:         Supply the Enable password, then press Enter
Hostname#
```

The visual evidence that you now have Enable privilege is that the command prompt has now changed to a # character alone.

Before we proceed, you also need to be aware that the router can be in one of two modes. The first is what I will term *view mode*. With this mode, you can enter the `show` and `debug` commands. This allows you to view the status of interfaces, protocols, and other items related to the router. It is the mode that the router will be in after you first log on. The second is *configuration mode*. This allows you to alter the configuration running in the router at that time. This is important to realize, because as soon as you press the Enter key after entering a configuration command, that command takes immediate effect even before you leave configuration mode. You can get into configuration mode only after gaining Enable privilege. This is achieved as follows:

```
Hostname#config terminal   Press Enter
Enter configuration commands, one per line. End with Ctrl/Z.
Hostname(config)#
```

Note that the line telling you to end with Ctrl-Z is echoed back by the computer. The command to get into configuration mode in this case tells the router that it is to be configured from the terminal. The router also can be told to get its configuration from a network server; this will be covered later. You will notice that the prompt changes to remind you that you are in configuration mode.

The following is an example of how to enter configuration commands for the Ethernet 0 interface:

```
Hostname(config)#interface ethernet0   Press the Enter key
Hostname(config-int)#
```

To move back one level, type in the following:

```
Hostname(config-int)#exit   Press the Enter key
Hostname(config)#
```

If you wish to exit configuration mode from any level, simultaneously hold down the Ctrl and press the Z key:

```
Hostname(config-int)<Ctrl-Z>   Press the Enter key
Hostname#
```

To exit Enable mode, type in the following:

```
Hostname#exit   Press the Enter key
Hostname>
```

You now have the basics for navigating the user interface.

Shortcuts. The following lists the more useful of the available keystrokes for the Cisco IOS. If <Ctrl-*x*> appears, it means you should hold down the Ctrl while pressing the character *x* key.

Arrow Keys. The arrow keys are useful only with an ANSI/VT100-emulating terminal. The up and down keys display the command history; for example, pressing the up arrow will display the previous command. By default, 10 commands are kept in the history. If you want to change that, go into configuration mode and type in `terminal history` *xx*, where *xx* is the number of commands to remember. The down arrow key will go forward in the command history.

If you are not using an ANSI/VT100 terminal or emulation, the command history can still be accessed by using the <Ctrl-N> and <Ctrl-P> key combinations, for *N*ext and *P*revious command in the command history.

Backspace or DEL. Either of these keys deletes the character before the cursor.

Tab or Enter. Each of these keys executes the command entered.

The ? Key. Possibly the most useful key in the user interface, the "?" key, can be entered at any time to find out what can be entered next. This is best illustrated with an example:

`Hostname>`**`show ip route ?`**	Press the Enter key
`bgp`	Border Gateway Protocol
`Connected`	Connected networks
`egp`	Exterior Gateways protocol
`eigrp`	Enhanced Interior Gateway Routing Protocol
`igrp`	Interior Gateway Routing Protocol
`isis`	ISO is-is
`ospf`	Open Shortest Path First
`rip`	Routing Information Protocol
`static`	Static routes
`summary`	summary of all routes
`supernets-only`	show supernet entries only
`Hostname>`**`show ip route`**	

After the question mark is entered, the router informs you of the options available to complete the command, and re-enters the command typed in so far, so that all you need to do is select the appropriate option. As soon as you see a `<cr>` option in the available command listing, you know that you can press the Enter key and the router will execute the command.

A point to note here is that if the list of options extends past one screen, the last line of the display will show `More`. Pressing the keyboard space bar will show the next page of information, and pressing the Enter key will show the next single line of information.

The following key combinations illustrate useful commands:

- <Ctrl-A> Move cursor to beginning of line.
- <Ctrl-B> Move cursor back one character.
- <Ctrl-D> Delete the character the cursor is on.
- <Ctrl-H> Same as backspace, i.e., delete the character before the cursor.
- <Ctrl-K> Delete characters to end of line. The characters are held in a buffer and can be recalled for later insertion in a command line.
- <Ctrl-U> Delete to end of line; again, the characters go to a buffer.

- <Ctrl-V> Used to insert control characters in the command line. It tells the user interface to treat the next character literally, rather than as an editor command.
- <Ctrl-W> Delete the previous word.
- <Ctrl-Y> Paste the character from the buffer (same as the `yank` command in Unix).
- Esc < Show the first line from the history buffer.
- Esc > Show the last line from the history buffer.
- Esc b Move cursor back one word.
- Esc d Delete the word in front of the cursor.
- Esc f Move the cursor forward one word.
- Esc Del Delete the word before the cursor.

Many administrators with either a PC or Unix background ask about a full-screen editor for altering configurations. This is unlikely ever to be available. A full-screen editor raises questions of when command syntax is checked, at what time the changed configuration takes effect, and so forth. Once you are familiar with the user interface, it does seem efficient and simple to use. Subsequent sections will cover using *TFTP servers* to load and save configuration files over a network, which saves a lot of typing when multiple routers must be configured.

Summary

This chapter looked at the role of a router in an internetwork, and contrasted that with the operation of other network devices, such as PCs and bridges. We also saw how to connect a terminal to the console port of a router, so that the basics of the Cisco user interface could be explored.

CHAPTER 2

TCP/IP Communications

Objectives

The objectives of this chapter are as follows:

- Introduce the TCP/IP and OSI communication models.
- Define the protocols of the TCP/IP protocol suite.
- Explore the addressing schemes used by the different layers of the TCP/IP protocol suite.
- Examine how the protocols and reference tables maintained by the protocols cooperate to transport a packet through an internetwork.
- Serve as a technology primer. (Chapter 3 deals with the practical aspects of implementing the protocols discussed here on Cisco router equipment.)

What Is TCP/IP?

TCP/IP (Transmission Control Protocol/Internet Protocol) is a suite of network protocols. *TCP* and *IP* are only two of the protocols within this suite; they are, however, two of the most important. A protocol specification is comparable to a language. As with any spoken language, there are rules regarding the meaning of certain sounds, and which words signal the beginning or ending of a conversation.

TCP/IP is a set of rules that can be considered computer language, equivalent in human terms to English or French. Just as a human who speaks only English and a human who speaks only French will find it difficult to have a meaningful conversation, so a computer that speaks only TCP/IP will have difficulty exchanging information with a computer that speaks only Novell's IPX.

With TCP/IP enabled, computers using dissimilar operating systems are able to exchange data in an orderly fashion.

The most commonly quoted model for describing data communications is the *Open Systems Interconnection* (OSI) model. This seven-layer model was defined for the OSI set of protocols and gives us a framework for examining the roles and responsibilities of each protocol within the TCP/IP suite. Throughout the remainder of this book, protocols will be referred to as belonging to a specific OSI model layer, such as layer 2 or layer 3. The following gives a brief definition of the OSI model and then compares it to the Department of Defense four-layer data communications model that originally was used to classify protocols within the TCP/IP protocol suite. In order for you to communicate effectively with network engineers, you need at least a basic understanding of this OSI model.

The OSI Data Communications Model

The *OSI Reference Model* provides a model for computer networking. The OSI Reference Model was defined by the International Standards Organization (ISO) and consists of seven layers. Each layer has a task to perform. The layers are: *Application, Presentation, Session, Transport, Network, Data Link,* and *Physical.* The layers from Application through Network generally are implemented in software. The Data Link and Physical layers are implemented with both hardware and software. Table 2.1 outlines the responsibilities of these seven layers.

TABLE 2.1

OSI Reference Model Layer Definitions

Layer	Description
Layer 7: Application layer	The Application layer consists of application programs and the user interface. It is through features in this layer that all exchange of meaningful information occurs between users.
Layer 6: Presentation layer	The Presentation layer defines the representation of data, so that data is exchanged in an understandable format.
Layer 5: Session layer	The Session layer sets up and terminates communications on the network. It also manages the dialogue between users and systems. It is at this level that user and machine names are interpreted.
Layer 4: Transport layer	The Transport layer controls the quality and reliability of the data transmission. Packets are sequenced and acknowledged at this layer. An example of a layer 4 protocol is TCP.
Layer 3: Network layer	The Network layer routes data through the network. It allows any properly configured pair of nodes on an internetwork to communicate. The Network layer calculates routes and controls congestion. An example of a layer 3 protocol is Net Ware's IPX.
Layer 2: Data Link layer	The Data Link layer packages and unpackages data for transmission across a single link. It deals with data corruption (through checksumming) and coordination of shared media. An example of a layer 2 protocol is Ethernet.
Layer 1: Physical layer	The Physical layer establishes the physical connection between a computer and the network. It also controls the transmission of information and specifies the mechanical and electrical characteristics of the protocol in terms of connector size, pin assignments, and voltage levels. An example of a layer 1 protocol is RS-232.

The concept behind this model of network computer communication is that, at the Application layer, an application will want to send some data to another application residing on another machine on the network. An example may be a workstation mail program wishing to send mail to another user via a mail server. The workstation mail application has to take the text of the message to be sent and package it in some way with an address of its destination. This information must somehow be encoded into electrical signals representing binary 1s and 0s that can be transmitted over a network cable.

In this example, the application at layer 7 will define what text has to be sent. To reach its destination on another machine, the message must descend through the layers of this model, through software layers, through the network card and cable hardware, across a network cable of some kind, and ascend through the corresponding layers on the destination machine to the destination application.

As the message descends through the layers, it looks less like human language and more like the 1s and 0s that a computer understands.

The terminology used by the ISO to describe this process is as precise and as abstract as one would expect of a large international committee. It will be used in this example for the sake of clarification.

The two key ideas to absorb from the following discussion are that each layer will only "talk" to its corresponding layer on another machine, and each layer *encapsulates* information from the layer above as the message descends through the layers for transmission.

The message that each layer on the sending machine will send to its corresponding layer on the receiving machine is termed a *Protocol Data Unit* (PDU). The message that passes between layers on the same machine is called a *Service Data Unit* (SDU). To make it clear about which type of data unit we are talking, each PDU and SDU has a prefix attached. For example, referring to Fig. 2-1, consider the Transport layer sending a Transport PDU from the sending to the receiving machine. To get the TPDU from the sending to the receiving machine, the sending machine's Transport layer sends a Network SDU to its Network layer. The Network layer passes an LSDU to the Data Link layer, which passes a PhSDU to the Physical layer for transmission on to the network cable.

At the receiving machine, the process is reversed, until the Network layer sends a Network SDU to the Transport layer, at which point we can say that the receiving machine's Transport layer has received a TPDU from the sending machine.

An important concept about this layered model is that as the information passes down through the layers, the software responsible for each layer

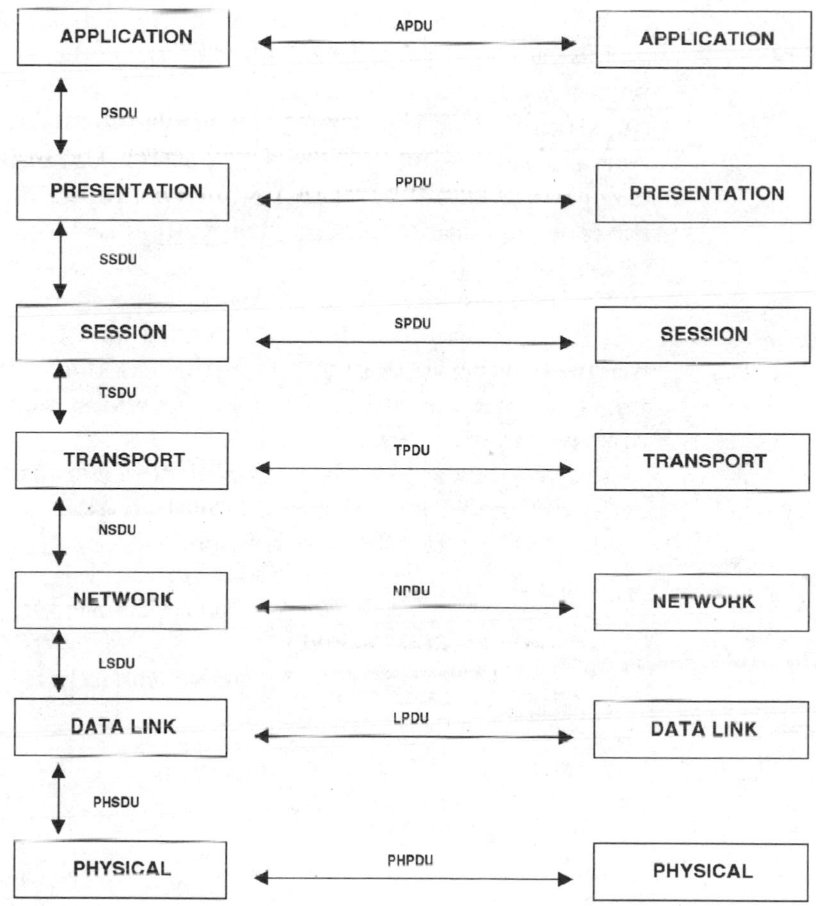

Figure 2-1 Units of communication described in the OSI data communications model

will add its own header information. This concept is referred to as *encapsulation;* each layer is said to encapsulate the information from a higher layer.

Consider Fig. 2-2. Using the example of a mail message, "Hello Fred," that is sent from the sending machine to the receiving machine, we can describe the communications process as follows:

The "Hello Fred" message, along with other Application data, will be delivered to the layer 6 protocol as a PSDU. The layer 6 protocol adds its header information and passes an SSDU down to the layer 5 protocol. The layer 5 protocol cannot interpret the layer 6 header or anything else in the SSDU, and treats all of the SSDU as user data. To pass a TSDU to the layer 4 protocol (the Transport layer), the layer 5 protocol adds a layer 5 header in front of the SSDU, and this process continues until a PhSDU is given to the Physical layer, where binary 1s and 0s are converted into electrical signals for transmission over the network media.

At the receiving machine, the electrical signals are translated into 1s and 0s by the Physical layer, and the layer 2 (Data Link) protocol interprets these 1s and 0s as frames, removes the layer 2 header generated by the sending machine's layer 2 protocol, and passes an LSDU up to its Network layer. Again, this process of each layer removing its own header and passing the information upwards continues until "Hello Fred" and the other Application data are delivered to the receiving machine's Application layer.

The ISO designed protocols for all layers in this model. These protocols, however, have not become as widely quoted or used as the model that defines their operation. The main reason for this is that the TCP/IP protocol suite was already defined, in widespread use, and proven to work well in many environments.

Next we look at how the Department of Defense in the United States defined a model for computer communications and implemented this model with the TCP/IP protocol suite.

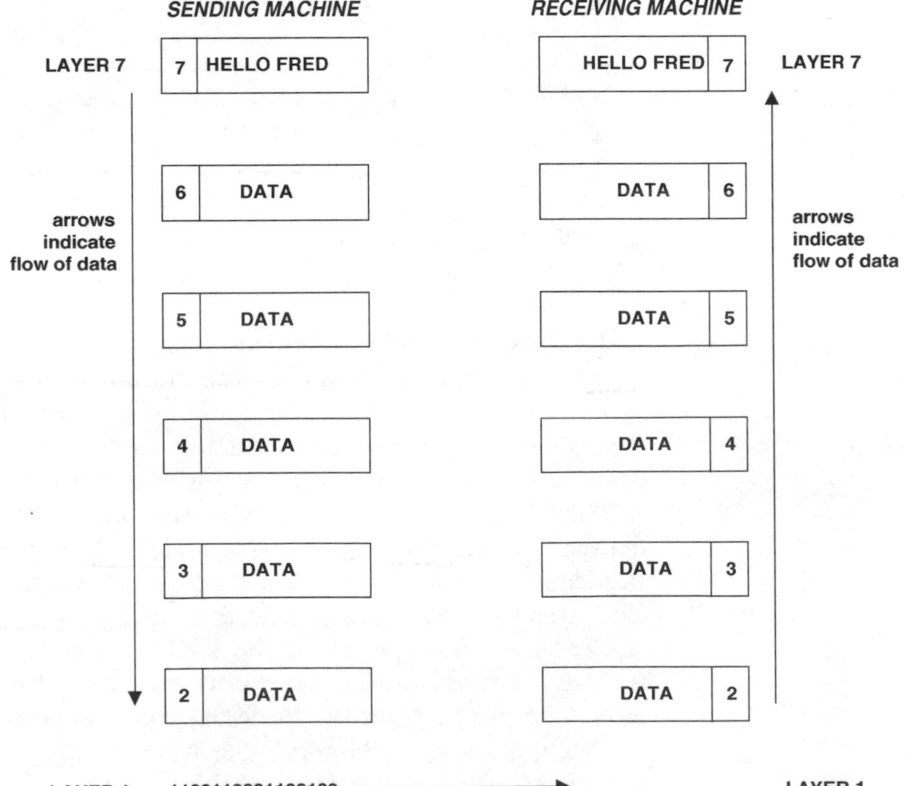

Figure 2-2 Encapsulation through the layers of the OSI model

TABLE 2.2

The DoD Data Communications Model

Layer	Description
Layer 4: Application layer	The Application layer consists of application programs and serves as the window, or network interface. It is through this window that all exchange of meaningful information occurs between communication users. Examples includes Telnet and SMTP.
Layer 3: Host-to-Host Transport layer	Provides end-to-end data delivery services. The protocols at this layer are TCP and UDP.
Layer 2: Internet layer	Defines the datagram or frame format and handles routing data through an internetwork. Examples include IP and ICMP.
Layer 1: Network Access layer	Defines how to access a specific network topology such as Ethernet or Token-Ring.

Department of Defense Model

The Department of Defense (DoD) has defined a four-layer networking model. Each layer of this model consists of a number of protocols that are collectively referred to as the TCP/IP protocol suite.

The specifications for each protocol within the TCP/IP suite are defined within one or more *Requests for Comments* (RFC). The RFCs are submitted by various Internet users who are proposing new protocols, suggesting improvements of existing protocols, or even offering comments on the state of the network. These documents are online on various systems on the Internet, and are available to anyone.

Table 2.2 shows the DoD's four-layer model. You can see that the layers of the DoD model do not precisely match those of the OSI model. For example, in DoD terms IP is a layer 2 protocol, whereas in OSI terms it is a layer 3 protocol. Throughout the rest of this book, when a protocol function is referred to as belonging to a particular layer, it is the OSI layer definition that is used.

Application Layer. Several protocols make up the Application layer of the TCP/IP suite. This layer of the TCP/IP protocol suite corresponds roughly to the Application, Presentation, and Session layers of OSI Reference Model. The protocols implemented at the Application layer are:

- *Telnet* This a terminal emulation service that provides remote login over the network.
- *FTP* File Transfer Protocol is used for interactive file transfer.

- *SMTP* The Simple Mail Transfer Protocol delivers electronic mail on a system.
- *DNS* Domain Name Service maps host names to IP addresses.
- *RIP* Routing Information Protocol advertises routes to different network numbers on the internetwork.
- *NFS* The Network File System allows directories on a host computer to be shared by other machines on the network.

Each application normally requires two separate programs: a client program and a server program (often referred to as a *daemon*).

The daemon program runs in the background on the host server and may start when the system starts. More often, daemon programs are started by the INETD process, which starts and stops these programs as required by the system. A user, on the other hand, executes the client program to gain access to the server.

As we shall see, some Application layer protocols use different Transport layer protocols; for example, Telnet and SMTP rely on TCP, whereas RIP and DNS rely on UDP.

Host-to-Host Transport Layer. The *Host-to-Host Transport layer* is often referred to simply as the Transport layer; for convenience, I will do this also. This layer is responsible for delivering packets between the Internet layer and an application. An important concept in the world of TCP/IP communications is that of *port numbers* (sometimes referred to as *socket numbers*). Each application running in the computer will be given a unique port number at the Transport layer.

This can be thought of as the application's address within the host machine. The most common port numbers assigned can be viewed on any Unix machine in the */etc/services* file. This file lists common applications, and which Transport layer protocol and port number each application uses.

There are two types of protocol within the Transport layer. The first we shall look at is TCP, which is a *connection-oriented protocol*. The type of communication this protocol delivers is known as *reliable data delivery*. When this type of protocol sends data between two machines, the sending machine first informs the network that it needs to start a conversation with some other machine on the network. The network then informs the intended receiving machine that a connection is requested, and the request either is accepted or refused. This is similar to using the telephone system in that the sender knows whether the intended recipient is there and available before data is sent. Typically, a connection-oriented protocol has the following features:

- The network guarantees that all packets sent will be delivered in the correct order, without loss or duplication. If this is not possible, the network will terminate the call.
- If a network becomes overly busy, future call requests are refused in order to preserve the integrity of existing calls.

Thus it is not possible to send a *broadcast packet* using a connection-oriented protocol. By definition, a broadcast packet is sent to multiple hosts on the same network. The first thing a connection-oriented protocol tries to do is contact the intended destination machine and see if it will accept new calls. In a properly designed network addressing scheme, no computer will claim to own a broadcast address.

The second type of protocol at the Transport layer is a *connectionless protocol*, which in the case of TCP/IP is the *User Datagram Protocol* (UDP). A connectionless protocol transmits its data onto the network with a destination address, and assumes that it will get there. This is similar to using the postal service. The network does its best to deliver the data intact and in the correct order, but if multiple paths exist between sender and receiver, out-of-sequence packet delivery is likely. Connectionless protocols assume that the application running in the Application layer takes care of these things.

The choice of using a connection-oriented or a connectionless protocol is not always as straightforward as it might seem. A connection-oriented protocol may seem attractive because of the guarantees it gives, but often the overhead (particularly in terms of packet acknowledgment) can make certain system implementations impossible. It is generally an application developer issue and will not be discussed further here.

Transmission Control Protocol (TCP). The Transmission Control Protocol is the DoD's connection-oriented Transport layer protocol and provides a reliable connection for data exchange between different hosts. With this protocol, all packets are sequenced and acknowledged, and a virtual circuit is established for communications. Upper-level applications using TCP include the following:

- Virtual Terminal Protocol (Telnet)
- File Transfer Protocol (FTP)
- Simple Mail Transfer Protocol (SMTP)

TCP provides reliability through the use of acknowledgments with retransmission. The idea of an *acknowledgment* is that the receiving machine has to reply to the sending machine that the message sent was received intact. If an acknowledgment is not received, the sending machine will assume that the message was not received and will retransmit it.

If the receiving machine had to reply to every packet, the result would be a lot of overhead on the network (assuming that most packets get through in a well-designed network). To reduce overhead, TCP employs a concept called *windowing*.

The window size advertised by a receiving machine tells the sending machine how many bytes it can accept—essentially how much space is available in its receive buffer. The sending machine uses the window size to determine how much data can be sent before it must receive another acknowledgment. If an acknowledgment is not received within the specified window size, retransmission occurs beginning with the last acknowledged data. Typically, if the receiving machine's receive buffer is getting full, it will advertise a decreasing window size to slow the rate of incoming traffic. If a window size of zero is advertised, the sender will not send any further data until it receives an acknowledgment with a nonzero window value.

The window size normally is determined by an algorithm coded into the TCP protocol stack, and varies according to the characteristics of the host machines and network in use.

To establish a TCP connection, a three-step handshake is exchanged between sender and receiver to establish a dialogue before data is transmitted. This process is illustrated in Fig. 2-3.

To initiate communications, the sending machine transmits a *Synchronize Sequence Numbers* (SYN) packet to the receiving machine, to inform the receiving machine that a new connection is requested and to state which number will be used as the starting point for numbering the messages sent. These sequence numbers are used to ensure that packets

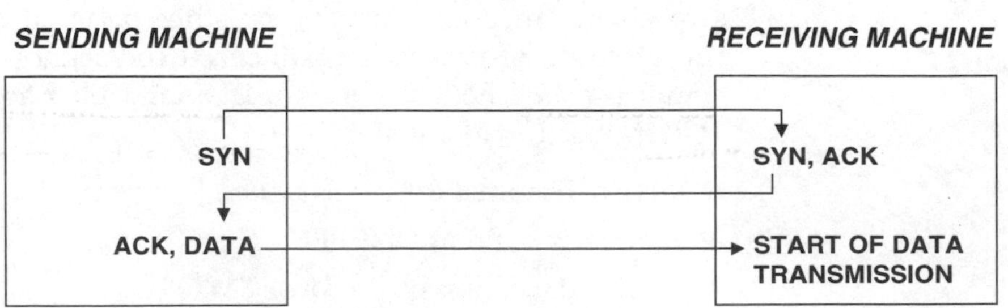

Figure 2-3 The TCP three-way handshake to initiate a connection

received are processed in the order sent. For the process to continue, the receiving machine must acknowledge this SYN packet and tell the sender the sequence number at which it will start sending data. This is achieved by the receiving machine returning a SYN ACK packet to the sending machine. Finally, the sending machine sends an acknowledgment of the information sent by the receiving machine and sends the first data.

This process provides proof positive, before any message transmission occurs, that the receiving machine is alive and ready to receive data. To close the connection, a similar three-step handshake is exchanged, using the FIN packet.

TCP views the data sent as a continuous stream of information. Fragmenting information into discrete packets to be sent over a network is the responsibility of the DoD Internet layer.

User Datagram Protocol (UDP). The *User Datagram Protocol* provides unreliable, connectionless delivery service. It lets the upper-level applications send sections of messages, or *datagrams,* without the overhead involved in acknowledging packets and maintaining a virtual connection. The one similarity between TCP and UDP is that UDP also uses port numbers to identify applications running in the sending and receiving machines.

With UDP you have no way of knowing whether or when the message arrives at its destination, or the order in which messages sent are received. Because there are no acknowledgments or three-step handshakes to begin data transmission with UDP, it is possible to use this protocol for broadcast messages that are sent to all hosts on a network.

Upper-level applications using UDP include the following:

- Trivial File Transfer Protocol (TFTP)
- Network File System (NFS)
- Broadcasts

Internet Layer. The *Internet Protocol* (IP) is the most important protocol of the Internet layer. All traffic, incoming and outgoing, goes through IP. The primary purpose of the Internet layer is to route packets between different hosts, which is accomplished by the addressing scheme of IP. The Internet layer consists of four protocols, as shown in Table 2.3.

Internet Protocol (IP). IP is a connectionless protocol and does not guarantee delivery of packets across a network. IP relies on higher-layer

TABLE 2.3 DoD Model Internet Layer Protocols

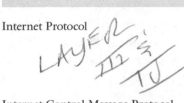

Protocol	Description
Internet Protocol	The Internet Protocol (IP) provides datagram service between hosts. It is responsible for addressing packets, packet routing, fragmentation, and reassembly, and moving data between the Transport and Network Access layers.
Internet Control Message Protocol	The Internet Control Message Protocol (ICMP) lets routers and hosts send error or control messages to other routers or hosts.
Address Resolution Protocol	The Address Resolution Protocol (ARP) translates a host's software address to a hardware address.
Reverse Address Resolution Protocol	The Reverse Address Resolution Protocol (RARP) determines a software address from a hardware address. Diskless workstations often use this protocol when booting up, to find out what their IP address will be. DHCP, which is a superset of BOOTP, is more commonly deployed than RARP for this functionality these days.

protocols either in the Transport or Application layers to provide connection-oriented service if necessary. (In some older implementations, the Data Link layer is used; see the section on X.25 and LAPB in Chap. 6.) The IP header contains many fields, the most important of which are the Source Address, Destination Address, and Time To Live. The format of IP addresses is explained later in this chapter.

Delivering a packet from one machine on the internetwork to another is handled by IP. Based on the network depicted in Fig. 2-4, we can examine the difference in IP operation when an application on PC1 needs to send data first to PC2, and then to PC3.

In the first instance, where PC1 needs to send to PC2, examination of the destination address tells IP that the destination is on the same network number. In this case, the packet is sent directly to PC2. In the case in which PC1 needs to send a packet to PC3, examination of the destination address tells IP on PC1 that PC3 is on a different network. In this case, PC1 will examine its configuration and send the packet to its default gateway for routing to the final destination. The terms *gateway* and *router* are interchangeable in most TCP/IP documentation. A gateway or router (however one refers to it) is responsible for routing packets between different physical networks.

The Time To Live field is used to ensure that a packet caught in a routing loop (i.e., a packet circulating between routers and never reaching a destination) does not stay in the internetwork forever. Each time a packet travels through a router, its Time To Live field is reduced by one. If this value reaches zero, a router will discard the packet. Different routing protocols have different initial values for the Time To Live field; for example, RIP has an initial value of 15.

ICMP. The Internet Control Message Protocol performs four main functions, which are:

- *Flow control* When a receiving machine is too busy to accept the incoming stream of data from a sending machine, it sends a Source Quench Message to temporarily stop the stream of data.
- *Unreachable destination alerts* If a machine on the network detects that a destination is unreachable, either because the destination address does not match an operating machine on the network, or due to a link failure, it will send a Destination Unreachable message to the sending machine.
- *Redirecting routes* A gateway sends an ICMP redirect message to tell a sending machine to use another gateway. Consider an example in which a gateway receives from a sending machine a packet that is destined for a given network. If the gateway knows that the destination network can be reached more efficiently by the sending machine using a different gateway, it will tell the sending machine so, by issuing an ICMP redirect.
- *Checking remote hosts* ICMP echo messages are used to check the physical connectivity of machines on an internetwork. The ICMP echo packet is more commonly known as a *ping* packet.

ARP and RARP. Spanning the Internet and Network Access layers are two protocols, the *Address Resolution Protocol* (ARP) and the *Reverse Address Resolution Protocol* (RARP). ARP is an Internet protocol used to associate an

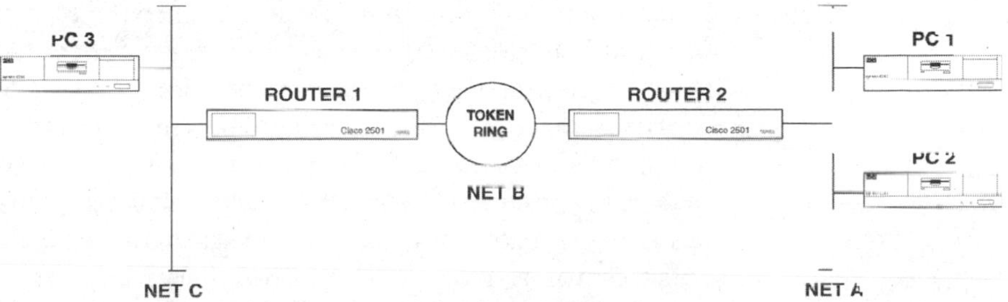

Figure 2-4 Delivering packets on the same segment and across routers

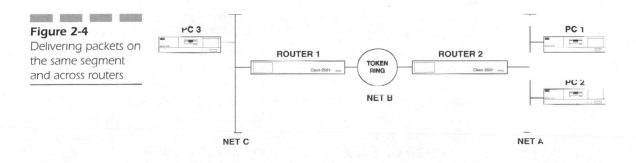

IP address to a physical address, typically Ethernet or Token-Ring 802.2 MAC addresses. (MAC addresses are discussed more fully in Chap. 3.) Each IP device on the network maintains an *address resolution table.* This table maps MAC addresses to IP addresses. When a computer that uses IP for network communication wants to deliver a message to another computer on the same network segment, the MAC address is responsible for getting the packet to the correct workstation.

You do not manually maintain the address resolution table. ARP creates entries in this table as they are needed. If your workstation's ARP table does not contain the MAC address of your destination, a broadcast requesting the address goes out to every host on the network. If the destination host is online and supports ARP, it will hear the broadcast and respond by sending back its MAC address, which then is added to the ARP table. This process is transparent to the user.

RARP is used to supply an IP address to a diskless workstation at boot time. A diskless workstation will know its MAC address, and will request an IP address at boot time from a RARP server via a broadcast.

Network Access Layer. The *Network Access layer* relates the Internet software layer to the hardware that carries the data, and it is the lowest layer in the DoD data communications model. The key point to understand is that network numbers are not understood at this layer; the addresses used at the Network Access layer have significance only for the network segment on which the packet is transmitted. The addresses at the Network Access layer do not traverse a router.

Unlike the other layers in the DoD model, the Network Access layer must know the details of the underlying network so that packets can be formed correctly and sent across the physical network in place.

The functions performed at this layer include forming network packets and using MAC addresses to deliver packets on a network segment. It is here that the protocols define those electrical and mechanical specifications of communication that allow a packet to be transported on a given network.

By means of a *Frame Check Sequence* (FCS), this layer ensures that packets that have been subjected to interference during transmission are not accepted at their layer 2 destination. The FCS is calculated by the sending machine and attached to the message sent. The receiving machine performs the same calculation and assumes that, if its FCS matches that received with the packet, that packet is okay. If the FCS values do not match, the packet is discarded. Typically, at this layer protocols do not re-request the transmission of damaged and discarded frames. (An exception is X.25's LAPB protocol, discussed in Chap. 6.)

The Network Access layer specifies the physical (hardware) medium for data transmission. The Institute of Electrical and Electronics Engineers (IEEE) Project 802 established standards that define interface and protocol specifications for various network topologies.

The people on Project 802 split the OSI Data Link layer in two. Project 802 created the *Logical Link Control* (LLC) sublayer and the *Media Access Control* (MAC) sublayer. The LLC sublayer defines how a receiving machine discards damaged packets. The MAC sublayer handles issues of supplying globally unique hardware addresses to device interfaces.The following sections list MAC specifications defined by the 802 committees. Each of these MAC standards defines a unique packet (or frame) format.

802.3 (Ethernet). The following Ethernet protocols use a bus topology and the media types listed:

- 10Base5 Thick Ethernet, 50-Ω coaxial, 10 Mbps
- 10Base2 Thin Ethernet, 50-Ω coaxial, 10 Mbps
- 1Base5 Twisted-pair, 1 Mbps
- 10Base-T Twisted-pair, 10 Mbps

802.4 (Token Bus). Common token bus protocols include the following:

- Carrierband 1 Mbps, phase continuous, FSK, 75-Ω coaxial
- Carrierband 5–10 Mbps, phase coherent, FSK, 75-Ω coaxial
- Broadband 1, 5, 10 Mbps, multilevel, duobinary, AM/PSK, 75-Ω coaxial

802.5 (Token Ring). Token ring networks (such as IBM's Token-Ring) use the following protocols:

- 1 Mbps, shielded twisted-pair (IEEE)
- 4 Mbps, shielded twisted-pair (IEEE)
- 16 Mbps, shielded twisted-pair (IBM)
- 16 Mbps, early token release (IBM)

TCP/IP Addressing

As previously illustrated, when connecting two systems using TCP/IP, each protocol layer on one host communicates directly with the corresponding layer on the other host. For example, the DoD Network Access layer on one host communicates directly with the Network Access layer on another host. Each layer will use its own addressing scheme:

- The Application layer uses a hostname.
- The Transport layer uses a port number.
- The Internet layer uses an IP address.
- The Network Access layer uses a MAC address.

Now that all the terms we need to use have been introduced, we start to look at how things really work in an internetwork. The goal of the seven OSI layers of communication protocols is to form a packet that is correctly encoded for the network topology in use (such as Ethernet or Token-Ring), and to direct the packet to the correct destination—or at least to the next router in sequence to reach the desired destination. Figure 2-5 shows how the various addresses have to be assembled before a packet can be transferred on a network.

We will now examine in more detail the addressing used at each layer of the DoD model, and conclude the chapter with a summary that illustrates how all the addresses work together to deliver a packet.

Application Layer Addressing

The Application layer is the interface to the user. At this layer, computers are addressed by hostnames, as it is easier for humans to refer to computers by name rather than by IP address. For example, you could call the VAX system in the sales department *Sales-VAX*, or use any other name that is convenient.

In the case of the Internet, which contains thousands of systems, two different computers could well have the same name assigned by a local administrator. For example, two different companies might both choose to name the VAX system in their sales departments *Sales-VAX*. To avoid confusion, the Internet has a number of domains. Each domain has sub-

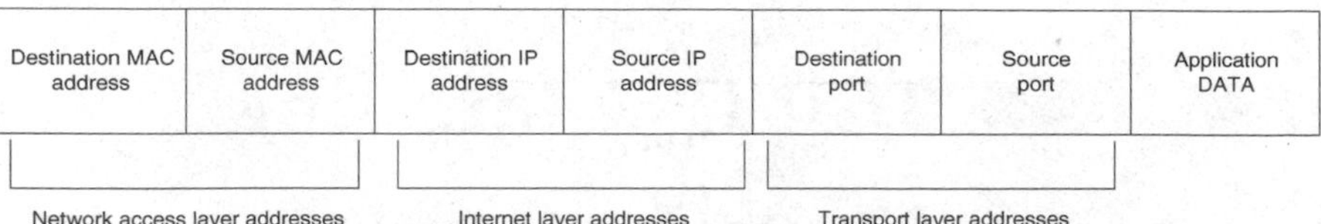

Figure 2-5 Addresses used in a packet to deliver application data across a network

domains that can have further divisions as necessary. The Internet includes the following domains and usages:

- MIL Used by the Department of Defense
- EDU Used by colleges and universities
- COM Used by corporations and other commercial entities
- NET Used by those managing the Internet

The domain name for a host consists of a set of subdomains separated by periods. For example, the computer *Sales-VAX* located at the Acme company might have a *Sales-VAX.acme.com* domain name. This is referred to as a *fully qualified hostname*. If one wishes to communicate with a host that is at another Internet site, the fully qualified hostname must be used.

Hostnames cannot be used as an address in forming a packet to be sent over a network, so they are converted to IP addresses, which are used in addressing a packet. To translate a hostname to an IP address, a computer typically will refer to a *hosts* file (normally stored locally in the */etc* subdirectory) or a Domain Name Service server on the internetwork, which is, effectively, a centralized *hosts* file.

The *hosts* file contains three columns: hostname, IP address, and alias. (There can be multiple aliases.) Here's an example:

```
123.45.45.45   Host1       Host1.acme.com
345.12.12.12   Host2       Host2.acme.com
173.23.6.4     Host3       Host3.acme.com
127.0.0.1      localhost
```

Manually keeping all hosts files on all machines on an internetwork the same can become quite a headache. DNS enables you to point hosts to a DNS server on the network, which will resolve hostnames to IP addresses for many hosts. This reduces administration, as you only have to maintain one database, not multiple hosts files.

Transport Layer Addressing

The Transport layer addresses are quite simple: They consist of a destination and source port number. A portion of an */etc/services* file from a Unix machine that lists certain well-known port numbers is shown below:

```
ftp      21/tcp
telnet   23/tcp
smtp     25/tcp
```

tftp 69/udp
snmp 161/udp

For each Application layer protocol, this tells us the port number and whether the Transport layer protocol is TCP or UDP. The port numbers given are destination port numbers. If, for example, a computer needs to establish a Telnet session to another computer, it will set a destination port address of 23 and pick a random source port address of value greater than 1023. Port numbers lower than 1023 are reserved as "well-known" destination port numbers.

Internet Layer Addressing

At the Internet layer, all hosts must have a software address. In TCP/IP the software address for a host is the Internet or IP address. This address identifies the network to which the host is attached. Routers use this address to forward messages to the correct destination. This layer of addressing is the most labor-intensive for network administrators, so we will spend more time on this than any other layer.

The Internet address of a host consists of 4 bytes or *octets*, which contain both a network and a node address. For every computer, the network portion of its address must match the network address of every other computer on that network. The host portion, however, must be unique for that network number.

If a computer is on the Internet, it is using a network address assigned by the *Network Information Center* of Chantilly, VA, known as the *InterNIC*, which operates under the authority of the *Internet Assigned Numbers Authority*. Typically an Internet service provider assigns the numbers for organizations or individuals. Normally the address is in dotted decimal notation.

The Internet Protocol supports three classes of Internet network addresses: A, B, and C, as shown in the following table. The important point here is that the value of the first octet defines the class to which the address belongs. These classes are summarized in Table 2.4, and shown graphically in Fig. 2-6.

Examples of network numbers (in bold) followed by host addresses for each of the classes appear below.

Class A **100.**1.1.1
Class B **165.8.**1.1
Class C **199.119.99.**1

To keep track of all the network numbers on an inter
machine maintains a routing table.

The Routing Table. Each entry in a routing table provides a variety of information, including the ultimate destination network number, a metric, the IP address of the next router in sequence to get to the destination (if appropriate), and the interface through which to reach this destination. The metric is a measure of how good the route is—basically, the lower the metric, the better the route. Other information can be present

TABLE 2.4
Internet Address Classes

Address Class	Characteristics
Class A Networks	In a class A network, the first byte is the network address and the final 3 bytes are for the host address. There are 126 Class A networks, each having up to 16,777,216 hosts. On the Internet, all Class A addresses have been assigned.
Class B Networks	In a class B network, the first byte is in the 128 to 191 range. The first 2 bytes identify the network and the last 2 bytes identify the host within that network.
Class C Networks	In a class C network, the first byte is in the 192 to 223 range. The first 3 bytes define the network and the last byte defines the host within that network.

Figure 2-6
Class A, B, and C network numbers

Class A

network 1-126	host	host	host

Class B

network 128-191	network	host	host

Class C

network 192-223	network	network	host

in routing tables, including various timers associated with the route. The routing table can have entries from the following sources:

- RIP, IGRP, or some other routing protocol
- Manual entries that can be default or static

Static routes are routes that are added manually; a destination and gateway address are specified for either a specific host (such as 193.1.1.1), or for an entire network (such as 193.1.1.0). A default route can be added by specifying a destination address of 0.0.0.0 when entering a static route. If a packet is destined for a network number not listed in the routing table, the default route entry tells the router to which IP address it should forward packets. It is assumed that the router to which the packet is forwarded will know how to get the packet to its ultimate destination.

Life gets more complicated when we use *netmasks* to split a network number into several subnets. A specific example of applying and changing subnet masks on a Cisco router is given in Chap. 3, but we will discuss the basic theory here. Most people new to the subject have some difficulty understanding how netmasks work. If the following discussion does not help you, don't panic. When we get to Chap. 3 and see the effect that changing netmasks has on a real network, things should become more clear.

Subnet Masks. Netmasks are used to split a network into a collection of smaller subnetworks. This may be done to reduce network traffic on each subnetwork, or to make the internetwork more manageable. To all intents and purposes, each subnetwork functions as if it were an independent network.

Communication between a node on a local subnetwork and a node on a different subnetwork is like communication between nodes on two different networks. To a user, routing between subnetworks is transparent. Internally, however, the IP software recognizes any IP addresses that are destined for a subnetwork and sends those packets to the gateway for that subnetwork.

In an internetwork without netmasks, the routing table keeps track of network numbers. In an internetwork with netmasks, the routing table maintains a list of subnets and how to reach them. When netmasks are used, an IP address is interpreted as follows:

IP address = Network address.Subnetwork address.Host address

This shows that when a network is divided into subnetworks, the host address portion of the IP address is divided into two parts, the subnetwork address and the host address.

For example, if a network has the Class B IP network address portion 129.47, the remainder of the IP address can be divided into subnetwork addresses and host addresses. The network administrator controls this division to allow for maximum flexibility for network development at the site.

A *subnet mask* is the mechanism that defines how the host portion of the IP address is divided into subnetwork addresses and local host address portions. The subnet mask is a 32-bit (4-byte) number, just as an IP address is.

To understand the mechanics of the netmask, it is important to know a little binary arithmetic. We will go through the process of working out how netmasks work. Then I will show you a shortcut.

In binary, the only digits available are 0 and 1. This means that the rightmost digit of a binary number represents the amount of 1s in the number, either 0 or 1. The next digit represents the number of 2s the next digit the number of 4s, etc. To convert the 8-bit binary number 01101001 to the more familiar decimal, we need to use the map below:

128	64	32	16	8	4	2	1
0	1	1	0	1	0	0	1

This binary number is in fact 105 in the more familiar decimal. You can check this by using a scientific calculator. If you have eight 0s in a binary number, the decimal value is obviously 0. If you have eight ones, the decimal value is 255.

To see how a netmask splits up the host portion into subnet address and host address, it is necessary to convert both the IP address and the netmask to binary.

Once the IP address and netmask have been converted to binary, a logical AND is performed between the address and netmask (which means the resultant value is 1 if both IP and netmask value are a 1; otherwise the result is 0). Let's look at the example computation in Fig. 2-7.

Thus the resultant subnet address is 201.222.5.120. This netmask is said to have 5 bits in the subnet field, which leaves 3 bits to define hosts. Note that the last 3 bits of the fourth byte are separated off to show the effect of the netmask. With 3 binary bits, there are eight

Figure 2-7
Calculating a subnet mask

IP address:	201.222.5.121				
Subnet mask:	255.255.255.248				
	Network Number	Subnetwork Number			Host Address
201.222.5.121:	11001001	11011110	00000101	01111	001
255.255.255.248:	11111111	11111111	11111111	11111	000
Subnet:	11001001	11011110	00000101	01111	000
	201	222	5		120

possible values (0 through 7). There are, however, only six of these addresses that can be used for hosts on this subnet. This is because the first and last values are reserved. The first is reserved for identifying the subnet number itself, and the last is the broadcast address for that subnet. This is shown for our example IP address and netmask below:

IP address	= 210.222.5.121
Subnet mask	= 255.255.255.248
Subnet address	= 201.222.5.120
Usable subnet host addresses	= 201.222.5.121 – 201.222.5.126
Subnet broadcast address	= 201.222.5.127

It is good to work through a few examples to understand how it works. Try to work out the subnet address, usable host addresses, and broadcast address for the following:

IP address = 164.2.34.35
netmask = 255.255.255.224

IP address = 101.2.3.18
netmask = 255.255.0.0

The answers are given at the end of this chapter.

A quicker way to work it out, which you can use once you are happy with what is going on, is as follows:

- Write down the netmask in binary.
- Look at the decimal value of the rightmost 1 in the netmask.

This decimal value tells you what increment in the IP address puts you into a new subnet.

This is best explained by using an example. Let's say we have a netmask of 255.255.255.224. Converting this to binary, we get:

11111111.11111111.11111111.11100000

We can see that the 1s end in the spot that represents the number of 32s we have in the number. This means that with every increment of 32 in the IP address, we go into a new subnet. We can illustrate this by applying this netmask to the following IP address:

150.2.3.56

With the 255.255.255.224 netmask, we get a new subnet every 32 addresses, so the subnets will start at:

150.2.3.0
150.2.3.32
150.2.3.64
150.2.3.96
150.2.3.128
150.2.3.160
150.2.3.192
150.2.3.224

So, for the address 150.2.3.56, with a netmask of 255.255.255.224, the subnet address is 150.2.3.32.

Tables 2.5 and 2.6 show how many hosts and subnets result when a range of subnet masks is applied to both class B and C networks. Always note that the first and last address for a host or a subnet cannot be used.

Network Access Layer Addressing

The Network Access layer addresses can be referred to by several names, which include *MAC, hardware,* and *physical* addresses. I refer to them as MAC addresses. A MAC address is used by one of the network types defined by the Project 802 committee, basically either an Ethernet or token-passing network.

A MAC address is a collection of 6 bytes of information, usually represented with hexadecimal numbers and looking something like this:

08:CA:00:12:34:56

Every MAC address in the world is unique. The way this is ensured is that a central body assigns the first 3 bytes to manufacturers as a prefix, and the manufacturer then numbers the devices with 3 additional bytes that are numbered sequentially. If a manufacturer runs out of numbers to assign, it can always get a new prefix. If you ever see a device on a network with a MAC address that begins with 00.00.0C, you know it is a Cisco device.

TABLE 2.5

Class B Subnetting

#Bits	Subnet Mask	Subnets	Hosts
2	255.255.192.0	2	16382
3	255.255.224.0	6	8190
4	255.255.240.0	14	4094
5	255.255.248.0	30	2046
6	255.255.252.0	62	1022
7	255.255.254.0	126	510
8	255.255.255.0	254	254
9	255.255.255.128	510	126
10	255.255.255.192	1022	62
11	255.255.255.224	2046	30
12	255.255.255.240	4094	14
13	255.255.255.248	8190	6
14	255.255.255.252	16382	2

TABLE 2.6

Class C Subnetting

Bits	Subnet Mask	Subnets	Hosts
2	255.255.192	2	62
3	255.255.224	6	30
4	255.255.240	14	14
5	255.255.248	30	6
6	255.255.252	62	2

MAC addresses are used to deliver packets to their destination on one network. People often ask, "If there is a guaranteed-unique MAC address on the internetwork, why bother assigning IP addresses?"

The answer goes back to the analogy of delivering a letter via the postal service, discussed in Chap. 1. The postal service is efficient because it uses distribution points, generally located in each city. An internetwork is the same in that it uses a router as a distribution point for a network number. If there were no IP addresses, each router would have to keep track of the location of every MAC address on the internetwork. This soon becomes unwieldy in an internetwork of any size.

So, we have IP addresses that are responsible for getting a packet delivered to the correct network (or subnet if netmasks are used), and MAC addresses are then used to deliver the packet locally. What actually happens as a packet is transported through an internetwork is that the source and destination MAC addresses change each time the packet travels through a router, whereas the IP source and destination addresses remain constant. This is illustrated in Fig. 2-8.

This figure shows that when PC1 sends a packet to PC2 through the router, the source and destination IP addresses remain constant, but the MAC addresses change as the packet moves from one network segment to another through the router.

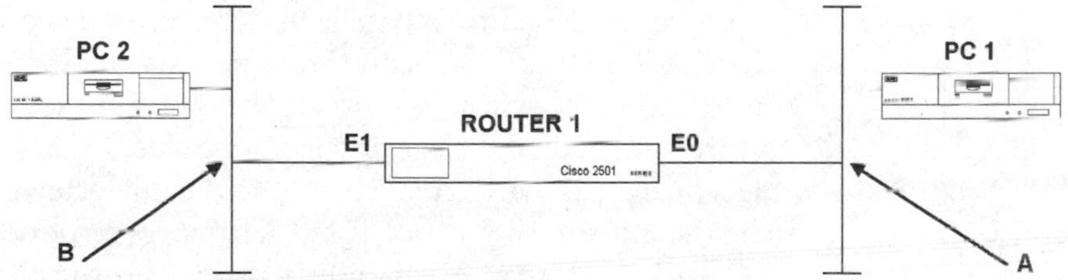

Figure 2-8 How the MAC addresses used in addressing a packet change as it traverses an internetwork

	PC 1	Router E0	Router E1	PC 2
MAC- Address	M1	M2	M3	M4
Software (IP) address	I1	I2	I3	I4

A packet sent from PC1 to PC2 will look like this at point A:

destination MAC	source MAC	destination IP	source IP	data
M2	M1	I4	I1	1001001

A packet sent from PC1 to PC2 will look like this at point B:

destination MAC	source MAC	destination IP	source IP	data
M4	M3	I4	I1	1001001

Note that the source and destination IP address remain constant as the packet traverses the internetwork.

Putting It All Together

We have covered all the issues necessary to be able to explain how the TCP/IP protocols and reference tables (the routing and ARP tables) cooperate to transport a packet through an internetwork.

In the following explanation, we take the example of a PC trying to establish a Telnet session with a host machine that is located on the other side of a router.

Assuming the PC is running a Telnet client application, the command `Telnet Sales-VAX` is entered into the PC. By selecting the Telnet application, the destination port number is set to 23. Next, the hostname *Sales-VAX* needs to be resolved, meaning that its IP address needs to be found. This is done by either referencing *Sales-VAX* in the locally held *hosts* file, or requesting the IP address for *Sales-VAX* from a DNS server on the network.

Once the IP address has been determined, the PC looks to see if the destination IP address is on the same network (or subnet if netmasks are used). In this case it is not, so the PC will set the destination MAC address to that of its default gateway. The PC refers to its ARP table to determine the MAC address of the default gateway. If the IP address of the default gateway is not listed with a corresponding MAC address, the PC will issue an ARP broadcast to determine the MAC address. Once the MAC address of the default gateway is determined, all source and destination addresses are known and the packet is forwarded to the default gateway.

The default gateway will now receive the packet, examine the destination IP address and immediately look at its routing table. If the destination is on a directly connected segment, the default gateway will reference its ARP table, find the MAC address associated with the destination IP address of the *Sales-VAX* machine, and forward the packet to its final destination.

This process is re-examined in Chap. 3, when you will have a chance to see the previously described processes work in a Cisco router environment.

Summary

In this chapter we defined what a protocol is and explored two models for data communications, the OSI and TCP/IP (DoD) model. Specific protocols within the TCP/IP protocol stack were identified and the relevant addressing schemes used by each were explained. The discussion on addressing also introduced the concept of the subnet mask and how that can be used to divide a network into many subnetworks. Finally, we saw an overview of how TCP/IP protocols and reference tables cooperate to deliver a packet across an internetwork.

Answers to Netmask Questions

IP address	= 164.2.34.35
netmask	= 255.255.255.224
subnet address	= 162.2.34.32
usable host addresses	= 162.2.34.33 to 62
broadcast address	= 162.2.34.63

IP address	= 101.2.3.18
netmask	= 255.255.0.0
subnet address	= 101.2.0.0
usable host addresses	= 101.2.0.1 to 101.2.255.254
broadcast address	= 101.2..255.255

CHAPTER 3

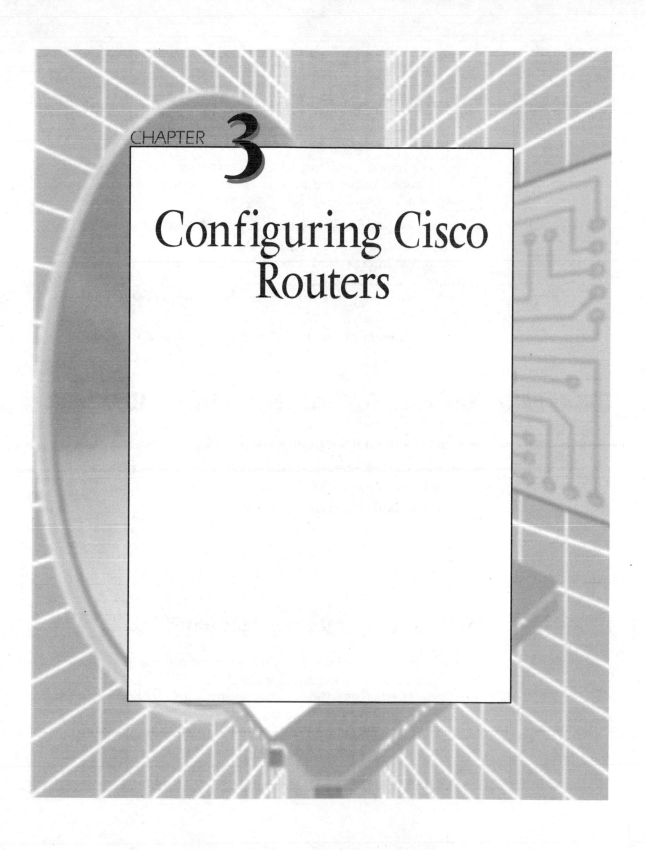

Configuring Cisco Routers

Objectives

The objectives of this chapter are to

- Illustrate how to configure a Cisco router using the Setup feature, configuration mode, and how to retrieve a configuration file from a network server.
- Understand and be able to modify router configuration files.
- Build a lab that will be used to explore how Cisco routers interact on a simple internetwork and see how the Cisco IOS reports some simple faults. This lab will be used in later chapters to explore Cisco router configurations for implementing various network protocols and systems.
- Perform elementary troubleshooting of the lab internetwork.

Sources for Configuring a Router

A router can be configured from three sources:

- Manually, using a terminal connected to the console port (or logged in over a network via a Telnet session).
- Through commands stored in nonvolatile memory.
- Through commands stored in a file residing on a TFTP server somewhere on the network.

A summary of these commands is given in Table 3.1.

Configuring a Router Manually

When a router is configured manually, we can use the Cisco Setup utility, provided that the router does not have a configuration file already in existence. Alternatively, we can change an existing configuration using the `configure terminal` command.

Configuring a Router Using Setup. This first example of configuring a router assumes that you are attaching a terminal to your router and configuring it for the first time.

TABLE 3.1 Configure Commands

Command	Description
configure terminal	Executes configuration commands from the terminal. Use this command to make changes to the configuration file from the console port or a telnet session. Once changes are entered press <Ctrl-Z> to end the update mode session. Note that the shortest unique command identifier may be used; in this case, configuration mode can be invoked by entering conf t.
Configure memory	Executes configuration commands stored in NVRAM.
Configure network	Retrieves configuration commands are stored in a network server and load that configuration into memory. You will be prompted for the IP address of the TFTP server to connect to, as well as the configuration filename.

When you connect a router to a terminal and power it up for the first time, the text displayed will be similar to that shown in Fig. 3-1. If this is a new router that has not been configured, there will be no configuration in memory and the router will go into the initial configuration dialog. If you wish to return a configured router to this state, type in `write erase` when in privileged user mode to erase the configuration in memory. In Fig. 3-1, the text in bold is that which was entered.

We will now explain all the entries and modify this to be a working configuration.

Deciphering the Initial Configuration File. A *router configuration file* is plain ASCII text. This text file is read at boot time and put into effect as a working configuration by the router operating system, the IOS. By entering router configuration mode, commands can be entered that will add, modify, or delete configuration options while the router is running. Router configuration files can be saved as plain text on a TFTP server, modified by a full-screen text editor, and reloaded via TFTP.

Having completed the exercise for giving our new router a random configuration, let's take a more detailed look at what this configuration file means.

The first entry, `hostname Router1`, defines the text the router will use as a prompt; this router will generate a prompt `Router1>`.

The `enable secret` entry indicates that a secret password has been supplied to get into Enable mode. The password is encrypted and cannot be viewed from the configuration file.

The `enable password enter` tells us that the password "enter" can be used to get into Enable mode. On later versions of Cisco IOS, configuring both an enable secret and an enable password means that only

Figure 3-1
The Cisco setup utility

Notice: NVRAM invalid, possibly due to write erase.
--- System Configuration Dialog --

At any point you may enter a question mark ? for help.
Refer to the Getting Started Guide for additional help.
Use ctrl-c to abort configuration dialog at any prompt.
Default settings are in square brackets [].
Would you like to enter the initial configuration dialog? [yes]: **y**

First, would you like to see the current interface summary? [yes]: **y**
Any interface listed with OK? value "NO" does not have a valid configuration

Interface	IP-Address	OK?	Method	Status	Protocol
Ethernet0	unassigned	NO	not set	up	down
Serial0	unassigned	NO	not set	down	down
Serial1	unassigned	NO	not set	down	down

Configuring global parameters

Enter host name [Router]: **router1**

The enable secret is a one-way cryptographic secret used
instead of the enable password when it exists.

Enter enable secret: **test**

The enable password is used when there is no enable secret
and when using older software and some boot images.

Enter enable password: enter
Enter virtual terminal password: access
Configure SNMP Network Management? [yes]: **n**
Configure IP? [yes]: n
Configure IGRP routing? [yes]: **n**
Configure RIP routing? [no]: **n**

Configuring interface parameters:

Configuring interface Ethernet0:
Is this interface in use? [yes]: **y**
Configure IP for this interface? [yes]: **y**
Configure IP Unnumbered on this interface? [no]: **n**
IP address for this interface: 123.45.45.45

Number of bits in subnet filed [0]: **0**
Class A network is 123.0.0.0, 0 subnet bits; mask is 255.0.0.0

Configuring interface Serial0:
Is this interface in use? [yes]: **y**
Configure IP on this interface? [yes]: **y**
IP address for this interface: 122.22.22.22
Number of bits in subnet field [0]: **0**
Class A network is 122.0.0.0, 0 subnet bits; mask is 255.0.0.0

Figure 3-1 continued

```
Configuring interface Serial1:
  Is this interface in use? [yes]: n

The following configuration command script was created:

hostname router1
enable secret 5 $1$UtL7$KqpczYUWglg4pnWYbNYD0.
enable password enter
line vty 0 4
password access
no snmp-server
!
ip routing
!
interface Ethernet0
ip address 123.45.45.45 255.0.0.0
!
interface Serial0
ip address 122.22.22.22 255.0.0.0
!
interface Serial1
shutdown
no ip address
!
end

Building configuration...yes/no]: y
Use the enabled mode "configure" command to modify this configuration.
```

the enable secret will allow you into Enable mode. Earlier versions of IOS did not recognize an enable secret and would allow entry to Enable mode with the enable password only.

The next entries that require explanation are those that refer to router access via virtual terminals (Telnet access). These entries are shown as follows:

```
line vty 0 4
password access
```

The first line defines five allowable Telnet accesses (numbered 0 through 4), and the next line states that a password "access" will be required before a command prompt is presented to any Telnet session requesting access to the system.

The next configuration command, `no snmp-server`, disables the Simple Network Management Protocol process on the router. SNMP is an Application level protocol that runs atop UDP, and will be covered in more detail in Chap. 7. Unless you are implementing a secure SNMP system, it is recommended that you disable SNMP on the router. If you enable the default SNMP process on a Cisco router, any intruder who knows SNMP will be able to retrieve the router configuration and enable password. The intruder then could cause serious disruption to your network, from which you might not be able to recover without physically replacing all the routers in the network.

The `ip routing` entry simply enables IP routing on the router. The next set of entries shown configures the Ethernet 0 port.

```
interface ethernet0
ip address 123.45.45.45 255.0.0.0
```

This configuration defines an IP address of 123.45.45.45 for the Ethernet 0 port, with a netmask of 255.0.0.0. This is the default mask for a class A network number and was selected by the router because we stated that 0 bits should be contained in the subnet field when the router was configured.

The next two lines define the basic configuration of the Serial 0 port to have an IP address of 122.22.22.22, again with a default class A netmask.

```
interface serial0
ip address 122.22.22.22 255.0.0.0
```

The next section defines the configuration for the Serial 1 port, which is not in use on this router. The `shutdown` entry defines this port as being closed and not in operation. The `no ip address` indicates that an IP address has not yet been assigned to this port.

```
interface serial1
shutdown
no ip address
```

The exclamation points shown in the configuration file are merely separators used to display router component configurations in sections.

Configuring Routers from the Command Prompt. Now that we know how to give a router a basic configuration file and understand the contents of this configuration file, we can modify the file so that it becomes useful.

When configuring Cisco routers, you need to be aware that there are three classes of commands:

- **`Global`** A single-line command that affects the function of the whole unit.

- **Major** A command that indicates a particular interface or process that is being configured. Each major command must have at least one subcommand.
- **Subcommand** Subcommands are used after a major command to configure a process or interface.

To display router configurations, the commands shown in Table 3.2 can be used.

Global commands. The first class of command we will examine are global commands. Global commands normally appear at the top of the router configuration file, and are used to address configuration details that affect the operation of the router as a whole. The global commands defined in the configuration file above are as follows:

```
hostname router1
enable secret 5 $1$UtL7$KqpczYUWgIg4pnWYbNYD0
enable password enter
no snmp-server
ip routing
```

To modify a global parameter, type the following at the enable prompt:

```
Router1#conf t
```

The router will reply with the following:

```
Enter configuration commands, one per line. End with Ctrl/Z.
Router1(config)#
```

TABLE 3.2

Configuration Display Commands.

Command Syntax	Command	Description
sh conf	Show Configuration	Displays the contents of NVRAM. The configuration file loaded at boot time is stored here. Upon boot, the router copies the configuration file from NVRAM into RAM. This is the configuration that the router was started with, or the configuration the last time the `write mem` command was executed, which writes the running configuration to NVRAM.
wri term	Write Terminal	Displays current configuration on the terminal that is running in memory.

You now can type configuration commands that affect global parameters on the router. When you press the Enter key at the end of a line, the command takes effect and is entered into the configuration file.

The following are examples of global commands you might wish to enter in the router configuration.

```
Router1(config)#hostname Newname
Newname(config)#
```

The `hostname` command changes the hostname of the router and immediately is reflected in the prompt when the command is entered, as shown above.

The router can be told to configure at boot time from system ROM, flash memory, or a configuration file held on a TFTP server on the network. A router configuration file can list all three options and the router will try to boot from the source listed first. If that fails, it will try the second source, and so forth. The commands to boot from these sources are as follows:

- **Boot System ROM** This indicates that the router will be booted from ROM chips on the Route Processor. These chips are read-only and cannot be written to. You can update these chips by requesting new ones from Cisco.
- **Boot System Flash** The router will be booted from flash. Flash memory can contain more than one version of the IOS. Routers can be ordered with additional flash memory.
- **Boot System** *Filename IP-Address* Boot from the network. The most typical option is to configure a 2500-series router to boot from flash, if available, or from ROM.
  At the configuration prompts, type the following:

```
Newname(config)#boot system flash
Newname(config)#boot system rom
```

Press <Ctrl-Z> to exit configuration mode. This will enter the above commands in the sequence shown in the configuration file. The new configuration can be viewed with the `write terminal` command.

Another global command you will most likely want to enter is shown as follows:

```
Newname(config)#no ip domain-lookup
```

This command is useful, particularly if, like me, you are not the world's greatest typist. If you make a spelling mistake when trying to enter a command (when you are in View rather than Configuration mode), the router does not recognize the command. It will assume that this strange word is the name of a host on the network and that you wish to establish a Telnet session with it. The router will not find the strange hostname in its own host table and will try to find a Domain Name Server on the network in the hope that the DNS machine will know the IP address of the strange host. Either you do not have an available DNS machine or, if one is available, it will not have details of this strangely named host. The router, therefore, fails to establish a Telnet session. This takes some time. To stop an unnecessary search, enter the `no IP domain-lookup` command in Configuration mode. It just makes life easier.

Major Commands and Subcommands. The thing that differentiates a global command from a major command on a router configuration file is that the global command is on one line. A major command is followed by, at the least, a one-line subcommand that relates to the major command.

The major commands in the initial configuration file are listed next, with the associated subcommands indented:

```
line vty 0 4
  password access
interface Ethernet0
  ip address 123.45.45.45 255.0.0.0
interface Serial0
  ip address 122.22.22.22 255.0.0.0
interface Serial1
  shutdown
  no ip address
```

To experiment with configuring major commands, and their associated subcommands, we will look at configuring the following:

- Give the Ethernet port an IP address of 192.1.1.1, with a subnet mask of 255.255.255.192.
- Configure Serial 0 to have an unnumbered IP address.
- Configure Serial 1 with an IP address of 193.1.1.1 and a subnet mask of 255.255.255.0.
- Configure Serial 1 to have a secondary IP address of 194.1.1.1, with a netmask of 255.255.255.0.

At the Enable prompt, type the following:

```
Newname#conf t
Newname(configure)#int eo
Newname(config-if)#ip address 192.1.1.1  255.255.255.192
Newname (config-if)#<Ctrl-Z>
```

This completes the configuration for the Ethernet 0 port. Note that the prompt changes when you have entered a major command and are about to enter subcommands.

The *IP unnumbered* feature, which we are about to configure for the Serial 0 port, is discussed in more detail in Chap. 7; however, a basic introduction is useful here. IP unnumbered is a Cisco proprietary feature that has many uses on an internetwork. IP unnumbered is used when two router serial ports are connected on a point-to-point link via a leased line (Fig 3-2).

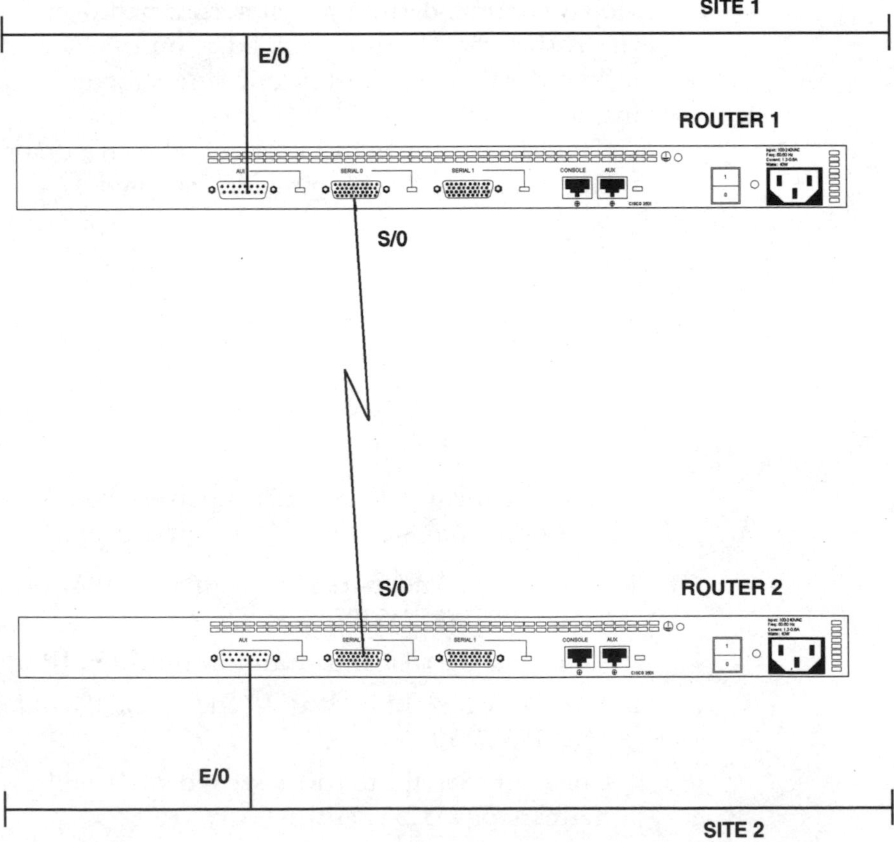

Figure 3-2 Example of a point-to-point link used with IP unnumbered

Assuming that IGRP is the routing protocol used on this network, subnet mask information is not transmitted in routing updates; therefore all interfaces that have IP addresses assigned to them must use the same netmask in order for the routing tables to be updated properly. Let's say that at both site 1 and site 2 we want to apply a netmask that will allow 62 usable IP addresses in the subnet (remember the first and last address in a subnet cannot be assigned to a host or router interface). The netmask in this case will be 255.255.255.192.

If limited address space is available (meaning that the network has to use Internet-compatible addresses, which were assigned to a corporation by an Internet service provider), applying a netmask of 255.255.255.192 to both serial ports will waste 60 addresses on the internetwork. This is because a separate subnet is assigned to the link between router 1 and router 2, but only the serial ports on these routers need an IP address.

IP unnumbered gets around this problem by letting the router know that the serial port is on a point-to-point link, and allows each serial port to use the address of its respective router's Ethernet port for communications across the link. Using IP unnumbered in this fashion prevents us from having to allocate a whole subnet to a point-to-point link.

```
Newname#conf t
Newname(config)#int S0
Newname(config-if)#ip unnumbered E0
```

The Serial 1 line will be configured by entering the following:

```
Newname(config)#int S1
Newname(config-if)#ip address 193.1.1.1  255.255.255.0
Newname(config-if)#ip address 194.1.1.1  255.255.255.0 sec
```

A secondary IP address may be assigned to a router port if the number of host machines on that segment is about to exceed the number allowable by the current IP address and subnet scheme. By assigning a secondary IP address, new hosts may be added to that segment without the need to reconfigure all the host's IP addresses already on the segment.

Configuring a Router from a Network Server

What typically happens when a Cisco router network is being rolled out is that a base configuration for all routers is defined, and has the modified IP addresses for each location. It makes life easier if this base configuration can be loaded into each router from a network server each time a new router is installed. It is more time-efficient to modify an existing configuration than to create one from scratch.

There is a simple way to achieve this, using any machine that can act as a TFTP (Trivial File Transfer Protocol) server. Many of the more full-featured TCP/IP stacks available commercially provide TFTP server functionality. Any Unix machine also can act as a TFTP server.

TFTP is a simple file transfer protocol that is not as complex or as fully functional as FTP. TFTP has little in the way of security, user authentication, or end-to-end reliability, because it uses UDP rather than TCP as the layer 4 protocol.

Let's look at setting up a Unix machine as a TFTP server, saving the configuration file of a router to this TFTP server, and then reloading the configuration.

TFTP is called into action by the INETD daemon process whenever the server machine receives a request on UDP port 69, which is the port number permanently assigned to TFTP.

To have TFTP started in the "secure" mode, the appropriate line in the *inetd.conf* must be uncommented. In a standard *inetd.conf* file in a Unix machine, there are two TFTP entries, as shown below:

```
#tftp   dgram   udp   wait   nouser   /etc/tftpd   tftpd
tftp    dgram   udp   wait   root     /etc/tftpd   tftpd-s   /cisco
```

The line containing the *tftpd-s* is the one in which we are interested. The only modification you need make to this line is to specify which directory you want to become the TFTP secure directory. In this case, it is the */cisco* directory. The only thing that makes this "secure" is that the specified directory is the only one that can be written to or read from; it does not offer user-level security in terms of usernames and passwords. These entries correctly show the insecure option for starting TFTP as commented out, by starting that line with the # character.

Once we have secure TFTP available, and a configuration similar to that shown in Fig. 3-3, we can store and retrieve configurations as plain ASCII text. In the last section we used the `conf t` command to configure from the terminal and the `wri t` command to display the running configuration on the terminal. Now we will look at the `wri net` command to write the configuration to a network server and the `conf net` command to configure the router from a network server.

To successfully write a router configuration to a TFTP server, the file name used to store the file must already exist in the secure directory and have read, write, and execute privileges. In the following example,

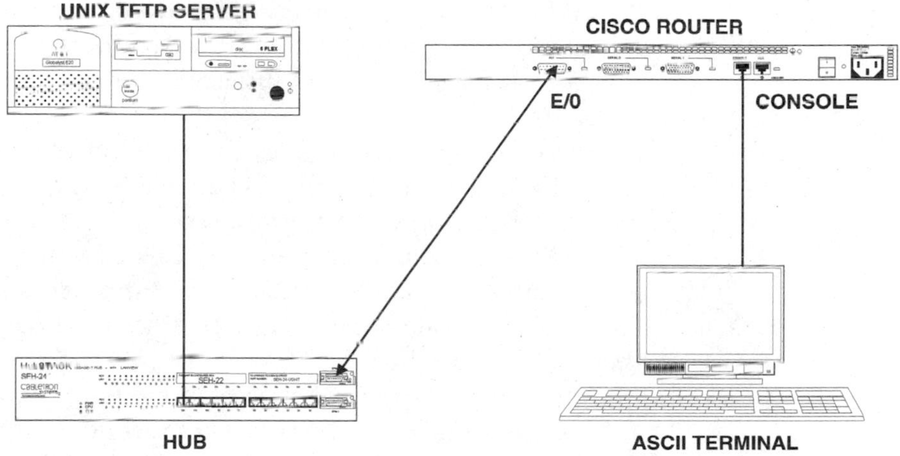

Figure 3-3 Network configuration for storing and retrieving router configuration files

the file *router.conf* must exist in the */cisco* directory of the TFTP Unix server (which has address 209.1.1.1), with *rwxrwxrwx* rights. The following is taken from a Cisco router screen being told to save its configuration to a network server. Note the !!!! characters indicate a file transfer is occurring. Once the file *router.conf* is stored on the TFTP server, it can be edited and stored as any other file name, and is ready to be loaded into another computer.

```
Router1#wri net
Remote host[]? 209.1.1.1
Name of configuration file to write [router-confg]?router.conf
Write file router.conf on host 209.1.1.1 [confirm]? (press enter to confirm)
Writing router.conf: !!!!! [OK]
```

To configure a router from a network server, the following commands have to be input to the router:

```
Router1#conf net
Host or network configuration file[host]? (press enter to accept default)
Address of remote host [255.255.255.255]?209.1.1.1
Name of configuration file [router-confg]?router.conf
Configure using router.conf from 209.1.1.1 [confirm]? (press enter to confirm)
Loading router.conf from 209.1.1.1 (via ethernet 0) !!!!!!!!!
Router#
```

Configuring a Router using Auto-Install

Auto-install is a feature of Cisco routers that was designed to enable a new router to come out of its box, get connected to a leased line at a site, download the correct configuration from a network TFTP server, and be up and running without any intervention from the remote site staff. This idea is useful for initial installation or maintenance replacement of faulty router hardware.

This is a very attractive idea for a typical organization that has centrally located network engineering staff responsible for connecting remote offices to the corporate network. In practice, it is not always a good idea to depend on this to work in a first-time installation. The reason has nothing to do with the Cisco implementation, but relates to the fact that telephone company leased lines tend to have problems when they are first installed.

If anything disrupts the process of configuration file download, such as a spike or some other interruption to service on the line, the configuration file will be corrupted (remember that TFTP uses UDP and therefore does not have error recovery or retransmissions). When a configuration file is corrupted, the newly installed router will not be reachable over the leased line network connection, and will not use the auto-configuration procedure at boot time once it has a configuration file.

Auto-configuration is useful for getting the correct configuration file to a replacement router. When a router is replaced in the field, it is assumed that the initial line problems have been solved and the configuration file will be safely transmitted over the line.

Let's discuss how auto-configuration works. It is assumed that a network configuration similar to that defined in Fig. 3-4 is available for this process. Step 1 is that the new router to receive the configuration is connected via a DTE/DCE cable to what we will call the *staging router.* In this configuration, the staging router Serial 0 port must be connected to the DCE end of the cable and be configured to supply a clock signal. (The details of this configuration are given later in this chapter when we build the lab environment.) When the new router is powered on, it will issue what is known as a *broadcast SLARP request* out of its serial port.

SLARP stands for *Serial Line Address Resolution Protocol.* When the staging router serial port receives the SLARP request, it replies by giving the new router its IP address. Once the new router receives this IP address, it will add 1 to it and take that IP address as its own. A word of caution: This works only for the first two addresses in a network or subnetwork. An example will clarify this.

Suppose the Serial 0 port on the staging router has address 1.1.1.1, and through the SLARP process, the serial port on the new router will configure itself to have address 1.1.1.2.

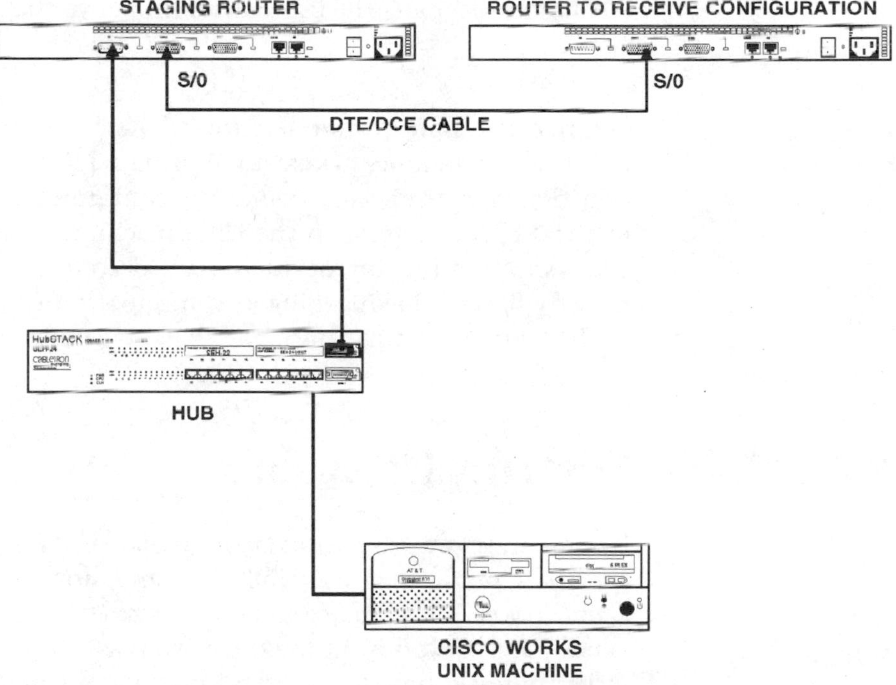

Figure 3-4 Using auto install to configure a router

Once the new router has an IP address, the auto-configuration process configured into the IOS operating system will seek out a file named *network-confg* (located on the Cisco Works Unix machine), and reference a hostname associated with the 1.1.1.2 address. The new router does this by issuing a broadcast on UDP port 69. The staging router must have a global command to forward UDP broadcasts, and the Serial 0 port must have an IP-helper entry on the serial port directing this broadcast to the IP address of the Cisco Works management station. The Forward Protocol command and the Serial 0 IP-helper command appear in the configuration of the staging router as follows (assume the management machine has an IP address of 151.3.5.5):

```
!
interface serial 0
ip address 1.1.1.1  255.0.0.0
ip-helper 151.3.5.5
!
ip forward-protocol udp
!
```

The effect of these two commands is to take a broadcast sent on the 1.0.0.0 network and direct it to the IP address 151.3.5.5.

The *network-confg* file lists entries similar to the following

```
iphost newrouter      1.1.1.2
```

Once the new router has found its hostname ("newrouter," for instance), for argument's sake it will issue a TFTP request for a configuration file named *newrouter-config*. The configuration file must be located in the TFTP directory on the Unix machine, as must the *network-confg* file. Assuming the appropriately named configuration file is there, the router will start downloading its configuration from the TFTP directory of the Cisco Works machine.

Setting Up a Lab

By this stage, we have covered the basics of TPC/IP operation, how to use the Cisco router user interface, and how to change addresses on router ports. What we are going to do is to set up a lab for purposes of experiment. If you want to do this yourself, you need three Cisco 2500-series routers, a hub, and what is known as a Cisco DTE/DCE cable. (We will define a DTE and DCE, and explain their importance, later in this section.) This is a minimal set of equipment, which allows us to do meaningful work without the need to dedicate a high-end router to this task.

The physical connections for the internetwork on which we are going to experiment are shown in Fig. 3-5. The router configurations are shown in Fig. 3-6.

The only entry that should be unfamiliar in these router configurations is the `clockrate 64000` entry in router 3. To understand why this is there, we need to understand how router serial ports normally communicate via *digital modem devices* (normally referred to as CSU/DSU).

To permanently connect two routers located in disparate locations, with a data transmission rate of 56 kbps or higher, you normally will use a digital leased line. The digital leased line terminates in a CSU/DSU, which is then connected to the router serial ports at both ends of the link, as shown in Fig. 3-7.

In datacomm-speak, the router serial port will be configured as a *DTE,* which stands for *Data Terminal Equipment.* The CSU/DSU will be configured as *DCE,* for *Data Communications Equipment.* Why is this important? Because of the functions of the connector pins on each device.

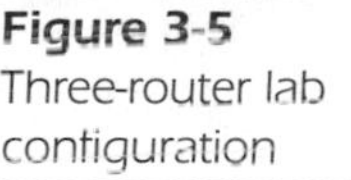

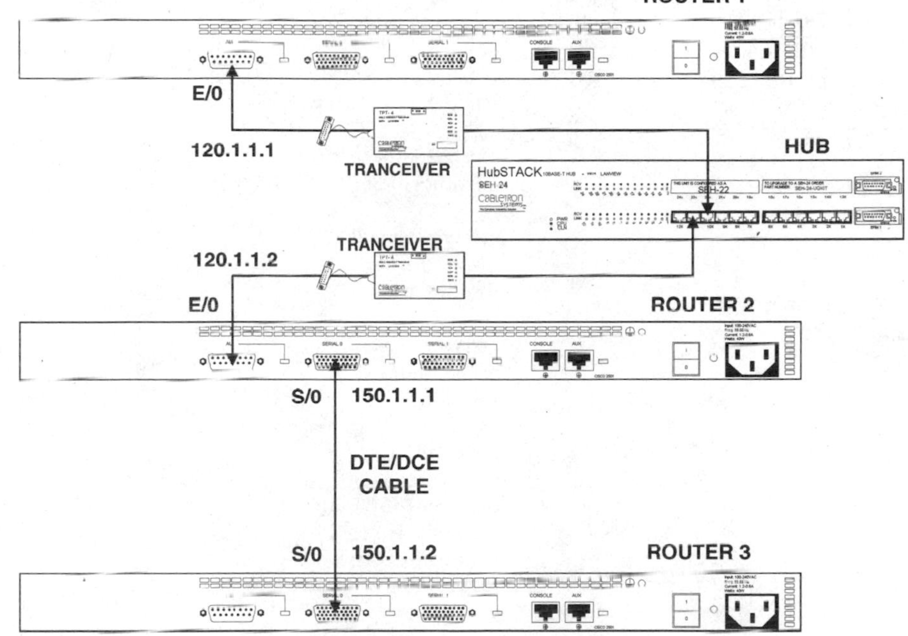

Figure 3-5 Three-router lab configuration

Most people are somewhat familiar with the RS-232 serial interface specification. In this specification, pin 2 is *transmit data* (Tx) and pin 3 is *receive data* (Rx). When a PC is connected to a modem, we have a DTE connected to a DCE and use a *straight-through* cable, meaning that pins 1 through 25 on one end of the cable are connected to the corresponding pins on the other end of the cable. If we want to connect a PC serial port to a printer serial port, we would be connecting two DTE devices, so we'd use a *crossover* cable. This cable eliminates the need for a modem by physically connecting pin 2 on one end of the cable to pin 3 on the other end, and vice versa.

This is necessary; otherwise both DTE devices would try to transmit data on the same connector pin. This is a problem because each pin has only unidirectional functionality, meaning that it can be used either for sending or receiving signals. The simple rule to remember is that a DTE communicates with a DCE; DCE-to-DCE or DTE-to-DTE connections need something devious in the cabling to make them work.

The same concept holds true in the Cisco world. The Cisco serial port has 60 connector pins; the function of each pin depends on whether the port is configured as a DTE or a DCE. The next question is how a port decides whether it should be a DTE or DCE, and how you can tell.

Figure 3-6
Initial configuration files for the three lab routers

Configuration for router 1

```
hostname router2
!
enable secret 5 $1$W6qH$DTNrEHmJm6QqYcMu5PRh.
enable password test
!
interface Ethernet0
 ip address 120.1.1.1 255.0.0.0
!
interface Serial0
 no ip address
 shutdown
!
interface Serial1
 no ip address
 shutdown
!
line con0
line aux 0
 transport input all'
line vty 0 4
 password access
 login
!
end
```

Configuration for router 2

```
version 10.3
!
hostname router2
!
enable secret 5 $1$/P2r$ob00lmzYqpogV0U1g1O8U/
enable password test
!
interface Ethernet0
 ip address 120.1.1.2 255.0.0.0
!
interface Serial0
 ip address 150.1.1.1 255.255.0.0
!
interface Serial1
 no ip address
 shutdown
!
!
line con 0
line aux 0
line vty 0 4
 password ilx
 login
!
end
```

Figure 3-6
continued

```
Configuration for router 3
    Current configuration:
    !
    version 10.3
    !
    hostname router3
    !
    enable secret 5 $1$cNaQ$a4jcvrXlzVO4cwJB7RP5j1
    enable password test
    !
    interface Ethernet0
     ip address 193.1.1.1 255.255.255.0
     shutdown
    !
    interface Serial0
     ip address 150.1.1.2 255.255.0.0
     clockrate 64000
    !
    interface Serial1
     no ip address
     shutdown
    !
    !
    line con 0
    line aux 0
     transport input all
    line vty 0 4
     password ilx
     login
    !
    end
```

The Cisco serial port has 60 pins, far more than you need to transmit and control data, and some of the pins are dedicated to "sensing" which cable is connected. The way it works is that each Cisco cable has a certain number of pins connected together (effectively looping pins together on each end of the cable), giving every cable a unique configuration. When the cable is plugged into the serial port, the port can tell which pins are looped together, and as a result, decides whether it will be a DTE or DCE.

With a Cisco 2500 and a Cisco DTE/DCE cable, this effect easily can be seen; plug one end of the DTE/DCE cable into the Serial 0 port of the router, and issue the following command:

```
Router2>show controllers serial 0
```

The displayed output will be as shown in Fig. 3-8.

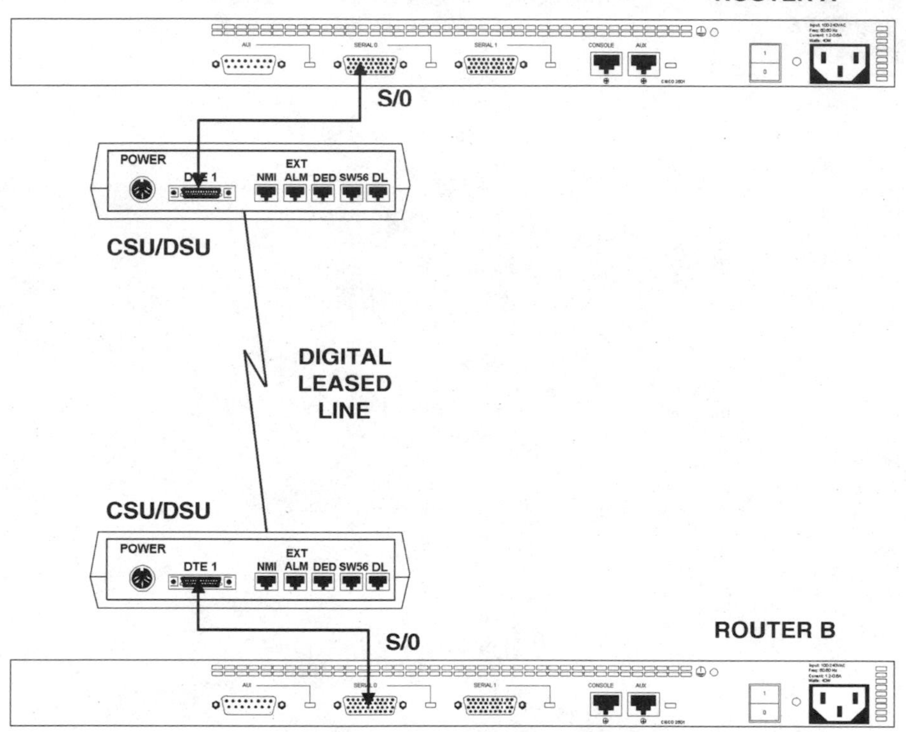

Figure 3-7
Router to CSU/DSU connection

Look at the shaded line and disregard the rest of the screen output for the moment. With this end of the cable, the port is sensing that it should assume a DTE configuration. Now disconnect the DTE/DCE cable and plug the other end into the serial port. Issuing the same command displays the information shown in Fig. 3-9.

As you can see, the port has sensed a different cable connector configuration and has configured itself to be a DCE.

By using the DTE/DCE cable to connect router 2 and router 3 together (Fig. 3-5), the two serial ports will be able to communicate, with one configured as DTE and the other as DCE.

So far, so good. The question remains, however, as to why there is the `clockrate 64000` entry in the configuration of router 3. Referring back to Fig. 3-7, we see that router serial ports normally are connected to a CSU/DSU. Cisco serial ports use *synchronous communication*, which means a separate clock source is used to synchronize the router interaction with the CSU/DSU. Normally that clock signal is supplied by the CSU/DSU (which, in turn, is normally configured to take its clock signal from the network of the telephone company supplying the leased line).

In the lab environment there are no CSU/DSUs, so we have to tell one of the ports to generate a clock signal, to mimic what the CSU/DSU would normally provide. The `clockrate` command only takes effect for a port that is configured as a DCE.

The `clockrate 64000` command tells the port (if it is configured as a DCE) to generate a clock signal that simulates the port being connected to a 64 kbps line. Other values to simulate other line speeds are available.

We now will begin to explore the TCP/IP communication process between these three routers.

The ICMP *ping* command, which stands for *Packet Internet Groper*, sends a packet to a specified destination and requests a response. Let's see what happens if we try to ping router 2 from router 1. At the command prompt of router 1, input the following:

```
Router1>ping 120.1.1.2
```

Figure 3-8 Output of *show controllers* command with DTE cable

```
HD unit 0, idb = 0x80668, driver structure at 0x820E8
buffer size 1524 HD unit 0, V.35 DTE cable
cpb = 0x11, eda = 0x4800, cda = 0x4814
Rx ring with 16 entries at 0x114800
00 bd_ptr=0x4800 pak=0x084018 ds=0x11D840 status=80 pak_size=22
01 bd_ptr=0x4814 pak=0x083BB0 ds=0x11C418 status=80 pak_size=0
01 bd_ptr=0x4814 pak=0x083BB0 ds=0x11C418 status=80 pak_size=0
02 bd_ptr=0x4828 pak=0x083D28 ds=0x11CAD0 status=80 pak_size=0
03 bd_ptr=0x483C pak=0x083EA0 ds=0x11D188 status=80 pak_size=0
04 bd_ptr=0x4850 pak=0x084190 ds=0x11DEF8 status=80 pak_size=0
05 bd_ptr=0x4864 pak=0x084308 ds=0x11E5B0 status=80 pak_size=0
06 bd_ptr=0x4878 pak=0x084480 ds=0x11EC68 status=80 pak_size=0
07 bd_ptr=0x488C pak=0x0845F8 ds=0x11F320 status=80 pak_size=0
08 bd_ptr=0x48A0 pak=0x082D00 ds=0x1180E8 status=80 pak_size=0
09 bd_ptr=0x48B4 pak=0x082E78 ds=0x1187A0 status=80 pak_size=0
10 bd_ptr=0x48C8 pak=0x082FF0 ds=0x118E58 status=80 pak_size=0
11 bd_ptr=0x48DC pak=0x083168 ds=0x119510 status=80 pak_size=0
12 bd_ptr=0x48F0 pak=0x0832E0 ds=0x119BC8 status=80 pak_size=0
13 bd_ptr=0x4904 pak=0x0835D0 ds=0x11A938 status=80 pak_size=0
14 bd_ptr=0x4918 pak=0x083748 ds=0x11AFF0 status=80 pak_size=0
15 bd_ptr=0x492C pak=0x0838C0 ds=0x11B6A8 status=80 pak_size=0
16 bd_ptr=0x4940 pak=0x083A38 ds=0x11BD60 status=80 pak_size=0
cpb = 0x11, cda = 0x5000, cda = 0x5000
TX ring with 4 entries at 0x115000
00 bd_ptr=0x5000 pak=0x000000 ds=0x000000 status=80 pak size=0
01 bd_ptr=0x5014 pak 0x000000 ds=0x000000 status=80 pak_size=0
02 bd_ptr=0x5028 pak=0x000000 ds=0x000000 status=80 pak_size=0
03 bd_ptr=0x503C pak=0x000000 ds=0x000000 status=80 pak_size=0
04 bd_ptr=0x5050 pak=0x000000 ds=0x000000 status=80 pak_size=0
0 missed datagrams, 0 overruns
0 bad datagram encapsulations, 0 memory errors
0 transmitter underruns
```

Figure 3-9 Output of *show controllers* command with DCE cable

```
HD unit 0, idb = 0x7AA6C, driver structure at 0x7C528
buffer size 1524 HD unit 0, V.35 DCE cable clockrate 64000
cpb = 0x21, eda =  0x4940, cda = 0x4800
Rx ring with 16 entries at 0x214800
00 bd_ptr=0x4800 pak=0x07E030 ds=0x214C418 status=80 pak_size=0
01 bd_ptr=0x4814 pak=0x07E1AC ds=0x21CAD0 status=80 pak_size=0
02 bd_ptr=0x4828 pak=0x07E328 ds=0x21D188 status=80 pak_size=0
03 bd_ptr=0x483C pak=0x07E4A4 ds=0x21D840 status=80 pak_size=0
04 bd_ptr=0x4850 pak=0x07E620 ds=0x21DEF8 status=80 pak_size=0
05 bd_ptr=0x4864 pak=0x07E79C ds=0x21E5B0 status=80 pak_size=0
06 bd_ptr=0x4878 pak=0x07E918 ds=0x21EC68 status=80 pak_size=0
07 bd_ptr=0x488C pak=0x07EA94 ds=0x21F320 status=80 pak_size=0
08 bd_ptr=0x48A0 pak=0x07D158 ds=0x2180E8 status=80 pak_size=0
09 bd_ptr=0x48B4 pak=0x07D450 ds=0x218E58 status=80 pak_size=0
10 bd_ptr=0x48C8 pak=0x07D5CC ds=0x219510 status=80 pak_size=0
11 bd_ptr=0x48DC pak=0x07D748 ds=0x219BC8 status=80 pak_size=0
12 bd_ptr=0x48F0 pak=0x07D8C4 ds=0x21A280 status=80 pak_size=0
13 bd_ptr=0x4904 pak=0x07DA40 ds=0x21A938 status=80 pak_size=0
14 bd_ptr=0x4918 pak=0x07DBBC ds=0x21AFF0 status=80 pak_size=0
15 bd_ptr=0x492C pak=0x07DD38 ds=0x21B6A8 status=80 pak_size=0
16 bd_ptr=0x4940 pak=0x07DEB4 ds=0x21BD60 status=80 pak_size=0
cpb = 0x21, eda = 0x503C, cda = 0x503C
TX ring with 4 entries at 0x215000
00 bd_ptr=0x5000 pak=0x000000 ds=0x200078 status=80 pak_size=22
01 bd_ptr=0x5014 pak=0x000000 ds=0x200078 status=80 pak_size=22
02 bd_ptr=0x5028 pak=0x000000 ds=0x200078 status=80 pak_size=22
03 bd_ptr=0x503C pak=0x000000 ds=0x200078 status=80 pak_size=22
04 bd_ptr=0x5050 pak=0x000000 ds=0x200078 status=80 pak_size=22
0 missed datagrams, 0 overruns
0 bad datagram encapsulations, 0 memory errors
0 transmitter underruns
```

The router will display the following on the screen:

```
Type escape sequence to abort.
Sending 5, 100-byte ICMP Echos to 120.1.1.2, timeout is 2 seconds:
.!!!!
Success rate is 80 percent (4/5), round-trip min/avg/max = 28/75/112 ms
```

Why are only four of five packets returned? Could it be that a packet gets lost occasionally? Well, let's try it again.

```
Router1>ping 120.1.1.2
Type escape sequence to abort.
Sending 5, 100-byte ICMP Echos to 120.1.1.2, timeout is 2 seconds:
!!!!!
Success rate is 100 percent (5/5), round-trip min/avg/max = 1/2/4 ms
```

This time all five packets sent receive a reply. Try it as many times as you like and you'll see that every packet sent gets a reply. To understand why this happens, we must consider what the router is doing when a ping packet is sent. The router has to construct a correctly formatted Ethernet packet, with the necessary addresses to get from source to destination.

To do this, the router must identify the following four addresses:

- Source MAC address
- Source IP address
- Destination MAC address
- Destination IP address

The router knows its own MAC and IP address, and the ping command defined the destination IP address. What is missing is the destination MAC address. In Chap. 2 we discussed the ARP protocol, which maintains the ARP table that maps MAC addresses to IP addresses. When router 1 first tries to send out a ping packet, it does not have the MAC address of router 2, so it cannot complete the construction of the first ping packet. It then sends out a broadcast ARP request to find out the MAC address of router 2. (Router 1 actually tries to find out the MAC address associated with the destination IP address specified in the ping command.) Once router 2 replies, the MAC/IP address pair is put in the ARP table. When router 1 tries to send a packet to router 2 a second time, it has all the information and the ping packet can be correctly constructed. That is why only the very first ping fails and all other pings succeed.

We can demonstrate this interaction as follows. Input the following on router 1:

```
Router1>show ip arp

Protocol   Address     Age (min)  Hardware Addr    Type   Interface
Internet   120.1.1.1   -          0000.0c47.42dd   ARPA   Ethernet0
Internet   120.1.1.2   2          0000.0c47.0457   ARPA   Ethernet0
```

Turn off router 1 and then turn it back on. When presented with the router prompt, input the same command. The output now shows the following:

```
Router1>sho ip arp

Protocol   Address     Age (min)  Hardware Addr    Type   Interface
Internet   120.1.1.1   -          0000.0c47.42dd   ARPA   Ethernet0
```

As you can see, after the router is rebooted, only its own MAC address is in the ARP table. To ping router 2, an ARP broadcast must be sent to determine the MAC address of router 2.

Now, try the same thing from router 2 to ping router 3. Input the following to router 2:

```
Router2>ping 150.1.1.2
Type escape sequence to abort.
Sending 5, 100-byte ICMP Echos to 150.1.1.2, timeout is 2 seconds:
!!!!!
Success rate is 100 percent (5/5), round-trip min/avg/max = 28/30/32 ms
```

The success rate is 100 percent the first time out. Why did this work on the first try, and the ping from router 1 to router 2 didn't? The answer is that the communication from router 2 to router 3 uses the Cisco default Data Link protocol for a serial port, which is HDLC. HDLC is used for point-to-point links that do not have MAC addresses associated with them. Therefore router 2 has all the information it needs to send a ping packet out on a serial port.

We have reached the point where router 1 can ping router 2 and router 2 can ping router 3. Should router 1 be able to ping router 3? Try that by entering the following into router 1:

```
Router1>ping 150.1.1.2
Type escape sequence to abort.
Sending 5, 100-byte ICMP Echos to 150.1.1.2, timeout is 2 seconds:
......
Success rate is 0 percent (0/5)
```

As you can see, it does not work. To solve this problem, we need to look at the routing table, often a good place to start when troubleshooting router problems. We can display the routing table by inputting the following to router 1:

```
Router1>show ip route
Codes: C - connected, S - static, I - IGRP, R - RIP, M - mobile, B - BGP
       D - EIGRP, EX - EIGRP external, O - OSPF, IA - OSPF inter area
       E1 - OSPF external type 1, E2 - OSPF external type 2, E - EGP
       i - IS-IS, L1 - IS-IS level-1, L2 - IS-IS level-2, * - candidate default
Gateway of last resort is not set

C120.0.0.0 is directly connected, Ethernet0
```

As you can see, the routing table has entries only for the 120.0.0.0 network. (Remember, we configured the port with default subnet masks, so having a first octet value of 120 means we have a class A network, and therefore only the first octet is used to identify the network number.) In this instance, the router realizes that the destination address, 150.1.1.2, is on the 150.1.0.0 network (a class B network). The router will realize that this is not a directly connected network and will refer to its routing table to determine which router should get the ping packet in order to reach the 150.1.0.0 network. Clearly, without an entry in its routing table for the 150.1.0.0 network, the router can go no further.

You can enter the route directly into the router's routing table with the following input:

```
Router1>ena
Password:
Router1#conf t
Enter configuration commands, one per line. End with Ctrl/Z.
Router1(config)#ip route 150.1.0.0 120.1.1.2
Router1(config)#<Ctrl-Z>
Router1#
```

This tells router 1 that the next router to go to on the way to the 150.1.0.0 network is that with the address 120.1.1.2. This is shown in the routing table as follows:

```
router1>show ip route
Codes: C - connected, S - static, I - IGRP, R - RIP, M - mobile, B - BGP
       D- EIGRP, EX - EIGRP external, O - OSPF, IA - OSPF inter area
       E1 - OSPF external type 1, E2 - OSPF external type 2, E - EGP
       i- IS-IS, L1 - IS-IS level-1, L2 - IS-IS level-2, * - candidate default
Gateway of last resort is not set

       C120.0.0.0 is directly connected, Ethernet0
       S150.1.0.0 [1/0] via 120.1.1.2
```

So what happens if we now try to ping 150.1.1.2 from router 1?

```
Router1>ping 150.1.1.2
Type escape sequence to abort.
Sending 5, 100-byte ICMP Echos to 150.1.1.2, timeout is 2 seconds:
......
Success rate is 0 percent (0/5)
```

It still fails. What happens is that router 1 now knows to pass the packet to router 2 to get to the 150.1.0.0 network. Once the packet is delivered to router 3, router 3 will try to reply to 120.1.1.1. Router 3 does not have a route to the 120.0.0.0 network, so the ping fails again. To resolve this, we need to add a route to the 120.0.0.0 network in the routing table of router 3. This is done as follows:

```
Router3(config)#ip route 120.0.0.0 150.1.1.1
Router3(config)#<Ctrl-Z>
Router3#
```

The routing table of router 3 now looks like this:

```
Router3#sho ip route
Codes: C - connected, S - static, I - IGRP, R - RIP, M - mobile, B - BGP
      D- EIGRP, EX - EIGRP external, O - OSPF, IA - OSPF inter area
      E1 - OSPF external type 1, E2 - OSPF external type 2, E - EGP
      i- IS-IS, L1 - IS-IS level-1, L2 - IS-IS level-2, * - candidate default
Gateway of last resort is not set

S120.0.0.0 [1/0] via 150.1.1.1
C150.1.0.0 is directly connected, Serial0
```

Note that the routes entered are either *static* (meaning they are in the router's configuration), or *connected* (meaning they are directly connected to one of the router's interfaces).

Now if we go back to router 1 and ping router 3, we see what we wanted to see all along:

```
Router1>ping 150.1.1.2
Type escape sequence to abort.
Sending 5, 100-byte ICMP Echos to 150.1.1.2, timeout is 2 seconds:
!!!!!
Success rate is 100 percent (5/5), round-trip min/avg/max = 28/30/32 ms
```

Adding routes manually in this fashion rapidly becomes cumbersome for a growing network. To automate the routing table update process, routing protocols are run on the routers. Chapter 4 covers routing protocols in depth; at this time, however, we shall look in overview at the configuration of Cisco's *Interior Gateway Routing Protocol* (IGRP).

We are now going to remove the static routes we configured in the routers and configure IGRP on each router so that it will make the required entries in the routing table for us.

First, remove the static routes. To do this type the following into router 1:

```
Router1#no ip route 150.1.0.0 120.1.1.2
```

Into router 3, type the following:

```
Router3#no ip route 120.0.0.0 150.1.1.1
```

This introduces the "no" form of command. Whenever you need to remove an entry in the router's configuration, simply enter configuration mode and type the word "no" followed by the configuration entry you want to remove.

Making standard IGRP a running process on all three routers is a simple configuration change, and can be executed as follows for router 2:

```
Router2#conf t
Router2(config)#router igrp 9
Router2(config-router)#network 150.1.0.0
Router2(config-router)#network 120.0.0.0
Router2(config-router)#<Ctrl-Z>
```

Once you have entered configuration mode, you define the router process IGRP as belonging to an *Autonomous System number* 9. It does not matter what number you assign as the Autonomous System number in this case. All you need do is assign the same number to all three router IGRP processes. IGRP processes simply will exchange route information with other processes belonging to the same Autonomous System number.

The two network entries are there to tell IGRP what networks to advertise in its initial IGRP packet. The rule to follow is that you must configure a network entry for each directly connected network number. Note that, because IGRP does not send subnet mask information in its updates, the entries here are concerned only with network (not subnetwork) numbers.

The entries for router 1 and router 3 are made as follows:

```
Router1#conf t
Router1(config)#router igrp 9
Router1(config-router)#network 120.0.0.0
Router1(config-router)#<Ctrl-Z>

Router3#conf t
Router3(config)#router igrp 9
Router3(config-router)#network 150.1.0.0
Router3(config-router)#<Ctrl>Z
```

The three router configurations now appear as shown in Fig. 3-10.

After a few minutes have elapsed, IGRP will have advertised the network numbers throughout this small internetwork and have updated the routing tables with appropriate entries. The routing table for router 1 is as shown here:

```
Router1>show ip route
Codes: C - connected, S - static, I - IGRP, R - RIP, M - mobile, B - BGP
       D- EIGRP, EX - EIGRP external, O - OSPF, IA - OSPF inter area
       E1 - OSPF external type 1, E2 - OSPF external type 2, E - EGP
       i- IS-IS, L1 - IS-IS level-1, L2 - IS-IS level-2, * - candidate default
Gateway of last resort is not set

C120.0.0.0 is directly connected, Ethernet0
I150.1.0.0 [100/8576] via 120.1.1.2, 00:01:20, Ethernet0
```

And the routing table for router 3 is as follows:

```
Router3>show ip route
Codes: C - connected, S - static, I - IGRP, R - RIP, M - mobile, B - BGP
       D - EIGRP, EX - EIGRP external, O - OSPF, IA - OSPF inter area
       E1 - OSPF external type 1, E2 - OSPF external type 2, E - EGP
       i - IS-IS, L1 - IS-IS level-1, L2 - IS-IS level-2, * - candidate default
Gateway of last resort is not set

I120.0.0.0 [100/8576] via 150.1.1.1, 00:01:14, Serial0
C150.1.0.0 is directly connected, Serial0
```

The thing to note is that the routing table indicates that the routes necessary for router 1 and 3 to ping each other were learned from IGRP and are no longer static routes as they were originally.

Figure 3-10 Lab router configuration with IGRP enabled

```
Router 1
router1#wr t
Building configuration...
Current configuration:
!
version 10.3
!
hostname router1
!
enable secret 5 $1$W6qH$DTNrEHmJrn6QqYcMu5PRh.
enable password test
!
interface Ethernet0
 ip address 120.1.1.1 255.0.0.0
!
interface Serial0
 no ip address
 shutdown
!
interface Serial1
 no ip address
 shutdown
!
router igrp 9
 network 120.0.0.0
!
line con 0
line aux 0
 transport input all
line vty 0 4
 password ilx
 login
!
end

Router 2
Building configuration:
Current configuration:
```

Figure 3-10
continued

```
!
version 10.3
!
hostname router2
!
enable secret 5 $1$/P2r$ob00lmzYqpogV0U1g1O8U/
enable password test
!
interface Ethernet)0
 ip address 120.1.1.2 255.0.0.0
!
interface Serial0
 ip address 150.1.1.1 255.255.0.0
!
interface Serial1
 no ip address
 shutdown
!
router igrp 9
 network 120.0.0.0
 network 150.1.0.0
!
line con 0
line aux 0
line vty 0 4
 password ilx
 login
!
end

Router 3
Building configuration:
Current configuration:
!
version 10.3
!
hostname router3
!
enable secret 5 $1$cNaQ$a4jcvrX1zVO4cwJB7RP5j1
enable password test
!
interface Ethernet0
 ip address 193.1.1.1 255.255.255.0
!
interface Serial0
 ip address 150.1.1.2 255.255.0.0
 clockrate 64000
!
interface Serial1
 no ip address
 shutdown
!
```

Figure 3-10 continued

```
router igrp 9
 network 150.1.0.0
!
line con 0
 exec-timeout 0 0
line aux 0
 transport input all
line vty 0 4
 password ilx
 login
!
end
```

It is now worth exploring the application of subnets in a real environment. What we are about to do is configure all ports on this small internetwork to be in subnets of the network number 160.4.0.0. To accomplish this, we need to change the address and netmask of all ports and the IGRP configuration for each router. For router 1, these changes are put into effect by the following input:

```
Router1(config)#int e0
Router1(config-int)#ip address 160.4.1.33 255.255.255.224
Router1(config-int)#exit
Router1(config)#router igrp 9
Router1(config-router)#no network 120.0.0.0
Router1(config-router)#network 160.4.0.0
Router1(config-router)#<Ctrl-Z>
```

The configuration for router 1 is illustrated in Fig. 3-11. To configure router 2 and view its configuration, follow the commands shown in Fig. 3-12. In order to configure router 3, use the commands shown in Fig. 3-13.

Note that when configuring IGRP, the same network number is defined on each router. In this case, when IGRP advertisements are received, it is assumed that the same subnet mask is used on all interfaces on the internetwork and the correct entries in the routing tables are then made. The routing tables now appear as follows:

```
Router1>show ip route
Codes: C - connected, S - static, I - IGRP, R - RIP, M - mobile, B - BGP
       D - EIGRP, EX - EIGRP external, O - OSPF, IA - OSPF inter area
       E1 - OSPF external type 1, E2 - OSPF external type 2, E - EGP
       i - IS-IS, L1 - IS-IS level-1, L2 - IS-IS level-2, * - candidate default
Gateway of last resort is not set

160.4.0.0 255.255.255.224 is subnetted, 2 subnets
C 160.4.1.32 is directly connected, Ethernet0
I 160.4.1.64 [100/8576] via 160.4.1.34, 00:00:00, Ethernet0
```

```
Router2>show ip route
Codes: C - connected, S - static, I - IGRP, R - RIP, M - mobile, B - BGP
       D - EIGRP, EX - EIGRP external, O - OSPF, IA - OSPF inter area
       E1 - OSPF external type 1, E2 - OSPF external type 2, E - EGP
       i - IS-IS, L1 - IS-IS level-1, L2 - IS-IS level-2, * - candidate default
Gateway of last resort is not set

160.4.0.0 255.255.255.224 is subnetted, 2 subnets
C  160.4.1.32 is directly connected, Ethernet0
C  160.4.1.64 is directly connected, Serial0

Router3>show ip route
Codes: C - connected, S - static, I - IGRP, R - RIP, M - mobile, B - BGP
       D - EIGRP, EX - EIGRP external, O - OSPF, IA - OSPF inter area
       E1 - OSPF external type 1, E2 - OSPF external type 2, E - EGP
       i - IS-IS, L1 - IS-IS level-1, L2 - IS-IS level-2, * - candidate default
Gateway of last resort is not set

160.4.0.0 255.255.255.224 is subnetted, 2 subnets
I  160.4.1.32 [100/8576] via 160.4.1.65, 00:01:07, Serial0
C  160.4.1.64 is directly connected, Serial0
```

Figure 3-11 Router 1 configured for subnets

```
!
version 10.3
!
hostname router1
!
enable secret 5 $1$W6qH$DTNrEIImJrn6QqYcMu5PRh.
enable password test
!
interface Ethernet0
 ip address 160.4.1.33 255.255.255.224
!
interface Serial0
 no ip address
 shutdown
!
interface Serial1
 no ip address
 shutdown
!
router igrp 9
 network 160.4.0.0
!
line con 0
line aux 0
 transport input all
line vty 0 4
 password ilx
 login
!
end
```

Figure 3-12
Router 2 configured for subnets

```
router2# conf t
Enter configuration commands, one per line. End with CNTL/Z.
router2(config)# int e0
router2(config-if)# 160.4.1.34 255.255.255.224
router2(config-if)# ip address 160.4.1.34 255.255.255.224
router2(config-if)# int s0
router2(config-if)#ip address 160.4.1.34 255.255.255.224
router2(config-if)# exit
router2(config)#router igrp 9
router2(config-router)# no net 120.0.0.0
router2(config-router)#no net 150.1.0.0
router2(config-router)# net 160.4.0.0
router2(config-router)# <ctrl>Z
router2#
```

The configuration for router 2 now looks like the following:

```
router2# wr t
Building configuration...
        Current configuration:
!
version 10.3
!
hostname router2
!
enable secret 5 $1$/P2r$ob00lmzYqpogV0U1g1O8U/
enable password test
!
interface Ethernet0
 ip address 160.4.1.34 255.255.255.224
!
interface Serial0
 ip address 160.4.1.65 255.255.255.224
!
interface Serial1
 no ip address
 shutdown
!
router igrp 9
 network 160.4.0.0
!
line con 0
line aux 0
line vty 0 4
 password ilx
 login
!
end
```

An interesting point is that the network number that is tracked in the routing table is a derived value. By looking at both the assigned IP address and the subnet mask, the subnetwork number is calculated. This effect can be clearly illustrated by changing the IP address of the serial port on router 3, keeping the subnet mask the same, then viewing the new routing table:

```
Router3(config)#interface serial 0
Router3(config-int)#ip address 160.4.1.100 255.255.255.224
```

The routing table now looks like this:

```
Router3>show ip route
Codes: C - connected, S - static, I - IGRP, R - RIP, M - mobile, B - BGP
       D - EIGRP, EX - EIGRP external, O - OSPF, IA - OSPF inter area
       E1 - OSPF external type 1, E2 - OSPF external type 2, E - EGP
       i - IS-IS, L1 - IS-IS level-1, L2 - IS-IS level-2, * - candidate default
Gateway of last resort is not set

160.4.0.0 255.255.255.224 is subnetted, 2 subnets
I  160.4.1.32 [100/8576] via 160.4.1.65, 00:01:07, Serial0
C  160.4.1.96 is directly connected, Serial0
```

As you can see, the routing table automatically adjusted to keep track of a new network number associated with that interface, simply because you changed the IP address of that interface.

As a point of interest, this is the exact opposite of the way that NetWare protocols work. In NetWare, you assign one network number to a server and all workstations on that network work out their own address. With TCP/IP, you assign addresses and a subnet mask to all workstation interfaces and the network number is calculated from that. We will be discussing the NetWare protocols more fully in Chap. 5.

Lab Exercises

We will now alter the configuration to make things stop working and look at how these problems can be identified and resolved.

Make these changes to the lab environment and we will troubleshoot the network and get it back into a working state.

1. Change the encapsulation on router 3 Serial 0 port to ppp.
2. Change the polarity of the DTE/DCE cable, so that the end of the cable connected to the router 2 Serial 0 port is connected to the router 3 Serial 0 port

Figure 3-13 Router 3 configured for subnets

```
router2# conf t
Enter configuration commands, one per line. E
router3(config)# int s0
router3(config-if)# ip address 160.4.1.66 255.2
router3(config-if)# exit
router3(config)#router igrp 9
router3(config-router)#no net 150.1.0.0
router3(config-router)# net 160.4.0.0
router2(config-router)# exit
router3(confug)#
```

The configuration for router 3 now looks

```
router3# wr t
Building configuration...
        Current configuration:
!
version 10.3
!
hostname router3
!
enable secret 5 $1$cNaQ$a4jcvrXlzV
enable password test
!
interface Ethernet0
 ip address 193.1.1.1 255.255.255.0
 shutdown
!
interface Serial0
 ip address 160.4.1.66 255.255.255.2
 clockrate 64000
!
interface Serial1
 no ip address
 shutdown
!
router igrp 9
 network 160.4.0.0
!
line con 0
line aux 0
 transport input all
line vty 0 4
 password ilx
 login
!
end
```

3. Configure the Ethernet 0 port on router 1 to be shut down.
4. Change the Autonomous System number of the IGRP process on router 2 to 15.
5. Disconnect the Ethernet 0 port on router 2 from the hub.

To effect the router configuration changes, perform the following:

```
Router3#conf t
Router3(config)#int s0
Router3(config-if)encapsulation ppp

Router1#conf t
Router1(config)#int e0
Router1(config-if)shutdown

Router2#conf t
Router2(config)#no router igrp 9
Router2(config)#router igrp 15
Router2(config-router)network 160.4.0.0
```

A troubleshooting procedure should follow the previously described OSI seven-layer model of communications. You need to check the Physical layer first, then the Data Link and so forth, until the system is communicating properly.

Overview of Physical Layer Troubleshooting

A visual check shows whether cables are connected, but may not show a cable break. The best way to determine whether a router port is physically connected is to use the `show interface` command and interpret the screen output. Perform the following on router 2:

```
Router2#show interface ethernet 0
Ethernet0 is up, line protocol down
```

This is the first line of the output, and shows you that the port is okay, but was not able to establish a protocol session. This is either due to an unplugged/broken cable, or a broken transceiver. In this case, the cable is simply unplugged; replugging the cable brings the line protocol up. The problem generated by change number 5 has been detected and corrected.

Next on the Physical level you should check the serial port connections. Entering the following in router 2 will bring up a screen display, the last line of which is as shown.

```
Router2#show interface serial 0
   .
   .
DCD=up DSR=up DTR=up RTS=up CTS=up
```

This indicates that the physical connectivity to this port is working, and all the expected EIA signals are present. The port is, however, showing that the line protocol is down. This is due to either clocking problems or mismatched encapsulation. To resolve this, we issue the `show controllers serial 0` command on both router 2 and 3, and check that the router configuring its Serial 0 port as a DCE has the `clockrate 64000` entry in its configuration. By changing the polarity of the DTE/DCE cable, we match the DCE port with the "`clockrate 64000`"-configured serial port and resolve the problem caused by change 2.

The final Physical layer issue to determine whether any ports that need to be in use are physically shut down. Enter the following on router 1.

```
Router1#show interface ethernet 0
Ethernet0 is administratively down, line protocol down
```

The first line of the screen output as shown indicates that the port has been shut down by the administrator, by the `shutdown` entry in the port's configuration. This can be fixed by issuing the `no shutdown` command in interface configuration mode, which resolves the problem caused by change 3.

Overview of Data Link Layer Troubleshooting

For Data Link layer troubleshooting, we refer to the router configuration. The only thing to check here is that connected ports share the same Data Link layer encapsulation. By issuing the `wri t` command to both router 2 and 3, we see mismatched layer 2 encapsulations. By viewing the configurations, we see PPP as the encapsulation for Serial 0 on router3, but the Serial 0 port of router 2 shows no encapsulation. With no encapsulation, the Cisco HDLC default is used. Taking out the `encapsulation ppp` entry from the Serial 0 port of router 3 resolves problem 1.

Overview of Network Layer Troubleshooting

Once the layer 1 and 2 problems have been resolved, only the Network layer remains to be checked in our scenario. We know that with IGRP, routing information is exchanged only between systems belonging to the same Autonomous System number. By reviewing the router configurations, we see that router 2 has a different AS number than router 1 and 3. Changing the AS to match enables all routers to share route information, which resolves problem 4. All routers can now ping one other again, because IGRP can now update each router's routing table with the necessary information.

Summary

This chapter covered how to configure a new router using Cisco's Setup feature, viewing and understanding the configuration file that this generates, and modifying this file using the Cisco configuration mode. How to store and retrieve these files from a network TFTP server was covered, including use of the auto configuration routine.

The chapter concluded with instructions on how to build a simple laboratory of three Cisco routers to enable us to explore how routers interact in a small internetwork.

CHAPTER 4

Routing Protocols Used in TCP/IP

Objectives

This chapter examines various routing protocols popular in the TCP/IP world. By the end of this chapter you should have a good theoretical understanding of the following protocols and know how they are implemented in a Cisco environment.

- RIP version 1
- IGRP
- EIGRP
- OSPF
- Integrated IS-IS
- EGP and BGP

Additionally, you should be able to choose which routing protocol to use for different situations. Finally, the process of redistribution, which enables multiple routing protocols to communicate on one internetwork, will be explained, and examples of implementation given. We will discuss the theory of each protocol, its good and bad points, and examine how the protocol can be configured on Cisco routers.

Routing Protocol Responsibilities

Routing protocols exist to keep routing tables accurate, even though the internetwork they are operating on will be changing due to equipment or line failures and the addition of new network segments.

To keep tables accurate, a routing protocol operation has two parts. The first sends advertisements (referred to as *routing updates*) out from a router, regarding the location of network numbers it knows about. The second receives and processes these routing updates in a way that keeps the router's routing table directing traffic efficiently.

There are two main types of routing protocols, the *Interior Gateway Routing Protocol* and the *Exterior Gateway Routing Protocol.* To understand the difference between these two, we need to define what an *autonomous system* is on an internetwork. Figure 4-1 shows a large internetwork split into three autonomous systems.

The idea behind autonomous systems is as follows. Imagine there are three different internetworks, one managed by an American-based team,

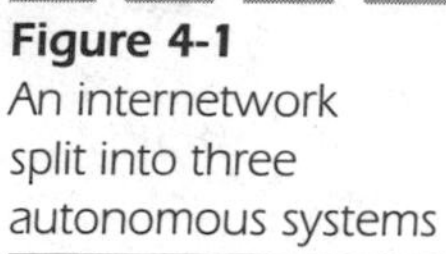

Figure 4-1
An internetwork split into three autonomous systems

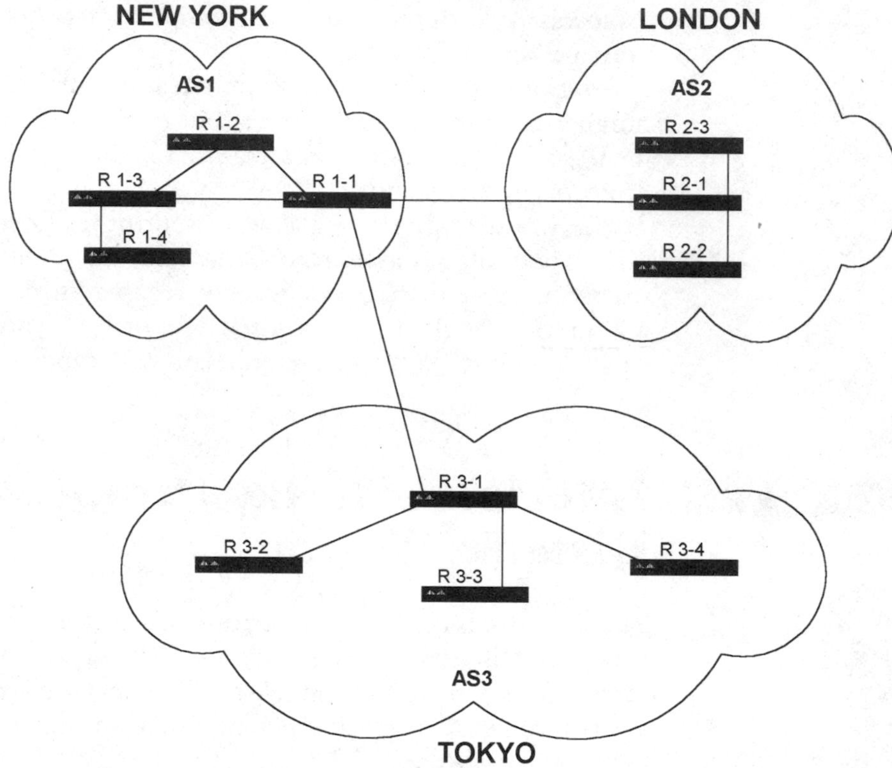

one by a UK-based team, and one by a team based in Japan. Each of these internetworks is managed in a different way and has different policies. Suppose these three internetworks need to be connected so they can exchange information, but the separate network management teams want to retain their own policies and want to control the routing updates received from the newly connected internetworks.

One way to meet these goals is to define an Exterior Gateway Routing Protocol process on the routers that connect the three internetworks. In Fig. 4-1, these are routers R1-1, R2-1 and R3-1. The Exterior Gateway Protocol limits the amount of routing information that is exchanged among these three internetworks and allows them to be managed differently.

Within each autonomous system, all routers would run an Interior Gateway Routing Protocol, which assumes that the whole internetwork is under the management of one body and, by default, exchanges routing information freely with all other routers in the same autonomous system. Sophisticated Interior Gateway Routing Protocols, such as Cisco's IGRP, however, have the functionality to act as Exterior Gateway Routing

Protocols. As with most things in computer networking, clear-cut definitions are hard to come by.

Exterior Gateway Routing Protocols and multiple autonomous system numbers are used on the Internet but rarely in the commercial environment, so we shall concentrate mainly on the Interior Gateway Routing Protocols in this chapter.

The world of Interior Gateway Routing Protocols is split into two camps, one known as *distance vector* and the other as *link state*. In the next section, we discuss two distance vector routing protocol algorithms, *RIP* and *IGRP*, followed by a discussion of the hybrid *EIGRP*. After that, we shall look at two link state protocols, *OSPF* and *Integrated IS-IS*.

Interior Gateway Protocols: Distance Vector

The first distance vector protocol was the *Routing Information Protocol*, (RIP). The discussion that follows on RIP fully explains how a distance vector routing protocol works. We will review the generic distance vector algorithm, followed by discussion of RIP version 1 as the first protocol of this type.

Generic Distance Vector

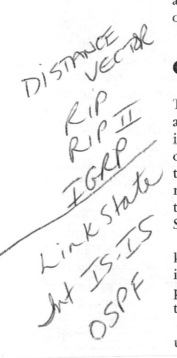

The *distance vector algorithm* (sometimes referred to as the *Bellman-Ford* algorithm for the people who invented it), requires each machine involved in the routing process to keep track of its "distance" from all other possible destinations. What happens is that a router is programmed to construct a table of all possible destinations (in terms of network numbers) and measure the distance to each location. The only information a router has at boot time is what networks are directly attached to it. So how can it find out about all other possible destinations?

Each router is programmed so that it announces all the destinations it knows about, along with the distance to each. Once a router starts hearing all the advertisements from other routers, it can start to list all the possible destinations and calculate the shortest path to these destinations—the one kept in the routing table.

So a distance vector protocol will, on a regular basis, send out an update that contains all the information contained in the machine's

routing table. These updates are sent only to neighboring routers on directly connected segments. One of the key differences between distance vector and link state routing is that link state protocols send information to routers on remote segments.

Once these updates get to a router, the router will then use a collection of algorithms and timers to decide what entries should be put into the routing table of the machine that is receiving the updates. Another key aspect of distance vector protocols is that any given machine knows only the next hop in the sequence to deliver the packet to its ultimate destination. In link state protocols, each machine has a complete map of the network it is in (or, more accurately, the routing area it is in—but we will come to that later).

To finish this introduction, let's take a high-level overview of the code behind the distance vector algorithm:

1. Each router has a unique identification on the internetwork.
2. Every router will identify a metric to be associated with each link directly connected to itself.
3. All routers will start advertising directly connected links with a metric of zero.
4. Every router transmits to neighbors the complete information regarding all destinations and their metric when the router first boots, then periodically, and whenever a router becomes aware of a change.
5. Each router determines which directly connected neighbor offers the lowest metric to each location.

RIP: The Routing Information Protocol

The first Interior Gateway Protocol (IGP) was the Routing Information Protocol, or "RIP" as it became known. RIP was designed for an environment that had only a relatively small number of machines, and these machines were connected with links that had identical characteristics.

As the first IGP, RIP gained widespread use and was distributed free with BSD Unix as the *routed* daemon process. As today's heterogeneous networks grow and become more diverse, RIP has been improved upon with more modern, more full-featured distance vector protocols. RIP is still in widespread use and is the only routing protocol that Unix machines universally understand.Okay, before we get into the workings of RIP, let's refresh our memories regarding what a routing table looks like. To display a Cisco router's routing table, do the following:

```
Router1>show ip route
Codes:  C - connected, S - static, I - IGRP, R - RIP, M - mobile, B - BGP
   D - EIGRP, EX - EIGRP external, O - OSPF, IA - OSPF inter area
   E1 - OSPF external type 1, E2 - OSPF external type 2, E - EGP
   i - IS-IS, L1 - IS-IS level-1, L2 - IS-IS level-2, * - candidate default
Gateway of last resort is not set

 160.4.0.0 255.255.255.224 is subnetted, 2 subnets
C  160.4.1.32 is directly connected, Ethernet0
R  160.4.1.64 [120/1] via 160.4.1.34, 00:00:12, Ethernet0
```

In the first column, the router tells us how it learned about the routing table entries. The legend at the top of the display explains what these abbreviations mean. For example, C means that the network is directly *connected* to the router on the specified interface. S stands for *static route* and means that the route to this destination network is hard-coded into the router's configuration. R means that the router learned of this destination network via a *RIP update*.

The rest of the entry in the router's routing table states which interface to use for the specified network, and which router to send the packet to next if the destination network is on another part of the internetwork. In this case, the RIP entry is telling us to use the router with address 160.4.1.34 in order to get to the 160.4.1.64.subnet, and that this router is connected to the Ethernet 0 interface.

Let's look at the rest of this entry in more detail. The `[120/1]` entry in the RIP line first gives the value of the administrative distance, and then the metric. The *administrative distance* is a value assigned to routing protocols. RIP has a value of 120, OSPF of 110, IGRP of 100, EIGRP of 90, static of 1, and directly connected of 0.

This administrative distance is used if two routing protocols advertise the same route to the same router. In this case, the router will prefer the route supplied by the routing protocol with the lowest value for administrative distance. The logic behind this is that, because Cisco routers give you the ability to have multiple routing protocols running on the same router, you need some way of deciding which routing protocol is advertising the best route. Clearly the metrics used by different routing protocols are not comparable; RIP only goes up to a metric of 16, while IGRP goes to more than 16 million, so this other measure is used to show preference for the routing protocols in use. EIGRP is most preferred, IGRP next, then OSPF and finally RIP.

The 00:00:12 value is a counter that indicates the amount of time that has passed since the router received an advertisement for this route.

We will now discuss how RIP handles its responsibilities as a routing protocol in more detail.

The Basics of How RIP Works. Once configured on an internetwork, the operation of RIP and its interaction with the routing table is fairly straightforward. By default, every 30 seconds each RIP-enabled device sends out a RIP update message, comprising routing information from the machine's routing table. This message includes the following:

- Destination address of host or network.
- The IP address of the gateway sending the update.
- A metric that indicates the distance (in terms of hops) to the destination.

It is worth noting that interfaces on a Unix machine or a router can be defined as passive. If that is done, the interface in question does not send out any RIP updates; it merely listens for updates from other machines.

Once a routing device receives an update, it processes the new information, which it compares with that in the existing routing table. If the routing update includes a new destination network, it is added to the routing table. If the router receives a route with a smaller metric to an existing destination, it replaces the existing route. If an entry in the update message has the same destination network and gateway but a different metric, it will use the new metric to update the routing table.

This covers how routers handle a static network using RIP; some additions to the protocol are in place to handle changes in topology, such as a downed link. If the preceding were the only logic coded into a router, it would not recover from a downed link because it remembers only the best route to any given destination. If the gateway, or link to that gateway, should fail, the routing table might never reflect the change.

That's because, so far, the logic defined depended upon a gateway notifying its neighbors of whether its metrics had changed. If the gateway could no longer communicate, it could not notify its neighbors of a change. To handle such situations, RIP employs timers: It sends out messages (every 30 seconds by default), and the protocol assumes that if a gateway or specific route is not heard from within 180 seconds, it no longer is available. Once it determines that a route is unavailable, the router sends a special message that notifies its neighbors of the unavailable route. After 270 seconds, if nothing is heard from the gateways or route, this information is flushed from the router's routing table. These timers are known as the *update, invalid,* and *flush* timers, respectively.

To understand fully how a router deals with link or other failures on the internetwork, we need to explore other issues, starting with the *count to infinity* problem. With a router that uses RIP as its routing protocol, "infinity" turns out to be 16. Clearly, some further explanation is needed here.

RIP's interpretation of infinity as the number 16 relates to the Time To Live (TTL) field in the IP layer header. Each time a packet travels through a router, its TTL field (with initial value of 15) is decreased by one. When the TTL value reaches 0, the packet is discarded and no longer exists in the internetwork. This feature is there to stop a packet caught in a routing loop from being switched back and forth forever between routers. Obviously we want the TTL value to be high enough to allow us to send correctly routed packets through whatever network size we want to implement, but small enough so that packets are not kept in a routing loop for too long. In a RIP-based network, this value is fixed at 15. With IGRP, we can set the value to whatever we like.

Let's see how this situation of a circulating packet can occur, and what features in RIP have been implemented to minimize its occurrence. Referring to Fig. 4-2, consider the situation wherein a PC on network 3 needs to send a message to a PC on network 1.

First let's examine what happens with RIP during normal operation. Router A initially will advertise that it knows about networks 1 and 2. Router B will advertise that it knows about networks 2 and 3. (This is similar to the lab we set up in Chap. 3.) After these initial advertisements, both routers know about all three networks. If router B sends an update to router A, stating that it knows how to get to network 1, we can run into some problems. Here's how this can happen.

Suppose the interface on router A goes down and router A cannot contact network 1. If router B is advertising to router A a route to net-

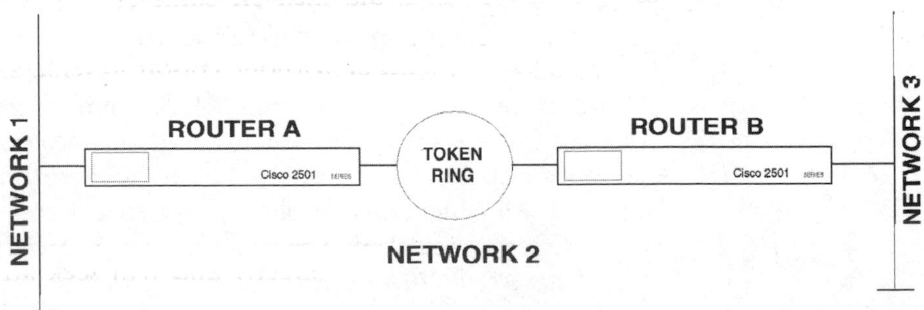

Figure 4-2
An internetwork in which Split Horizon prevents routing loops

work 1, router A will think that it can get to network 1 by sending a packet to router B. So, if a PC on network 3 wants to send a packet to a PC on network 1 and the interface on router A to network 1 goes down, the packet will get caught in a routing loop. This happens because router B will decide that to get to network 1, it must send the packet to router A. Router A knows that its directly connected interface to network 1 is down and that network 1 cannot be reached that way. Since router A has received an update from router B stating that it knows how to get to network 1, the packet will get sent back to router B and the process starts all over. The only thing that stops this process is the count to infinity.

The *Split Horizon* algorithm was designed to counter this problem. The effect of the Split Horizon rule is that a router will send out different routing update messages on different interfaces. In effect, a router never sends out information on an interface that it learned from that interface. The logic is that if a router first learns of a network from an adjacent router, that adjacent router must be nearer the network. The effect of this rule in the sample internetwork of Fig. 4-2 is that router B will have learned about network 1 from router A, and therefore, according to Split Horizon, router B will not include network 1 in its routing updates sent to router A.

RIP version 1 implemented Split Horizon with *Poison Reverse Update*. This formidable sounding title is, in fact, a small modification to the Split Horizon algorithm described above. All it means is that, instead of not advertising routes to the source, routes are advertised back to the source with a metric of 16, which will make the source router ignore the route. It is perceived that explicitly telling a router to ignore a route is better than not telling it about the route in the first place.

All this means in practice (if the fault condition is in effect) is that a PC will know that it cannot send a message to a PC on network 1 more quickly. This could mean that a user knows he cannot send his message, or this knowledge could kick off some dial-backup facilities to restore service more quickly.

Split Horizon, with or without Poison Reverse, only counters routing loops between adjacent routers. Let's look at Fig. 4-3 and see a situation in which Split Horizon will not save us from a routing loop.

Suppose router C gets a packet destined for network 1; then, in normal operation, the packet is sent to router A for delivery. If the interface on router A to network 1 goes down, router A knows it cannot deliver the packet to network 1 directly and will seek an alternate route. Split Horizon stops router C from telling router A that it knows how to get to

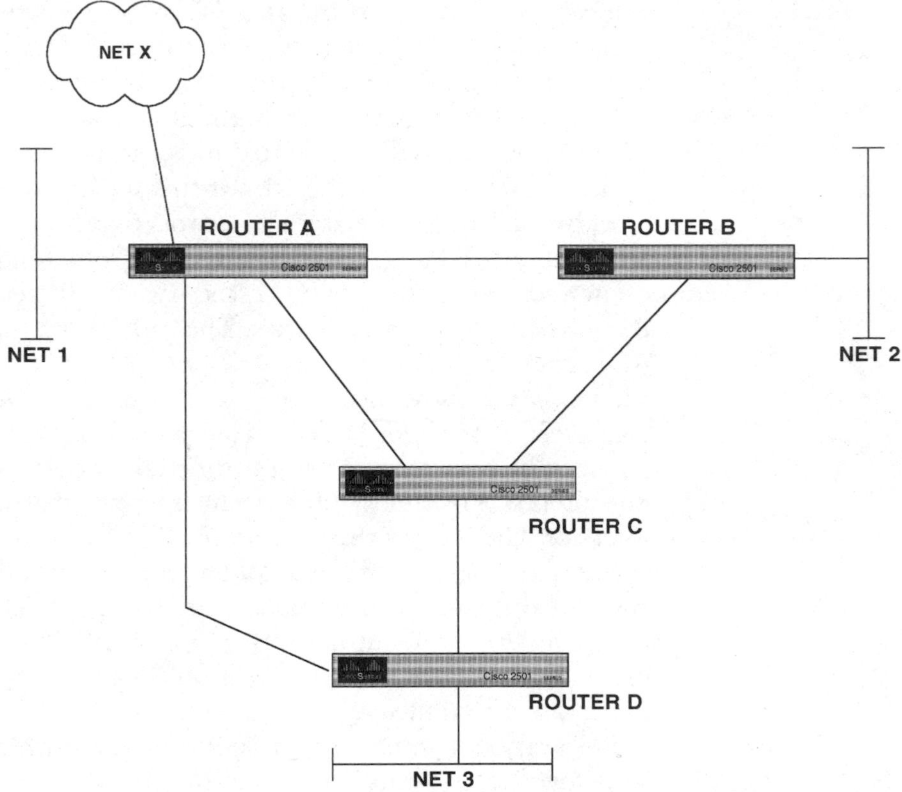

Figure 4-3 An internetwork in which RIP's maximum metric value causes problems

network 1, but it will tell router B. After the network 1 interface failure on router A, router B will no longer hear about network 1 from router A, but will hear about it from router C. Therefore, router B will be free to advertise a route to network 1 to router A, stating that it can get to network 1 via router C. This leads to a routing loop between routers A, B, and C, even though Split Horizon is in effect.

Another time when the value 16 has significance in a RIP-based network is when a network has been built that has a path through more than 15 routers from source to destination.

Router D will hear about two ways to get to Network 1, one from router A and one from router C. Router A will advertise network 1 to both C and D with a metric of 1. Router C will increment this metric by 1 (to indicate the packet has traveled through a router) and will readvertise this route to D. Router D will get both of these updates and select router A as the best way to get to network 1, because it has the lowest metric. Now suppose router A had received a routing update from network X, which had a route with a metric of 15. Router A will add 1 to the metric, making it 16. The next router to receive this in an update from A will declare that it is infinity and will eliminate this route from its routing table (if the route existed there in the first place)—or, at the very least, fail to add this route to its routing table.

This means that routers B, C, and D will not be able to reach anything on network X, because RIP will think that network X is too far away. This is annoying, particularly if all of the links and routers are functioning correctly.

Triggered Updates and Hold-Downs. The larger a network grows, the more difficult it is to get all the routing tables on all the routers updated correctly. The time it takes for all the routing tables to get adjusted by a routing protocol is called the *convergence time*. To speed up this process, RIP employs *triggered updates*, which means that whenever a RIP-enabled router learns of a topology change, such as a link becoming unavailable, it will not wait for the next scheduled routing update to be sent out, but will instead send out a triggered update immediately.

Unfortunately, this does not work for all situations. Look at Figure 4-4 to examine what happens if the link between A and B becomes unavailable. When routers A and B realize that they are no longer connected, they will notify their neighbors of the link failure via a triggered update. All router devices receiving this news will issue triggered updates to their neighbors, indicating the change in topology. Problems occur if, for example, router E is made aware of the change before router D. Router E adjusts its routing table to reflect that the A-to-B link is no longer available; however, if router D has not heard of this change and sends to E a regular update message (assuming that the A-to-B link is still available), E will reinstate the A-to-B link in its routing table.

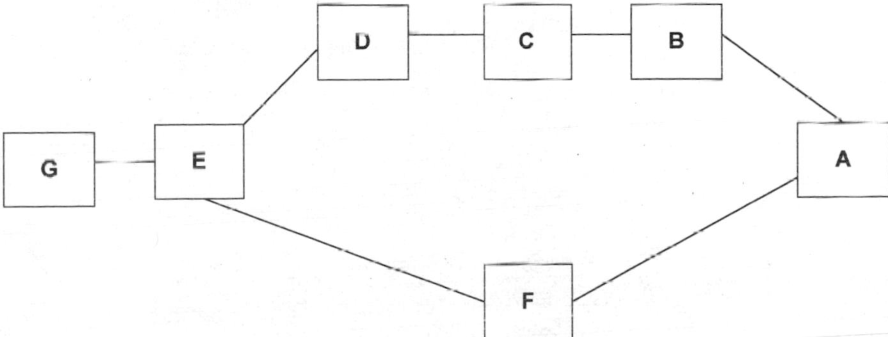

Figure 4-4
A larger internetwork in which the use of hold-downs is necessary

In this situation, the benefit of using triggered updates has been negated, and we still have to wait for the A-to-B route to expire in all the routing tables in the network. A method for improving the convergence time in this type of situation is the *hold-down timer.*

The *hold-down rule* states that when a route is removed, no update to that route will be accepted for a given period of time. In our example, this means router E will ignore the update from router D attempting to reinstate the A-to-B route. This gives the triggered updates time to get to all other routers, ensuring that any new routes are not just reinstating an old link. The downside of this scheme is that the system will not reach convergence in the quickest possible time. However, convergence time with triggered updates and hold-downs is much better than without.

Now that we have explained the operation of RIP, we can go back to the lab and explore the information that the router will give us regarding RIP.

The command `show ip route 160.4.1.64` gives some explanation of the summarized display given when a `Show ip route` is executed.

```
router1#sho ip route 160.4.1.64
Routing entry for 160.4.1.64 255.255.255.224
   Known via "rip", distance 120, metric 1
   Redistributing via rip
   Last update from 160.4.1.34 on Ethernet0, 00:00:26 ago
   Routing Descriptor Blocks:
   * 160.4.1.34, from 160.4.1.34, 00:00:26 ago, via Ethernet0
   Route metric is 1, traffic share count is 1
```

The point of interest is that the display tells us the netmask used in determining subnet values, in this case 255.255.255.224. In addition, it explains that the 120 value is the administrative distance and the metric is 1. Further, it explains that the last update for this route was obtained 26 seconds ago from address 160.4.1.34 on Ethernet 0.

The next command, `show ip protocols`, gives us the timer values, discussed in the preceding section, for this specific RIP system.

```
router1#sho ip protocols
Routing Protocol is "rip"
   Sending updates every 30 seconds, next due in 22 seconds
   Invalid after 180 seconds, hold down 180, flushed after 240
   Outgoing update filter list for all interfaces is not set
   Incoming update filter list for all interfaces is not set
   Redistributing: rip
   Routing for Networks:
   160.4.0.0
   Routing Information Sources:
GatewayDistance        Last Update
160.4.1.34      120     0:00:16
Distance: (default is 120)
```

Problems with RIP. In today's large, heterogeneous networks that connect Ethernet segments to serial-line wide area links and dial-up links, the following problems make the use of RIP far from ideal.

- As the network grows, destinations that require a metric of more than 15 become unreachable. This is particularly bad if a network administrator applies a metric of more than 1 to a link, to indicate a slow transmission time.
- The overly simplistic metric generates a suboptimal routing table, resulting in packets being sent over slow (or otherwise costly) links when better paths are available. Other routing protocols use a more complex metric to include the throughput of each link in use.
- RIP-enabled devices will accept RIP updates from any device. This enables a misconfigured device to disrupt an entire network quite easily. Other protocols allow "neighbors" to be defined as the only ones from which to accept routing updates.
- RIP does not carry subnet mask information in updates. It assumes all interfaces on the network have the same mask. Because of this, the network can run out of usable Internet-compatible addresses earlier than is necessary.
- On larger internetworks, convergence time is unacceptably slow (greater than 5 min) for most commercial applications such as database access or financial transactions.
- The Split Horizon with Poison Reverse Update algorithm in RIP only counters routing loops between adjacent routers. Other routing protocols employ more sophisticated mechanisms to counter larger routing loops, thereby allowing the safe use of a zero hold-down value, which speeds up convergence time considerably.
- RIP updates use more bandwidth than other protocols, mainly because the whole routing table is sent in updates.

Even though it may not be the best protocol available, there are still those who have to introduce Cisco routers into a largely Unix-based routing environment, and the only routing protocol that routers can use to exchange information reliably with Unix machines is RIP. With that in mind, let's see what needs to be done to configure RIP on a Cisco router.

The first step is to enable the process on the router, which is achieved as follows:

```
Router1(config)#router rip
Router1(config-router)network A.B.C.D
```

The first line defines RIP as a running process, and the second defines the whole network number that will be advertised by RIP on initial startup of the routing process. You need to add entries for all the network numbers that are directly connected. If there may be interfaces on the router that you do not want to send routing updates through, consider Fig. 4-5.

In this figure, the Ethernet 0 port is connected to a local area network. This network may contain routers advertising routes that you do not want to get to the global wide area net. To stop the router sending any of these local routes over the global net, use the `passive interface` command as shown next. This command stops the router from sending out any updates on the specified interface.

```
Router1(config-router)#passive interface S0
```

RIP is a broadcast protocol, so in order for routing updates to reach routers on nonbroadcast networks, you must configure the Cisco IOS to permit this exchange of routing information. This is a fairly rare occurrence. Consider Fig. 4-6.

Suppose you have two sites connected via a public frame relay network and want router 1 to send RIP updates to router 2. With a default configuration for RIP, the frame relay network will not broadcast the RIP update to all connected devices, so we have to tell router 1 to send a directed RIP update message to router 2. This is achieved as follows:

```
Router1(config-router)#neighbor W.X.Y.Z
```

where `W.X.Y.Z.` is the IP address of router 2.

In summary, the RIP configuration utilizing all these features is shown as follows:

- `router rip`
- `network A.B.C.D`
- `passive interface serial 0`
- `neighbor W.X.Y.Z`

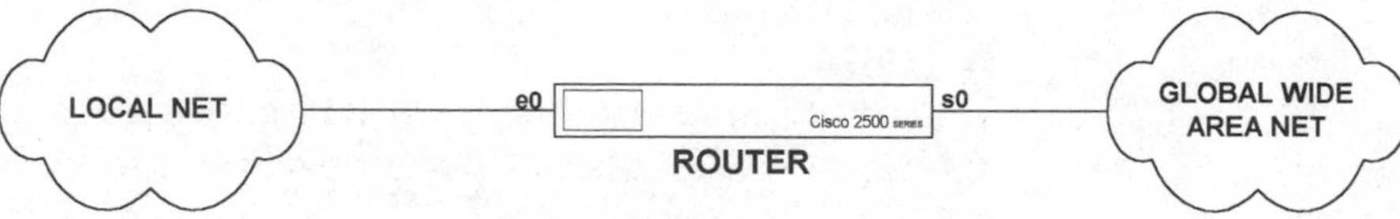

Figure 4-5 The use of passive interfaces on a RIP internetwork

NET 1
e0
ROUTER 1
s0
PUBLIC
FRAME RELAY
NETWORK
s0
Cisco 2500
e0
ROUTER 2
NET 2
ROUTER 1 # CONFIG TERM
ROUTER 1 (CONFIG)# ROUTER RIP
ROUTER 1 (CONFIG-ROUTER)# NEIGHBOR W.X.Y.Z
WHERE W:X.Y.Z. IS THE IP ADDRESS OF s0 ON ROUTER 2

Figure 4-6 Configuring RIP to send routing updates to a specified router

It is possible to change the value of the update, invalid, and flush timers along with the value of hold-down. I do not recommend you do this for RIP. The only reason to use RIP on a router is if you are exchanging routing information with a Unix machine, and it is likely that the timers and hold-down value for the Unix machine are not easily configurable. If you are concerned enough about the performance of your routing protocol to adjust the timers, you should not be using RIP, but rather something such as IGRP, and use redistribution (discussed later in this chapter) to exchange route information with Unix machines.

RIP performed its job well, given what it was designed for, but its time as the only routing protocol to run on a large and diverse network is over. Let's look at how Cisco improved things with the Interior Gateway Routing Protocol, IGRP.

IGRP: Interior Gateway Routing Protocol

Cisco's stated goals for IGRP include the following:

- Stable, optimal routing for large internetworks, with no routing loops occurring.
- Fast response to changes in network topology.
- Ability to handle multiple "types of service" (though not currently implemented).
- Low overhead in terms of bandwidth and router processor utilization.
- Ability to split traffic among several parallel routes when they are of roughly equal desirability.

The key differences between RIP and IGRP are in the metric, poisoning algorithm, and use of default gateway. IGRP's Split Horizon, triggered updates, and hold-downs are implemented in a fashion similar to RIP.

IGRP Metrics. IGRP computes a vector of metrics that is used to characterize paths. This metric value can exceed 16 million, which allows a great deal of flexibility when mathematically describing link characteristics. This composite metric (as defined by Cisco) is calculated as follows:

$$[(K1/B) + (K2 \times D)] \times R$$

where

K1, K2 = constants

B = unloaded path bandwidth *x* (1–channel occupancy). This is for the narrowest bandwidth segment of the path.

D = Topological delay

R = reliability

Two additional data elements are passed in routing updates: *hop count* and *Maximum Transmission Unit,* although neither currently are used in the calculation.

K1 and K2 indicate the weight to be assigned to bandwidth and delay, and are defined by the type of service requested for a packet. In reality, the metric calculation is much simpler than this equation would suggest. If two routers are connected via their Serial 0 ports, the default bandwidth assumed for the metric calculation is 1.544 Mbps (T-1 speed). For a T-1, IGRP assigns a composite delay of 21,000 μs. By default K1 = 10,000,000; K2 = 100,000; and R = 1. This gives a metric of 8576 for every serial port connection on a network, regardless of the actual line capacity in place. This metric value can be viewed by using the `show ip route A.B.C.D` command, in which `A.B.C.D` is the IP address of a device on the other side of the serial port link. An example is shown as follows:

```
router1#sho ip rout 160.4.1.64
Routing entry for 160.4.1.64 255.255.255.224
  Known via "igrp 9", distance 100, metric 8576
  Redistributing via igrp 9
  Last update from 160.4.1.34 on Ethernet0, 00:00:33 ago
  Routing Descriptor Blocks:
  * 160.4.1.34, from 160.4.1.34, 00:00:33 ago, via Ethernet0
  Route metric is 8576, traffic share count is 1
  Total delay is 21000 microseconds, minimum bandwidth is 1544 Kbit
  Reliability 255/255, minimum MTU 1500 bytes
  Loading 1/255, Hops 0
```

Metric values can be customized using the `bandwidth interface` command for each serial port, to factor in actual bandwidth available for each link for metric calculations. This is a good idea.

As stated, the Cisco IOS, unless it is configured otherwise, will decide that each serial link is using a T-1 for the purposes of metric calculation.

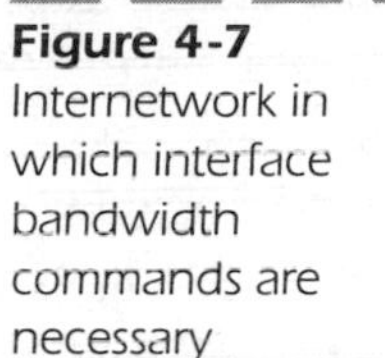

Figure 4-7 Internetwork in which interface bandwidth commands are necessary

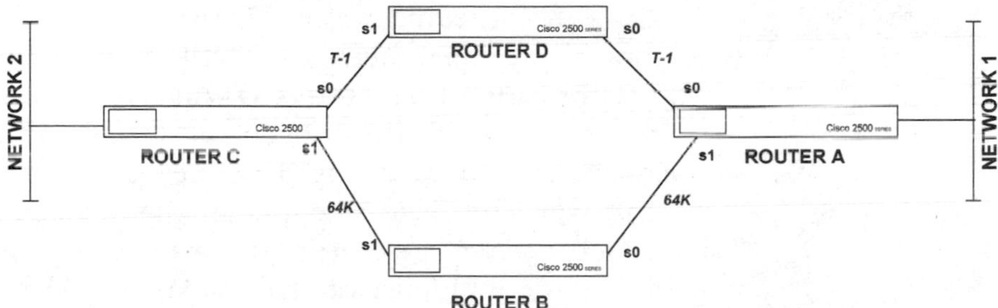

This can be verified by issuing the following command on router A (see Fig. 4-7).

```
RouterA>show interface serial 1
Serial1 is up, line protocol is up
   Hardware is HD64570
   Internet address is 160.4.1.65 255.255.255.224
   MTU 1500 bytes, BW 1544 Kbit, DLY 20000 usec, rely 255/255, load
1/255
```

The first four lines of command output are shown. As you can see, the bandwidth assumed is that of a T-1, even though a 64 kbps line is in use. It would have been nice if this bandwidth value had used what was actually there by default; because the router is getting the clock signal from the line CSU/DSU, it does have the information to do so—but the connection in the Cisco IOS is not made.

Why is this important? As previously stated, IGRP will split traffic between paths that it thinks are of equal value in terms of the composite metric. If no adjustments are manually made to the router configuration to change the value of bandwidth used for the 64 kbps links in the metric calculation, router A will calculate the metric from network 1 to network 2 as 17152 (8576 + 8576) for both the route through router D and the route through router B. Transferring a file from a machine on network 1 to a machine on network 2 will mean that the traffic is split equally between these two paths. As you can see, the available bandwidth of these two paths is actually very different, which will lead to a suboptimal rate of file transfer.

The way to fix this is to assign appropriate bandwidth values to each link. This is achieved as follows:

```
RouterA(config)#interface serial 1
RouterA(config-int)#bandwidth 64000
```

The same should be done for the Serial 1 interface on router B. The result of this is that the route from network 1 to network 2 will have a far lower metric through router D than through router B. As the routes no longer have equal metrics, for a file transfer from network 1 to network 2, the path through router D will carry all the traffic.

In the Cisco IOS, the concept of *variance* can be used to define unequal-cost load balancing. This means that if up to four paths are roughly equal, traffic will be split among them, in inverse proportion to their metric value. These alternative path metrics must be within a specified variance multiplier of the best metric. The variance value multiplied by the best metric defines the upper value of the metric of the links that will be considered for unequal-cost load balancing. In Fig. 4-8, we see an internetwork that, with appropriate settings of variance, will allow traffic between network 1 and network 2 to be split between routes through router B and D, in proportion to the bandwidth available.

In this instance it is desirable to have traffic between network 1 and 2 split between the two paths. If the variance is set to a value greater than 1, traffic may be split over paths of unequal metric. A value of 1 is the default and means that traffic will only be sent over the best path, or split between equal paths. If the variance is set to 1.5, it means that any path with a metric up to 1.5 times the metric of the best path will be added to the routing table and used when sending traffic.

The variance multiplier is set as follows:

```
RouterA(config-router)#variance 1.5
```

Caution must be taken with network design due to IGRP's ability to use load balancing. As long as either the Data Link or Transport layer protocol can handle receiving out-of-sequence packets, everything is fine. If one is using frame relay, for example, to transport UDP packets in an internetwork with multiple routes between networks, however, the IGRP feature will cause problems, because neither frame relay nor UDP guarantee correct sequencing of packets. In this instance, using TCP as

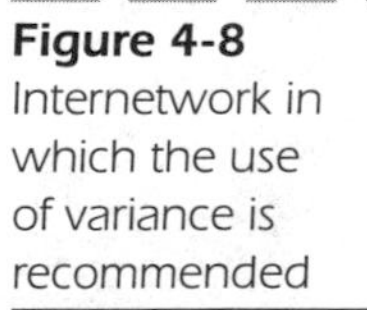

Figure 4-8 Internetwork in which the use of variance is recommended

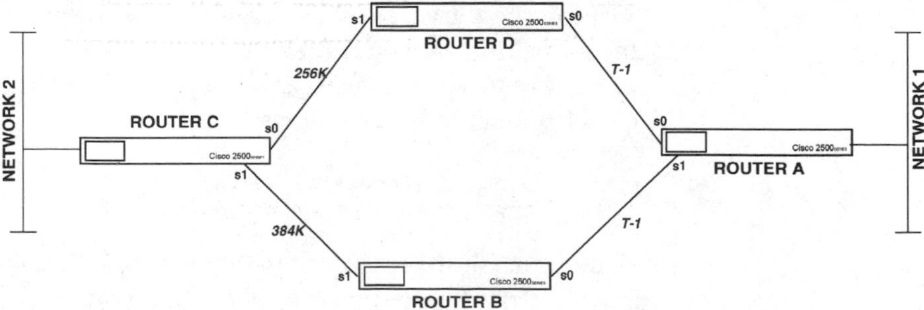

the transport protocol, or swapping to LAPB for the link-level protocol, will resolve the problem.

IGRP Route Poisoning. The poisoning algorithm used in IGRP can counter larger routing loops than can the Split Horizon with Poison Reverse used by RIP. RIP's poisoning algorithm only counters routing loops between adjacent routers. IGRP will poison routes in which metric increases by a factor of 10 percent or more after an update. This is based on the logic that routing loops generate continually increasing metrics. Using this type of poisoning rule will mean that certain valid routes will be erroneously deleted from routing tables. If routes are valid, however, they will be reinstated by the next regular update message. The key advantage to this type of poisoning is that it safely allows a zero hold-down value, which speeds up network convergence time considerably.

IGRP Default Gateway. For routers, the network number 0.0.0.0 has special significance to identify a specified router as the *default gateway*. A default gateway is used by the router when it has to forward a packet destined for a network that is not explicitly listed in the routing table. Consider this routing table from a Unix machine:

```
Network          Gateway          Flags  RefCnt  Use     Interface
123.0.0.0        134.4.4.1        UG     40      5000    le0
134.4.0.0        134.4.4.1        UG     50      7000    le0
0.0.0.0          134.4.4.5        UG     10      2000    le0
```

This router knows about two real networks (the 123.0.0.0 and 134.4.0.0), as well as the default network of 0.0.0.0. If the router has to forward a packet to anything other than the two real networks about which it knows, it will send the packet to the router with IP address 134.4.4.5, hoping that it will know how to get the packet to its final destination. This function is useful if you want to reduce the amount of network numbers a Unix machine must know about, but still have it participate in routing decisions. Consider Fig. 4-9, which shows an internetwork that would generate the routing table shown above.

In this internetwork, the Unix machine is effectively delegating all the WAN routing decisions to the WAN router, which is acting as a *boundary router* to the global network. Routing protocols will circulate information about this default route in routing updates as if it were a real network. This can cause problems if this one gateway, defined as the default, becomes unavailable. With RIP, 0.0.0.0 is the only way to define a default gateway.

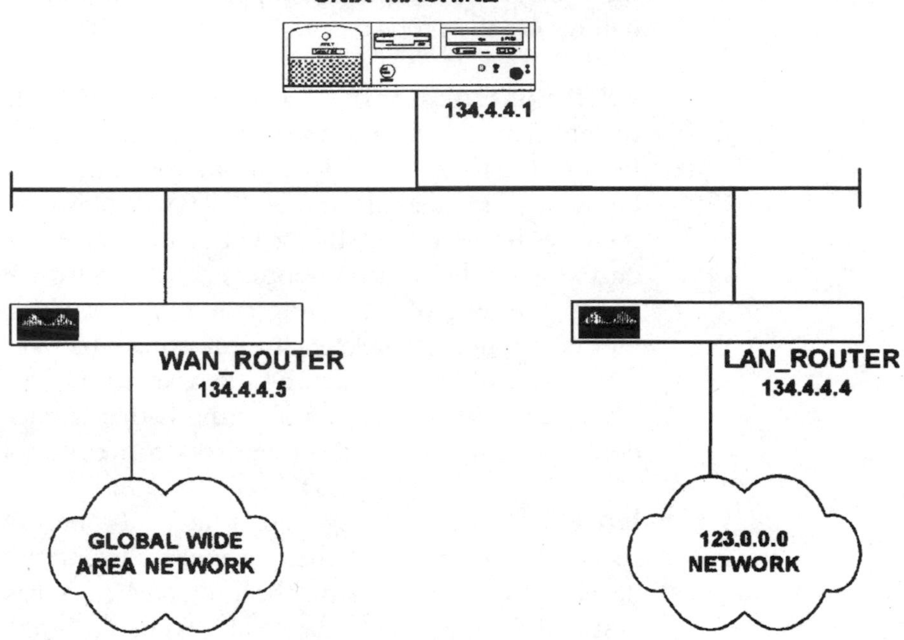

Figure 4-9 Internetwork with one router operating as the default

IGRP takes a different approach that allows real networks to be flagged as candidates for being a default. This is achieved by turning on a bit associated with those networks, marking the networks as being a candidate. Periodically IGRP scans the routers offering a path to this flagged network, selects the path with the lowest metric, and uses that as the default (Fig. 4-10).

In this figure, two routers, router 1 and router 2, both have a connection to the global Internet, which in this case is accessed via the 130.6.0.0 class B network. In this internetwork, the network number that is used to access the Internet will be flagged as the default in both of the routers that are connected to the Internet. This is done by entering the following global configuration command into both router 1 and router 2:

```
Router(config)#ip default-network 130.6.0.0
```

In this case, an asterisk will appear in the routing table of all routers against the entry for the 130.6.0.0 network, indicating that this is the default network. All routers should choose router 1 as the way to access this network number.

Now suppose host 1 has router 5 configured as its default gateway. This means that it will send all packets not destined for the local network to router 5. Router 5 will have selected router 1 as the way to get to the default network. Thus, if host 1 has to send a packet to 202.14.5.3, which is on the Internet, it will send the packets to router 5. Router 5 will realize it does not have a route to the 202.14.5.0 network and will send the packet to router 1, which it already has chosen as its route to the default network. As long as router 1 has an entry to the 202.14.5.0 network, the packet will be delivered.

The concept is that if a default network is identified, and a router does not have a route to a given network, it will send the packet to the default network, assuming that some router on the way to the default network will have a routing table entry for the ultimate destination.

This keeps local routers, such as router 5 in Fig. 4-10, from having to maintain very large routing tables.

One command that could be confusing is the `ip default-gateway` command. You might think that it defines a default gateway for the

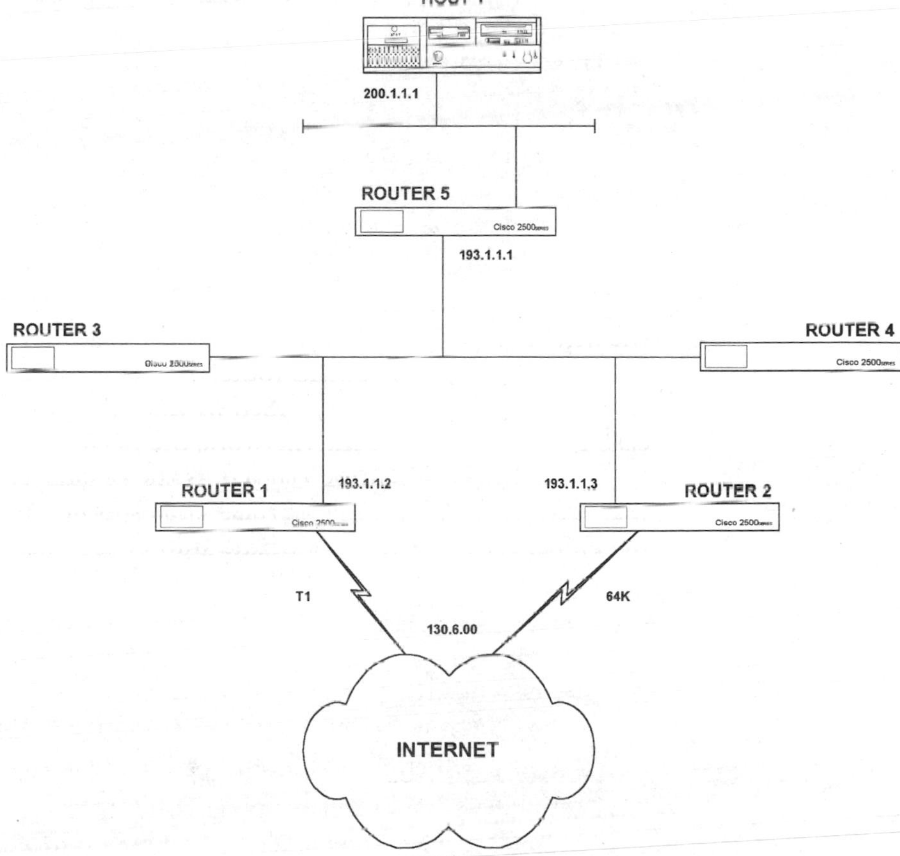

Figure 4-10 Internetwork using Cisco's default-network feature

routing table to use during normal operation. It does not. This command is there for upgrading routers remotely; we will revisit it in Chap. 7.

Before we move on, let's just see the `default-network` command operate in the lab we used in Chap. 3. If we configure the routers as previously shown in Chap. 3 and Fig. 3.5, and connect the Ethernet 0 port on router 3 to the hub, we will bring the Ethernet 0 port on router 3 into the *up* state, which means it can participate in the routing processes. Router 1 does not have a routing process configured, but is configured with a static route to 150.1.0.0 via 120.1.1.2. Router 2 is running IGRP with network subcommands for 120.0.0.0 and 150.1.0.0. Router 3 has a router IGRP process with network subcommands for 150.1.0.0 and 193.1.1.0. Finally, router 1 is configured to have the following entry in its configuration:

```
Router1(config)#ip default-network 150.1.0.0
```

We want router 1 to be able to ping the 193.1.1.1 interface on router 3 by sending a ping packet to router 2, which is marked as the router to go to for the default network 150.1.0.0.

This will cause router 1 to mark with an asterisk the entry for the 150.1.0.0 network in its routing table, denoting that this is a candidate for default.

The routing tables for routers 1, 2, and 3 now look like this:

```
Router1>show ip route
C  120.0.0.0 is directly connected, Ethernet 0
S* 150.1.0.0 [1/0] via 120.1.1.2

Router2>show ip route
C  120.0.0.0 is directly connected, Ethernet 0
C  150.1.0.0 is directly connected, Serial 0
I  193.1.1.0 [10018576] via 150.1.1.2, 00:00:40, Serial 0

Router3>show ip route
I  120.0.0.0 [10018576] via 150.1.1.1, 00:00:52, Serial 0
C  150.1.0.0 is directly connected, Serial 0
C  193.1.1.0 is directly connected, Ethernet 0
```

If we try to ping 193.1.1.1 from router 1, the following happens:

1. Router 1 sees that the 193.1.1.0 network is not listed in its routing table. It then sees that network 150.1.0.0 is flagged as default, so the router sends the packet destined for 193.1.1.1 to the router that knows the way to the default network, that being router 2.
2. Router 2, which knows about network 193.1.1.0, receives the packet, so the packet is forwarded on to router 3.
3. Router 3 receives the packet and delivers it to 193.1.1.1.

4. To reply to 120.1.1.1, router 3 has an entry in its routing table to pass the packet to router 2, which passes the reply packet back to router 1.

This feature is useful because it minimizes the number of entries needed in the routing table of router 1.

Configuring IGRP. The following is a typical configuration to define IGRP as a routing protocol on a Cisco router:

```
router igrp 12
timers basic 15 45 0 60
network 162.4.0.0
network 193.1.1.0
no metric holddown
metric maximum-hop 50
```

The first line defines the routing protocol to be IGRP, for the autonomous system 12. An *autonomous system* is a network that is administered by one person or one group. For most organizations, every routing device will have the same autonomous system number. IGRP will not exchange updates with routers from different autonomous system numbers.

The second line shortens the default value of IGRP timers. The values indicated here use: 15 seconds for the basic time constant, for when regular update messages are broadcast; 45 seconds for route expiry, if no updates for that route are received; 0 seconds for hold-down, and 60 seconds for flushing the route from the routing table.

The third and fourth lines identify the networks directly attached to the routing device being configured.

The fifth line disables hold-downs, meaning that after the route for a given network has been removed, a new route for that destination network will be accepted immediately.

The sixth line removes packets if they have passed through 50 routers. This number should be large enough to allow all valid routes within your network, but as low as possible to speed up the removal of any packets caught in a routing loop.

When used with appropriate entries in the interface configurations to identify the correct bandwidth value to use in metric calculations, the foregoing configuration should serve most internetworks well. This configuration for IGRP timers is known as *Fast IGRP*, as it speeds up network convergence time considerably, compared to standard IGRP timers.

As with RIP, a neighbor can be defined if routing updates need to be sent to a router that is only reachable over a network that does not support a broadcast protocol.

IGRP will service most networks very well. There are only a few instances when IGRP causes problems on an internetwork. These problems are endemic to all distance vector protocols. If the following scenario fits the description of your internetwork, you should consider reviewing the use of a link state protocol, or the hybrid EIGRP.

Suppose that your organization is using an InterNIC-assigned class B network number, split into several hundred subnets allocated to geographically dispersed sites. Each site has a dial backup link to a central location. If the link to a site goes down and the site equipment dials in to the central location, all routers on the network need to know that this has happened, and also the new way to reach this site. Triggered updates get sent around the whole network and all routing tables are adjusted.

A distance vector protocol will send out periodically all the information from its routing table (with some minor adjustments for the Split Horizon rule). If there are enough subnets in the routing table, these periodic updates can swamp a dial-up link. Link state and hybrid protocols send updates that contain only the information relevant to the change that has occurred on the internetwork.

The question of distance vector versus link state is not an easy one to answer. We shall revisit how to make this choice at the end of the chapter.

EIGRP: The Hybrid Protocol

In the early 1990s, Cisco introduced Enhanced IGRP, which uses the same distance vector technology found in IGRP for the underlying metric calculations. What has changed are the route advertising procedures, and the calculation of entries into the routing table. These procedures are like those of a link state protocol. The key components of EIGRP are:

- Neighbor discovery/recovery
- Reliable transport protocol
- DUAL finite state machine
- Variable-length subnet masks

Neighbor discovery is the process by which a router learns of other routers on directly attached links. EIGRP uses small hello packets for neighbor discovery (as long as a router receives hello messages from a neighboring router, it assumes that the neighbor is functioning and they can exchange routing information). The key point is that EIGRP uses partial updates. When the state of a link or router changes, EIGRP sends out only the information necessary to those needing to hear about it, instead of sending the entire routing table to all neighbors. This clearly minimizes the bandwidth used by EIGRP regular update messages when compared to those used by IGRP.

At the heart of EIGRP is the *Diffusing Update Algorithm* (DUAL), the decision process for all route computations. DUAL uses distance information to select efficient, loop-free paths and selects the best route for insertion into the routing table, as well as a feasible successor. This feasible successor is used if the primary route becomes unavailable, thus avoiding a complete recalculation of the algorithm in the event of a link failure, and hence lowering convergence time. EIGRP also introduced a *Reliable Transport Protocol* to ensure guaranteed, ordered delivery of routing updates, rather than relying on broadcasts.

A key design feature of EIGRP is that it will support routing for protocols other than IP. EIGRP also supports routing for IPX and AppleTalk network protocols. This has some advantages in a mixed networking environment in that only one routing protocol need be configured.

EIGRP supports *variable-length subnet masks* (VLSM), which increase flexibility for the use of netmasks in internetwork design. Previously we discussed why an internetwork could have only one value of netmask assigned, as neither RIP nor IGRP carried netmask information in routing updates. EIGRP does carry this information.

The functionality afforded by VLSM is most useful when an organization has a limited address space assigned by the InterNIC, and has to supply these addresses to several sites of varying size (see Fig. 4-11).

We can see that network 2 must support 50 usable addresses, and network 1 must support 10. If network 2 has the most hosts at one site on the internetwork, and we are using RIP or IGRP, we would have to assign a netmask of 255.255.255.192, which gives us 62 usable addresses on each subnet. This would waste 52 usable addresses on network 1. With

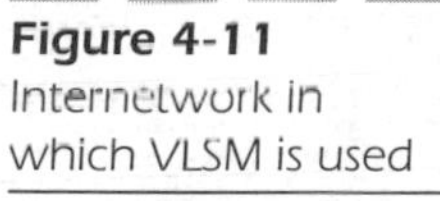

Figure 4-11 Internetwork in which VLSM is used

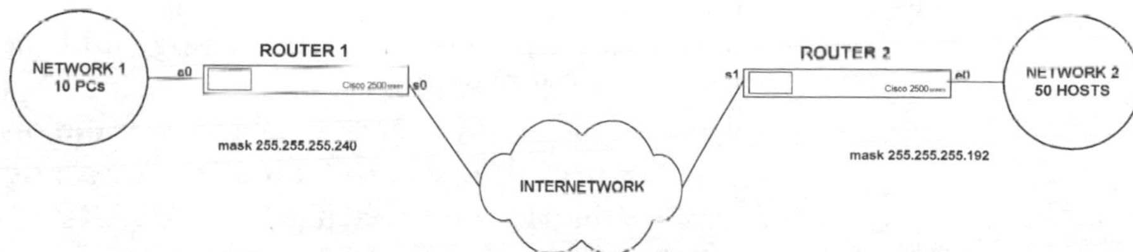

EIGRP we can assign a netmask of 255.255.255.192 to the Ethernet 0 port of router 2 and a 255.255.255.240 to the Ethernet 0 port of router 1. EIGRP will transmit this netmask information in its updates and routing table integrity will be maintained.

Inside EIGRP

The first table we will look at is the neighbor table. Neighbors are discovered when they send a hello packet to a neighboring router. All hello packets are used to form the neighbor table, which is where routers keep information regarding the state of adjacent neighbors. Hello packets include a *HoldTime,* the amount of time in which a router receiving the hello packet will treat the sender of the hello as reachable. If another hello is not received within the HoldTime, DUAL is informed of the change of state. This table also keeps track of *Reliable Transport Protocol* (RTP) sequence numbers and estimates an appropriate time for retransmission requests for RTP packets.

EIGRP has a topology table that contains all destinations advertised by neighboring routers, along with the metric value for each destination. This topology table forms the basis for input to the DUAL calculations. The output of DUAL feeds into the routing table. A topology table entry for a destination can be in one of two states, either active or passive (the normal condition). A route only becomes active when an event occurs to cause a route recalculation due to some router or link becoming unavailable.

An entry in the topology table gets moved to the routing table when what is known as a *feasible successor* has been found. A feasible successor can be thought of as the best alternative path to a destination, if the best path fails. If there is a feasible successor for an entry in the topology table, and the neighbor chosen for this entry stops sending hello packets, the entry will not go active in the topology table. Having a feasible successor therefore is a good thing, because it avoids a full recalculation of the DUAL algorithm in the event of a network failure.

EIGRP is a proprietary Cisco technology, and therefore has good compatibility with IGRP. EIGRP updates are not backwardly compatible with IGRP updates, but there is an automatic redistribution scheme for interoperability of IGRP and EIGRP routes, and there exist directly translatable metrics between IGRP and EIGRP. (Redistribution will be discussed later in this chapter.)

Configuring EIGRP

The following is a typical configuration to define EIGRP as a routing protocol on a Cisco router:

```
router eigrp 13
network 170.4.0.0
network 200.10.1.0
```

The first line defines EIGRP as a process on the router for autonomous system 13. The second and third lines identify the directly attached networks that participate in the routing process.

EIGRP supports unequal-cost load balancing by the variance command in a fashion similar to that discussed for IGRP; in fact, the same command is used to specify the variance multiplier.

One area of configuration that differs between IGRP and EIGRP is the option to disable route summarization. Route summarization is explained below.

In Fig. 4-12 we have two companies, Company A and Company B. Let's say Company A has to provide an information service to two locations of

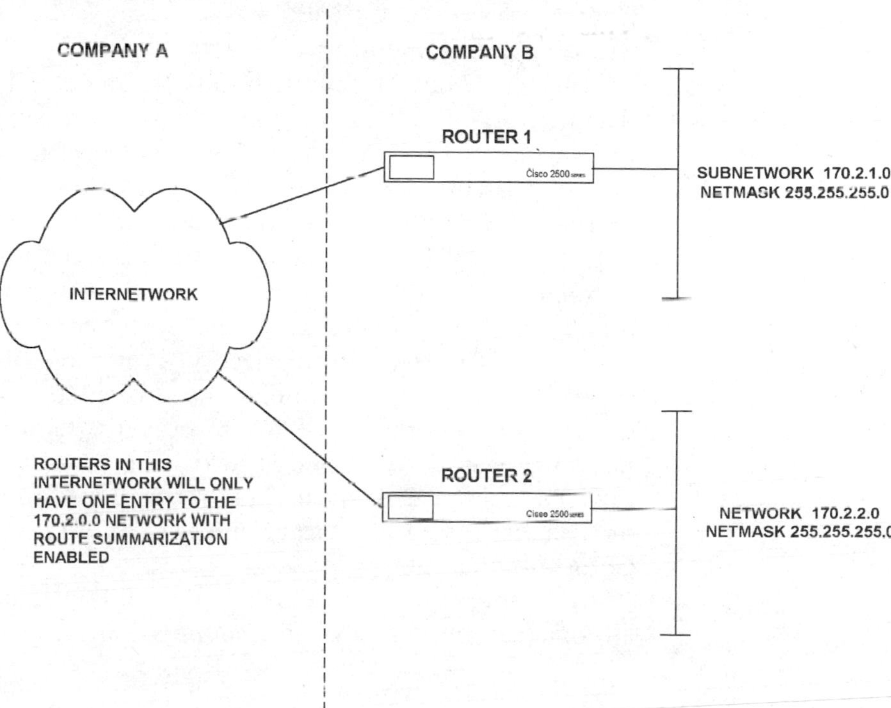

Figure 4-12 Internetwork in which route summarization causes a problem

Company B. Company B uses the 170.2.0.0 network, with a netmask of 255.255.255.0, which means it can provide 254 subnets, each capable of supporting 254 hosts with this one network number. Company A uses the 150.1.0.0 network, with subnet masks applied, so that this one network number can be used to connect many client sites to its internetwork.

If both companies are using EIGRP with a default configuration, the internetwork addressing shown in Fig. 4-12 will not work properly. The reason for that is that whole network numbers are summarized at their boundary. This means that the routers in the 150.1.0.0 internetwork do not see the 170.2.0.0 subnets, but rather see only an advertisement for the entire route. With IGRP or RIP, nothing can be done to change this, but with EIGRP there is an option we can use.

This can be a difficult concept for network administrators who have been accustomed to using netmasks on one network number and expect separate subnets to be treated as separate networks.

EIGRP provides the option to turn off route summerization, which means that network 150.1.0.0 will be able to accommodate more than one connection to the 170.2.0.0 network.

To help understand why this is so, let's consider the decision-making process a router within the 150.1.0.0 network goes through when it has to forward a packet to, say, 170.2.4.4 as an example. The first thing the router will do is determine the whole network number that the destination is on, which is 170.2.0.0. It will then look for an entry in its routing table for that network. The routing table will keep track of individual subnets within the 150.1.0.0 network, but does not do the same for external networks by default. This is so because it will not receive subnet information for the 170.2.0.0 network from the routers at the Company B locations.

In the case of Fig. 4-12, there will be two equal-cost routes in Company A's router to 170.2.0.0, so traffic will be split between them, irrespective of which subnet is the packet's real destination.

With EIGRP, route summarization can be disabled; the routing tables in 150.1.0.0 routers will maintain the two entries for the two subnets in the 170.2.0.0 network and be able to properly deliver packets to both subnets. The way this is done is to disable route summarization for all EIGRP processes. This means that router 1 and router 2 in Fig. 4-12 will send subnet information regarding the 170.2.0.0 network to the routers in Company A's routers.

To do this, enter the following EIGRP configuration commands for all routers involved in accessing subnets on multiple network numbers:

```
Router1(config)#router eigrp 11
Router1(config-router)no auto-summary
```

Routing Protocols: Link State

Distance vector and link state are just two different ways of automatically updating routing tables in routers. A link state protocol has totally different mechanisms for gathering route information and calculating which route will be put into the routing table. The fact is, both distance vector and link state protocols should choose the same next-hop router to put in the routing table for most destinations.

We can introduce the concepts of link state routing as follows:

1. A router will find out which routers are directly connected to it.
2. Each router will send out *link state advertisements* (LSAs), which list the names and cost to each of its neighbors.
3. The LSA sent to a given router's neighbors will be forwarded to every other router.
4. Each router now knows the complete topology of the internetwork and computes optimal routes for every destination for entry into the routing table.

Before we consider implementations of the link state type routing protocol, it is worth finding the answers to two questions: How do we ensure that a router interprets link state packets in the correct order? And how are actual routes computed once the LSAs have been received?

A timestamp could be put on each LSA, but that would require very accurate synchronization of every router on the internetwork. What is implemented now is a combination of sequence number and age. Each router will start sending LSAs with sequence number 0 and increment this value each time an LSA is sent. In addition, any given LSA may not exist in the system longer than a predetermined time, normally an hour.

Once a router has a complete LSA database (referred to by Cisco as a *Topological database*), it may compute routes for entry into the routing table. This is done using *Dijkstra's algorithm*. Because you cannot alter anything within Dijkstra's algorithm when configuring a router, I will not go in to its logic. In concept, it is a kind of trial-and-error mechanism in that it tries different routes to get to the same destination, calculates the metric for each, and then selects the route with the lowest metric. Clearly, the larger the internetwork, the more possible permutations the algorithm must try out before finding the optimal route. This can place a heavy burden on a router's processor when a link state protocol is used in a large internetwork. This burden can, however, be reduced through proper design.

OSPF: Open Shortest Path First

OSPF was designed by the Internet Engineering Task Force in the late 1980s because it was clear that RIP was increasingly unable to serve large heterogeneous networks, particularly the Internet. OSPF is an open standard, implemented by all major router manufacturers. OSPF is a classic link state routing protocol and requires that the network be physically configured in a routing hierarchy; this means that a central backbone connects different routing areas together. OSPF received its name as it is an open standard and uses the Shortest Path First algorithm (otherwise known as the Dijkstra algorithm).

It should be noted that OSPF only supports routing for IP. OSPF was designed as an Interior Gateway Protocol, but it is capable of receiving routes from and sending routes to different autonomous systems.

An OSPF internetwork normally is divided into a number of areas that contain hosts and routers. These areas should be designed so that cross-area communication is kept to a minimum. Within the autonomous system, some routers with multiple interfaces can be configured as *border area routers,* which means one interface will be in one area, a second interface in another. In this case, the router keeps a topological database for each area that it is in.The only way to get from one area to another area is via the *backbone,* which is always configured as *area 0.* It must be noted that the backbone can be noncontiguous to make routing more efficient. In this case, backbone connectivity is restored by virtual links that are configured between any backbone routers that share a link to a nonbackbone area and function as if they were direct links.

In OSPF, link state advertisements are sent to all other routers within a given area. This contrasts with a distance vector protocol (such as RIP or IGRP) that sends all of the routing tables in updates messages, but only to their neighbors. LSAs include data such as metrics used, interface address, and other variables. A topological database is present in each router and contains the collection of LSA information, giving an overall picture of networks in relation to routers. Note that all routers within a given area have identical topological databases.

As previously mentioned, an OSPF backbone area is used to connect all other areas together and is responsible for transferring routing information among areas. As might be expected, there are two types of routing within OSPF, one for within a given area (*intra-area routing*), and the other for between areas (*inter-area routing*). Figure 4-13 shows a simple OSPF hierarchical internetwork.

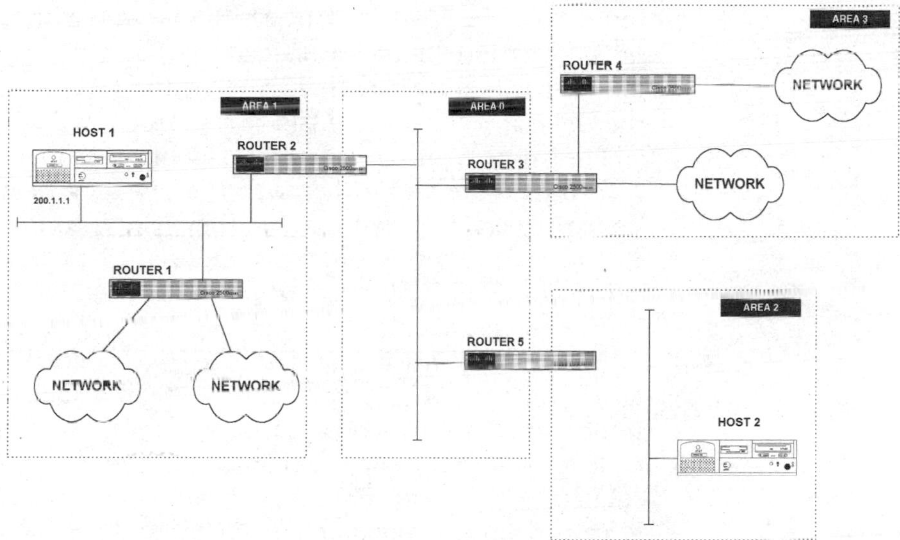

Figure 4-13
An OSPF hierarchial internetwork

In order for the host 1 in area 1 to transmit data to host 2 in area 2, the packets must be sent to router 2, which connects area 1 to the backbone, which then forwards the packet to router 5, which connects area 2 to the backbone, which finally gives the packet to its ultimate destination, host 2. The backbone area is labeled area 0 and, as far as the routing algorithms go, acts much like any other area.

It should be noted that the internal topology of any area is invisible to every other area. This means that each router within a given area will know how to get to every other router within its area, and how to get to the backbone. It will not know how many routers exist or how they are connected for any other area. This is important to keep in mind when designing dial backup systems for OSPF-based internetworks. (This issue will be revisited in Chap. 7.)

As you can see, an internetwork based around a true link state protocol such as OSPF is considerably more complex to design and operate than one based on a distance vector protocol. As with all things in life, there are tradeoffs. With a distance vector routing protocol, the internetwork can be designed, deployed, and troubleshot fairly easily; within larger networks, however, problems occur with the size of routing table updates and speed of convergence. With link state routing, an internetwork is more complex to design and troubleshoot, and uses more router processor time, but it does converge quickly.

This covers protocol initialization for routers connected on point-to-point circuits. On LANs, things are a little different. On a LAN, several routers may be connected, in which case one will be elected as the *designated router* and another as its backup. The designated router is responsible primarily for generating LSAs for the LAN to all other networks in the OSPF area. (Note that OSPF areas can be termed *domains*.)

The concept of *adjacencies* also is important in the world of OSPF. Two routers are said to be *adjacent* when they have synchronized their link state databases, that is to say, they have the same map of the routing area to which they belong. It is important that pairs of routers become adjacent, because routing information protocol packets will only be transferred between routers that have become adjacent.

Another key feature of OSPF is *route aggregation*, which minimizes entries in the routing table and topological database in the receiving routers and keeps protocol traffic to a minimum (Fig. 4-14). The routing table for router B shows entries learned about via OSPF for two adjacent subnets, 200.1.1.8 and 200.1.1.12, that both exist in area 1. Because router B is an area border router, it can aggregate these two subnets, using a different subnet mask, so that router C needs only one entry in its routing table to reach both subnets.

Configuring OSPF. In OSPF, there are three types of routers:

- A *backbone router* has its interface connected only to the backbone.
- An *area border router* attaches to multiple areas.
- An *internal router* has all directly connected interfaces within the same area.

The following is a typical configuration to define an OSPF internal or backbone router process on a Cisco router:

```
router ospf 50
network140.8.0.0  0.0.255.255  area 0
```

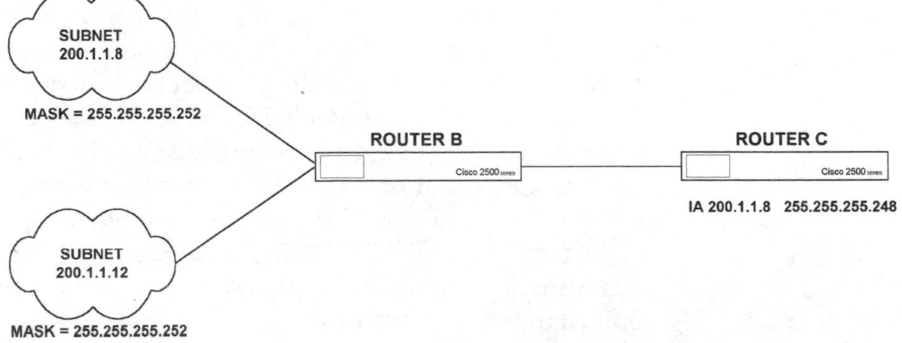

Figure 4-14 An example of OSPF route aggregation

The first line defines OSPF as a routing process with process ID 50; this is an internally used identification number for each instance of the OSPF routing process run on a router. The second line identifies all interfaces that will participate in the OSPF routing process. In this case, all interfaces belonging to the 140.8.0.0 network participate. The *wildcard mask* (in this case 0.0.255.255) can be thought of as an inverse subnet mask, meaning that, in this instance, it masks out any bits in the third and fourth octet when determining if an interface will run OSPF. The second line also identifies the area to which the router belongs (in this case area 0, the backbone).

The following is a typical configuration to define an OSPF inter-area router process on a Cisco router:

```
router ospf 62
network 180.8.2.0  0.0.0.255 area 0
network 180.8.0.0  0.0.255.255 area 2
```

In this instance, all interfaces with 180.8.2 as the first 3 octets are considered part of area 0. All interfaces that have 180.8 as the first 2 octets of their addresses are considered to be part of area 2.

Let's use the lab we built in Chap. 3 to explore OSPF configuration, as shown in Fig. 4-15.

To configure the routers for this network configuration to be serviced by OSPF, delete any router IGRP, or IP default-network commands left in the router configurations. Next insert the following commands: In router 1:

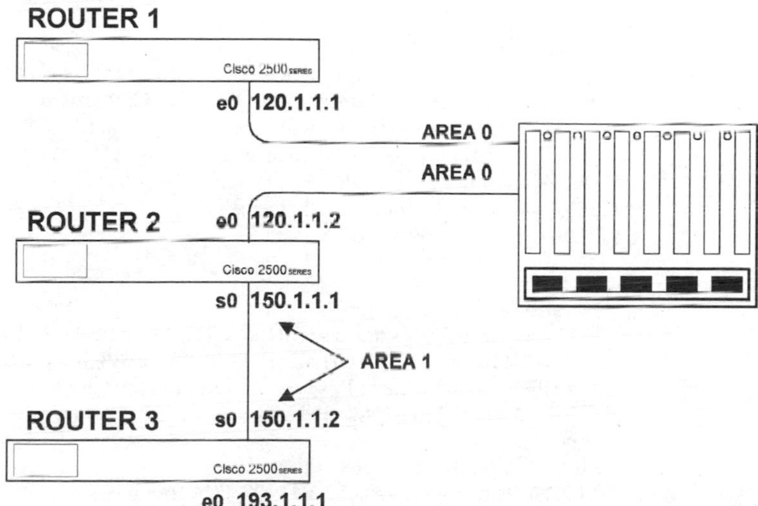

Figure 4-15 Basic configuration for an OSPF internetwork

```
Router1(config)#router ospf 10
Router1 (config-router)network 120.0.0.0 0.255.255.255 area 0
```

In router 2:

```
Router2(config)#router ospf 10
Router2(config-router)#network 120.0.0.0 0.255.255.255 area 0
Router2(config-router)#network 150.1.0.0 0.0.255.255 area 1
```

In router 3:

```
Router3(config)#router ospf 10
Router3(config-router)#network 150.1.0.0 0.0.255.255 area 1
```

In this configuration, OSPF will produce the same results as IGRP in terms of route selection for entry into the routing table. Let's look at the routing tables of each router, as shown in Fig. 4-16.

These routing tables show that routers 1 and 3 learned of networks via an OSPF inter-area routing process. The administrative distance for

Figure 4-16 Routing tables generated by OSPF

```
Router 3
router3#sho ip route
Codes: C - connected, S - static, I - IGRP, R - RIP, M - mobile, B - BGP
    D - EIGRP, EX - EIGRP external, O - OSPF, IA - OSPF inter area
    E1 - OSPF external type 1, E2 - OSPF external type 2, E - EGP
    i - IS-IS, L1 - IS-IS level-1, L2 - IS-IS level-2, * - candidate default
Gateway of last resort is not set
O IA 120.0.0.0 [110/74] via 150.1.1.1, 04:45:33, Serial0
C 150.1.0.0 is directly connected, Serial0

Router 2
router2>sho ip route
Codes: C - connected, S - static, I - IGRP, R - RIP, M - mobile, B - BGP
    D - EIGRP, EX - EIGRP external, O - OSPF, IA - OSPF inter area
    E1 - OSPF external type 1, E2 - OSPF external type 2, E - EGP
    i - IS-IS, L1 - IS-IS level-1, L2 - IS-IS level-2, * - candidate default
Gateway of last resort is not set
C 120.0.0.0 is directly connected, Ethernet0
C 150.1.0.0 is directly connected, Serial0

Router 1
routerl >sho ip rout
Codes: C - connected, S - static, I - IGRP, R - RIP, M - mobile, B - BGP
    D - EIGRP, EX - EIGRP external, O - OSPF, IA - OSPF inter area
    E1 - OSPF external type 1, E2 - OSPF external type 2, E - EGP
    i - IS-IS, L1 - IS-IS level-1, L2 - IS-IS level-2, * - candidate defauft
Gateway of last resort is not set
C 120.0.0.0 is directly connected, Ethernet0
O IA 150.1.0.0 [110/74] via 120.1.1.2, 04:49:28, Ethernet0
```

OSPF is shown, along with the metric for the route (110/74). As usual, the routing table shows the next-hop IP address and the interface to use to get to this next hop.The interesting thing is that the time specified for when the route was last updated is 4 hours, 49 minutes, 28 seconds. This is how long the routers have been up. Essentially there have been no updates to the routes because nothing on the internetwork has caused the routes to be recalculated. With OSPF, each router knows that every other router is there and available through the use of hello packets. In a distance vector protocol, updates to routes typically occur every minute, and if this timer increases to more than 3 minutes or so, it is assumed that the route is no longer valid.

There are three other useful commands for OSPF systems, which we will examine in turn. These are:

- `show ip ospf neighbor`
- `show ip ospf interface`
- `show ip ospf database`

Entering the following command will produce the display shown:

```
Router1>sho ip ospf neighbor

Neighbor ID    Pri   State      Dead Time   Address      Interface
150.1.1.1      1     FULL/DR    0:00:32     120.1.1.2    Ethernet0
```

This display shows the neighbor IP address, its OSPF priority and state, the time the router will wait for another hello packet before this neighbor will be declared dead, and the address and interface through which this neighbor is reachable.

Figure 4-17 The *show ip ospf interface* command

```
routerl > sho ip ospf interface
Ethernet0 is up, line protocol is up
  Internet Address 120.1.1.1 255.0.0.0, Area 0
  Process ID 10, Router ID 120.1.1.1, Network Type BROADCAST, Cost: 10
  Transmit Delay is 1 sec, State BDR, Priority 1
  Designated Router (ID) 150.1.1.1, Interface address 120.1.1.2
  Backup Designated router (ID) 120.1.1.1, Interface address 120.1.1.1
  Timer intervals configured, Hello 10, Dead 40, Wait 40, Retransmit 5
  Hello due in 0:00:08
  Neighbor Count is 1, Adjacent neighbor count is 1
    Adjacent wdh neighbor 150.1.1.1 (Designated Router)
Serial0 is administratively down, line protocol is down
  OSPF not enabled on this interface
Serial1 is administratively down, line protocol is down
  OSPF not enabled on this interface
```

The command shown in Fig. 4-17 gives more information on the specific OSPF setup on each interface, such as:

- The interface address, netmask, and area ID.
- The OSPF process ID (synonymous with the autonomous system number), ID used by the router (in this case its IP address), network type, and link cost.
- The timers used in the hello neighbor discovery process.
- Acount of the number of neighbors and a list of the routers that have achieved an adjacent condition. (Adjacency is achieved if two routers have the same topology table.)

The final command to look at for this configuration is the `show ip ospf database` command, which shows us the table of link state advertisements the router uses as input to the Dijkstra algorithm to determine the routing table (Fig. 4-18).

This supplies fairly straightforward information. The Link ID is the router's IP address for which information is being given. The ADV Router is the router that advertised the Link ID previously listed. (In this case, router 150.1.1.1 advertises the 150.1.0.0 network, the 120.1.1.2 interface, and the 150.1.1.1 interface.) The sequence number is used to detect old, duplicate, or out-of-sequence link state advertisements. The link count identifies the number of interfaces running OSPF in the router.

Now that we have seen what the topology database looks like during normal operation, let's try the following. If we connect the Ethernet interface on router 3 to the hub for the configuration shown in Fig. 4-15, an interesting situation arises. This is the configuration used to test the `IP default-network` command earlier in this chapter. In that situa-

Figure 4-18 The *show ip ospf database* command

```
router1> show ip ospf database
    OSPF Router with ID (120.1.1.1) (Process ID 10)
        Router Link States (Area 0)
Link ID     ADV Router    Age   Seq#          Checksum   Link count
120.1.1.1   120.1.1.1     62    0x8000000E    0x8AC3     1
150.1.1.1   150.1.1.1     58    0x8000000F    0x30C      1
        Net Link States (Area 0)

Link ID     ADV Router    Age   Seq#          Checksum
120.1.1.2   150.1.1.1     58    0x8000000D    0x4DD5
        Summary Net Link States (Area 0)

Link ID     ADV Router    Age   Seq#          Checksum
150.1.0.0   150.1.1.1     58    0x8000000D    0xC31C
```

tion, connecting the Ethernet 0 interface on router 3 to the hub did not adversely affect the operation of IGRP.

In OSPF, things are a little different due to the use of LSAs.

To perform this experiment, add an entry to the `ospf 10` section on router 3 for the 193.1.1.0 network to area 0, as follows:

```
Router3(config)#router ospf 10
Router3(config-router)#network 193.1.1.0 0.0.0.255 area 0
```

Now try to ping 120.1.1.1 from router 3.

```
Router3#ping 120.1.1.1
Type escape sequence to abort.
Sending 5, 100-byte ICMP Echos to 120.1.1.1, timeout is 2 seconds:
......
Success rate is 0 percent (0/5)
```

This happens because the routing table has changed, so let's look at the routing table of router 3 and see what happened.

```
Router3#sho ip route
Gateway of last resort is not set
C150.1.0.0 is directly connected, Serial0
C193.1.1.0 is directly connected, Ethernet0
```

The reason for this is that the topology database is now supplying information to the Dijkstra algorithm, which prevents the 120.0.0.0 network from being entered in the routing table. The topology database knows about the 120.0.0.0 network, but it does not make it into the routing table, so router 3 no longer can send packets there. This topology database is now shown as follows:

```
Router3#sho ip ospf database
Router Link States (Area 1)

Link ID ADV Router      Age      Seq#      Checksum         Link count
150.1.1.1       150.1.1.1       77       0x80000010       0x2E5D  2
193.1.1.1       193.1.1.1       96       0x80000012       0x5409  2

Summary Net Link States (Area 1)
Link ID ADV Router      Age      Seq#      Checksum
120.0.0.0       150.1.1.1       76       0x8000000E       0x37FC
193.1.1.0       193.1.1.1       395      0x80000001       0xFCCD

Router Link States (Area 0)
Link ID ADV Router      Age      Seq#      Checksum         Link count
193.1.1.1       193.1.1.1       390      0x80000003       0xFEF9  1

Summary Net Link States (Area 0)
Link ID ADV Router      Age      Seq#      Checksum
150.1.0.0       193.1.1.1       395      0x80000001       0x5769
```

Clearly, the OSPF link state advertisement mechanism and Dijkstra algorithm are less forgiving than the distance vector system.

Optional OSPF Configuration Commands. The preceding configurations covered what was necessary to get OSPF up and running with default values. The following commands are optional if you want to customize your environment. This should be done with caution, because many of the commands need all interfaces on the internetwork to have the same values applied for correct routing.

- `ip ospf retransmit-interval`
- `ip ospf priority number`
- `ip ospf hello-interval`
- `ip ospf dead-interval`
- `area n stub`
- `area n range aa.aa.aa.aa mm.mm.mm.mm`
- `no ospf auto-cost-determination`

The `ip ospf retransmit-interval` command specifies the number of seconds between link state advertisement retransmissions for adjacencies on an OSPF interface.

The `ip ospf priority number` command sets the priority of a given router, which is used during router initialization to determine the designated and backup router for a LAN.

The `ip ospf hello-interval` command is used to define the interval in seconds between hello packets sent out by a router.

The command `ip ospf dead-interval` defines the length of time a router waits to hear hello packets from another OSPF router before declaring it down.

In the command `area n stub`, the *n* here is the area number. A *stub area* is one into which no route information regarding other area numbers is sent. Instead, the stub area border router generates a default route for any router in the stub area to use if a packet needs to be sent to another area number. This reduces the amount of LSA packets in a routing area.

The `area n range aa.aa.aa.aa mm.mm.mm.mm` command is used by area border routers to reduce the number of subnets advertised between areas. This is the command used to implement the route summarization shown in Fig. 4-14. In this figure, an area border router summarizes two adjacent subnets into one subnet for advertisement to another router. In this example, the command would be:

```
area 2 range 200.1.1.8 255.255.255.248
```

To explain the `no ospf auto-cost-determination` command, it must be noted that prior to release 10.3 on Cisco IOS, OSPF assigned a default cost to each serial link, much the same way IGRP operated in the lab of Chap. 3. With IGRP, we had to assign bandwidth commands for each interface, so that the route calculation used appropriate metrics. The same was true in OSPF, where specific `ip ospf cost` entries had to be put in for each interface to associate the correct cost for the bandwidth available. Cisco's OSPF implementation now assigns cost values based on the bandwidth of the link in use. For example, a 64 kbps link gets a cost (metric) of 1562, whereas a T-1 gets a cost of 64. The `no ospf auto-cost-determination` command disables this feature and allows a network administrator to customize the cost of links used in the internetwork.

Variable-Length Subnet Masks in OSPF. Previously we mentioned that VLSM can save address space on an internetwork. An example of VLSM is given in Fig. 4-19. In this figure, OSPF will distribute information regarding the two netmasks identified throughout the internetwork. This is useful, because we might need to assign a netmask of 255.255.255.0 to the 160.4.3.0 subnet to accommodate all the hosts on this subnet. If we only need a 255.255.255.224 netmask for the number of hosts on the 160.4.4.32 subnet, however, we can assign this netmask and use addresses in the range 160.4.4.65 to 160.4.4.254 elsewhere in the internetwork.

OSPF will keep track of all these subnets and treat them as if they were separate network numbers. This type of network configuration would not be possible with IGRP, because IGRP would summarize the major network number 160.4.0.0 on both entry points to the 150.1.0.0 network, potentially leading to packets destined for the 160.4.3.0 subnet (this is using a netmask of 255.255.255.0) being delivered to the 160.4.4.0 subnet.

The ability to use different values for the subnet mask and have discontinuous subnets is useful for an internetwork like the Internet; on a private internetwork, however, they can easily cause severe problems that

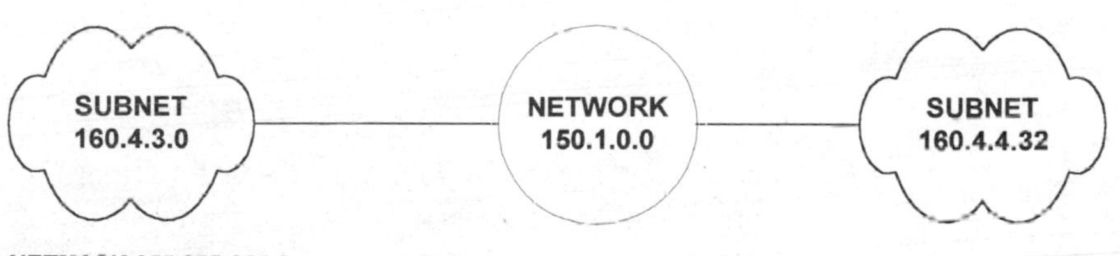

Figure 4-19 Variable-length subnet masks in OSPF

are difficult to resolve. Let's explore what could happen to the configuration of the routers in Fig. 4-20 that would cause severe problems.

This numbering scheme means that for subnet A, we can assign host addresses from 160.4.8.49 to 160.4.8.62. For subnet B, we can assign host addresses within the range 160.4.8.65 to 160.4.8.126. This is a correct configuration, but it is easy to make mistakes and get into serious trouble, even on a very simple internetwork such as this. Suppose the administrator for router 1 realizes he is running out of addresses for subnet A hosts, and, knowing that OSPF supports VLSM, decides to change the mask used on subnet A to 255.255.255.192. The effect of this causes an interesting problem.

With a 255.255.255.192 mask, the first subnet, from 160.4.8.0 to 160.4.8.63 should not be used, because as with all subnet and host values, the first and last in a subnet are not usable. This means that all the hosts numbered from 49 to 62 are no longer valid in subnet A.

Suppose this error is recognized and the administrator decides to reinstate the original subnet A values and generate another subnet off a different interface on router 1. This time the administrator chooses subnet 160.4.8.96 with a mask of 255.255.255.224, giving addressable hosts in the range 160.4.8.97 to 160.4.8.126. This will cause a problem with subnet B, because this range of addresses is legal for subnet B and the new subnet. With this new configuration, routers 1 and 2 will not know where to send packets destined for these hosts. Unless you really need it, VLSM can cause problems on complex internetworks.

Integrated IS-IS

The *IS-IS protocol* has its origins in OSI. IS-IS stands for *Intermediate System to Intermediate System*, which means it is used by routers to talk to each other; in OSI terms, an *Intermediate System* is OSI-speak for a router. IS-IS is a link state protocol and is utilized in Digital Equipment Corporation's DECnet Phase V. To give the protocol a wider appeal, it was made "integrated" so that it would carry route information for protocols other than OSI, most notably the TCP/IP protocols.

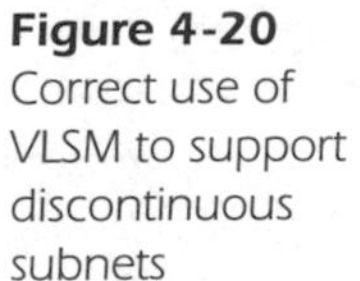

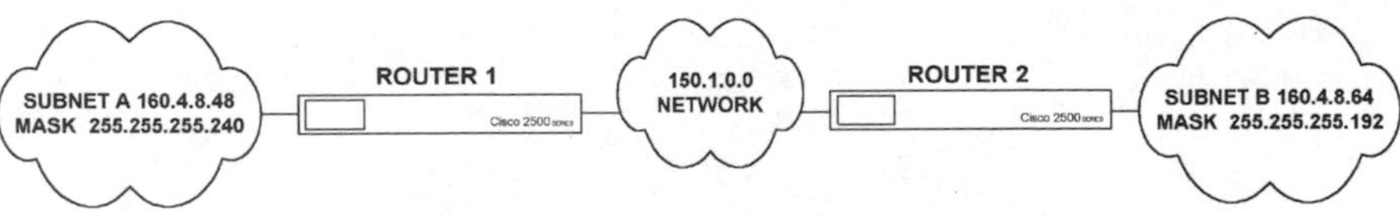

Figure 4-20 Correct use of VLSM to support discontinuous subnets

The technology behind the protocol is similar to OSPF; it uses LSAs sent to all routers within a given area and hello packets to detect whether a router is still functioning.

Nothing more will be said of Integrated IS-IS, because I recommend that if you want to use a link state protocol, you use OSPF.

Exterior Gateway Routing Protocols

These protocols are designed to regulate what traffic can travel between different autonomous systems and protect each from any bugs in another AS. The mechanisms we will examine here are static routing, the Exterior Gateway Protocol, and the Border Gateway Protocol.

Static Routing

Usually an experienced network administrator will seek to minimize any manual configuration. In the case of exterior routing, this might be different, because static routing offers a number of advantages when routing between autonomous systems. These advantages can be summarized as follows:

- Complete flexibility over the advertisement of subnets and their next-hop routers.
- No routing protocol traffic travels over the link connecting autonomous systems.
- Because no routing protocol is operating over the inter-AS link, there is no possibility of a faulty router in one AS affecting the other AS.

The down sides are obvious. Static routes do not adapt to link failures, and manual configuration can be a headache to maintain. Despite these down sides, static routing often is a popular choice for connecting internetworks that do not "trust" one another. Let's say autonomous system 1 consists of network numbers 45.0.0.0 and 46.0.0.0, and autonomous system 2 consists of network numbers 47.0.0.0 and 48.0.0.0. This is illustrated in Fig. 4-21.

To complete static routing for connecting these two autonomous systems together, use the following commands:

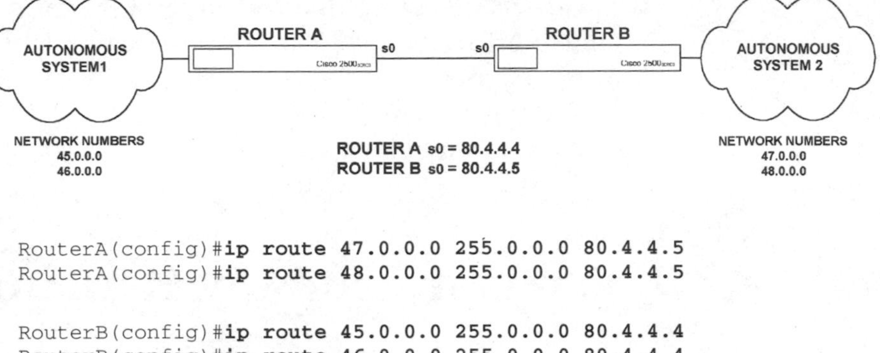

Figure 4-21 Internetwork used to discuss static routing

```
RouterA(config)#ip route 47.0.0.0 255.0.0.0 80.4.4.5
RouterA(config)#ip route 48.0.0.0 255.0.0.0 80.4.4.5

RouterB(config)#ip route 45.0.0.0 255.0.0.0 80.4.4.4
RouterB(config)#ip route 46.0.0.0 255.0.0.0 80.4.4.4
```

This tells each autonomous system how to get to networks in the other autonomous system.

Exterior Gateway Protocol

The Exterior Gateway Protocol, or EGP, has three components, *neighbor acquisition, neighbor reachability,* and *routing information.* EGP was designed to add a measure of automation to the configuration of routes between different autonomous systems. EGP has been superseded by the Border Gateway Protocol, (BGP), so we will not spend too much time on it.

EGP Neighbor Acquisition. We can use Fig. 4-21 to discuss how EGP works. Suppose router A has been configured to initiate a neighbor relationship with router B. This will initiate a *neighbor acquisition packet* to be sent from router A to router B. If router B has been configured to accept a neighbor relationship with A, this packet is accepted. The neighbor reachability mechanism is the hello packet, used to verify that a router that is accepted as a neighbor is still functioning. The routing information of EGP is similar to distance vector protocols, but it omits the metric for routes advertised. EGP was implemented like this because it was designed for the Internet, when it was assumed that there would be a core network with separate routing domains connected to this core by one router.

The major problem with using EGP in a more generalized network is that, because no use is made of metrics, if there is more than one path to a destination, packets can easily get caught in routing loops (Fig. 4-22).

If router R4 receives a packet for AS1, it will have two routes to AS2, one via R3 and one via R6. Because there are no metrics involved, the

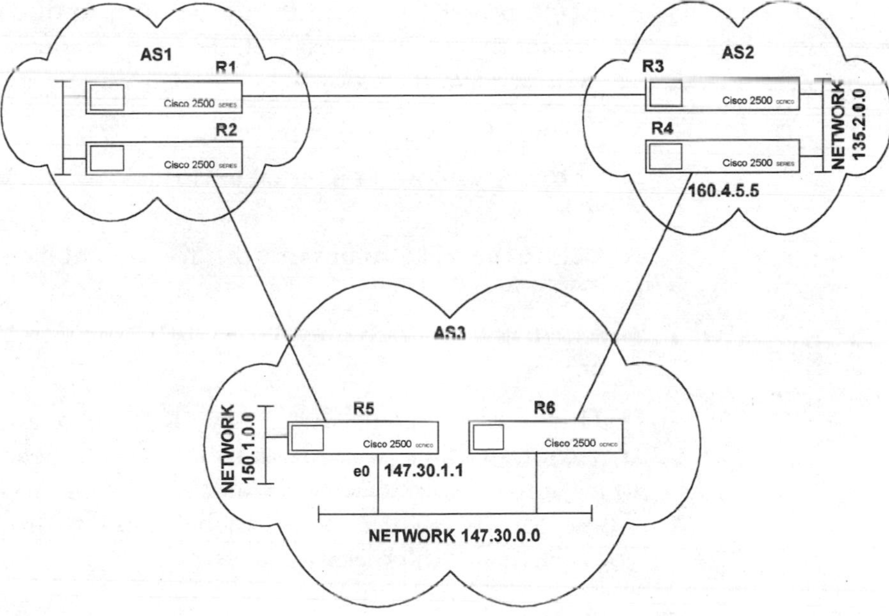

Figure 4-22 A sample internetwork in which EGP does not work

routes are equal in R4's determination, so it may choose either. Let's say it chooses to send the packet to R3. R3 also has two routes to AS1, one via R4 and one to R1. Again, these routes are equal in R3's consideration, so the packet could be returned to R4, where the cycle starts over again. Clearly, EGP has problems for a general environment, so I would recommend leaving it alone.

BGP: Border Gateway Protocol

BGP was introduced to improve upon EGP. One of BGP's main features is that it introduces a reliable transport protocol to ensure that route updates are received. BGP also implements a keep-alive mechanism, ensuring that BGP routers know if neighboring BGP routers fail. BGP does not transmit metrics with its route updates, but does transmit a path for each AS that lists the autonomous systems to be visited on the way to the destination AS. BGP thus avoids the circulating-packet problem of EGP.

BGP works on the principle of enforcing policies. A *policy* is manually configured and allows a BGP-enabled router to rate possible routes to other autonomous systems, selecting the best path.

Configuring BGP. We can use Fig. 4-22 to discuss how to configure BGP on a router. In this example, let's take router R6. To configure BGP we will perform the following:

- Define BGP as a routing process.
- Define the networks internal to this AS that are going to be advertised.
- Define the relationships that this router will have with its neighbors.
- Assign administrative weights to paths to control the path selection process.

This is a basic configuration for BGP. There are, however, many further configuration customizations that can be made. If you really want to get into complex BGP configuration, I would recommend talking to a Cisco Systems engineer who can help you with customizing BGP for your particular internetwork.

For a basic configuration, the following commands are entered into router R6:

```
Router6(config)#router bgp 3
Router6(config-router)#network 147.30.0.0
Router6(config-router)#network 150.1.0.0
Router6(config-router)#neighbor 147.30.1.1 remote-as 3
Router6(config-router)#neighbor 160.4.5.5 remote-as 2
```

The first line in this configuration defines BGP for autonomous system 3 on router 6. The next two lines define the network numbers internal to AS 3 that will be advertised via BGP. The fourth line defines an internal neighbor that is in the same AS. The BGP process on router 6 will now exchange information with a BGP process defined on R5. The fifth line defines the neighbor in a different AS with which router 6 will exchange information.

The effect of this configuration is that R6 will share information about networks 147.30.0.0 and 150.1.0.0 with the two specified routers via BGP updates.The last thing left to do in our basic configuration of BGP is to assign administrative weights to control the path selection process. In the following example, a weight of 40,000 is assigned to the path to router R4.

```
Router6(config-router)#neighbor 160.4.5.5 40000
```

This administrative weight can vary between 0 and 65535, with the default being 32768. The effect of increasing the weight to R4 is to make it less attractive when R6 is calculating which paths to use.

Redistributing Route Information between Protocols

If you have the opportunity to build a network from scratch, and could design it such that the only devices to run routing protocols are routers, you could choose your favorite routing protocol and use that exclusively. Typically, however, the situation is that there is an existing network with an existing routing protocol in place and, more often than not, Unix machines have some routing responsibilities in a network. Because most Unix machines only support RIP, and it is unlikely that RIP will be the best choice of routing protocol for an internetwork of any size, the question arises of how more than one routing protocol can coexist on an internetwork, either permanently or during a period of migration.

The answer is *redistribution*. A router can be configured to run more than one routing protocol and redistribute route information between the two protocols. The idea is that the internetwork will have multiple domains, each operating with a different routing protocol. At the border between these domains, one router has the responsibility of running both routing protocols and informing each domain about the other's networks in the appropriate routing protocol. This is illustrated in Fig. 4-23.

In this figure, the router has to run both RIP and IGRP, then inform domain A about the networks in domain B with RIP updates and inform domain B about domain A's networks using IGRP updates. The router in this figure will only be able to assign one metric to all the routes that it redistributes from one domain to another; it cannot translate metrics between protocols. At first, this may seem to be a drawback, that all networks are redistributed with the same metric value, no matter where they are located in the other domain. In reality this is not a problem, because to get from domain A to domain B, all connections have to go through the same router; the initial part of the journey is identical when sending packets between domains.

In Fig. 4-23, a packet destined for domain A, originating in domain B, reaches router 1. Router 1 then has a routing table filled with entries for

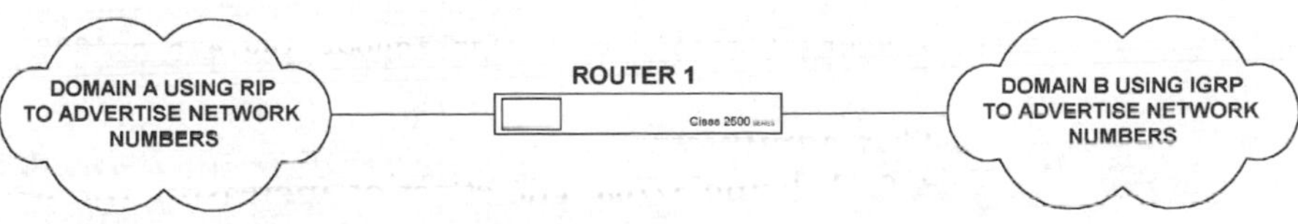

Figure 4-23 An internetwork where the use of redistribution is appropriate

the networks in domain A that have been calculated using RIP updates. The packet will follow the best path to its destination network.

The following is an example of how, in Fig. 4-23, the routing protocol processes could be configured on router 1 to redistribute routes between the RIP and IGRP domains.

If we take a basic configuration for both RIP and IGRP, we add the redistribute commands shown in bold type:

```
router igrp 12
timers basic 15 45 0 60
network 164.8.0.0
network 193.1.1.0
no metric holddown
metric maximum-hop 50
redistribute rip
default - metric 300 344 200 200 200
router rip
network 150.1.0.0
network 120.0.0.0
redistribute igrp 12
default-metric 3
```

This assumes that domain A has network numbers 150.1.0.0 and 120.0.0.0 in it, and domain B has networks 164.8.0.0 and 193.1.1.0 in it.

The five values following the `default-metric` entry in the router IGRP section are the metrics that will be sent out in IGRP updates, for routes learned about via RIP. In the router RIP section, routes learned from IGRP updates will be advertised with a metric of 3. It must be noted that the numbers shown here are random. In most instances this does not matter, because all cross-domain traffic has to go through router 1 as previously explained.

We will now look at a few more examples of redistributing route information between protocols of different types.

Redistributing between RIP and OSPF

Let's take the example of one RIP domain and one OSPF domain needing to exchange information (Fig. 4-24). This is very much like the last example we used to redistribute route information between RIP and IGRP.

As before, we have connected the Ethernet 0 ports of router 1 and router 3 to the same hub, so that the Ethernet 0 port of router 3 can be brought in to an *up* state and participate in the routing processes, even though these two Ethernet ports are on different network numbers. This is not good practice in general and should be used only in a lab environment.

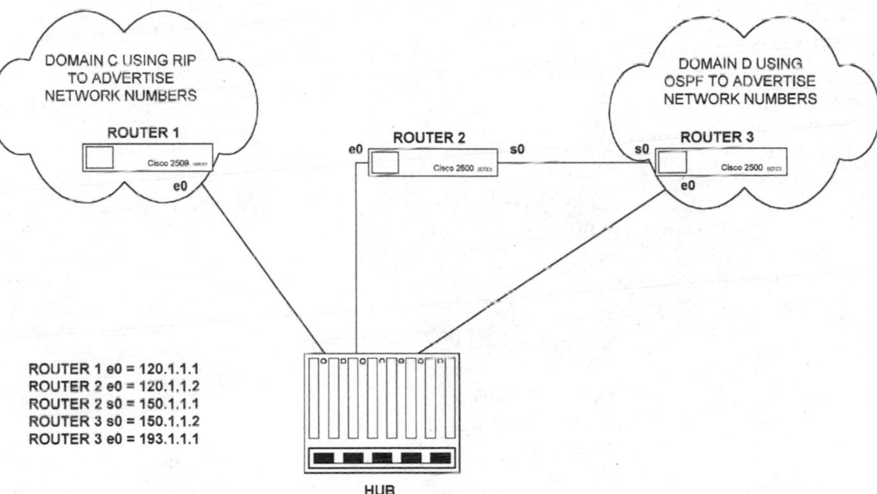

Figure 4-24 Internetwork redistributing between the OSPF and RIP protocols

The configurations and routing table for each router in this instance are shown in Fig. 4-25.

The routing tables of router 3 and 1 show that the redistribution process functioned as expected. Router 3 knows about 120.0.0.0 via the OSPF process on router 2, and uses the OSPF default metric set in router 2 for that destination. Router 3 considers 120.0.0.0 as an external network, as the RIP domain is considered a different autonomous system. Router 1 knows about network 150.1.0.0 from the RIP process on router 2, and uses the RIP default metric set on router 2 for this entry.

In this small internetwork, RIP does not need to send advertisements out the Serial 0 port of router 2, so it can be disabled on this port by adding the following entry in router 2.

```
Router2(config)#router rip
Router2(config-router)#passive-interface serial 0
```

If this setup were part of a larger internetwork, there would be the possibility of a route existing from router 3 to router 1, via some other router that also is performing redistribution. This could cause a routing loop under certain conditions. To prevent this possible loop condition, it is a good idea to tell the RIP process on all routers performing redistribution to prevent routes that originated in the RIP domain from being readvertised back in to the RIP domain from the OSPF domain. To achieve this, we use *access lists*. An access list is a useful feature that allows almost infinite customization of the operation of your network.

Figure 4-25
Router configurations and routing tables for OSPF and RIP redistribution

```
router1 #wri t
Building configuration...
Current configuration:
!
version 10.3
hostname router1
!
enable secret 5 $1$W6qH$DTNrEHmJrn6QqYcMu5PRh.
enable password test
!
!
interface Ethernet0
  ip address 120.1.1.1 255.0.0.0
!
interface Serial0
  no ip address
  shutdown
!
interface Serial1
  no ip address
  shutdown
!
router rip
  network 120.0.0.0
!
!
line con 0
line 1 16
  transport input all
line aux 0
  transport input all
line vty 0 4
  password ilx
  login
!
end
router1#sho ip route
Codes: C - connected, S - static, I - IGRP, R - RIP, M - mobile, B - BGP
     D - EIGRP, EX - EIGRP extemal, O - OSPF, IA - OSPF inter area
    E1 - OSPF external type 1, E2 - OSPF external type 2, E - EGP
    i - IS-IS, L1 - IS-IS level-1, L2 - IS-IS level-2, * - candidate defauft
Gateway of last resort is not set
C 120.0.0.0 is directly connected, Ethernet0
R 150.1.0.0 [120/4] via 120.1.1.2, 00:00:1 1, Ethernet0

Router 2
router2#wri t
Building configuration...
Current configuration:
version 10.3
!
hostname router2
```

Figure 4-25
Continued

```
!
enable secret 5 $1$/P2r$ob00lmzYqpogV0U1g1O8U/
enable password test
!
interface Ethernet0
  ip address 120.1.1.2 255.0.0.0
!
interface Serial0
  ip address 150.1.1.1 255.255.0.0
!
interface Serial1
  no ip address
  shutdown
!
router ospf 10
  redistribute rip
  network 150.1.0.0 0.0.255.255 area 1
  defauft-metric 64000
!
router rip
  redistribute ospf 10
  network 120.0.0.0
  default-metric 4
!
!
line con 0
line 1 16
line aux 0
line vty 0 4
  password ilx
  login
!
end
router2#show ip route
Codes: C - connected, S - static, I - IGRP, R - RIP, M - mobile, B - BGP
     D - EIGRP, EX - EIGRP external, O - OSPF, IA - OSPF inter area
    E1 - OSPF external type 1, E2 - OSPF external type 2, E - EGP
    i - IS-IS, L1 - IS-IS level-1, L2 - IS-IS level-2, * - candidate default
Gateway of last resort is not set
C 120.0.0.0 is directly connected, Ethernet0
C 150.1.0.0 is directly connected, Serial0


Router 3
router3#wri t
Building configuration...
Current configuration:
!
version 10.3
hostname router3
!
enable secret 5 $1$cNaQ$a4jcvrXlzVO4cwJB7RP5j1
enable password test
```

Figure 4-25
Continued

```
!
!
interface Ethernet0
  ip address 193.1.1.1 255.255.255.0
!
interface Serial0
  ip address 150.1.1.2 255.255.0.0
  clockrate 64000
!
interface Serial1
  no ip address
  shutdown
!
router ospf 10
  network 150.1.0.0 0.0.255.255 area 1
!
!
line con 0
  exec-timeout 0 0
line 1 16
  transport input all
line aux 0
  transport input all
line vty 0 4
  password ilx
  login
!
end
router3#sho ip route
Codes: C - connected, S - static, I - IGRP, R - RIP, M - mobile, B - BGP
     D - EIGRP, EX - EIGRP external, O - OSPF, IA - OSPF inter area
     E1 - OSPF external type 1, E2 - OSPF external type 2, E - EGP
     i - IS-IS, L1 - IS-IS level-1, L2 - IS-IS level-2, * - candidate defauft
Gateway of last resort is not set
O E2 120.0.0.0 [110/64000] via 150.1.1.1, 02:03:51, Serial0
C 150.1.0.O is directly connected, Serial0
C 193. 1. 1.0 is directly connected, Ethernet0
```

An access list contains a series of commands that either permit or deny specific types of packets from getting through a given interface. These access lists are applied to either inbound or outbound packets.

The objective of the access list here is to tell all routers redistributing from OSPF into RIP not to send information regarding the 150.1.0.0 network from the OSPF domain back to the RIP domain. The entries in the configuration of router 2 to achieve this are as follows:

```
router rip
distribute-list 9 out ospf 12
!
access-list 9 deny 150.1.0.0 0.0.255.255
access-list 9 permit 0.0.0.0 255.255.255.255
```

The first line in the router RIP section specifies the access list number, 9, to be applied to packets coming out of the OSPF autonomous system 12. The access list itself contains two entries, the first of which is to deny any packets from the 150.1.0.0 network. The 0.0.255.255 is a mask value. The second entry permits all other packets. This is necessary because the last, and unseen, line in any access list denies all packets.

Another, potentially more useful example is to examine how OSPF could be added to the backbone of a simple internetwork that uses RIP for nonbackbone locations. This can be done if we reconfigure our lab a little, by using two more DTE/DCE cables. The configuration that we will build in our routers is shown in Fig. 4-26.

In this configuration, RIP does not communicate between routers over the OSPF area 0 backbone, so we will use the `passive-interface` command to stop those RIP advertisements coming out of the serial interfaces of all routers with the following configuration entries.

```
Router rip
passive-interface serial 0
passive-interface serial 1
```

RIP routes can then be redistributed in to the OSPF area 0 with the following commands:

```
router ospf 9
redistribute rip subnets
```

This differs from previous redistribution commands because we are explicitly telling OSPF to redistribute subnet information. Without this

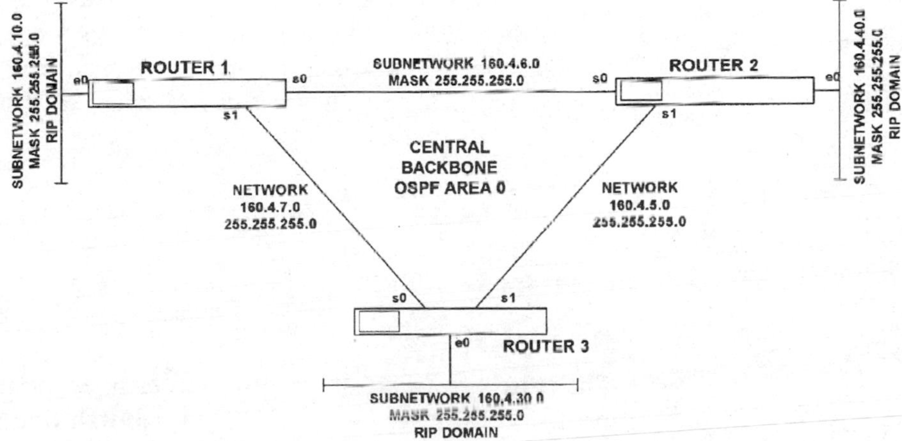

Figure 4-26 OSPF as a backbone protocol for a RIP internetwork

command, OSPF will redistribute only those networks without netmask information.

All RIP domains receive route information from other RIP domains and the OSPF backbone via the following configuration entries:

```
router rip
redistribute ospf 9
default-metric 10
```

The final configurations and routing tables for this example are given in Fig. 4-27.

This gives us the results we expect, with each router knowing about all six subnets on the internetwork. As you can see from these routing tables, OSPF will share traffic between paths of equal metric. This is illustrated by looking at the routing table for router 3. In this routing table, 160.4.6.0 has two equal-cost paths, one via router 1, and one via router 2.

Routing between Autonomous Systems

Let's now look at a different situation, one in which we have different autonomous systems, both running EIGRP, that need to exchange route information. In this example, it is assumed that both autonomous systems are under common administration and the use of an exterior gateway protocol is not necessary.

By default, EIGRP will only send route advertisements to the one autonomous system; if two EIGRP processes for two autonomous systems are running on the same router, however, redistribution can be used to transfer information between each AS routing database.

Let's say we have a router with one interface in autonomous system 15, network 120.0.0.0, and one in autonomous system 16, network 150.1.0.0. Our objective is to transfer information regarding 120.0.0.0 into AS 16. The route protocol sections for this router are shown as follows:

```
router eigrp 15
network 120.0.0.0
redistribute eigrp 16
distribute-list 5 out eigrp 16
router eigrp 16
network 150.1.0.0
!
access-list 5 permit 120.0.0.0
```

The third line of this configuration enables the router to redistribute information from AS 16 into AS 15. The fourth line, in conjunction with

Figure 4-27 Router configurations and routing tables for redistribution between an OSPF backbone and RIP domains

```
router 1
routerl #wri t
Building configuration...
Current configuration:
!
version 10.3
hostname router1
!
enable secret 5 $1$W6qH$DTNrEHmJrn6QqYcMu5PRh.
enable password test
!
!
interface Ethernet0
  ip address 160.4.10.1 255.255.255.0
!
interface Serial0
  ip address 160.4.6.2 255.255.255.0
!
interface Serial1
  ip address 160.4.7.2 255.255.255.0
!
router ospf 9
  redistribute rip subnets
  network 160.4.6.0 0.0.0.255 area 0
  network 160.4.7.0 0.0.0.255 area 0
!
router rip
  redistribute ospf 9
  passive-interface Serial0
  passive-interface Serial1
  network 160.4.0.0
  default-metric 3
!
!
line con 0
line 1 16
  transport input all
line aux 0
  transport input all
line vty 0 4
  password ilx
  login
!
end
router1#sho ip route
Codes: C - connected, S - static, I - IGRP, R - RIP, M - mobile, B - BGP
    D - EIGRP, EX - EIGRP external, O - OSPF, IA - OSPF inter area
   E1 - OSPF external type 1, E2 - OSPF external type 2, E - EGP
  i - IS-IS, L1 - IS-IS level-1, L2 - IS-IS level-2, * - candidate default
Gateway of last resort is not set
  160.4.0.0 255.255.255.0 is subnetted, 6 subnets
O E2    160.4.40.0 [110/20] via 160.4.6.1, 00:05:59, Serial0
O       160.4.5.0 [110/128] via 160.4.7.1, 00:05:59, Serial1
```

Figure 4-27
Continued

```
          [1 10/1 28] via 160.4.6.1, 00:05:59, Serial0
C       160.4.6.0 is directly connected, Serial0
C       160.4.7.0 is directly connected, Serial1
C       160.4.10.0 is directly connected, Ethernet0
O E2    160.4.30.0 [110/20] via 160.4.7.1, 00:05:59, Serial1

router 2
router2#wri t
Building configuration...
Current configuration:
!
version 10.3
!
hostname router2
!
enable secret 5 $1$/P2r$ob00lmzYqpogVOU1g1O8U/
enable password test
!
interface Ethernet0
  ip address 160.4.40.1 255.255.255.0
!
interface Serial0
  ip address 160.4.6.1 255.255.255.0
  clockrate 64000
!
interface Serial1
  ip address 160.4.5.2 255.255.255.0
  clockrate 64000
!
router ospf 9
  redistribute rip subnets
  network 160.4.5.0 0.0.0.255 area 0
  network 160.4.6.0 0.0.0.255 area 0
!
router rip
  redistribute ospf 9
  passive-interface Serial0
  passive-interface Serial1
  network 160.4.0.0
  defauft-metric 6
!
!
line con 0
line 1 16
line aux 0
line vty 0 4
  password ilx
  login
!
end
router2#show ip route
Codes: C - connected, S - static, I - IGRP, R - RIP, M - mobile, B - BGP
    D - EIGRP, EX - EIGRP external, O - OSPF, IA - OSPF inter area
```

Figure 4-27
Continued

```
    E1 - OSPF external type 1, E2 - OSPF external type 2, E - EGP
    i - IS-IS, L1 - IS-IS level-1, L2 - IS IS level-2, ' - candidate default
Gateway of last resort is not set
    160.4.0.0 255.255.255.0 is subnetted, 6 subnets
C       160.4.40.0 is directly connected, Ethernet0
C       160.4.5.0 is directly connected, Serial1
C       160.4.6.0 is directly connected, Serial0
O       160.4.7.0 [110/128] via 160.4.6.2, 00:06:58, Serial0
            [110/1 28] via 160.4.5.1, 00:06:58, Serial1
O E2    160.4.10.0 [110/20] via 160.4.6.2, 00:06:58, Serial0
O E2    160.4.30.0 [110/20] via 160.4.5.1, 00:06:58, Serial1

router 3
router3#wri t
Building configuration...
Current configuration:
!
version 10.3
!
hostname router3
!
enable secret 5 $1$cNaQ$a4JcvrX1zVO4cwJB7RP5j1
enable password test
!
interface Ethernet0
  ip address 160.4.30.1 255.255.255.0
!
interface Serial0
  ip address 160.4.7.1 255.255.255.0
  clockrate 64000
!
interface Serial1
  ip address 160.4.5.1 255.255.255.0
!
roader ospf 9
  redistribute rip subnets
  network 160.4.7.0 0.0.0.255 area 0
  network 160.4.5.0 0.0.0.255 area 0
!
router rip
  redistribute ospf 9
  passive-interface Serial0
  passive-interface Serial1
  network 160.4.0.0
  defauft-metric 4
!
line con 0
  exec-timeout 0 0
line 1 16
  transport input all
line aux 0
  transport input all
line vty 0 4
```

Figure 4-27 Continued

```
  password ilx
  login
!
end
router3#sho ip route
Codes: C - connected, S - static, I - IGRP, R - RIP, M - mobile, B - BGP
     D - EIGRP, EX - EIGRP external, 0 - OSPF, IA - OSPF irder area
    E1 - OSPF external type 1, E2 - OSPF external type 2, E - EGP
    i - IS-IS, L1 - IS-IS level-1, L2 - IS-IS level-2, * - candidate default
Gateway of last resort is not set
    160.4.0.0 255.255.255.0 is subnetted, 6 subnets
O E2   160.4.40.0 [110/20] via 160.4.5.2, 00:07:45, Serial1
C      160.4.5.0 is directly connected, Serial1
O      160.4.6.0 [110/128] via 160.4.7.2, 00:07:46, Serial0
               [1 10/1 28] via 160.4.5.2, 00:07:46, Serial1
C      160.4.7.0 is directly connected, Serial0
O E2   160.4.10.0 [110/20] via 160.4.7.2, 00:07:46, Serial0
C      160.4.30.0 is directly connected, Ethernet0
```

the final line, restricts the information that is redistributed from AS 16 to only those routes in the 120.0.0.0 network.

Summary

In this chapter we examined how routers automatically update their routing tables to keep optimal routes to all network numbers, in spite of a changing internetwork topology. At the high level, there are two types of routing protocol, Interior and Exterior Gateway Protocols.

Interior Gateway Protocols are designed to exchange full routing information between all routers in the same autonomous system. An autonomous system is the largest entity in a routing hierarchy. Exterior Gateway Protocols are designed to transfer information between different autonomous systems in a controlled fashion.

Interior Gateway Protocols are further subdivided into distance vector and link state protocols.

Distance vector protocols only exchange information with neighbors on directly connected segments, using broadcast routing updates. It is the duty of each router to pass on route information learned from one neighboring router to another. These routing updates perform the function of transferring route information and act as keep-alives. Virtually all the routing table entries are sent in each routing update. Distance vector protocols require the use of several mechanisms to maintain an optimal routing environment, including Split Horizon, Poison Reverse, triggered updates, and hold-downs.

Link state protocols use separate mechanisms to update other routers and to send keep-alive messages. Routes are advertised using link state advertisements, which are explicitly sent to every other router in a given routing area. Keep-alives are sent in the form of small hello packets between routers. Sending LSAs to all routers in a given area enables each router to generate a complete map of that routing area. Link state protocols apply the Dijkstra algorithm to this database to generate routes for entry into the routing table.

In general, link state protocols scale better for very large internetworks, producing acceptable convergence times and less routing protocol traffic in the event of link failures. By "very large," I mean an internetwork servicing over 1500 locations. Link state protocols, however, have to deal with more internal structures to process and thus require more router CPU and memory.

In a Cisco environment, you have the choice of IGRP, EIGRP, or OSPF as the Interior Gateway Routing Protocol. In most cases, IGRP is adequate and is the most familiar to network administrators who have been accustomed to RIP. EIGRP and OSPF can provide better convergence times, but are more complex to customize. EIGRP, and particularly OSPF, require more RAM and a faster processor in the router device for adequate performance.

For most users, if an External Gateway Protocol is necessary at all, static routing is normally adequate.

CHAPTER 5

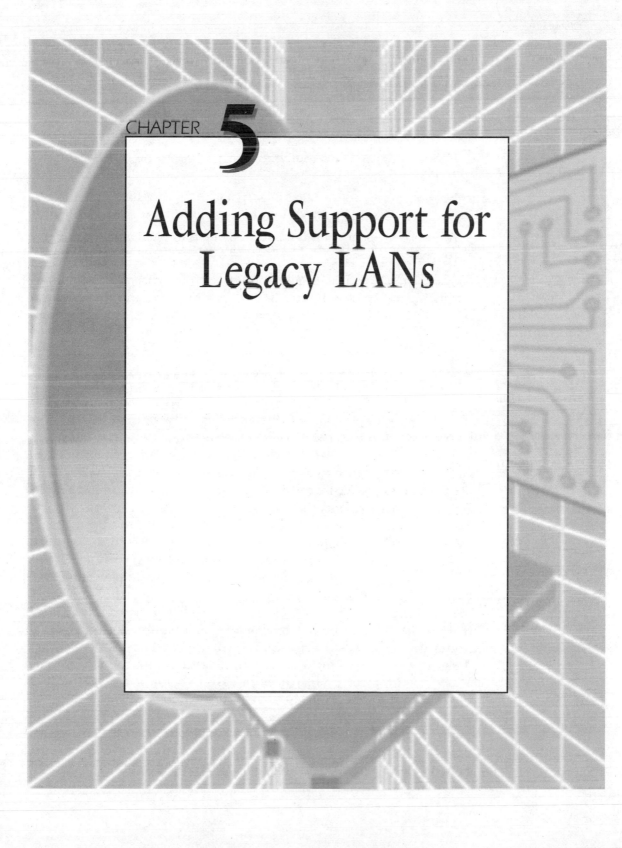

Adding Support for Legacy LANs

Objectives

In this chapter we will examine:

- How we can use Cisco routers to transport protocols other than TCP/IP.
- Network protocols included in corporate networks, such as Novell NetWare's IPX, the IBM SNA protocols, and Windows NT NetBEUI.
- An overview of how bridging technology is implemented on Cisco routers.

The approach will be to give an overview of each technology, discuss integrating each protocol into a TCP/IP environment, and then give configuration examples of how to implement these protocols on Cisco routers.

Novell NetWare's IPX/SPX Protocols

Novell's NetWare product, which is installed in more than 50 percent of LANs worldwide, uses the IPX/SPX (Internetwork Packet Exchange and Sequenced Packet Exchange) protocol as its basis for communications. NetWare was designed as a departmental server operating system, originally meant to service up to 100 users. Novell's marketing strategy was to aim for the departments that did not want to wait in line for corporate MIS departments to deliver systems that they could instead buy off the shelf. This strategy was well-timed—it coincided with cheap, powerful PCs becoming available—and became phenomenally successful.

To make it as easy as possible for departments to implement a LAN protocol, Novell designed the IPX/SPX protocols, which eliminate the need to number individual nodes in a network. Because it was assumed that NetWare would be implemented in an environment in which all nodes were connected via a high-capacity Ethernet LAN, NetWare designers also programmed a number of features into the original NetWare Core Protocol set that made it easy to connect a NetWare LAN, but fairly costly in terms of bandwidth utilization.

As a result of NetWare's success, IPX became a de facto standard and many third-party developers developed applications for it. This was all well and good until it became necessary to transport NetWare traffic over wide area networks that do not have the bandwidth available that an Ethernet LAN does. To resolve these issues, protocols such as the NetWare Link State Protocol and IPXWAN were developed.

NetWare is a client/server system; as such, all communications pass between the client software on a workstation PC and the server. Client PCs do not communicate directly. This contrasts with the TCP/IP communications model, which is designed to allow any machine to send information directly to any other machine without the need to go to a central server first. The TCP/IP communications model is often referred to as *peer-to-peer networking*.

We will look at an overview of NetWare protocol technology before discussing specific router implementations of these protocols.

Overview of IPX and SPX

IPX and *SPX* span the layer 3 and layer 4 protocol functions in OSI terms and, as such, do have fields in the header for network numbers. IPX is a connectionless datagram protocol, similar in many ways to IP; SPX provides connection-oriented delivery similar to TCP. A packet containing an IPX destination and source address also will contain the MAC destination and source in the layer 2 header, as previously described for TCP/IP communications. The major difference between NetWare and TCP/IP implementations is that on a NetWare LAN, you assign a network number for a given segment and all nodes use their MAC address in combination with this network number to generate their own station address. In TCP/IP every workstation is given an IP address, and the network number is derived from that value and any subnet masks applied.

The IPX header always starts with the hexadecimal value FFFF. The IPX header is somewhat similar to an IP header, carrying essentially the same information. The key information carried is as follows:

- Destination network, node and socket numbers
- Source network, node and socket numbers
- Transport Control byte
- Length of IPX header and data

These are fairly self-explanatory, except for the *Transport Control byte*. To propagate route information, IPX uses a version of RIP that closely resembles that implemented by the Xerox Networking System. As with other RIP implementations, the maximum number of hops a packet is allowed to traverse is 15, and the 16th router will discard the packet. When a packet is originated, this value is set to 0 and is incremented as the packet passes through each successive IPX router. As you can see, the IPX Transport Control byte performs the same function as the IP Time To Live field.

The destination network value is obvious; however, this value is set to 00-00-00 if the destination server is on the same network number as the client sending the packet.

The destination node address has a differing value depending on whether a NetWare client or server is sending the packet. If the packet was sent by a server, it will contain the destination workstation's MAC address, and if it was sent by a workstation to a server, it will contain the value 00-00-00-00-00-01. It must be noted that the MAC information in the layer 2 header will contain the appropriate MAC address for the destination machine, whether that is a server or a workstation.

Source and destination sockets are used in IPX/SPX communications in the same way as in TCP/IP, i.e., a socket identifies the address of a program running in a machine.

SPX adds additional fields to the layer 3 header, which include source and destination connection IDs, and sequence and acknowledgment numbers. Since SPX operates as a connection-oriented protocol, it operates on a handshake principle to initiate and close connections, similar to TCP.

With SPX, a constant stream of traffic between the client and server is generated by the protocol and is independent of any user data that needs to be transmitted between the two. This stream of traffic uses timers to decide when to re-request responses if none are received. The timers you may wish to adjust on the workstation or server software are:

- SPX listen timeout
- SPX verify timeout
- SPX abort timeout
- SPX Ack wait timeout
- SPX watchdog verify timeout
- SPX watchdog abort timeout

In Novell documentation, the default values for these timers are given in ticks, with one tick being the standard PC clock tick, roughly 1/18th of a second.

NetWare Client-to-Server Communication

The NetWare client protocols are implemented in two parts: The first is the IPX/SPX protocol, the second is the *shell*, or *redirector*. Applications that need only to use the services of IPX/SPX need only to load the first part (typically the IPXODI.COM file). To communicate with a NetWare server, the NetWare shell or redirector must be loaded as well. The purpose of this shell is to intercept all requests from a workstation application and to determine if the request will be serviced by the local OS or the server resources.

The workstation shell handles all interaction with the server, including interpreting route information and server service advertising. Novell did a good job with the design of this software, given its intended market, because it hides the process of address assignment and routing issues from the person installing the network. There is a price to be paid for this, however. The price paid is in the amount of network bandwidth consumed by the *Service Advertising Protocol* (SAP), *Routing Information Protocol* (RIP), and *NetWare Core Protocol* (NCP), roughly in that order.

The NetWare Core Protocol is the language that NetWare clients and servers use to talk to one another. Typical NCP functions are to deliver file reads or writes, set drive mappings, search directories, and so forth. Novell does not publish many details about NCP because it is considered to be confidential.

The area of NetWare communications that is of most interest to us is the Service Advertising Protocol (SAP). It is via SAPs that a workstation finds out what servers are available on the network to connect to. There are three types of SAP packet:

- Periodic SAP information broadcasts
- SAP service queries
- SAP service responses

In essence, the SAP *information broadcasts* are used to advertise information that a server has within its *bindery* if it is a NetWare 3.*x* server, or *NetWare Directory Service* (NDS) if it is a 4.*x* server. A NetWare server's bindery is a flat-file database of resources and clients on a network, whereas the directory service keeps this information as objects in a hierarchical database. These SAP broadcasts occur by default every 60 seconds.

When a service is broadcast, it is given a server type number, the most common of which are listed as follows:

Type	Function
4	File server
7	Print server
21	NAS SNA gateway
98	NetWare Access Server

With many (more than 20) NetWare servers interconnected, the size of these SAP broadcasts can become troublesome for heavily utilized WAN links. Overutilization during broadcast phases can cause packets to be dropped by a router attempting to forward traffic on the link.

The service queries performed by SAP are executed when a workstation wants to find a particular service on the network. Service queries effectively are queries of the network database file kept on the server (be this a bindery or directory service). The most common example of this is the *Get Nearest Server* query.

When a client starts the NetWare shell, a Get Nearest Server SAP is broadcast on the network, and either a NetWare server or router can answer these broadcasts. When this broadcast is sent out, all servers on the network reply, but the client will establish a connection only with the first one to reply. The first to reply will not necessarily be the server defined as the "preferred" server in the client's configuration. In this case, the workstation will connect to the first server to reply, just to query its database to find out how to get to the preferred server.

The IPX header previously described has a destination network number field that is used for routing purposes. NetWare servers and routers provide information on the networks they know about by using a version of RIP, in the normal distance vector protocol fashion, via broadcasts. This routing information is contained in routing information tables located at each router and server on the internetwork.

NetWare's RIP operates much the same way as does the RIP version 1 described previously for IP networks. RIP update broadcasts are sent out when a router initializes, when specific route information is requested, periodically to maintain tables, when a change occurs, or when a router is going down. In addition, NetWare RIP employs Split Horizon, although Poison Reverse and hold-down timers are not used. The metric used by NetWare RIP is the number of ticks to get to a destination. If two routes have the same tick value, the number of hops is used as a tie-breaker. This is an improvement on IP RIP, as the tick value is a better measure of the speed of delivery of a given route.

RIP is used on initial startup of the client shell. After the SAP Get Nearest Server broadcast sequence is completed, and the quickest server replies first, the workstation must find a route to that server. This is achieved by using the RIP request broadcast. When this broadcast is sent out, the workstation is requesting route information for the network number it needs to reach. The router servicing routes to this network number will respond.

Configuring Basic IPX Routing

With few exceptions, Cisco's implementation of Novell's IPX provides full routing functionality. The only part that is proprietary to Cisco is the use of IPX over X.25 or T-1 connections. For these connections, you must have Cisco routers on both ends of the connection.

One of the most useful features of Cisco IPX routing is that you can use EIGRP as the routing protocol. EIGRP provides automatic redistribution between RIP and EIGRP domains, the opportunity to traverse up to 224 routers in a network, and use of incremental SAP updates. Incremental SAPs are used when EIGRP routers exchange information. Because EIGRP utilizes a reliable transport mechanism for updates, a router does not need to continuously send out all SAP information in regular broadcasts. With incremental SAPs, SAP information is sent out only when it changes.

Assuming that you have a version of Cisco IOS loaded that is licensed to run IPX, the first task involved in getting IPX routing functional is to use the global `ipx routing` command as follows:

```
Router1(config)#ipx routing
```

Once this is done, IPX network numbers can be assigned to the router's interfaces. Care must be taken when installing a new router on an existing IPX network. If one of the router's interfaces is connected to an existing IPX network with an address that does not match that already in use, the NetWare servers will complain, displaying error messages that another device is disagreeing with them. This situation stops the new router from participating in IPX routing on the network.

When the IPX network number is assigned, you have the opportunity to define the encapsulation type used for frames on that interface. This is of particular interest on an Ethernet LAN interface, in which the encapsulation used for the layer 2 Ethernet frame can take any one of four values.

By default, NetWare servers prior to version 4 used a Novell-specific implementation of the IEEE 802.3 Ethernet frame. This type of frame only supported IPX as the network layer 3 protocol. To use this type of encapsulation for an Ethernet port, type the following (assuming that we use an IPX network number of 5):

```
Router1(config)#interface E0
Router1(config-int)ipx network 5 encapsulation novell-ether
```

Note that the Ethernet encapsulation is specified for the IPX protocol on this interface, but other protocols such as IP may be routed on this interface using a different encapsulation.

On many LANs, TCP/IP connectivity had to be added after the original IPX installation. The default NetWare frame type could not support TCP/IP, so many network administrators configured their NetWare servers to use both the default and Ethernet_II frame type for IPX communications. This allowed individual client workstations to be migrated from Novell 802.3 to Ethernet_II. The drawback is that it doubled SAP, RIP, and other NetWare administration packets on the network, so typically Novell 802.3 was removed from the server when all workstations had been converted to Ethernet_II.

To change the Ethernet encapsulation on an Ethernet interface to Ethernet_II, perform the following:

```
Router1(config)#interface E0
Router1(config-int)#ipx network 5 encapsulation arpa
```

Novell realized that the single protocol restriction of its proprietary encapsulation was a significant drawback, so for NetWare 3.12 and 4.*x* Novell changed the default encapsulation to conform to the 802.2 standard.

To implement this encapsulation on an Ethernet interface, input the following configuration:

```
Router1(config)#interface E0
Router1(config-int)#ipx network 5 encapsulation sap
```

The final encapsulation is rarely used for Ethernet interfaces, but you may come across it. It is the *Sub Network Access Protocol* (SNAP). Ethernet SNAP can be configured as follows:

```
Router1(config)#interface E0
Router1(config-int)#ipx network 5 encapsulation snap
```

The way to determine which encapsulation is running is to use the `show interface` command that we have seen before. The encapsulation type is given on the fifth line of the display for an Ethernet interface.

Viewing Potential Problems

By enabling global IPX routing capability and assigning a network number to interfaces, the basic configuration for a Cisco router to participate in IPX routing is complete. It is only now, however, that the real work begins in order to get IPX routing working efficiently over a variety of network media.

We need to explore some commands that will show us potential problems and see the effects of optimization commands that we will execute. The first (and often the most telling) command display is that shown by issuing the `show ipx servers` command, shown in Fig. 5-1.

This shows the servers advertising SAP messages to the router. If this display is empty and you know there are functional NetWare servers on the same LAN as the router, it is a good indication that the encapsulation set on the router is different from that used by the servers to advertise SAPs. As you can see, the same server can advertise a number of services; for example, server NWARE1 advertises many services, including types 4, 107, 115, 12E, 12B, and 130. The `show ipx servers` command output also tells you the source of the information (in this case all

Figure 5-1 Screen output of the *show ipx servers* command

router1>**show ipx server**
Codes: S - static, P - periodic, E - EIGRP, N - NLSP, H - Holddown, + = detail
11 total IPX servers

Table ordering is based on routing and server info

	Type	Name	Net Address Port	Route	Hops	ITF
P	4	Nware1	789A.0000.0000.0001:0451	2/01	1	E0
P	4	Nware2	78A.0000.0000.0001:0451	3/02	2	E0
P	4B	SER4.00-4	789A.0000.0000.0001:8059	2/01	2	E0
P	77	Nware1	789A.0000.0000.0001:0000	2/01	2	E0
P	107	Nware1	789A.0000.0000.0001:8104	2/01	2	E0
P	115	Nware1	789A.0000.0000.0001:4005	2/01	2	E0
P	12B	Nware1	789A.0000.0000.0001:405A	2/01	2	E0
P	12E	Nware1	789A.0000.0000.0001:405D	2/01	2	E0
P	130	Nware1	789A.0000.0000.0001:1F80	2/01	2	E0
P	23F	Nware1	789A.0000.0000.0001:907B	2/01	2	E0
P	44C	1095U1	789A.0000.0000.0001:8600	2/01	2	E0

entries are by periodic updates), the source network, node number and port number of the entry, route metric in terms of ticks and hops, and the interface through which it is reachable.

It is quite easy for periodic SAP advertisements to completely overwhelm a WAN link for many seconds. Let's perform some calculations to show how this happens. A SAP packet can contain up to seven 64-byte entries, which, along with IPX and other information, gives a total of 488 bytes. Let's say that, including file servers, database servers, and print servers, there is a total of 50 NetWare devices on an internetwork. Each NetWare device typically will be advertising 10 different SAP services, giving a total of 500 SAPs. If we are using a 64 kbps line, let's work out the impact these regular SAP updates will have.

For 500 SAPs you need a total of 72 packets (71 packets each carrying 7 SAPs and 1 packet carrying 3 SAPS).

This means that for the fully loaded advertisements we need $71 \times 488 =$ 34,648 bytes, plus 49 bytes for the one partially filled SAP packet, for a total of 34,697 bytes.

To convert this in to a number of bits, multiply by 8, which gives us a total of 277,576 bits.

This can be viewed in two ways. First, we know these updates are sent out every minute, so we can work out the bits sent out per second to get the amount of bandwidth consumed by the updates. This is 277,576/60 = 4626 bits per second.

Alternatively, because these updates are sent out all at once every 60 seconds, we can see how long it will take to send this number of bits. This is calculated as follows;

$$277{,}576 \text{ bits} / 64 \text{ kbps} = 4.4 \text{ seconds}$$

Therefore with this many SAPs communicating on a 64 kbps line, you know that for at least 4.4 seconds out of every minute, total bandwidth will be consumed by the SAP advertisements.

Now let's look at the regular RIP updates. To view the known routes, issue the `show ipx route` command shown in Fig. 5-2, which also gives an explanation of the display entries.

This display is similar to the IP routing table examined earlier. The table shows how the route was discovered, what the network number is, which interface is nearest that network, and the next hop, if appropriate.

Each RIP update contains 40 bytes of header and up to fifty 8-byte network numbers. If there are 200 RIP routes, we get four full RIP packets, which is $4 \times 440 = 1760$ bytes. To convert this into bits, we multiply by

Figure 5-2 Screen output of the *show ipx route* command

```
router1>show ipx route
Codes: C - connected primary network, c - connected secondary network
S - Static, F - Floating static, L - Local (internal), W - IPXWAN, R - RIP, E - EIGRP, N - NLSP,
X - External, s - seconds, u - uses

3 total IPX routes. Up to 1 parallel paths and 16 hops allowed

No default route known

C   800    (SAP)           E0
C   111    (PPP)           As1
R   789A   [03/02] via     890.0000.0010.062a   30s   E0
```

8, which yields 14,080. If you divide 14,080 by 60, this is 235 bits per second. Transferring this amount of data at 64 kbps speed takes less than a second, so you can see that SAP updates are far more of a concern than are RIP updates.

To view a summary of the IPX traffic that has passed through this interface, issue the `show ipx traffic` command shown in Fig. 5-3.

This display is useful for viewing the amount of traffic generated by all the different types of NetWare communications protocols. It shows 158,054 packets received, of which 18,644 were SAPs. This is normal, but if SAPs become 20 percent of traffic, you should seek to reduce the SAPs by the methods discussed later in this chapter.

Optimizing IPX Routing and Service Advertising

There are many ways to reduce the overhead of IPX-based communications on an internetwork. You will get the best return immediately by setting up an access list that restricts transmission of SAPs over the wide area link to only those that are absolutely necessary. A typical access list and its application are shown as follows:

```
interface Ethernet0
ipx input-sap-filter 1000
!
access-list 1000 permit 123.0000.0000.0001 4
```

The first entry is part of the configuration for the Ethernet 0 port, and applies access list number 1000 to any packets coming into this port. The second section is the access list itself. This access list permits the device on network 123 with the IPX address of 0000.0000.0001 to pass type-4 SAPs

Figure 5-3
Screen output of the *show ipx traffic* command

```
router1>show ipx traffic
System traffic for 0.0000.0000.0001 System-Name: router1
Rcvd:   155098 total, 40 format errors, 0 checksum errors, 0 bad hop count,
        90 packets pitched, 90212 local destination, o multicast
Bcast:  90345 received, 14789 sent
        1333 encapsulation failed, 305 no route
SAP:    470 SAP requests, 231 SAP replies, 7 servers
        18332 SAP advertisements received, 7200 sent
        0 SAP flash updates sent, O SAP poison sent
        0 SAP format errors
RIP:    439 RIP requests, 403 RIP replies, 3 routes
        59338 RIP advertisements received, 4769 sent
        620 RIP flash updates sent, 0 RIP poison sent
        0 RIP format errors
Echo:   Rcvd 0 requests 0 replies
        Sent 0 requests, 0 replies
        760 unknown: 0 no socket, 0 filtered, 33 no helper
        0 SAPs throttled, freed NDB len 0
```

only. If the 4 were omitted, the list would allow the Ethernet port to pass all SAPs from this device. Clearly this device is a NetWare server, as all NetWare servers use the value 0000.0000.0001 for their *internal node address*. The result of applying this access list is that computers on the other end of this WAN link will hear only about this server on network 123.

This is what is known as a *SAP access list*, and is identified as such because it is numbered in the range 1000 to 1099. SAP access lists can be applied as input or output filters. If this list were being configured on an access router providing dial- up services, you would have a choice of applying an input filter on the Ethernet interface, which restricts the SAPs coming into the router and limits the entries in the output of the `show ipx servers` command, or placing an output list on each dial-up interface in use.

Applying an input list as shown in this example requires only one entry in the configuration of the Ethernet interface, but does restrict all other asynchronous interfaces on the router to being capable of connecting only to this one server. Applying an output list on each dial-up interface means that the router perceives all other servers on its Ethernet interface, giving you the flexibility of allowing different dial-up interfaces access to different IPX servers. However, it requires more work to configure access lists for each dial-up interface.

The next type of access list to add to further reduce WAN traffic is a *network filter list* to restrict which networks are added to the routing table and hence reduce the size of IPX RIP updates sent out every minute. The configuration to achieve this is shown as follows:

```
interface Ethernet 0
ipx input-network-filter 800
!
access-list 800 permit 234
```

In this example, standard access list 800 (standard access lists go from 800 to 899) permits routing updates from network 234, but denies all others.

If you are able to restrict WAN traffic to only those SAPs and RIP updates that are necessary for the remote servers and workstations to function correctly, you have gone a long way toward optimizing your internetwork, although there is more that can be done. As previously stated, SAP and RIP updates are sent out every minute; with many updates to be sent out at once, this update traffic can fill up all available bandwidth, cause buffers to fill, and in the worst case, cause the router to drop packets entirely. To alleviate this situation, you can have the router introduce a delay between SAP and RIP packets being sent out.

You can set the interpacket delay for SAPs by using the `ipx output-sap-delay` command. This command is configured on a per-interface basis and specifies the delay between packets in milliseconds. Novell recommends a value of 55 milliseconds for a Cisco router, because some older NetWare servers cannot keep up with Cisco's default delay of 0 milliseconds. If the problem you are trying to solve is related to WAN utilization, the best delay value to use will depend on the routers, traffic patterns, and links in use. Trial and error is the only real answer, but a value of 55 milliseconds is probably as good a starting point for experimentation as any.

The final thing you can do to optimize IPX SAP communication over a WAN link is to increase the amount of time between SAP updates. By using the `ipx sap-interval` command, you can set the SAP update period on specified WAN interfaces higher than the 1-minute default. NetWare workstations and servers on LANs require SAP updates every minute. As WAN interfaces typically connect two routers together over one link, you can configure the routers to exchange SAPs at intervals greater than a minute. The `ipx sap-interval` command can be applied to the router interfaces on both ends of a link to reduce WAN transmission of SAP information while maintaining the regular 1-minute updates on LAN interfaces for the NetWare workstation and servers. An example of the use of this command is:

```
interface serial 0
ipx sap-interval 10
```

This configuration sets the SAP update interval to 10 minutes for SAPs being sent out the Serial 0 port. A similar command, `ipx` update-time, can be used to increase the interval between RIP updates over a WAN link. This is an example of increasing the RIP update timer to 2 minutes:

```
interface serial 0
ipx update-interval 120
```

An alternative to relying on dynamic processes like RIP and SAP advertisements to control NetWare networking is to create static routing tables. This has the advantage of eliminating WAN bandwidth utilized by these protocols and is simpler to set up than configuring packet delays (which must be the same on all routers) and access lists. The down side is that routing information does not adjust automatically to link or other network failures. Static routing can be implemented by the use of the ipx route and ipx sap commands. Use the following to add a static route to the routing table:

```
Router1(config)#ipx route aa abc.0000.0010.2345
```

The *aa* in this command refers to the network number for which you wish to add a route. This is followed by the network number and node address of the device to use as the next hop to get to this network. The command structure and concept are exactly the same as adding a static route for a TCP/IP internetwork.

Static IPX SAP entries are added using the ipx sap command. Each static SAP assignment overrides any identical entry learned dynamically, regardless of its administrative distance, tick, or hop count. Within the ipx sap command you must specify the route to the service-providing machine. The Cisco router will not add this static SAP until it has learned a route to this machine, either by an IPX RIP update or a static route entry. An example of this command follows:

```
Router1(config)#ipx sap fserver 4 543.0000.0010.9876 451 1
```

This command first specifies the name of the machine to add to the SAP table, in this case fserver, which is then followed by the network number and node address of this machine. This information is followed by the IPX socket used by this SAP advertisement and the number of hops to the machine specified.

One final option to look at for reducing the bandwidth used by regular SAP and RIP updates is *snapshot routing*, which is a time-triggered routing update facility. Snapshot routing enables remote routers to learn route and SAP information from a central router during a prespecified active period. This information is then stored for a predefined quiet period until the next scheduled active period. In addition to specifying the active and quiet periods, a retry period also is set for snapshot routing. This retry period comes into effect if no routing information is exchanged during an active period, and is in place so that a device does not have to wait for an entire quiet period if routing information is missed during an active period.

Snapshot routing is implemented via the *snapshot client* on one side of the WAN link and *snapshot server* command on the other side of the WAN link.

Optimizing Periodic NetWare Maintenance Traffic

Novell NetWare is a complete network operating system and, as such, utilizes periodic updates in addition to those generated to keep routing and service tables updated. Although these updates do not consume significant bandwidth, they can be annoying if a *dial-on-demand routing* (DDR) solution is chosen for economic reasons. Clearly, if a local NetWare server is constantly sending updates to a remote server, the DDR link will be established and costs incurred even when no user data needs to be transmitted. These periodic updates comprise the following:

- NetWare IPX watchdog
- SPX keep-alives
- NetWare serialization packets
- NetWare 4 time synchronization traffic

The NetWare operating system has many protocols that are considered part of the NetWare Core Protocol; watchdog packets are considered part of the NCP set. The purpose of the watchdog packet is to monitor active connections and to terminate connections if the client machine does not respond appropriately to a watchdog packet request. The only two parameters of interest that can be altered for the watchdog service defined on the NetWare file server itself are in the AUTOEXEC.NCF file as follows:

```
set delay between watchdog packets = y
set number of watchdog packets = z
```

The default for *y* is 59.3 seconds, but can vary between 15 seconds and 20 minutes. The default for *z* is 10, but is configurable anywhere between 5 and 100. Clearly if these values are increased, less use will be made of WAN links by the watchdog protocol.

In place of changing these parameters on the server, you can configure a router to respond to the server's watchdog packets on behalf of a remote client. This is termed *IPX spoofing*. The obvious downside to doing this is that a router local to the NetWare server may keep connections open for remote client PCs that are in fact no longer in use. The effect this has is to use up one of the concurrent user accesses allowed within the NetWare server license. (Typically a NetWare server is sold with a license for 100 or 250 concurrent users.) To enable IPX spoofing, input the following global configuration command. (There are no arguments to specify for this command.)

```
Router1(config)#ipx watchdog spoof
```

The next periodic update we will examine is the *SPX keep-alive*. SPX is a connection-oriented protocol typically used by a network printer process (such as RPRINTER) or an application gateway (such as Novell's SAA gateway). To maintain an SPX connection during periods when no data is transmitted, both ends of an SPX connection transmit keep-alive messages every 3 seconds by default. (This is the NetWare 3.*x* default; NetWare 4.*x* sends SPX keep-alives every 6 seconds by default.) Keep-alive values on the server side cannot be user-configured, but they can be set on the client side, from a default of every 3 seconds up to one keep-alive every hour. An alternative to changing this default in the NetWare software is to implement SPX keep-alive spoofing on Cisco routers positioned between a client PC and NetWare server. Consider Fig. 5-4.

In this illustration, router 1 is spoofing onto IPX network A for the NetWare server and router 2 is spoofing onto IPX network C for the client PC SPX processes, and SPX keep-alives are kept off the WAN. SPX spoofing is implemented using the following global configuration commands:

```
Router1(config)#ipx spx-spoof
Router1(config)#ipx spx-idle-time 90
```

The first command enables SPX spoofing and the second command specifies the amount of time in seconds (90 in this case) before spoofing of keep-alive packets can occur.

Novell implements a 66-second unicast to all servers on the same internetwork to provide for comparison of license serialization numbers on servers in use. This is there to protect Novell from a user reinstalling

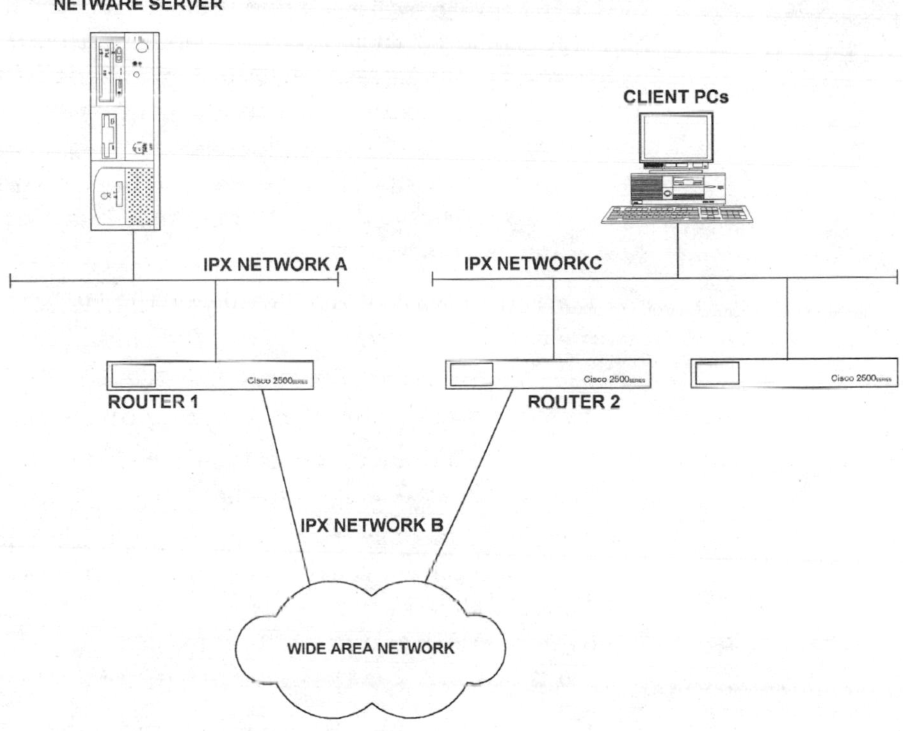

Figure 5.4 Network configuration for IPX/SPX spoofing

the same software license on multiple servers on the same internetwork. If a serialization packet is detected that has the same license number as the server receiving the packet, a server copyright violation message is broadcast to all users and the NetWare server consoles. There are no specific commands to stop these packets within the Cisco IOS, and the only way to block these serialization packets traversing a WAN is to use an access list.

NetWare 4.1 Considerations. The main administrative problem with NetWare 3 was that user accounts were defined on a per-server basis. In a LAN servicing several hundred or more users, several NetWare servers would have to be deployed and users would have to be given specific accounts on every NetWare server to which they needed access. This forced network managers to implement a maze of login commands to enable each user to get access to all the shared data needed.

To eliminate this problem, Novell introduced *NetWare Directory Services* (NDS), which replaced the flat-file user information database (the bindery) with a hierarchical, object-oriented replicated database. The advantage is that with the same database of user information on every server, a user can gain access to all resources needed with just one logon. With replication comes the problem of ensuring synchronization among these databases. To ensure synchronization, NetWare 4.1 timestamps each event with a unique code. (An *event* is a change to the database.) The timestamps are used to establish the correct order of events, set expiration dates, and record time values. NetWare 4.1 can define up to four different time servers:

1. *Reference time server* passes the time derived from its own hardware clock to Secondary time servers and client PCs.
2. *Primary time server* synchronizes network time with reference to at least one other Primary or Reference time server.
3. *Secondary time server* receives the time from a Reference or Primary and passes it on to client PCs.
4. *Single-reference time server* is used on networks with only one server and cannot coexist with Primary or Reference time servers. The Single-reference time server uses the time from its own hardware clock and passes it on to Secondary time servers and client PCs.

This synchronization of time between servers across a network can add to network congestion and activate dial-on-demand links unnecessarily. Novell offers a TIMESYNC.NLM program that can be loaded on a NetWare 4.1 server to reduce the amount of time synchronization packet traffic. The best way to limit the amount of this type of traffic over WAN links is to locate time servers appropriately on the network (Fig. 5-5.).

In this internetwork, there is one Reference time server, SA. This will supply time synchronization to servers SB and SC. Server SC will, in turn, supply time synchronization to server SD. Because SC was made a Primary time server, it is the only server that needs to communicate with the Reference server on network Y.

Configuring EIGRP for IPX

We already have discussed how RIP in the IP world can provide less-than-optimal routing. The same is true of RIP in the world of IPX routing. If you are implementing IPX over a wide area network, you should consider making the WAN routing protocol EIGRP. EIGRP is more efficient and provides quicker network convergence time over router-to-

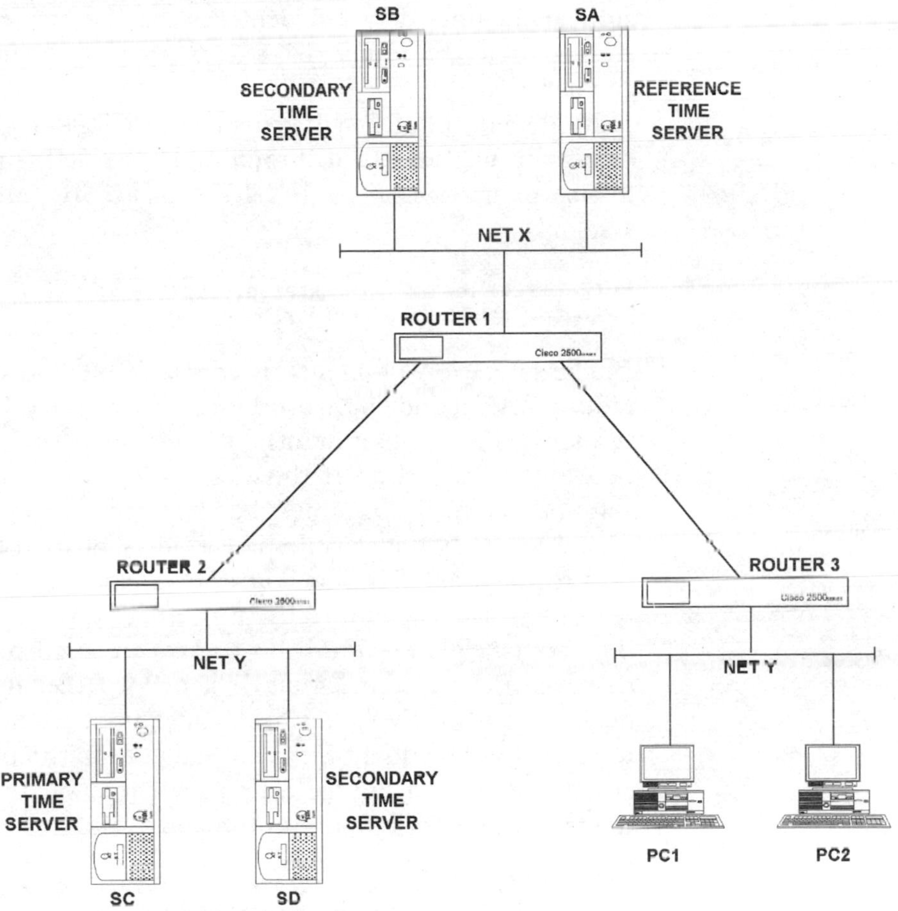

Figure 5-5 Locating NetWare time servers on an internetwork

router links than does IPX RIP. Because NetWare servers can only understand IPX RIP, however, we have the same issues in the Novell world as we did in the IP world when connecting Unix machines to an IGRP WAN.

We can make EIGRP the routing protocol for the WAN links, and use either static routes on the NetWare servers or redistribution on the routers, to enable the Novell servers to participate in routing across the WAN. To define IPX EIGRP on a Cisco router, enter the following commands:

```
Router1(config)#ipx router eigrp 22
Router1(config)#network aaa
```

The first line defines the IPX EIGRP routing process on the router to be part of autonomous system number 22. The second (and potentially subsequent lines defined) identifies the IPX network numbers directly connected to the router that will participate in the EIGRP route advertisements.

By default, EIGRP will redistribute IPX RIP routes into EIGRP as external routes and EIGRP routes into IPX RIP. An example of how to disable redistribution for IPX RIP updates into an EIGRP autonomous system is:

```
Router1(config)#ipx router eigrp 23
Router(config)#no redistribute rip
```

The operation of EIGRP is configurable and can be optimized to reduce WAN bandwidth utilization if necessary. The first step toward reducing EIGRP bandwidth utilization is to increase the interval between hello packets. If this value is increased, the hold time for that autonomous system also must be increased.

As previously stated, hello packets are sent by routers running EIGRP on a regular basis. These hello packets enable routers to learn dynamically of other routers on directly connected networks. In addition to learning about neighbors, the hello packets are used to identify a neighbor that has become unreachable. If a hello packet is not received from a neighbor within the hold time, the neighbor is assumed to have become unreachable. The hold time is normally set to three times the hello packet interval. To increase the hello packet interval and hold time, perform the following configuration commands:

```
Router1(config)#ipx hello-interval eigrp 22 15
Router1(config)#ipx hold-time eigrp 22 45
```

These commands executed on all routers within autonomous system 22 will increase the hello packet interval from the default 5 seconds to 15 seconds and the hold time from a default 15 seconds to 45 seconds.

In addition to the access list method of controlling SAP updates, EIGRP offers further opportunities to reduce the amount of WAN bandwidth consumed by SAP traffic. If an EIGRP neighbor is discovered on an interface, the router can be configured to send SAP updates either at a prespecified interval or only when changes occur. When no EIGRP neighbor is found on an interface, periodic SAPs are always sent. In Fig. 5-6, the default behavior of EIGRP for router 1 will be to use periodic SAPs on interface Ethernet 0, and send only SAP updates on Serial 0, when change to the SAP table occurs; this is an *incremental update*.

This default behavior is fine for most instances; however, we can optimize the SAP traffic sent out the Ethernet 0 port of router 2 by chang-

Figure 5-6
IPX EIGRP-based internetworks

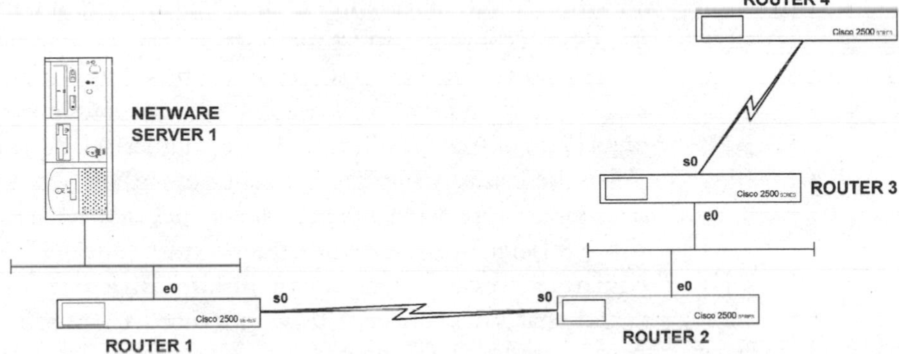

ing the default behavior. We want to do this because the default behavior assumes that a NetWare server will be connected to any LAN interface on the router and therefore periodic updates are sent out. But in this case, the only device on the Ethernet 0 port of router 2 is an EIGRP router, which gives us the option to use incremental updates. The following commands will implement this change to default behavior for autonomous system 24 on Ethernet 0.

```
Router2(config)#interface E0
Router2(config-int)#ipx sap-incremental eigrp 24
```

The Basics of NLSP and IPXWAN Operation

An alternative to using EIGRP over WAN links is the new *NLSP* and *IPXWAN* protocols designed by Novell. The *NetWare Link Services Protocol* (NLSP) was introduced to address the limitations of the IPX RIP and SAP update processes, and is equivalent to using a link state protocol such as OSPF for IP routing instead of a distance vector protocol like IGRP. IPXWAN was designed to reduce the WAN bandwidth utilization of IPX routing, and is a connection startup protocol. Once the IPXWAN startup procedure has been completed, very little WAN bandwidth is utilized by IPX routing over the WAN link. NSLP will operate over IPXWAN wide area links, as will other protocols like RIP and SAP. IPXWAN does not require a specific IPX network number to be associated with the serial link; it will use an internal network number.

NLSP is derived from the OSI's link state protocol, IS-IS. The key difference between NLSP and other link state protocols is that it does not currently support the use of areas. An NLSP network is similar to having all router devices in area 0 of an OSPF autonomous system. Using a link state protocol requires each router to keep a complete topology map of the internetwork in its memory.

As changes in topology occur, routers detecting the change send link state advertisements to all routers. This initiates execution of the Dijkstra algorithm, which results in the recalculation of the topology database. Since these advertisements are sent out only when a failure of some kind occurs, as opposed to every 60 seconds as in the distance vector RIP, more efficient use of bandwidth results. The RIP/SAP routing method continues to be supported for linking different NLSP areas. Novell has stated that NLSP soon will be enhanced to support linking of separate NLSP areas directly together.

The most significant challenge involved in implementing NLSP is the probable renumbering of IPX network numbers that will be necessary. Typically, IPX network numbers were assigned randomly, as address hierarchy is not important in IPX RIP/SAP networks. Address hierarchy is, however, essential to the efficient operation of a link state routing protocol. Renumbering to implement hierarchy in IPX is a serious undertaking and requires significant planning, which is the reason for the slow uptake of NLSP in the marketplace. Next, we discuss the operation of NLSP routing.

As with other link state routing protocols, NLSP routers must exchange hello packets on direct connections to determine who their neighbors are before exchanging route information. Once all the neighbors have been identified, each router sends a link state advertisement describing its immediate neighbors. After this, NLSP routers propagate network information via link state advertisements to other routers in the area. This process continues until routers become adjacent. When two routers are adjacent, they have the same topology database of the internetwork.

Once widespread adjacency is realized, the topology database is assumed correct if hello packets are continually received from all routers. Once three hello packets have been missed for a specific router, that router is assumed to be unreachable and the Dijkstra algorithm is run to adjust routing tables. Finally, a designated NLSP router on the internetwork periodically floods link state advertisements to all routers on the internetwork. This flood of packets includes sequence numbers of previous link state advertisements so that NLSP routers can verify they have the most recent and complete set of LSAs.

Before we consider specific router configurations for NLSP, we will look at the general operation of IPXWAN. Typically, NLSP and IPXWAN are implemented together, although they are not interdependent. One can be implemented without the other; NLSP does, however, require IPXWAN on serial links.

IPXWAN standardizes how IPX treats WAN links. IPXWAN can be implemented over the *Point-to-Point Protocol* (PPP), X.25, and frame relay. Before IPXWAN (a layer 3 protocol) can initiate, these layer 2 protocols must establish their WAN connection. Initialization of the layer 2 protocols starts a hello process to begin the IPXWAN process.

One of the routers will act as the primary requester, while the other acts as a slave that simply responds to these requests. The router having the higher internal network number value will be chosen as the primary requester. The two routers will agree on which routing protocol to use, typically RIP/SAP or NLSP, and then the requester proposes a network number to be assigned to the link. Finally the two routers agree on configuration details such as link delay and throughput available for the link.

Configuring NLSP and IPXWAN. To set up IPXWAN and NLSP, a number of global and interface configuration commands must be executed. The prerequisites for implementing the global and interface commands for these protocols are as follows:

- Global IPX routing must already be enabled before IPXWAN or NLSP commands will be accepted.
- NLSP LAN interfaces must already have an IPX network number entry.
- IPXWAN interfaces must have no IPX network number assigned.

The following input details the necessary global commands:

```
Router1(config)#ipx internal-network 8
Router1(config)#ipx router nlsp
Router1(config)#area-address 0 0
```

The first command defines the IPX internal network number that NLSP and IPXWAN will use to form adjacencies and to decide which router will be the primary requester. This number must be unique across the IPX internetwork. NLSP and IPXWAN will advertise and accept packets for this internal network number out of all interfaces, unless restricted by a distribute list. It is worth noting that the NLSP process adds a host address of 01 to this network number, which is a reachable address when using the `ipx ping` command. (IPX ping is not as useful as ICMP ping; not all NetWare devices support IPX ping.)

The second command line enables NLSP on the router and the third specifies the area address to use in the form of an address and mask. As NLSP supports only one area at the moment, zero values for both the area number and mask are adequate.

This completes global configuration. IPXWAN must be enabled for each serial interface, as must NLSP for each interface that is to participate in NLSP routing.

Let's now look at the interface configuration commands for IPXWAN.

```
Router1(config)#interface serial 0
Router1(config-int)#no ipx network
Router1(config-int)#ipx ipxwan
```

The first interface configuration command will not be reflected in the configuration file, and is input only as a safety measure to make sure that no network number is assigned to the link being used by the IPXWAN protocol. The second command simply enables the IPXWAN protocol. This second command can be followed by many option arguments, but the default option with no arguments normally is adequate. The configuration shown will use the Cisco default encapsulation for the layer 2 protocol, the Cisco-specific *HDLC*. If you want to change this to PPP, the `encapsulation ppp` interface command should be entered.

Optimizing NLSP. Although NLSP and IPXWAN are considerably more efficient than the older RIP/SAP method of disseminating network information, some optimization of IPX and NLSP operation is possible.

RIP and SAP are enabled by default for every interface that has an IPX configuration, which means that these interfaces always respond to RIP and SAP requests. When NLSP is enabled on an interface, the router only sends RIP and SAP traffic if it hears of RIP updates or SAP advertisements. This behavior can be modified by the following interface configuration commands:

- `ipx nlsp rip off` stops the router from sending RIP updates out the specified interface.
- `ipx nlsp rip on` has the router always send RIP updates out this interface.
- `ipx nlsp rip auto` returns the interface to default behavior.
- `ipx nlsp sap off` stops the router from generating periodic SAP updates.
- `ipx nlsp sap on` has the router always generate periodic SAP updates for this interface.
- `ipx nlsp sap auto` returns the interface to default behavior.

When SAP/RIP is used, the maximum hop count permissible is 15 by default, which can be restrictive for large internetworks. The maximum hop count accepted from RIP update packets can be set to any value up to 254 (the example shows 50 hops) with the following command:

```
Router1(config)#ipx maximum-hops 50
```

The process we will go through to customize an NLSP setup is outlined as follows:

- Configure the routers so that the least busy router is chosen as the *designated router* (DR).
- Assign predetermined metric values to a link to directly influence route selection.
- Lengthen the NLSP transmission and retransmission intervals to reduce NLSP network traffic.
- Lengthen the link service advertisement intervals to reduce LSA bandwidth utilization.

On each LAN interface, NLSP selects a designated router in the same way as other link state protocols do. A DR generates routing information on behalf of all routers on the LAN to reduce protocol traffic on the LAN segment. If the DR were not there, each router on the LAN would have to send LSA information to all the other routers. The selection of a DR usually is automatic, but it can be influenced by router configuration commands.

Because the DR performs more work than other routers on the LAN, you might wish to ensure that either the least busy or most powerful router always is chosen as the DR. To ensure that a chosen router becomes the DR, increase its priority from the default of 44 to make it the system with the highest priority. To give a router a priority of 55, input the following commands. (This is for a router with its Ethernet 0 port connected to the LAN determining its DR.)

```
Router1(config)#interface E 0
Router1(config-int)#ipx nlsp priority 55
```

NLSP assigns a metric to a link that is based on the link throughput (similar to IGRP). No account of load is taken into consideration. If you want to manually influence the selection of routes, you can change the metric assigned to any link with the following command (the example shows a metric of 100):

```
Router1(config)#interface Serial 0
Router1(config-int)#ipx nlsp metric 100
```

The NLSP transmission and retransmission timers are adequate for just about every installation. If you feel the need to alter these parameters, however, the following commands show how to set the hello packet interval to 20 seconds and the LSA retransmission time to 60 seconds:

```
Router1(config)#interface E 0
Router1(config-int)#ipx nlsp hello-interval 20
Router1(config-int)#ipx nlsp retransmit-interval 60
```

Similarly, the intervals at which LSAs are sent out and the frequency of the Dijkstra (the Shortest Path First) algorithm execution normally are adequate. If your network contains links that are constantly changing state from up to down, however, these values can be modified as follows to an LSA interval of 20 seconds and minimum time between SPF calculation of 60 seconds:

```
Router1(config)#lsp-gen-interval 20
Router1(config)#spf-interval 60
```

If these values are changed, they should be uniform across an entire internetwork for efficient operation.

Monitoring an NLSP/IPXWAN Internetwork. Let's look at the pertinent configuration details of the Cisco router at the center of the internetwork shown in Fig. 5-7. This router is set up to run NLSP on all interfaces and IPXWAN on its serial link to NetWare server 3, as shown in the excerpt from its configuration file also in Fig. 5-7.

The global configuration entries enable IPX routing, set the internal IPX network number, and enable NLSP routing with the appropriate area address and mask. On each Ethernet interface, a network number is assigned and NLSP is enabled. It is assumed that the default Ethernet encapsulation type is used both by the router and the NetWare servers. The serial interface uses PPP for its encapsulation and is enabled for both IPXWAN and NLSP. The serial link has no IPX network number associated with it; it uses an unnumbered link by default.

The operation of IPXWAN can be monitored by the `show ipx interface serial 0` command, which produces the output shown in Fig. 5-8.

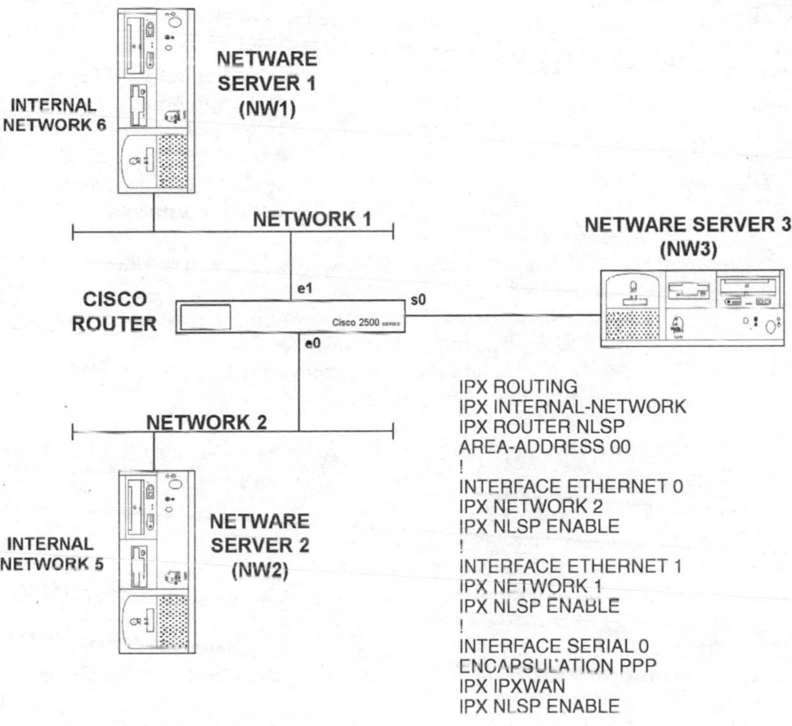

Figure 5-7 An NLSP- and IPXWAN-based internetwork

The IPXWAN node number is defined by the internal IPX network number and the router's configured hostname, which in this instance is `10/Router1`. The IPXWAN state indicates that it is a responder (slave), rather than a requester and is connected to a NetWare server named NW3, configured with an internal network number of 15.

To monitor the NLSP routes, issue the `show ipx route` command to view the IPX routing table, as shown in Fig. 5-9.

This routing table labels the internal network number with an L indicator, the directly connected Ethernet networks with a C indicator, NLSP routes with an N indicator, and the IPXWAN network with a W indicator. These two commands give you all the information that is necessary to determine the state of NLSP and IPXWAN routing.

NetBIOS over IPX

The IPX packet type 20 is used to transport IPX NetBIOS packets through a network. *NetBIOS* was designed as a fast and efficient protocol

Figure 5-8
The *show ipx interface serial command 0* for an IPXWAN interface

```
router1>show ipx interface serial 0
Serial 0 is up, line protocol is up
IPX address is 0 0000.0010.000 [up] line-up RIPPQ: 0, SAPPQ: 0
Delay of this IPXnetwork, in tcks is 31 throughput 0 link delay
Local IPXWAN Node ID:             10/router1
Network when IPXWAN master        0 IPXWAN delay (master owns):    31
IPXWAN Retry Interval:            20 IPXWAN Retry limit:            3
IPXWAN Routing negotiated:        RIP Unnumbered
IPXWAN State:                     Slave: Connecty
State change reason: Received Router Info Req as xlave
Last received remote node info: 15/NW3
Client mode disabled, Static mode disabled, Error mode is reset
IPX SAP update interval is 1 minute
IPX type 20 propagation packet forwarding is disabled
Outgoing access list is not set
IPX Helper list is not set
SAP GNS procerssing enabled, delay 0 ms, output filter list is not set
```

Figure 5-9
Monitoring NLSP routes

```
router1>show ipx route
Codes: C - connected primary network, c - connected secondary network
S - Static, F - Floating static, L - Local (internal), W - IPXWAN, R - RIP, E - EIGRP, N - NLSP,
X - External, s - seconds, u - uses

4 total IPX routes. Up to 1 parallel paths and 16 hops allowed

No default route known

L   800   (SAP              E0
C   111   (PPP)             As1
W   5     [20] [02/01] via  3.0000.0210.98bc   30s   E0
```

for small individual networks. As such, NetBIOS does not use a network number when addressing a destination node; it is assumed that the destination is on the same network segment. NetBIOS implements a broadcast mechanism to communicate between nodes. Broadcasts normally are blocked by a router, so if we want broadcasts to traverse a router, we must specifically configure it to do so. In NetBIOS networking, nodes are addressed with a unique alphanumeric name. If two NetBIOS nodes need to communicate via a Cisco router, it is possible to configure the router to forward IPX packet type 20 broadcasts between specified networks. Figure 5-10 provides an example of this.

Suppose that in this network we want NetBIOS nodes Eric and Ernie to communicate. This means we have to enable IPX packet type 20 to traverse the router between network *aaa* and *ccc*. As no NetBIOS nodes are on network *bbb*, no type 20 packets need to be sent onto that network. The relevant parts of a router configuration are shown in Fig. 5-11.

The command that enables reception and forwarding of NetBIOS packets on an interface is the `ipx type-20-propagation` command configured for interfaces Ethernet 0 and Ethernet 2.

Bridging Nonroutable Protocols

Some networking systems, such as Digital Equipment's LAT (*Local Area Transport*) do not define network numbers in packets sent out on a network. If a packet does not have a specific destination network number, a router will assume that the packet is destined for the local segment and will not forward it to any other network. In most cases this is the right thing to do; there are some instances, however, in which two devices need to communicate using a nonroutable protocol, and a router stands between them. One option to enable these two machines to communicate is to use the bridging capability of Cisco routers.

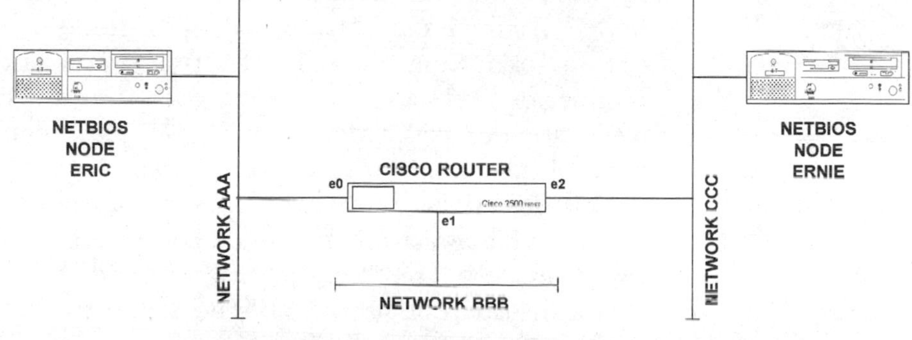

Figure 5-10 Forwarding NetBIOS packets through a Cisco router

Figure 5-11 Configuration for the router in Figure 5.10

```
INTERFACE ETHERNET 0
IPX NETWORK AAA
IPX TYPE-20-PROPAGATION

INTERFACE ETHERNET 1
IPX NETWORK BBB

INTERFACE ETHERNET 2
IPX NETWORK CCC
IPX TYPE-20-PROPAGATION
```

Before we get into the specifics of using a Cisco router as a bridge, let's review the operation of the two types of bridge that have been widely implemented in the market, *transparent bridges* and *source route bridges*. What has ended up being available in the marketplace are bridges that typically do both transparent and source route bridging. A device acting as this type of bridge will act as a transparent bridge if the layer 2 header does not contain a Routing Information Field, and will act as a pure source routing bridge if there is a Routing Information Field. The following will discuss the operation of transparent and source route bridging separately.

Transparent Bridges

The transparent bridge was developed to allow protocols that were designed to operate on only a single LAN to work in a multi-LAN environment. Protocols of this type expect a packet to be received by the destination workstation to arrive unaltered by its progress through the LAN. The basic job of a transparent bridge, therefore, is to receive packets, store them, and retransmit them on other LANs connected to the bridge, making it useful for extending the limits of a LAN.

In a Token-Ring environment, a transparent bridge can increase the number of workstations on a ring. Each time a token gets passed from workstation to workstation on a ring, the clock signal degrades. A transparent bridge can be used to connect two physical rings and allow more workstations to be connected because it uses a different clock and token for each ring. As far as any layer 3 software is concerned, however, the two rings are still on the same network number.

A transparent bridge will do more than this, though, because a learning bridge will "learn" which MAC addresses of workstations are on which LAN cable and either forward or block packets according to a list of MAC addresses associated with interfaces kept in the bridge. Let's examine how the bridge operates in the multi-LAN environment of Fig. 5-12.

First it must be noted that as far as any layer 3 protocols, such as IP or IPX are concerned, LAN 1 and LAN 2 in this figure are the same network number. The process operated by the transparent bridge is as follows:

- Listen to every packet on every interface.
- For each packet heard, keep track of the packet's source MAC address and the interface from which it originated. This is referred to as a *station cache*.

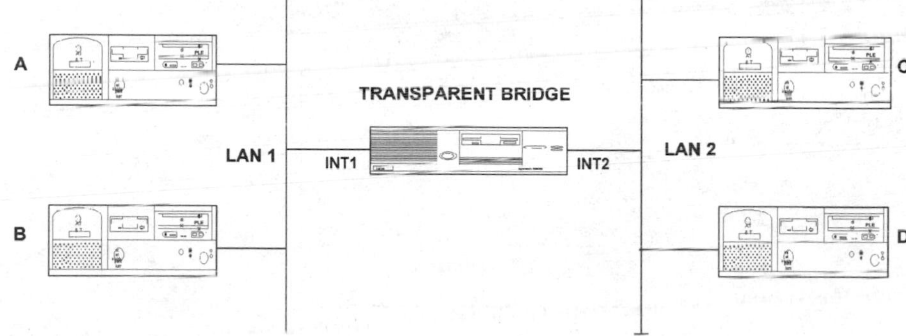

Figure 5-12 Transparent bridge operation

- Look at the destination field in the MAC header. If this address is not found in the station cache, forward the packet to all interfaces other than the one on which the packet was received. If the destination address is in the cache, forward the packet to only the interface the destination address is associated with. If the destination address is on the same interface as the device originating the packet, the packet is dropped; otherwise duplicate delivery of packets for that packet would result.
- Keep track of the age of each entry in the station cache. An entry is deleted after a period of time if no packets are received with that address as the source address. This ensures that if a workstation is moved from one LAN to another, the "old" entry in the station cache associating that address with a now incorrect interface is deleted.

Using this logic, and assuming that workstations A, B, C, and D in Fig. 5-12 all communicate with one another, the bridge will produce a station cache that associates workstations A and B with interface 1, then C and D with interface 2. This potentially relieves congestion in a network. All traffic that originates at and is destined for LAN 1 will not be seen on LAN 2 and vice versa.

This form of bridging works well for any LAN topology that does not include multiple paths between two LANs. We know that multiple paths between network segments is desirable to maintain connectivity if one path fails for one reason or another. Let's look at what a simple transparent bridge would do if implemented in a LAN environment such as that shown in Fig. 5-13.

Let's say this network is starting up and the station cache for both bridge A and B are empty. Suppose a workstation on LAN 1—let it be termed "workstation X"—wants to send a packet. Bridges A and B will

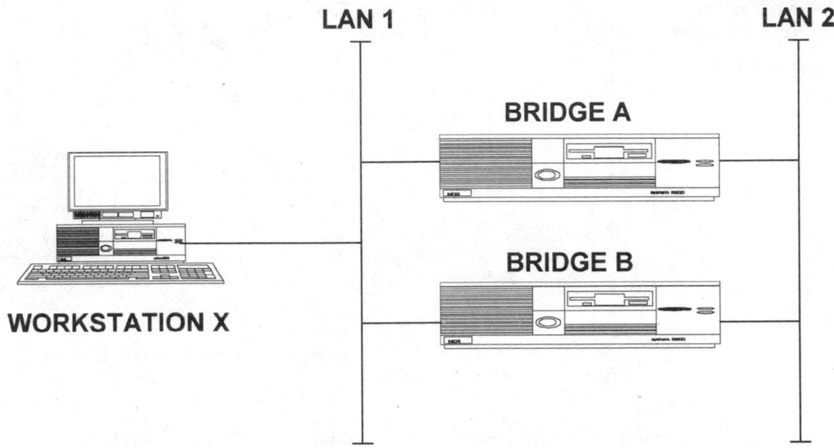

Figure 5-13 Network with multiple bridge paths between LANs

receive this packet, note that workstation X is on LAN 1, and queue the packet for transmission onto LAN 2. Either bridge A or bridge B will be the first to transmit the packet onto LAN 2; for argument's sake, say bridge A is first. This causes bridge B to receive the packet with workstation X as the source address on LAN 2, since a transparent bridge transmits a packet without altering header information. Bridge B will note that workstation X is on LAN 2 and will forward the packet to LAN 1. Bridge A will then resend the packet to LAN 2. You can see that this ends up a nasty mess.

Because a routed network typically will have multiple paths between LANs, turning on bridging capability could be as disastrous as in the example above if it were not for the *spanning tree algorithm* implemented on Cisco routers.

The Spanning Tree Algorithm. The spanning tree algorithm exists to allow bridges to function properly in an environment having multiple paths between LANs. The bridges dynamically select a subset of the LAN interconnections that provides a loop-free path from any LAN to any other LAN. In essence, the bridge will select which interfaces will forward packets and which will not. Interfaces that will forward packets are considered to be part of the spanning tree. To achieve this, each bridge sends out a configuration *bridge protocol data unit* (BPDU). The configuration BPDU contains enough information to enable all bridges to collectively:

- Select a single bridge that will act as the "root" of the spanning tree.

- Calculate the distance of the shortest path from itself to the root bridge.
- Designate, for each LAN segment, one of the bridges as the one "closest" to the root. That bridge will handle all communication from that LAN to the root bridge.
- Let each bridge choose one of its interfaces as its root interface, which will gives the best path to the root bridge.
- Allow each bridge to mark the root interface—and any other interfaces on it that have been elected as designated bridges for the LAN to which it is connected—as being included in the spanning tree.

Packets will then be forwarded to and from interfaces included in the spanning tree. Packets received from interfaces not in the spanning tree are discarded and packets are never forwarded onto interfaces that are not part of the spanning tree.

Configuring Transparent Bridging. When configuring a Cisco router to act as a transparent bridge, you need to decide the following before entering any configuration commands into the router:

- Which interfaces are going to participate in bridging and what the bridge group number for these interfaces will be.
- Which spanning tree protocol to use.

In Fig. 5-14 we have a router with four interfaces, three of which belong to bridge group 1. If the router had more interfaces, and if a second group of interfaces were chosen to form a bridge group, the two bridge groups would not be able to pass traffic between them; in effect, different bridge groups act as different bridges and do not pass configuration BPDUs between them. In the example of Fig. 5-14, IP traffic is routed between the interfaces and all other protocols are bridged.

In the configuration of the router in Fig. 5-14, the `bridge protocol` command defines the spanning tree algorithm to use; for transparent bridging that is either IEEE or DEC. This value must be consistent between all routers forming part of the same spanning tree. The *group number* is a decimal number from 1–9 that identifies the set of bridged interfaces. This configuration command option is implemented in case you want to set up on the same router sets of interfaces that belong to different bridging groups.

In Fig. 5-14, router A has been configured for Ethernet 0, Ethernet 1, and Serial 0 to be part of bridge group 1. This bridge group number has

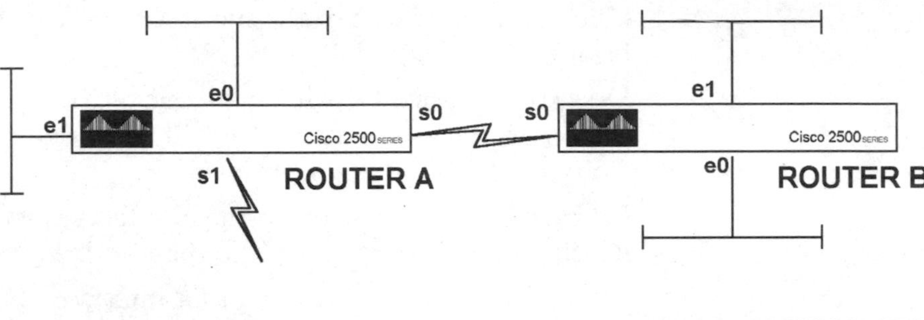


```
BRIDGE 1 PROTOCOL IEEE
!
INTERFACE ETHERNET 0
IP ADDRESS 193.1.1.1 255.255.255.0
BRIDGE - GROUP 1
!
INTERFACE ETHERNET 1
IP ADDRESS 194.1.1.1  255.255.255.0
BRIDGE GROUP 1
INTERFACE SERIAL 0
IP ADDRESS 195.1.1.1   255.255.255.0
BRIDGE - GROUP 1
!
INTERFACE SERIAL 1
IP ADDRESS 196.1.1.1
```

```
BRIDGE 1 PROTOCOL IEEE
!
INTERFACE SERIAL 0
BRIDGE - GROUP 1
!
INTERFACE ETHERNET 0
BRIDGE - GROUP 1
! INTERFACE ETHERNET 1
BRIDGE - GROUP 1
```

Figure 5-14 Network and router configuration for basic transparent bridging

significance only within router A, where it identifies the interfaces that will participate in bridging on that router. Router B has bridge group 1 defined as well. Again, this has relevance only within router B. Packets could just as well be bridged between routers A and B if the Serial 0, Ethernet 0, and Ethernet 1 interfaces on router B were made part of bridge group 2.

Extending transparent bridging to include dozens of Cisco routers is a simple matter, as the same configuration given here is replicated on each router to be included in the spanning tree. As long as each router to be included in the spanning tree has an interface that is configured to bridge transparently, and is connected to an interface on another router that is configured to bridge transparently, all such routers will be included in the spanning tree.

Source Routing Bridges

Source routing at one time competed with transparent bridging to become the 802.1 standard for connecting LANs at the layer 2 level.

When spanning tree bridges became the preferred 802.1 standard, source routing was taken before the 802.5 committee and was adopted as a standard for Token-Ring LANs. As such, it is only really used when connecting Token-Ring LANs.

The idea behind source routing is that each workstation will maintain in its memory a list of how to reach every other workstation; let's call this the *route cache*. When a workstation needs to send a packet, it will reference this route cache and insert route information in the layer 2 header of the packet, telling the packet the exact route to take to reach the destination. This route information is in the form of a sequence of LAN and bridge numbers that must be traversed in the sequence specified in order to reach the destination.

Let's look at Fig. 5-15, which shows the regular layer 2 header and one that is modified to participate in source route bridging. To inform a receiving node that the packet has source route information rather than user data after the source address, the multicast bit in the source address is set to 1. Prior to source route bridging, this multicast bit was never used.

If a workstation needs to send a packet to a destination not currently in the route cache, this workstation will send out an *explorer packet* addressed to that destination. An explorer packet traverses every LAN segment in the network. When an explorer packet reaches a bridge on its travels and could travel one of many ways, the bridge replicates the explorer packet onto every LAN segment attached to that bridge. Each explorer packet keeps a log of LANs and bridges through which it passes.

Ultimately the destination workstation will receive many explorer packets from the originating workstation and will, by some mechanism, tell the originating workstation the best route to enter into the route cache. Whether the destination or originating workstation actually

Figure 5-15 Layer 2 headers with and without the source multicast bit set

DESTINATION	SOURCE	DATA

DATA LINK LAYER HEADER WITH MULTICAST BIT IN SOURCE FIELD SET TO ZERO

DESTINATION	SOURCE	ROUTING INFORMATION	DATA

DATA LINK LAYER HEADER WITH MULTICAST BIT IN SOURCE FIELD SET TO ONE.
ROUTING INFORMATION IS IN THE FORM OF THE SEQUENCE OF LANs AND BRIDGES THE PACKET MUST TRAVERSE FROM SOURCE TO DESTINATION, eg. LAN1, BRIDGE2, LAN5, BRIDGE4, LAN10

calculates the route information, and what the exact details of the best route are, is open to vendor implementation and not specified in the standards.

Configuring Source Route Bridging. The first difference between transparent bridging and source route bridging becomes apparent when we look at the configuration commands. In transparent bridging, it was necessary only to identify the interfaces on each router that were to participate in transparent bridging and the spanning tree algorithm would work out which interfaces on each router in the spanning tree would be used for forwarding packets. Source route bridging is not so simple and requires every LAN and every source route bridge to be uniquely identified in the network. Configuration of a Cisco router for source route bridging is simple if we consider a bridge that has only two interfaces configured for source route bridging, as shown in Fig. 5-16. This then becomes a matter of bridging between pairs of Token-Ring LANs.

The following commands configure the Token-Ring 0 and Token-Ring 1 ports for source route bridging.

```
Router1(config)#interface to 0
Router1(config-int)#source-bridge 10 2 11
Router1(config-int)#interface to 1
Router1(config-int)#source-bridge 11 2 10
```

The first `source bridge` configuration command arguments for the Token-Ring 0 interface can be explained as follows:

- The local ring number for interface Token-Ring 0 is in this case 10, but it can be a decimal number between 1 and 4095. This number uniquely identifies the ring on that interface within the bridged network.
- The bridge number, which must be between 1 and 15, is in this case 2, and it uniquely identifies the bridge connecting the two rings within the bridged network.
- The target ring, which is the network number of the second ring in the ring pair, must be between 1 and 4095, and in this case is 11.

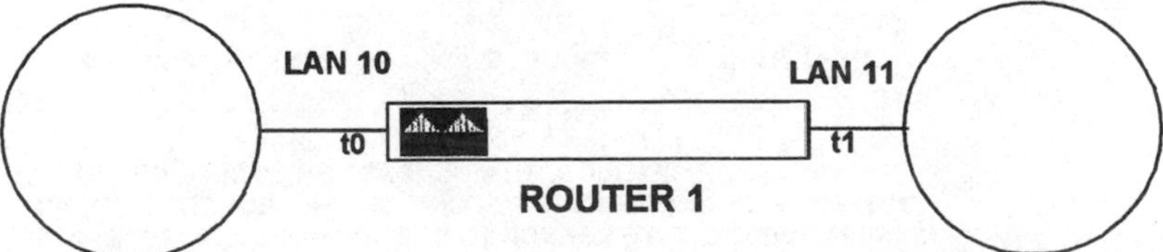

Figure 5-16
A simple source route bridge network

The second `source bridge` command is for the Token-Ring 1 port and merely reverses what this interface sees as the local and destination ring.

If a bridge has more than two interfaces that need source route bridging, an internal virtual ring needs to be defined and each "real" interface is bridged to the virtual ring. This configuration is shown in Fig. 5-17, with each external ring (100, 101, and 102) individually bridged to the internal ring 20, via router 1, which is identified with a source route bridging number of 5. ("Router 1" is the configured hostname of the router.)

It is worth noting that source route bridging has significance only on Token-Ring interfaces. If you are using a Cisco access server to provide remote dial-up services to a Token-Ring LAN, the dial-up ports will not use a Token-Ring encapsulation; they will probably use PPP. Network administrators may be forgiven for thinking that since all workstations on a LAN must have source routing enabled to get access to servers on remote rings, the dial-up workstations would need this too. This is, in fact, not the case. As the dial-up workstations are using PPP as a layer 2 protocol, there is no place to insert source route information in the layer 2 header.

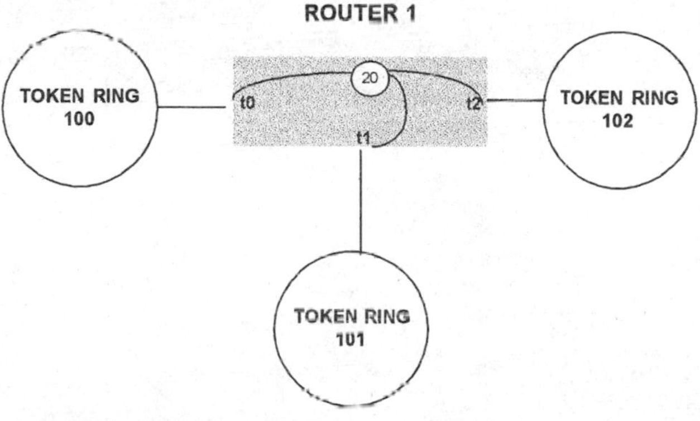

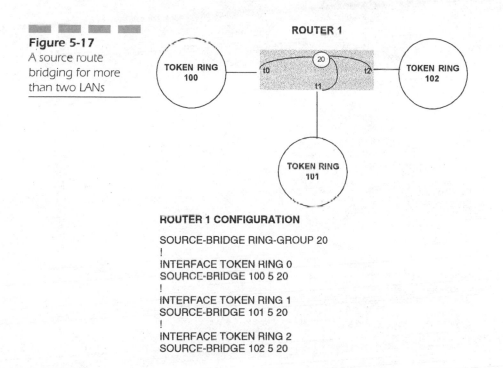

Figure 5-17 A source route bridging for more than two LANs

ROUTER 1 CONFIGURATION

```
SOURCE-BRIDGE RING-GROUP 20
!
INTERFACE TOKEN RING 0
SOURCE-BRIDGE 100 5 20
!
INTERFACE TOKEN RING 1
SOURCE-BRIDGE 101 5 20
!
INTERFACE TOKEN RING 2
SOURCE-BRIDGE 102 5 20
```

Source Route Transparent Bridging

What is implemented in the main is source route transparent bridging, in which a bridge will use source routing information if the multicast bit in the source address is set to 1 (this bit is now known as the *Routing Information Indicator*), and transparent bridging if the Routing Information Indicator is not set. Figure 5-18 shows a bridged network with a router configuration for both source route and transparent bridging.

The tasks to be accomplished when configuring a router to perform both transparent and source route bridging are as follows:

- For transparent bridging on Ethernet interfaces, define a transparent bridge process and associate a number with it.
- Define which spanning tree algorithm will be used by the Ethernet ports.

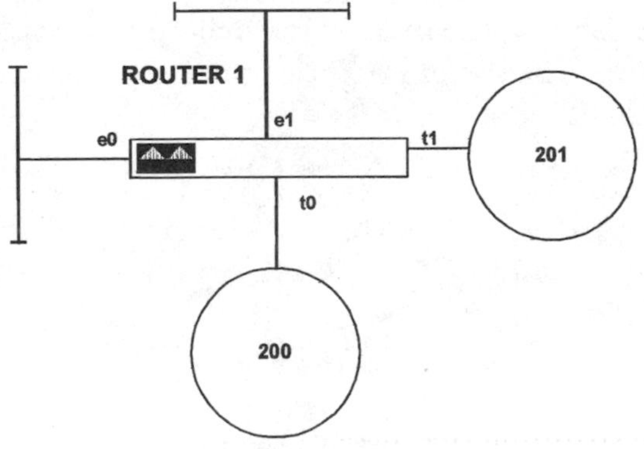

Figure 5-18 Router configuration for source route transparent bridging

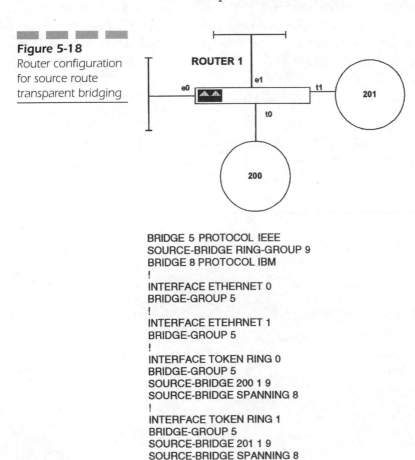

```
BRIDGE 5 PROTOCOL IEEE
SOURCE-BRIDGE RING-GROUP 9
BRIDGE 8 PROTOCOL IBM
!
INTERFACE ETHERNET 0
BRIDGE-GROUP 5
!
INTERFACE ETEHRNET 1
BRIDGE-GROUP 5
!
INTERFACE TOKEN RING 0
BRIDGE-GROUP 5
SOURCE-BRIDGE 200 1 9
SOURCE-BRIDGE SPANNING 8
!
INTERFACE TOKEN RING 1
BRIDGE-GROUP 5
SOURCE-BRIDGE 201 1 9
SOURCE-BRIDGE SPANNING 8
```

- Define an internal ring that can be paired with all external token rings.
- Define the automatic spanning tree function for the source route network. Note that the interfaces in a source route network can transparently bridge packets. The interfaces in a source route network will, however, define a separate spanning tree from the transparent bridge interfaces in the Ethernet network.
- Associate each Ethernet port with a specific bridge group.
- Enable the spanning tree function for each interface to be part of the source-route-based spanning tree.
- Associate each Ethernet and Token-Ring port with a transparent bridge group.

It seems complicated—and it is. I do not mind admitting that I do not like bridging, and I think that source route bridging does not scale well in a network of any size. Most people these days will use a layer 3 protocol (either IP or IPX), so there is little need to try to muscle layer 3 functionality into a layer 2 protocol. Having said that, if you really do have to implement source route transparent bridging and need to understand the commands shown in Fig. 5-18, an explanation follows.

The `bridge 5 protocol ieee` command defines a transparent bridge process with ID 5. This command partners with the interface command `bridge-group 5` that identifies all the interfaces to be part of this transparent bridge group. The `source-bridge ring-group 9` command defines the internal virtual ring with which all external rings will be paired. The `bridge 8 protocol ibm` command defines the spanning tree algorithm for this router and associates it with an ID of 8. This command partners with the interface command `source-bridge spanning 8` that identifies all Token-Ring ports that will participate in defining the spanning tree for the Token-Ring side of the network. The final command is the `source-bridge 200 1 9` command, which gives this bridge a source route bridging ID of 1 and links the Token-Ring network number on the specific interface (in this case 200) to the internal virtual token ring (number 9).

IBM Networking

IBM networking is a topic vast enough to justify the writing of many, many volumes. Here we have only one section in a chapter to give an overview of the most common things a network administrator will have to do when integrating IBM applications over a TCP/IP-based Cisco router network. Typically, Cisco routers are implemented to reduce or totally eliminate the need for IBM *front-end processors* (FEPs). FEPs direct SNA traffic over a network, typically using low-speed 9600 bps lines. The drive to reduce FEP utilization comes from an economic need to reduce the cost of FEP support and to provide a cost-effective WAN that can deliver client/server IP-based, as well as SNA, applications.

Typically Cisco routers get introduced in an IBM data center via direct channel attachment to replace a FEP and in each remote branch location connected to the data center. The data center router will route IP traffic over the WAN as normal and use a technology called *Data Link Switching* to transport SNA or NetBIOS traffic over the same WAN. At the remote branch end of the network, a small 2500-series router can be used both to connect LAN workstations to the WAN that can receive IP traffic, and to connect an IBM terminal controller that receives SNA traffic to service local IBM 3270 terminals.

Overview of IBM Technology

Let's face it, all this TCP/IP internetworking stuff may be fun, but what really delivers the benefits of computer technology to an organization is a well-designed, reliable, and responsive application. IBM technology has been the technology of choice for mission-critical applications for the past 20 years and will be with us for many more. The basic reason for this is that it works. With IBM's NetView management system, network managers also have an effective tool to monitor, troubleshoot, and (important for mission-critical applications), guarantee response times of applications.

IBM technology is hierarchical and fits well into an organization that works in a structured fashion, as everything is controlled by a central MIS department. Clearly, in today's faster-moving business environment, such central control with its inherent backlogs is not the favored approach for many organizations when planning future information systems development. Having said that, if an existing application is in place and serving its users well, there is little need to replace it just to make a network manager's life easier. Given that IBM applications will be around for a while, it is more cost-effective to integrate them into a multiprotocol network than to provide a separate network just for that traffic. Let's now look at IBM's communication technology in a little more detail.

IBM Networking Systems. The most prevalent IBM networking system is the *Systems Network Architecture* (SNA). SNA is a centralized hierarchical networking model that assigns specific roles to machines within the overall network. IBM mainframe operating systems (such as MVS, VM, or VSE) were designed to have access to an SNA network via *VTAM*, the *Virtual Telecommunications Access Method*, which defines which computers will connect to which applications. Applications in this environment are written to interface to VTAM through *Logical Unit* (LU) sessions. LU sessions are established, terminated, and controlled via a VTAM function called the *System Services Control Point* (SSCP). For IBM network staff, the terms *LU* and *PU* (*Physical Unit*) are frequently referenced terms. Defining an LU of 2 identifies a 3270 terminal session, for example. In addition, each type of terminating device (such as a printer or workstation) will have a different PU number associated with it.

IBM networkers are accustomed to having a method by which to allocate specific bandwidth resources to different types of traffic. This is not available as standard within TCP/IP, which relies on vendor-specific features such as Cisco's priority or custom queuing to duplicate that functionality. Being a centralized hierarchy, SNA provides good security with the RACF system, which is not matched very well by any security system currently implemented in the TCP/IP world. Again, TCP/IP standards rely on vendor-specific implementations such as Cisco access lists and TACACS+ (all of these extensions will be covered in subsequent sections).

A totally different IBM architecture is the *Advanced Peer-to-Peer Networking* scheme (APPN), which was designed for the AS/400 environment. In this architecture, the Logical Unit used is LU6.2, which applications use via a program interface called *Advanced Program-to-Program Communication* (APPC). Instead of 3270 sessions, the AS/400 operating system uses 5250 sessions to communicate between the server and workstation. A large part of why IBM systems lost popularity was due to these different architectures associated with different hardware platforms. In many organizations, network staff had to implement multiple cabling systems and users needed multiple terminals on their desks to access different IBM systems.

TCP/IP Support Provided by IBM. IBM mainframe and midrange computers will support TCP/IP connectivity directly via the TN3270 and TN5250 protocols. These protocols allow a user workstation running only TCP/IP communications software to run 3270 and 5250 applications over a TCP/IP network. Most of the functionality required by a user to run IBM applications is provided by the TN3270 and TN5250 protocols; however, some features are missing that might be important to some users.

In TN3270, the print job confirmation feature, important to users such as stockbrokers looking for trade confirmations, is not supported by the TCP/IP LPR/LPD printing mechanism. Also, the SysReq and Attn keys used to swap between mainframe applications is not fully supported under TCP/IP.

In TN5250, most terminal emulation, printing, and file-sharing functions are available, but file transfer has been a problem. APPN allows sophisticated querying of DB2 databases to retrieve data. With TN5250, there are no APPN functions, so it is much more difficult to retrieve query output from a DB2 database.

IBM has resolved these problems with a technology called *Multiprotocol Transport Networking* (MPTN). Using this technology, an APPC application can communicate over a TCP/IP network without the need for client workstations to load multiple protocol stacks. IBM achieves this by use of an application call translator that maps APPN to TCP/IP sockets function calls.

With an introduction to the IBM technology and an idea of some of the problems, let's look at how Cisco deals with them.

Cisco's Approach to IBM Technology Integration

Cisco provides many options for integrating IBM applications into a multiprotocol environment, ranging from direct channel attachment to a mainframe, to encapsulation of SNA protocols in IP packets using techniques such as STUN and DLSw.

If you decide to integrate IBM technology onto a multiprotocol network, the biggest concern of those responsible for delivering IBM application support is that they will lose the ability to guarantee response times. Typically, SNA applications have predictable low bandwidth consumption, whereas TCP/IP protocols are typified by bursts of traffic, often generating a need for high bandwidth availability. To alleviate these fears, Cisco implemented *priority output queuing*, which enables network administrators to prioritize traffic based upon protocol, message size, physical interface, or SNA device. If this mechanism is deemed inadequate, Cisco's custom queuing allows specific bandwidth to be allocated to different types of traffic, in effect providing separate channels on the one link for the different types of traffic carried.

Direct Channel Attachment. Let's take an overview of channel attachment, as shown in Fig. 5-19. In an IBM mainframe, Input/Output Processors (IOPs) communicate between the main CPU and the *mainframe channel,* which is an intelligent processor that handles communication with external devices. The Cisco *Channel Interface Processor* (CIP) can connect directly to a mainframe channel for high-speed communication between a mainframe and a router network. A CIP in a Cisco router replaces the need for an IBM 3172 controller to provide communication for terminal and printer devices. Channel attachment technologies that Cisco supports for CIP implementation are as follows:

- *ESCON,* a fiber optic link between an ES/9000 mainframe channel and the CIP.
- Parallel *bus-and-tag* for connecting to System 370 and subsequent mainframes.
- *Common Link Access for Workstation* (CLAW), which enables the CIP to provide the functionality of a 3172 controller.

The CIP works in conjunction with an appropriate interface adapter card, the *ESCON Channel Adapter* (ECA) for fiber connection, or the bus-and-tag *Parallel Channel Adapter* (PCA). One CIP supports two interface cards and up to 240 devices. When installed in a Cisco router, the CIP can be configured much like any other interface. The CIP will use TCP/IP to communicate with the mainframe channel, so the mainframe needs to be running TCP/IP. If the mainframe has VM for an operating system, it must be running IBM TCP/IP for VM version 2,

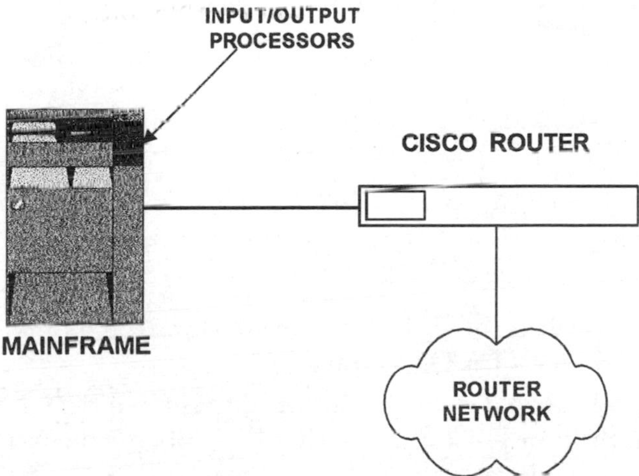

Figure 5-19 Connecting a mainframe and router via channel attachment

release 2; if it is running MVS, it must support IBM TCP/IP for MVS version 2, release 2.1.

To get the CIP up and working, a compatible configuration must be entered into the CIP interface and the IBM channel. Before we look at those configurations, it should be noted that the CIP can be installed only in a modular Cisco router. The modular series routers (the 4*x*00- and 7*x*00-series) are supplied as a chassis in which modules with different interfaces can be installed. The 2500-series routers come with a fixed configuration and have no slots for additional cards to be installed. So far, configurations given for routers have assumed a 2500-series router.

To configure an interface for a modular router, we first need to specify the slot number of the card. For example, if we have a four-interface Ethernet module inserted in the slot 0 of a 4700 router, the Ethernet interfaces will be addressed as Ethernet 0/1, Ethernet 0/2, Ethernet 0/3, and Ethernet 0/4. All `show` and `interface` configuration commands must reference the specific slot and Ethernet interface in this way. The same is true of a CIP card. The following shows how to select port 1 of a CIP interface card in slot 0:

```
Router1(config)#interface channel 0/1
Router1(config-int)#
```

Now that the router is in configuration mode for the CIP interface connected to the IBM channel, a basic configuration can be input to establish IP communication between the IBM channel and the CIP. The configuration commands to define a router process, and assign an IP address and CLAW parameters are shown as follows:

```
router eigrp 30
network 172.8.0.0
network 173.2.0.0
!
interface channel 0/1
ip address 172.8.5.1 255.255.255.0
claw 01 0 173.2.6.4 MVSM/C D100 tcpip tcpip
```

The CLAW parameters are not obvious and should be configured with help from a Cisco Systems engineer. Essentially, the CLAW arguments can be defined as follows:

- The 01 is the path that is a value between 01 and FE, which is always 01 for an ESCON connection.
- The next 0 value is a device address from the UNITADD value in the host IOCP file and should be obtained from the IBM host administrator.

- The rest of the values are derived from the Device, Home, and Link values from the host TCP/IP configuration files and refer to the host IP address, host name, device name, and host and device applications.

Once operational, the CIP can be monitored and controlled much the same as any other interface on a Cisco router. All the usual `show interface`, `show controller`, and `shutdown/no shutdown` commands work in the same fashion as for Ethernet or serial interfaces.

STUN and DLSw. Cisco's *Serial Tunnel* (STUN) feature was designed to allow IBM FEP machines to communicate with each other over an IP network. STUN encapsulates the SDLC frames used to communicate between FEPs within an IP packet for transmission over an IP internetwork. This provides flexibility in internetwork design and enables SNA and IP traffic to share the same wide area links, reducing costs and simplifying management. *DLSw,* which stands for *Data Link Switching*, provides a method for encapsulating IBM layer 2 LAN protocols within IP packets.

Using STUN to Interconnect FEP Machines. The most popular implementation of STUN provides local acknowledgment between the router and the FEP, to keep this traffic off the WAN. This does, however, require knowledge of the *Network Control Program* (NCP) SDLC addressing scheme setup in the connected FEP. Figure 5-20 shows how FEPs are connected with and without STUN-enabled routers between them.

As you can see, the Serial 0 port on both router 1 and router 2 takes the place of a modem that previously connected to the FEP. This means that the FEP is expecting to connect to a DCE device. Therefore the router-to-FEP cable must have the configuration that sets the router port as a DCE, and we must enter a `clockrate` command in the configuration of interface Serial 0, just as we did in the original lab setup in Chap. 3 when we were connecting two router ports directly together.

Before we see the configurations for router 1 and router 2, let's discuss what we need to achieve with the configuration.

STUN-enabled routers communicate on a peer-to-peer basis and we need some way of identifying each router to its STUN peer or peers. This is achieved by defining a *peer name* for each router. The peer name is defined as one of the IP addresses of an interface on that router. Typically a loopback interface is defined, and the address of the loopback interface is used as the router peer name. The reason for this is that loopback addresses are up only as long as the router is up; if we gave the

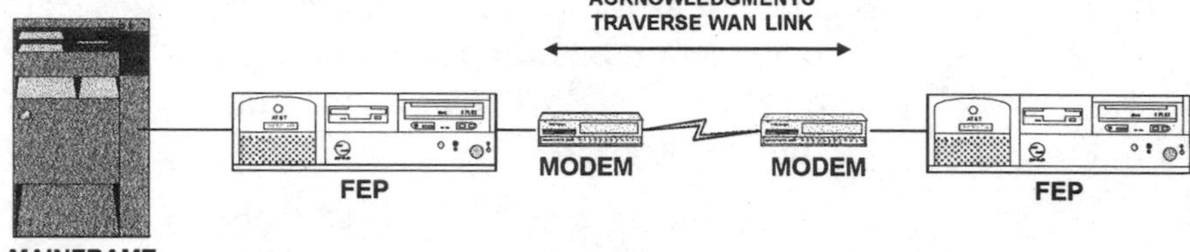

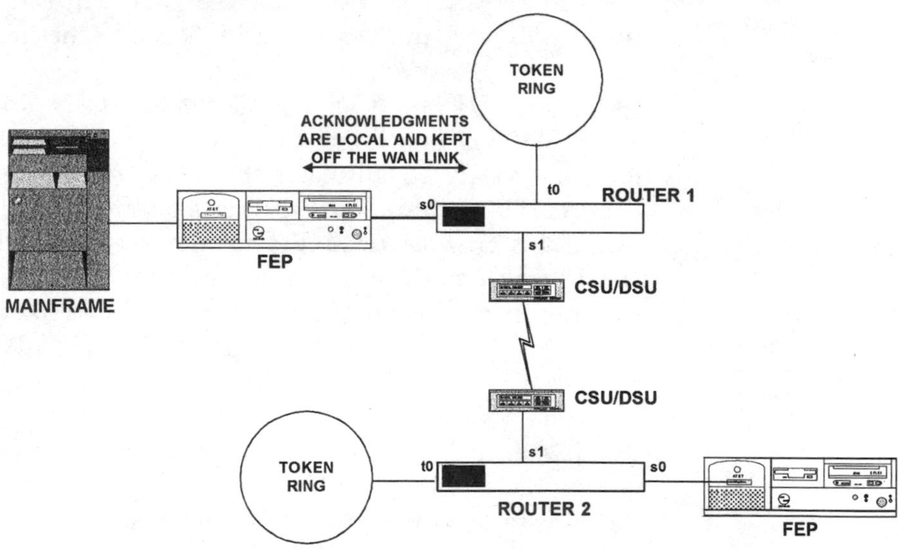

Figure 5-20 Connecting STUN-enabled routers between IBM FEPs

router a peer name of one of the serial interfaces, the peer name would become invalid if the serial interface was down for any reason.

Next, all the STUN peers that need to communicate as a group must be assigned the same STUN protocol group number. STUN peers will not exchange information with peers in another group number. The `stun protocol-group` command also defines the type of STUN operation for the link. The most popular option is the `SDLC` option, which provides local acknowledgment to the FEP and keeps this traffic off the serial link. The other popular option is the `basic` option of this command, which does not provide local acknowledgment, but does simplify router configuration slightly.

Using the `SDLC` option of the `stun protocol-group` command necessitates configuring the serial port connected to the FEP with an appropriate SDLC address number, which should be provided by the IBM FEP administrator. This option provides local acknowledgment of link-level packets, and therefore reduces WAN traffic. Once the SDLC address has been defined, we need to use the `stun route address x interface serial y` command, where *x* is the SDLC address number and *y* is the serial port through which you wish to direct STUN-encapsulated FEP frames. A `stun route address ff interface serial y` command directs broadcast SDLC traffic through the same STUN-enabled interface.

A typical STUN configuration for router 1 and router 2 in Fig. 5-20 is shown in Fig. 5-21.

Data Link Switching. Now let's look at the *DLSw* standard, as defined in RFC 1745. DLSw was designed to allow the transportation of SNA and NetBIOS traffic over an IP wide area network. The standard came into being largely as a result of problems encountered when trying to scale source route bridging to larger networks. Problems inherent in the source route bridge protocol include:

- Bridge hop-count limit of 7.
- Excessive generation of broadcast explorer packets, consuming WAN bandwidth.
- Unwanted timeouts at the Data Link level over WAN links.

It is important to realize that DLSw is not a layer 3 protocol and therefore does not perform routing. DLSw is a layer 2 protocol and works on the basis of establishing a DLSw circuit between two routers in an IP network. When DLSw is implemented, local Data Link level (layer 2)

Figure 5-21 Router 1 and router 2 configuration from Figure 5.20

ROUTER 1

```
STUN PEER-NAME 181.4.1.1
STUN PROTOCOL-GROUP 1 SDLC
!
INTERFACE SERIAL 0
NO IP ADDRESS
ENCAPSULATION STUN
SDLC ADDRESS 07
STUN ROUTE ADDRESS O7 INT SERIAL 1
STUN ROUTE ADDRESS FF INT SERIAL 1
CLOCKRATE 19200
!
INTERFACE TOKEN RING 0
IP ADDRESS 181.4.2.1 255.255.255.0
!
INTERFACE SERIAL 1
IP ADDRESS 181.4.3.1 255.255.255.0
!
INTERFACE LOOPBACK 0
IP ADDRESS 181.4.1.1 255.255.255.0
!
ROUTER IGRP
NETWORK 181.4.0.0
```

ROUTER 2

```
STUN PEER-NAME 181.4.6.1
STUN PROTOCOL-GROUP 1 SDLC
!
INTERFACE SERIAL 0
NO IP ADDRESS
ENCAPSULATION STUN
SDLC ADDRESS 07
STUN ROUTE ADDRESS O7 INT SERIAL 1
STUN ROUTE ADDRESS FF INT SERIAL 1
CLOCKRATE 19200
!
INTERFACE TOKEN RING 0
IP ADDRESS 181.4.5.1 255.255.255.0
!
INTERFACE SERIAL 1
IP ADDRESS 181.4.3.2 255.255.255.0
!
INTERFACE LOOPBACK 0
IP ADDRESS 181.4.6.1 255.255.255.0
!
ROUTER IGRP
NETWORK 181.4.0.0
```

communications are terminated at the local router, enabling that router to provide link-level acknowledgments. This functionality effectively turns a connection between two machines communicating via a DLSw router pair into three sections. At each end of the link, the machines will establish a connection with the DLSw router (typically a source route connection), and the two DLSw routers will establish TCP connections to carry the traffic over the IP WAN. In Fig. 5-22, PC A exchanges link-level acknowledgments with router 1, and PC B exchanges link-level acknowledgments with router 2; router 1 and router 2 exchange DLSw information via TCP connections.

In fact, before it is possible to switch SNA or NetBIOS traffic between two DLSw-enabled routers, these routers must establish two TCP connections. Once the TCP connections are established, various data will be exchanged between the routers, the most noteworthy of which are the MAC addresses and NetBIOS names each router can reach. So how does DLSw direct traffic through an IP network?

The process is essentially the same for both SNA and NetBIOS switching. Both protocols will seek out the location of a destination by

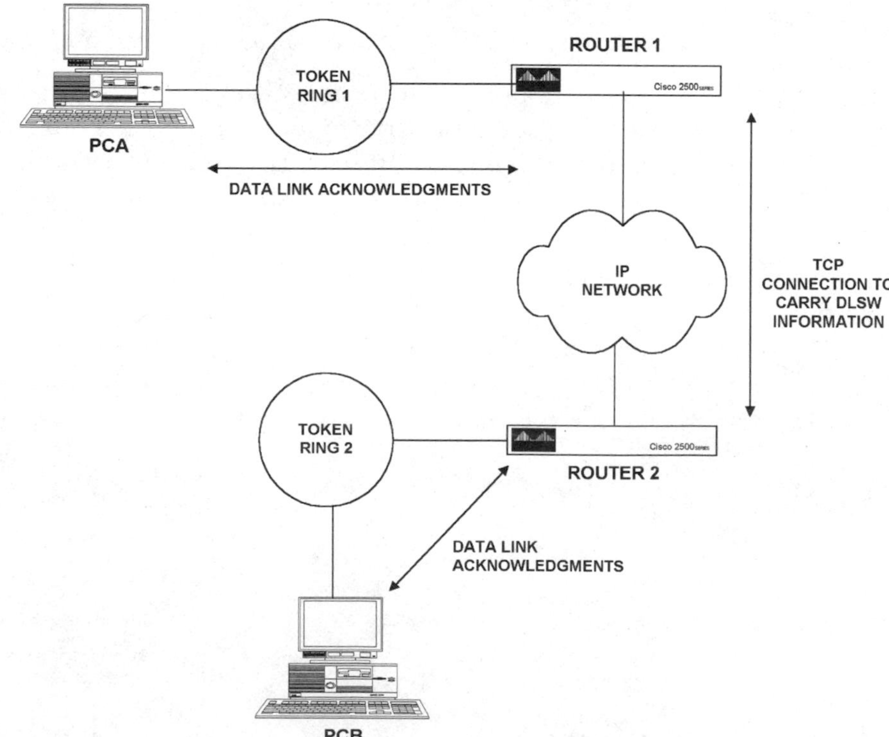

Figure 5-22 The three links used to establish a DLSw connection over an IP network

some type of explorer packet sent out on the network. The explorer packet asks all devices if they can get to the desired destination. One of the DLSw routers on the IP network should respond that it can reach the destination, at which time the TCP connections between the routers are made, and the packet can be sent from source to destination over the IP WAN.

There are many permutations and combinations of possible interconnects that might need to be made via DLSw links. We shall examine the example of connecting a remote Token-Ring LAN to a central SDLC IBM controller here, and in the next section on Windows NT, we will look at the example of connecting two Ethernet segments together via DLSw, so that NetBEUI traffic can be switched over an IP WAN.

The example shown in Fig. 5-23 is of a DLSw implementation that connects an SDLC controller to a remote Token-Ring LAN via an IP WAN.

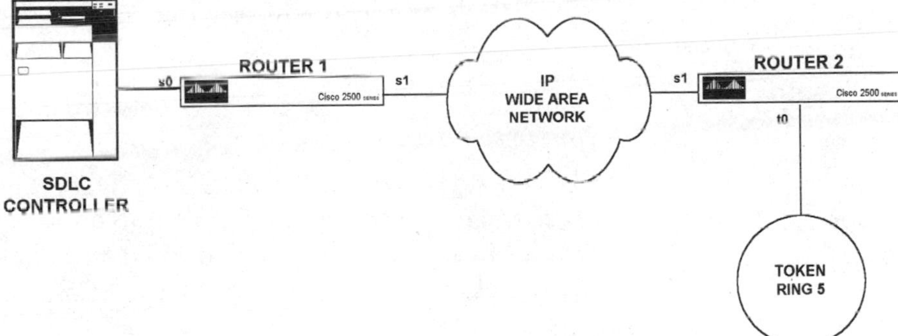

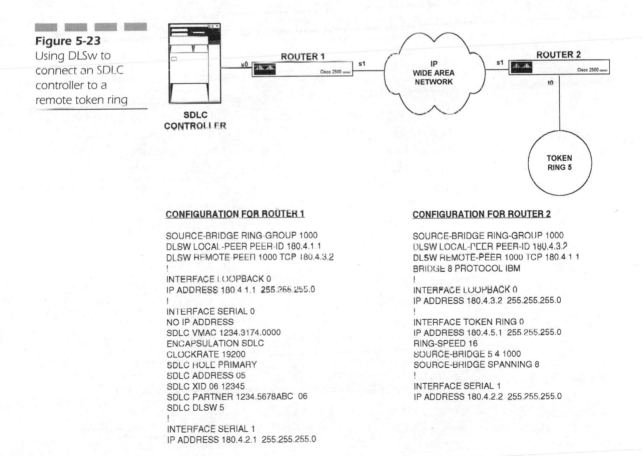

Figure 5-23 Using DLSw to connect an SDLC controller to a remote token ring

CONFIGURATION FOR ROUTER 1

```
SOURCE-BRIDGE RING-GROUP 1000
DLSW LOCAL-PEER PEER-ID 180.4.1.1
DLSW REMOTE-PEER 1000 TCP 180.4.3.2
!
INTERFACE LOOPBACK 0
IP ADDRESS 180.4.1.1  255.255.255.0
!
INTERFACE SERIAL 0
NO IP ADDRESS
SDLC VMAC 1234.3174.0000
ENCAPSULATION SDLC
CLOCKRATE 19200
SDLC ROLE PRIMARY
SDLC ADDRESS 05
SDLC XID 06 12345
SDLC PARTNER 1234.5678ABC  06
SDLC DLSW 5
!
INTERFACE SERIAL 1
IP ADDRESS 180.4.2.1  255.255.255.0
```

CONFIGURATION FOR ROUTER 2

```
SOURCE-BRIDGE RING-GROUP 1000
DLSW LOCAL-PEER PEER-ID 180.4.3.2
DLSW REMOTE-PEER 1000 TCP 180.4.1.1
BRIDGE 8 PROTOCOL IBM
!
INTERFACE LOOPBACK 0
IP ADDRESS 180.4.3.2  255.255.255.0
!
INTERFACE TOKEN RING 0
IP ADDRESS 180.4.5.1  255.255.255.0
RING-SPEED 16
SOURCE-BRIDGE 5 4 1000
SOURCE-BRIDGE SPANNING 8
!
INTERFACE SERIAL 1
IP ADDRESS 180.4.2.2  255.255.255.0
```

Let's discuss the configuration commands implemented one by one.

- Command `source-bridge ring-group 1000` defines a DLSw router group. Routers will establish DLSw connections only with other routers in the same ring group.
- Command `dlsw local-peer peer-id 180.4.1.1` enables DLSw on the router and gives the router a DLSw ID, which is taken from the loopback address defined, just as was done for STUN in the previous section.
- Command `dlsw remote-peer 1000 tcp 180.4.3.2` identifies a remote peer with which to exchange DLSw information using TCP. In this command, the 1000 value is the ring-group number and must match that set by the `source-bridge ring-group` command.
- Command `sdlc vmac 1234.3174.0000` sets a MAC address for the serial port connecting to the SDLC controller. This is a necessary part of enabling the link-level addressing for DLSw, enabling complete source-to-destination addressing using link-level addresses.
- Command `sdlc role primary` sets this end of the link as the primary.
- In command `sdlc xid 06 12345`, XID requests and responses are exchanged prior to a link between the router and the controller reaching an *up* state. The XID is derived from parameters set in VTAM and must be determined by the IBM administrator.
- Command `sdlc partner 1234.5678.9abc 06` defines the MAC address of the token ring on the remote router that will be communicated with, and the SDLC ID number of the link connecting the two DLSw routers together.
- Command `sdlc dlsw 5` associates the DLSw and SDLC processes, so that DLSw will switch SDLC ID 5 traffic.
- Command `source-bridge 5 4 1000` enables source routing for the token ring attached to router 2 and defines the token ring as ring number 5, router 2 as bridge number 4, and the destination ring as number 1000.
- Command `bridge 8 protocol ibm` defines the spanning tree algorithm for this router and associates it with an ID of 8.
- Command `source-bridge spanning 8` identifies all the Token-Ring ports that will participate in defining the spanning tree for the Token-Ring side of the network.

As you can see, this type of configuration is not trivial and takes significant cooperation between IBM data center staff and those responsible for Cisco router management.

Networking Windows NT

Windows NT has the fastest-growing market share of any network operating system (NOS) currently in the market. It seems that Microsoft has finally produced a NOS with which to challenge the leadership position of Novell's NetWare. NT bases much of its LAN communication on *NetBEUI*, the *NetBIOS Extended User Interface*, which is a legacy from Microsoft's LAN Manager and IBM's PC LAN products. NT, however, has built into the operating system the ability to interface to IPX/SPX, TCP/IP, and DLC (Data Link Control).

I will not go into the details of setting up these protocols using Windows NT utilities; there are plenty of Microsoft manuals and Microsoft Press publications to do that for you. What will be covered here is an overview of what NT servers use to communicate network information, and what the options and issues are for interconnecting NT servers and workstations over a WAN.

Windows NT Network Protocols

In this section we will examine the transport protocols of Windows NT, which are NetBEUI, NWLink, TCP/IP, and DLC.

NetBEUI. NetBEUI originally was designed for small LANs of around 20 to 100 workstations. As such, it was not designed with any concept of network numbers and is therefore a nonroutable protocol. Windows implements NetBEUI 3.0, which uses the NetBEUI Frame (NBF) protocol that is based on the NetBIOS frame type and therefore is compatible with previous versions of NetBEUI.

In communications based on NetBIOS, computers are referred to by name rather than address. Packets on the local segment are still delivered by MAC address, with each station on the network maintaining a computer-name-to-MAC-address translation. On a single LAN segment, NetBIOS communications deliver better performance than a routable protocol because the communication process is simpler. These days, however, there are very few networks installed that only ever need to connect to fewer then 100 other computers. Recognizing the problems of NetBEUI in larger environments, Microsoft chose TCP/IP as its strategic WAN protocol for Windows NT implementations.

NWLink. *NWLink* is the native Windows NT protocol for Novell's IPX/SPX protocol suite. NWLink provides the same functionality that IPX.COM or IPXODI.COM files did for a machine using the Open Data Link Interface (ODI) specification, namely the ability to use IPX as a transport protocol. To connect to a NetWare server requires the use of VLM programs for an ODI machine, or the *Client Services for NetWare* (CSNW) redirector for Windows NT.

NWLink is useful if you have a mixed environment of NT and NetWare servers and need an NT machine to communicate with both.

TCP/IP. In the Windows NT world, TCP/IP is used as a transport protocol, primarily for WAN connections. Later in this section we will be discussing functions of the NT server that generate network traffic, most of which can be encapsulated within TCP/IP. This is useful for minimizing the number of protocols that need to be supported on the WAN, but can be an issue if the encapsulated NetBEUI traffic starts to reach significant levels. We will discuss this later.

The NT implementation for TCP/IP includes SNMP and DHCP support, as well as the *Windows Internet Name Service* (WINS), which maintains a central database of computer-name-to-IP-address translations. *NetBT*, which stands for *NetBIOS over TCP/IP*, also is supported by NT for NetBIOS communication with remote machines via encapsulation in TCP/IP.

Data Link Control. An important difference between DLC and the other protocols supported by Windows NT is that DLC is not meant to be used as a primary means of workstation-to-server communication. That's because DLC does not have a NetBIOS interface. Even when other protocols such as TCP/IP are used for workstation-to-server communications, a NetBIOS interface is needed to encapsulate NetBIOS traffic within this other protocol, just as NT computers need to pass NetBEUI among themselves to function.

The DLC protocol needs to be implemented only on machines that either access IBM mainframes using certain emulation packages, or print to some older types of Hewlett-Packard printers.

Windows NT Network Traffic

In the world of NetWare servers, we saw that SAP advertisements primarily, and RIP updates secondly, are the means by which the NOS itself steals available bandwidth from the applications we wish to run over our internetwork. SAP and RIP were designed to advertise servers, available services, and the means to get to those services. In the world of Windows NT, there is the browser service that performs an equivalent function.

In our discussion of optimizing NetWare protocols for transmission over WANs, we saw that the Cisco IOS had many options for directly controlling the propagation of IPX SAP and RIP packets, because IPX is a routable protocol. Because the Windows NT browser service is based on NetBEUI transport, which is not routable, there is no opportunity for such a fine degree of control over the propagation of these packets by the Cisco IOS. We will, however, discuss the options for maintaining browser service over WAN links.

Windows NT Browser Service Overview. The Windows NT browser service is available to enable the sharing of resources across the network. This is achieved by the election of master and backup browser servers on each network segment. The browser servers keep track of shareable services on the network, and client computers query the browser servers to see what is available. The types of network traffic that this process generates are illustrated as follows.

- Each potential browser will advertise its candidacy via browser election packets, and an election process will take place to determine which machines become primary or backup servers.
- The master browser sends to backup browsers a new list of servers every 15 minutes.
- Nonbrowsers, potential browsers, and backup browsers announce their presence every 1 to 12 minutes.
- Workstations retrieve shareable resource information from their backup browsers on an as-needed basis.

Let's examine these concepts a little more closely.

Browser Types. A *browser* is a computer that holds information about services on the network, file servers, printers, shared directories, etc. The job of providing a browser service to nonbrowser machines is spread among several computers on a network, as defined in the following:

- *Master browser* maintains a list of all available network services and distributes the list to backup browsers. No client machine requests information directly of the master browser; client machines only request information directly from backup browsers. For each Windows NT workgroup or domain defined, there is only one master browser per Windows NT Workgroup or Domain.
- *Backup browsers* receive a copy of the browser list from the master browser and send it to client computers as requested.
- *Potential browser* is a computer that could be a browser if so instructed by the master browser.

An election process takes place to determine which computer will become the master browser and which computers will become backup browsers. An election is forced if a client computer or backup browser cannot locate a master browser, or when a computer configured to be a preferred master browser is powered on. The election is initiated by the broadcasting of an election packet to all machines on that network. The election process ensures that only one computer becomes the master browser; the selection is based on the type and version of the operating system each machine is running.

Browser Traffic. Assuming that browser election has taken place and the master browser and backups are operational, we can describe the traffic generated by the browser as follows.

After the initial boot sequence, a computer running the server process (workstations can run this process in addition to NT servers), will announce its presence to its domain's master browser. This computer is then added to the master browser's list of network services available. The first time a client computer wants to locate a network resource, it will contact the master browser for a list of backup browsers, and requests the list of network resources (domains, servers, etc.) from a backup server. The client computer now has what it needs to view, select, and attach to the available network resources.

The client PC now has a list of available resources. What happens if one of those resources becomes unavailable? There are browser announcements going on continually on a network. These announcements are similar in concept to routing update advertisements, i.e., as long as a router continually advertises route updates, it will still be considered usable by the other routers. Similarly, as long as a browser or server announces itself periodically, it will be considered available; if it stops announcing itself, however, it is deleted from the network resource list.

Initially every computer on the network will announce itself every minute to the master browser, although eventually this period is extended to 12 minutes. Backup servers request an updated resource list from the master browser every 15 minutes. When a master browser wins an election, it will request all systems to register with it. Systems will respond randomly within 30 seconds, to stop the master browser from becoming overwhelmed with responses.

If a nonbrowser machine fails, it could take up to 51 minutes for the rest of the machines on the network to find out about it. If a nonbrowser or backup browser computer does not announce itself for 36 minutes (three announcement periods), the master browser deletes it from its network resource list. It can take up to 15 minutes for this change to be propagated to all backup browsers. In the case of a master browser, the failure is detected the next time any machine tries to contact the master browser, and an election immediately takes place.

In addition to this traffic, master browsers broadcast network resource information between domains as well as within domains every 15 minutes. If a master browser that is sending its network resource information to another domain fails, it will take 45 minutes for that network resource information to be deleted from the domain receiving that information. Basically, a master browser will wait for three announcement periods before it deletes resource information coming from another domain.

Transporting Windows NT Traffic Over a WAN

We have seen that in a Windows NT-based network there is a lot of broadcast NetBEUI traffic that essentially is using NetBIOS frame types. NetBEUI is not routable, so should we connect sites together on a WAN-based network on Data Link level bridges?

I would not recommend it. We covered the issues of bridge-based networks earlier in this chapter, and outlined why building networks based on Data Link layer bridges is no longer popular.

We have two options, the first of which is the use of DLSw to transport the NetBIOS frames over the WAN links. The second is the use of a WINS server that will use unicast TCP/IP packets to announce specific services to prespecified servers across an IP WAN.

Connecting NT Networks via DLSw. Earlier we discussed using DLSw as a technology to carry Token-Ring-based NetBIOS traffic over TCP/IP WANs. This can be extended to the case for transporting NetBEUI traffic between Ethernet LANs via a TCP/IP WAN relatively easily. A typical internetwork for supporting this type of connectivity and corresponding router configurations are shown in Fig. 5-24.

We need to achieve a tunnel between router 1 and router 2 that will transport any NetBEUI packet between LAN 1 and LAN 2. The configuration for router 1 and router 2 to achieve this is given in Fig. 5-24, which we will discuss line by line.

The following commands configure router 1 for passing NetBIOS packets via DLSw over a TCP connection.

- Command `dlsw local-peer peer-id 162.8.5.1` enables DLSw on the router and identifies the interface with IP address 162.8.5.1 (in this case the Ethernet 0 interface) as the one being presented with NetBIOS packets.
- Command `dlsw remote-peer tcp 162.8.6.1` identifies the IP address of the remote device with which to exchange traffic

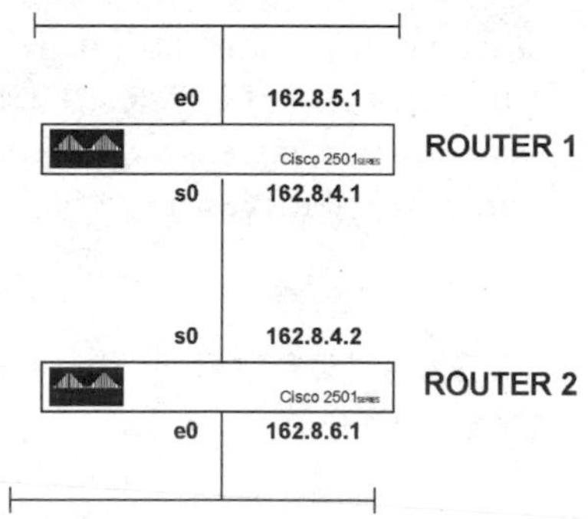

Figure 5-24 Transporting Ethernet-based NetBEUI packets over a router-based

CONFIGURATION FOR ROUTER 1

```
!
DLSW LOCAL-PEER PEER-ID 162.8.5.1
DLSW REMOTE-PEER TCP 162.8.6.1
DLSW BRIDGE-GROUP 1
!
INTERFACE ETHERNET 0
IP ADDRESS 162.8.5.1  255.255.255.0
BRIDGE-GROUP 1
!
INTERFACE SERIAL 0
IP ADDRESS 162.8.4.1  255.255.255.0
!
```

CONFIGURATION FOR ROUTER 2

```
!
DLSW LOCAL-PEER PEER-ID 162.8.6.1
DLSW REMOTE-PEER TCP 162.8.5.1
DLSW BRIDGE-GROUP 1
!
INTERFACE ETHERNET 0
IP ADDRESS 162.8.6.1  255.255.255.0
BRIDGE-GROUP 1
!
INTERFACE SERIAL 0
IP ADDRESS 162.8.4.2  255.255.255.0
!
```

using TCP. In this case, it is the Ethernet interface of router 2. In essence, the local peer and remote peer identify the two ends that will use TCP to carry NetBIOS packets between them.

- Command `dlsw bridge-group 1` is used to enable DLSw+ on the Ethernet interfaces that are assigned membership of bridge group 1 in interface configurations. In effect, DLSw+ is attached to a transparent bridge group, meaning the NetBIOS packets are exchanged transparently between all members of the bridge group.
- Commands `interface ethernet 0` through `bridge-group 1` identify this Ethernet interface as participating in the transparent bridge group 1.

The commands for router 2 are basically a mirror image of the commands entered for router 1, and you can see that the local peer for one router becomes the remote peer for its companion router, and vice versa.

This method of providing NetBIOS connectivity over a TCP connection works, but does not give you much control over which NetBIOS packets get forwarded and which do not. If there are multiple NT servers at each location, all the NetBIOS packets they generate will be forwarded over the link whether you want them to be or not. A slightly better option is to use the facilities within Microsoft's software to encapsulate NetBEUI traffic within TCP/IP directly within the NT server itself.

Using WINS to Announce Services Over an IP WAN. At the most basic level, a NetBIOS-based application needs to see computer names, while IP devices need to work with IP numbers. If the communication medium between two machines trying to communicate with each other via a NetBIOS- based packet is an IP network, there must be a mechanism for mapping NetBIOS names to IP addresses and converting the IP addresses back to NetBIOS names. This mechanism is the *NetBIOS over TCP/IP* protocol, otherwise known as *NBT.*

There are four types of node defined in NBT: the B, P, M, and H node. The B node issues a broadcast on the network every time it needs to locate a computer on the network that owns a given NetBIOS computer name. A P node uses point-to-point directed calls to a known NetBIOS name server, which will reply with the node address of a specified computer name. The M node is a mixture of B and P node operation. An M node will first issue a broadcast to locate a machine, and if that fails, it will query an identified name server. The H node does things the other way around, i.e., it will contact a known name server first, and if that fails, send out a broadcast to locate a host.

This procedure is similar in concept to how IP hosts resolve host names to IP addresses. An IP host will refer to either a local hosts file or a DNS server to resolve a hostname to an IP address. NetBIOS-name-to-IP-address resolution is executed by a broadcast, reference to a local LMHOSTS file or a central Windows Internet Name Service (WINS) server.

The order of search used by Microsoft clients for NBT name resolution is as follows:

1. The internal name cache is checked first.
2. NBT queries the WINS server specified in its configuration.
3. A broadcast is issued.
4. NBT searches the locally defined LMHOSTS file.
5. NBT issues a DNS query to a DNS server for name resolution (a last-gasp effort!).

The LMHOSTS file is a flat ASCII file that looks very similar to the hosts file used by IP nodes. A typical LMHOSTS entry is shown as follows.

```
193.1.1.1        My_server        #remote server
```

The `193.1.1.1` is the IP address of the computer using `My_server` as a NetBIOS name, while comments follow the # character.

Interestingly, NetBIOS does not use port numbers to identify processes running within a host. Each process running in a host must be assigned a different service name and have a separate entry in the LMHOSTS file. So if `My_server` is running an SNA gateway application and a client/server application, it will need two entries in the LMHOSTS file, each one mapping the appropriate NetBIOS service name of the application running to the IP address 193.1.1.1. In this respect, the IP model is more efficient because only one entry per machine needs to go into the host's file, and any applications running within a host are identified by port number by the transport layer protocol.

Managing LMHOSTS files distributed all around an internetwork presents the same problems as managing distributed hosts files. WINS was implemented as a service to offer the same functionality as DNS by providing a central repository for name resolution information. WINS is a proprietary Microsoft technology, and therefore does have some nicely integrated features if you are using an NT server. For example, if you are running both WINS and DHCP from the same NT server, WINS can read the DHCP databases to find out the NetBIOS names and IP addresses registered. A client configured for WINS and DHCP will also register coordinated computer name and IP address information as it comes online.

What all this means to a real internetwork is that by implementing either a WINS server or LMHOSTS file, and loading the NBT protocol on NT servers, you can have announcements made by NT servers over an IP network. Let's look at maintaining browser functionality if you have NT servers at distributed locations, interconnected by an IP WAN as shown in Fig. 5-25.

In Fig. 5-25 we assume that server 1 is running WINS and the workstations on that LAN are configured to use it for IP name resolution. With a default workstation configuration, WS1 will be able to contact directly any computer on LAN 1 and any remote computer with an IP address and name defined in the WINS server. Remote services, such as server 2, need to be configured to register with the server 1 WINS process. In a large environment, having all services register with one central WINS

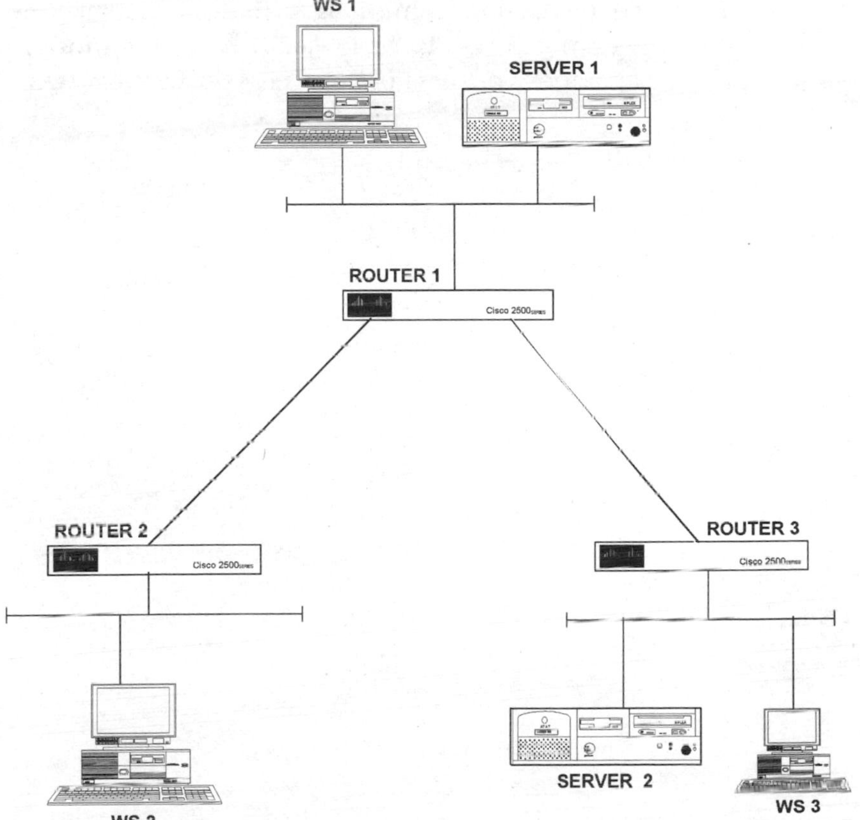

Figure 5-25 IP WAN connectivity in a Windows NT environment

server and keeping their listing alive with regular announcements can become burdensome. To counter this issue, Microsoft enables a distributed WINS strategy to be implemented, in much the same way that DNS operates as a distributed database.

Whichever way you choose to enable NT computers to use the browser service over a WAN, WAN bandwidth will be consumed. Every network mechanism uses some bandwidth to maintain information about connections. In each of Windows NT browsing, NetWare SAP/RIP or IPXWAN and NLSP, or IP routing protocols such as IGRP and OSPF, it comes down to how you configure the services for your particular installation. All of these options can work in the vast majority of cases.

Summary

In this chapter we explored the options available when using Cisco routers to interconnect IPX, IBM, nonroutable, and Windows NT networking protocols. We looked at how to minimize the effect that normal operations of these protocols has on available WAN bandwidth.

CHAPTER 6

Supporting Popular WAN Technologies

Objectives

This chapter will look at how Cisco routers are configured for the most popular WAN technologies used today. We will:

- Look at how the underlying technology works.
- Examine the Cisco router configuration commands available by looking at examples of how these commands can be used in real-world configurations.

Frame Relay

Frame relay is a layer 2 WAN protocol and, as such, does not understand the concept of network numbers. In a LAN, layer 2 addressing is normally defined by MAC addresses. In frame relay, addressing is defined by *Data Link Connection Identifiers* (DLCI, pronounced "del-see" by those familiar with frame relay implementations). DLCI numbers are not used as destination addresses such as LAN-based MAC addresses. A DLCI number only has significance locally, and not across the frame relay network.

Frame relay is a statistical multiplexed service. That means it allows several *logical connections* (often referred to as *channels*) to coexist over the same physical connection and allocates bandwidth dynamically among all users of that link. This is in contrast to a Time Division Multiplexed (TDM) service, which allocates a fixed amount of bandwidth to multiple channels on the same line. When frame relay was first introduced, many network engineers thought of it as a cut-down version of *X.25*. This was because frame relay is similar to X.25 in many ways, except it does not provide the same level of error correction. X.25 was designed as a packet switching network technology at a time when the wide area network links available were mainly analog lines that were prone to periods of poor transmission quality, and that introduced errors into packets transmitted across a network.

When frame relay was introduced, more and more digital circuits were available that provided better-quality transmission and, on average, higher reliability. Also, higher-level protocols such as TCP that performed error correction and flow control were becoming increasingly popular. The designers of frame relay decided, therefore, to cut out all the link-level acknowledgments and other overhead associated with X.25 connections that were there to deal with unreliable links.

Frame relay performs as much error checking as does Ethernet in that a *Frame Check Sequence* (FCS) derived from a *Cyclic Redundancy Check* (CRC) calculation is appended to each frame sent, which is checked by the receiving station. This FCS allows a receiving station to disregard a frame that has been altered in transit; however, neither frame relay nor Ethernet will re-request the damaged frame. Frame relay, therefore, offers better utilization of available bandwidth and is faster at transferring data than X.25, because it does not have to generate, receive, or process acknowledgments.

Frame relay does rely on the applications communicating over a frame relay link to handle error recovery. If an application uses a connection-oriented protocol such as TCP for its Transport layer protocol, TCP will handle error recovery and flow control issues. If an application uses a connectionless protocol such as UDP for its Transport layer protocol, specific programming within the application must be coded to handle error recovery and flow control.

X.25 as a specification merely dealt with how a DTE device will communicate with a DCE device and made no mention of how packets would get routed through a network. That's the same with frame relay. Frame relay networks may use a variety of mechanisms to route traffic from source to destination, and each one is proprietary to a vendor or group of vendors. What this means to us is that, typically, a Cisco router will be configured to connect to a public frame relay service without regard as to how the packets that are sent over that network are routed.

Frame relay and X.25 both operate using the concepts of *a permanent virtual circuit* (PVC) and a *switched virtual circuit* (SVC). An SVC uses a Call Setup procedure to establish a connection from source to destination in the same way a telephone does. A PVC is permanently connected between source and destination and operates in much the same way as a leased line. Although frame relay originally was proposed as a standard for packet transmission over ISDN using SVCs, it has gained far wider acceptance as a WAN technology using PVCs on a shared public network.

Let me say first of all that I see little point in implementing frame relay on a private network. Frame relay makes the most sense when the same network is going to be used by many organizations and sharing of the bandwidth between locations is called for. I therefore will restrict the rest of this discussion with the assumption that we are talking about connecting Cisco routers at one or more locations to a public shared frame relay service.

Before we look into the details of frame relay, let's look at when frame relay is appropriate and identify some of its pitfalls. Frame relay is ideally suited to networks that fit the following criteria:

- Many geographically dispersed locations need a permanent connection to a central site, but cannot cost-justify the provision of a leased circuit from each of the remote sites to the central location.
- The traffic to be transported tends to come in bursts or spurts, rather than in a constant stream.
- Applications accessed over the frame relay connection use a connection-oriented protocol to handle error recovery and flow control.
- Unpredictable application response time is not a big issue.
- Remote sites change location, or new sites are added on a regular basis.

If a network's goals match closely with the above, frame relay is a technology to consider. What makes frame relay attractive from the telephone company's point of view is that bandwidth can be allocated among many customers. When viewed statistically for a large population on the frame relay network, this makes sense. The probability that thousands of customers all want to use the network to the full extent at the same time is statistically quite small. Therefore, if everyone takes their proper turn at the bandwidth, the telephone company can sell more bandwidth than is available throughout the network. This enables the telephone company to offer a cheaper service via a shared frame relay network, but one that does not come with the same guarantees of throughput. This cheaper service often is billed at the same rate irrespective of location, and so is particularly attractive for connecting remote sites that may be thousands of miles away.

To counter user concerns over throughput guarantees, there is a frame relay feature called the *Committed Information Rate* (CIR). Prior to implementation of CIR, a user would get, for example, a 64 kbps line into a commercial frame relay service, but the throughput would vary, depending on other customer utilization of the frame relay network. Sometimes the throughput was unacceptable. The CIR guarantees a customer that the throughput on any given link would not drop below the CIR rate. In addition to the CIR, an agreement with a frame relay service provider generally allows a customer to have bursts of traffic up to another specified level, typically the speed of the connection into the frame relay service.

Shared frame relay services are certainly a cost-effective way to provide remote branches with occasional access to central e-mail, gateway, and application servers for internal users who can accept occasional slow response times. Frame relay is not appropriate for delivering mission-critical, bandwidth-intensive applications to external customers. If a frame relay service is to be used for an application that needs guaranteed throughput, the CIR must be set to the guaranteed bandwidth needed. This can be as expensive as getting dedicated bandwidth from the same telephone company.

There is a final concern I want to share with you before we move on to look at this technology in more detail. In Fig. 6-1, we see a typical frame relay implementation for a company with five remote branches.

Router 1 connects the central site with the servers to a commercial frame relay service. Routers 2 through 6 connect remote branches to the same frame relay service. Frame relay is not a broadcast medium, so any routing updates, or SAP updates for IPX traffic, need to be sent point-to-point to each location. This can tax the link from router 1 into the frame relay network as the number of branches grows. It is not uncommon to find 50 percent or more of a central site router's bandwidth into the frame relay service consumed with routing information packets. This situation can be avoided, as we shall see later, but requires careful design and a good knowledge of how the interconnected systems work. Frame relay should never be considered a plug-and-play technology.

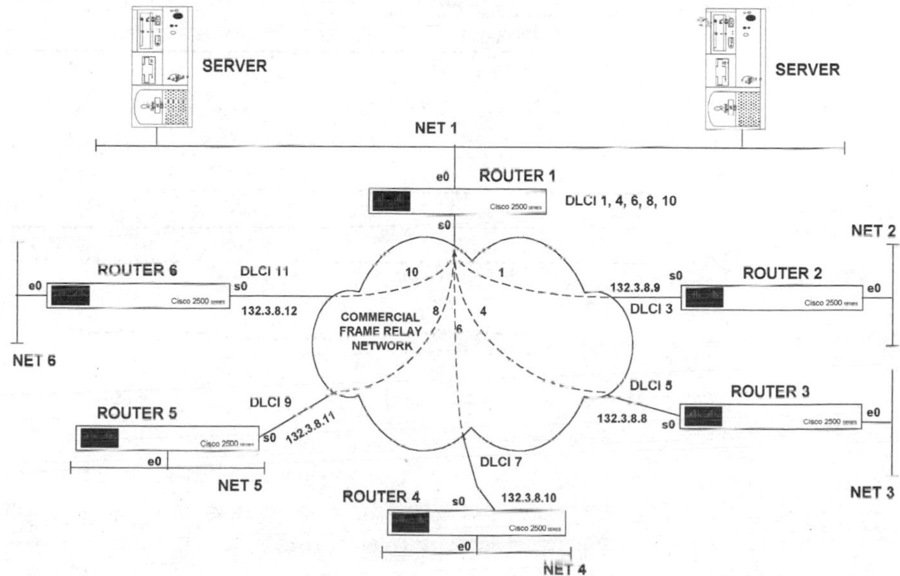

Figure 6-1 Typical frame relay network configuration

Frame Relay Terms

The first frame relay term you need to understand, the *DLCI*, already has been introduced. A DLCI is supplied for each end of a PVC by the frame relay provider. A DLCI number is used to identify each PVC defined at a location. At the central location shown in Fig. 6-1, there are DLCI numbers 1, 4, 6, 8, and 10. It is best to think of each DLCI as identifying a pipe that leads to a specific protocol address. For example, DLCI 1 leads to the IP address of Serial 0 on router 2, DLCI 4 leads to the IP address of Serial 0 on router 3, and so forth.

If you are implementing a TCP/IP solution over frame relay, remember that frame relay is a layer 2 protocol. All routers connected together via the *frame relay cloud* are peers. The key difference between a frame relay cloud and a LAN is that the frame relay cloud does not support broadcasts to all destinations as would a LAN. Referring to Fig. 6-1, this implies that all the Serial 0 ports on the routers shown would be in the same IP subnet and all the Ethernet 0 ports shown would have their own subnets. We will look at this in more detail in the section on "Configuring Frame Relay Features."

As with most networking technologies, there are several configuration options, and here we will look at the most common.

Basic frame relay is depicted in Fig. 6-2 and merely connects two locations together over a PVC. This is not very different from connecting these sites together via a leased line. The only difference is the fact that the bandwidth between the two sites is shared with other users of the frame relay network.

In this figure, router 1 is connected to router 2 via a PVC, which is defined within the frame relay cloud as existing from DLCI 1 to DLCI 2. In basic frame relay, other locations within the frame relay cloud could use these DLCI numbers because a DLCI has only local significance. This type of frame relay use is limited and has been superseded by use of what is known as the *LMI extensions*.

LMI stands for *Local Management Interface* and provides additional frame relay features that include:

- Use of Inverse ARP to automatically determine the protocol address of the device on the remote end of a DLCI.
- Simple flow control to provide XON/XOFF-type flow control for the interface as a whole. This is intended for applications communicating over frame relay that cannot use the congestion flags sent by frame relay networks.

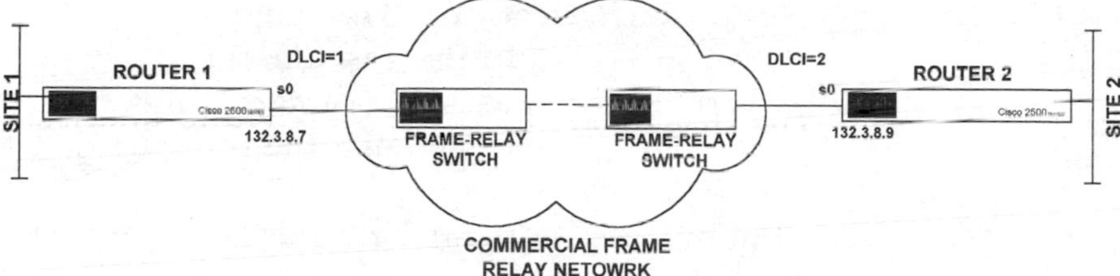

Figure 6-2 Simple frame relay connectivity

- Multicasting to allow the sender to send one copy of a frame that will be delivered to multiple destinations. This is useful for routing update and address resolution protocol traffic.
- Virtual Circuit Status messaging to allow LMI-enabled network connections to maintain information about the status of PVCs across the network, notifying other nodes if one node becomes unreachable.

Cisco joined with Northern Telecom, Stratacom, and DEC to define an LMI standard to deliver these benefits in anticipation of an open standard for LMI. The other commonly implemented LMI type is now *ANSI*, which was defined by that standards body some time after the four vendors above released theirs.

In addition to the LMI type, you can set the frame relay encapsulation to either Cisco or IETF if you are connecting to another vendor's equipment across a frame relay network. Cisco did not create these additional options to make an open standard proprietary or to make life difficult. Rather, Cisco created these standards in order to deliver benefits to users prior to standards bodies making a workable definition available to those wanting to deploy frame relay networks.

Configuring Frame Relay Features

As stated previously, frame relay is a technology that connects two end points across a network. These end points are identified within the network by DLCI numbers; the DLCI-to-DLCI connection is known as a PVC. We will examine configuration of a central Cisco router serial interface, first in a frame relay point-to-point connection, then in a multipoint connection, and finally with sub-interfaces. We also will explain how inverse ARP simplifies configuration and why the Split Horizon algorithm is not enabled on frame relay ports (unless sub-interfaces are used).

Basic Configuration. The simplest example of frame relay is that shown in Fig. 6-2. In that case, the frame relay provider assigns a DLCI address of 1 to the location of router 1, and 2 to the location with router 2. Let's look at how we build the configuration for the serial port of router 1.

In interface configuration mode for the Serial 0 port of router 1, type the following:

```
Router1(config-int)#ip address 132.3.8.7 255.255.255.0
Router1(config-int)#encapsulation frame relay
```

This defines frame relay encapsulation for the Serial 0 port. The only optional argument that can be supplied on this command is `ietf`, which would configure the interface to use the IETF rather than the Cisco encapsulation. Your frame relay provider will inform you if this argument is necessary.

The next configuration entry will be to define the LMI type. This command can have one of three values. The default is `Cisco`, while optional arguments can specify `ANSI` or `q933a`, the latter being the ITU standard. Again, your frame relay provider should let you know which to use.

```
Router1(config-int)#frame-relay lmi-type ansi
```

Next we have to tell the router which destination DLCI should be used to reach a given IP address. This discussion assumes that manual configuration of frame relay maps is necessary; in a subsequent section we will examine how inverse ARP makes this unnecessary. For router 1, the 132.3.8.0 subnet is reachable through the Serial 0 interface, so all packets for that subnet are sent out Serial 0. The frame relay supplier will have set up the PVC to send anything that originates at one end of the PVC out the other end.

The potential exists for many PVCs to be associated with one physical interface, so we must tell the serial port which DLCI number to use to get to which protocol address destination. Therefore, we have to tell it that to reach IP address 132.3.8.9, it will use DLCI 1. With this DLCI information, the frame relay network can deliver the packet to its desired destination. This configuration is achieved with the following command:

```
Router1(config-int)#frame-relay map ip 132.3.8.9 1 broadcast
```

The argument `broadcast` enables router 1 to send broadcast routing updates to router 2 through this PVC. If the Serial 0 port on router 2 were to be configured in the same way, the two routers could communicate via frame relay. With only one PVC, this level of configuration may seem like overkill—and it is—but the next example will show why it is necessary. Later in this chapter, when we use our three lab routers to configure a test frame relay network, we will see that a properly configured network and interface will remove the need to enter multiple `frame-relay map` commands.

This is all well and good, but it is not taking advantage of one of the main benefits of frame relay, which is the ability to multiplex many links onto one. This feature tends to be useful for a central router that must connect to many remote sites, a situation shown in Fig. 6-1. To enable router 1 in Fig. 6-1 to reach routers 2 through 6, the configuration we have so far can be extended with additional `map` statements. The first step, however, will be to buy the additional PVCs from the frame relay carrier and obtain the local DLCI numbers that identify PVCs to all the remote locations. Assume we are delivered the following DLCI assignments and IP address allocations:

Router	Serial 0 IP Address	DLCI at router 1	Remote DLCI
1	132.3.8.7		
2	132.3.8.9	1	3
3	132.3.8.8	4	5
4	132.3.8.10	6	7
5	132.3.8.11	8	9
6	132.3.8.12	10	11

To reach all remote routers, router 1 would need the configuration shown in Fig. 6-3. This shows that router 1 has 5 DLCIs configured, and tells it which DLCI to use to get the packets delivered to the appropriate IP address. At first it may seem that, by addressing packets to a DLCI number that is defined at the router 1 location, the packets are not really being sent anywhere. The best way to think of this, though, is to think of each DLCI as a pipe, and as long as router 1 puts the packet in the correct pipe, the frame relay network will deliver the packet to the correct destination.

Inverse ARP. As you can see, configuring all these frame relay map statements can become a bore, especially if you have upwards of 20 locations. Fortunately there is a mechanism that will save us from all this manual effort, and that is *Inverse ARP.* Inverse ARP works in conjunction with the LMI to deliver enough information to routers attached to a frame relay network, so that no frame relay map statements need to be manually configured.

Figure 6-3 Configuration for router 1 in Figure 6-1

```
INTERFACE SERIAL 0
IP ADDRESS 132.3.8.7 255.255.255.0
ENCAPSULATION FRAME RELAY
FRAME-RELAY LMI-TYPE ANSI
FRAME-RELAY MAP IP 132.3.8.9 1 BROADCAST
FRAME-RELAY MAP IP 132.3.8.8 4 BROADCAST
FRAME-RELAY MAP IP 132.3.8.10 6 BROADCAST
FRAME-RELAY MAP IP 132.3.8.11 8 BROADCAST
FRAME-RELAY MAP IP 132.3.8.12 10 BROADCAST
```

Upon startup, the LMI will announce to an attached router all the DLCI numbers that are configured on the physical link connecting the router to the network. The router will then send Inverse ARP requests out each DLCI to find out the protocol address configured on the other end of each DLCI's PVC. In this way, a router will generate its own list of what IP addresses are reachable through which DLCI number.

Fully Meshed Frame Relay Networks. For IP implemented over frame relay networks, the Split Horizon rule is disabled. This allows a central router to readvertise routes learned from one remote location on a serial interface to other remote locations connected to the same serial interface. In Fig. 6-1, this means that all routers will end up with entries in their routing tables for net 1 through net 6.

Some other protocols, such as those used in Apple networking, will not allow Split Horizon to be turned off, so routes cannot be readvertised out of the interface from which they were learned. To provide full routing capability across a frame relay network with these protocols requires a separate link from each location to every other location. This type of connectivity is referred to as a *fully meshed network* (Fig. 6-4).

A fully meshed network gives each router a specific DLCI number with which to reach every other router. This scheme does allow complete communication between all locations, but requires a large number of PVCs to be bought from the frame relay provider. As the number of nodes on the network increases, the number of PVCs needed grows exponentially, which can make this technology uneconomic to deploy. Now that Cisco has made sub-interfaces available, however, we have a method to get around this for these Apple protocols.

Frame Relay Sub-Interfaces. The simplest way to deploy sub-interfaces for full remote-branch-to-remote-branch connectivity is to implement sub-interfaces in a point-to-point configuration. Sub-interfaces can be deployed as point-to-point, or multipoint (the default).

A sub-interface allows you to effectively split one physical port into multiple logical ports. The advantage this gives is that if you configure the sub-interfaces as point-to-point links, each sub-interface is treated as if it were a separate connection by the layer 3 protocol and each sub-interface will appear as a separate entry in the routing table, with a different subnetwork ID associated with it. A sub-interface configured in multipoint mode behaves the same as the interfaces we have configured so far. Let's look at how a sub-interface configured in point-to-point mode allows us to configure a fully meshed network for protocols that cannot disable Split Horizon, without buying additional PVCs and DLCIs from a frame relay provider.

What we want to achieve with a sub-interface is to assign a complete subnet to each PVC, so that a router with multiple PVCs terminating in its serial port (that is, the serial port has multiple DLCI numbers associated with it in the frame relay network) will assign a separate entry in its routing table for each PVC link (Fig. 6-5).

If router 1 is appropriately configured with sub-interfaces, it will have a separate entry in its routing table for the PVC that goes from itself to router 2, and from itself to router 3. Let's take a look at the configuration of these three routers as shown in Fig. 6-6.

This configuration assumes that the default encapsulation and LMI type is in effect, and that Inverse ARP (enabled by default on a frame relay port) is not disabled. For router 1 we have sub-interface 0.1 and 0.2 on separate subnets.

Figure 6-4
Fully meshed frame relay network

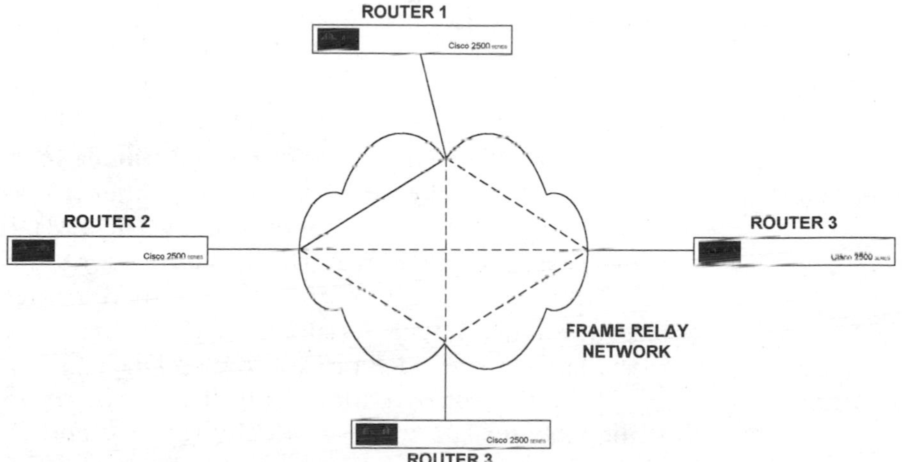

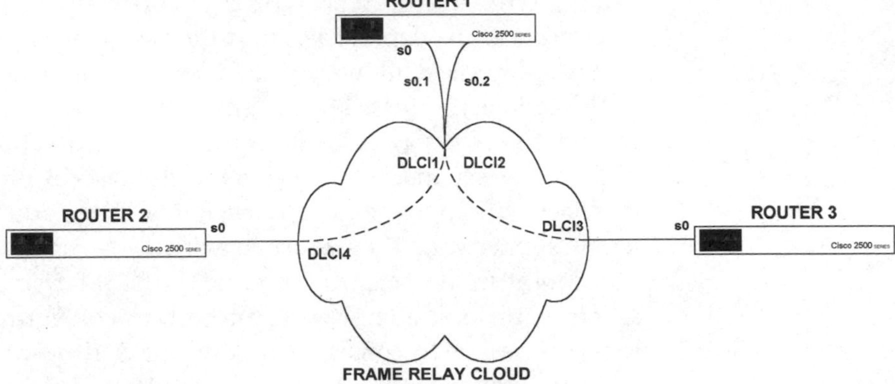

Figure 6-5 Sub-interfaces on a frame relay connection

Figure 6-6 Router configuration for frame relay sub-interfaces

CONFIGURATION FOR ROUTER 1

```
INTERFACE SERIAL 0
ENCAPSULATION FRAME RELAY
INTERFACES 0.1 POINT-TO-POINT
FRAME-RELAY INTERFACE-DLCI 1 BROADCAST
IP ADDRESS 164.8.5.1 255.255.255.0
!
INTERFACE S 0.2 POINT-TO-POINT
FRAME-RELAY INTERFACE DLCI 2 BROADCAST
IP ADDRESS 164.8.6.1 255.255.255.0
```

CONFIGURATION FOR ROUTER 2

```
INTERFACE SERIAL 0
IP ADDRESS 164.8.5.2 255.255.255.0
ENCAPSULATION FRAME RELAY
!
```

CONFIGURATION FOR ROUTER 3

```
INTERFACE SERIAL 0
IP ADDRESS 164.8.6.2 255.255.255.0
ENCAPSULATION FRAME RELAY
!
```

Sub-interface 0.1 is configured for subnet 164.8.5.0 and is associated with DLCI 1. The Serial 0 port on router 2 is configured for an IP address on the same subnet and by the LMI/Inverse ARP process described earlier will map DLCI 14 to IP address 164.8.5.1.

Similarly, the sub-interface 0.2 has an IP address configured on the same subnet as the Serial 0 port on router 3. Router 3 also will use the LMI/inverse ARP process to map DLCI 13 to IP address 164.8.6.1.

With this configuration, router 1 will have separate entries in its routing table for the subnets used by router 2 and router 3. Router 1 will broadcast routing updates to router 2 and router 3, so that both routers get their routing tables updated with entries for the 164.8.5.0 and 164.8.6.0. subnetwork. This allows router 2 and router 3 to communicate with each other via router 1.

This type of configuration makes the serial interface on router 1 appear as multiple interfaces to the layer 3 protocols, but on a Data Link and Physical layer it is considered one interface, with multiple PVCs multiplexed on it by the frame relay network.

Configuring a Test Frame Relay Network

We will now reconfigure our three lab routers to have one perform the function of a frame relay switch. Two other routers will be configured as remote branches connecting into the frame relay switch. The configuration we will use is shown in Fig. 6-7.

In this configuration, router 1 takes the place of a frame relay cloud. To build this lab environment, the first thing we must do is ensure that the DTE/DCE cables connecting router 1 to router 2 and router 3 are connected with the correct polarity. The goal here is to get both serial ports on router 1 to act as DCE rather than DTE, and the only way to do that in a lab environment—using cables instead of CSU/DSU devices to connect routers—is to connect the correct end of a DTE/DCE cable into the serial port. Use the `show controller serial 0` command after you have connected the DTE/DCE cable to the Serial 0 port. If the output from this command indicates a DTE configuration, use the other end of the cable to connect to router 1. The same goes for the Serial 1 port.

The configuration shown in Fig. 6-7 uses the default Cisco frame relay encapsulation and LMI, as well as leaving Inverse ARP functioning. Router 1 is configured as a pure frame relay switch. The following explains all the frame relay entries in this configuration.

- Global command `frame-relay switching` enables the frame relay switching process for this router and must be enabled before any interface configuration commands are entered.
- Command `encapsulation frame-relay` sets frame relay encapsulation for this interface.
- Command `frame-relay intf-type dce` sets the interface as a frame relay DCE device. The default is DTE; therefore routers 2 and 3, which need to be DTE, do not have a corresponding command.
- Command `frame-relay route 17 interface serial1 18` configures the static routing of the switch based on DLCI

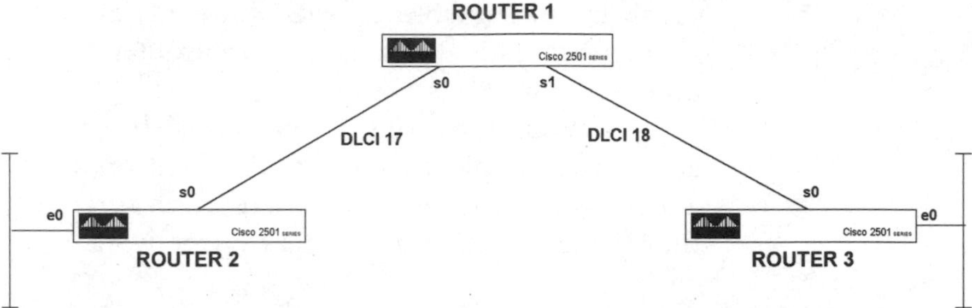

Figure 6-7 Configuration for a test frame relay network

CONFIGURATION FOR ROUTER 1

```
FRAME-RELAY SWITCHING
!
INTERFACE SERIAL 0
NO IP ADDRESS
ENCAPSULATION FRAME-RELAY
CLOCKRATE 1000000
FRAME-RELAY INTF-TYPE DCE
FRAME-RELAY ROUTE 17 INTERFACE SERIAL 1 18
!
INTERFACE SERIAL 1
NO IP ADDRESS
ENCAPSULATION FRAME-RELAY
CLOCKRATE 1000000
FRAME-RELAY INTT-TYPE OCE
FRAME-RELAY ROUTE 18 INTERFACE SERIAL 0 17
```

CONFIGURATION FOR ROUTER 2

```
INTERFACE ETHERNET 0
IP ADDRESS 200.1.1.1 255.255.255.0
!
INTERFACE SERIAL 0
IP ADDRESS 163.4.8.1 255.255.255.0
ENCAPSULATION FRAME-RELAY
!
ROUTER IGRP 12
NETWORK 163.4.0.0
NETWORK 200.1.1.0
```

CONFIGURATION FOR ROUTER 3

```
INTERFACE ETHERNET 0
IP ADDRESS 200.2.2.1 255.255.255.0
!
INTERFACE SERIAL 0
IP ADDRESS 163.4.8.2 255.255.255.0
ENCAPSULATION FRAME-RELAY
!
ROUTER IGRP 12
NETWORK 163.4.0.0
NETWORK 200.2.2.0
```

number. The command syntax configures the router so that any packets inbound on DLCI 17 will be routed out interface Serial 1, on DLCI 18 (note that DLCIs can have a value in the range 16—1007). The values shown are for the Serial 0 port; for the Serial 1 port, packets are inbound on DLCI 18 and routed to Serial 0 on DLCI 17.

The configuration for routers 2 and 3 should be self-explanatory by this stage; however, it is worth noting that the frame relay maps are generated through the LMI and Inverse ARP mechanism and require no explicit configuration of either router. Note that IGRP was configured for both router 2 and router 3, and because broadcasts are enabled by default, routing information traversed the frame relay switch, updating the routing tables of router 2 and 3. Therefore, router 2 is able to ping the

Ethernet port of router 3 and vice versa. Figure 6-8 shows the output of some interesting frame relay `show` commands that can be used to view the state of the frame relay network.

The first output shown in Fig. 6-8 is for the `show frame-relay route` command, which is useful when trying to troubleshoot PVC

Figure 6-8 Useful *show* commands for the test network

SHOW FRAME-RELAY ROUTE COMMAND ON ROUTER 1

INPUT INTT	INPUT DLCI	OUTPUT INTT	OUTPUT DLCI	STATUS
SERIAL 0	17	SERIAL 1	18	ACTIVE
SERIAL 1	18	SERIAL 0	17	ACTIVE

SHOW FRAME-RELAY PVC FOR ROUTER 1

PVC STATISTICS FOR INTERFACE SERIAL0 (FRAME RELAY DCE)
DLCI = 17, DLCI USAGE = SWITCHED, PVC STATUS = ACTIVE, INTERFACE = SERIAL0

```
INPUT PKTS 53               OUTPUT 56          IN BYTES 4378
OUT BYTES 4536              DROPPED PKTS 0     IN FECN PKTS 0
IN BECN PKTS 0              OUT FECN PKTS 0    OUT BECN PKTS 0
IN DE PKTS 0                OUT DE PKTS 0
PVC CREATE TIME 1:09:09     LAST TIME PVC STATUS CHANGED 1:00:29
NUM PKTS SWITCHED 53
```

PVC STATISTICS FOR INTERFACE SERIAL1 (FRAME RELAY DCE)
DLCI = 18, DLCI USAGE = SWITCHED, PVC STATUS = ACTIVE, INTERFACE = SERIAL1

```
INPUT PKTS 56               OUTPUT 53          IN BYTES 4536
OUT BYTES 4378              DROPPED PKTS 0     IN FECN PKTS 0
IN BECN PKTS 0              OUT FECN PKTS 0    OUT BECN PKTS 0
IN DE PKTS 0                OUT DE PKTS 0
PVC CREATE TIME 1:06:50     LAST TIME PVC STATUS CHANGED 1:03:01
NUM PKTS SWITCHED 56
```

SHOW FRAME-RELAY PVC FOR ROUTER 2

PVC STATISTICS FOR INTERFACE SERIAL0 (FRAME RELAY DTE)
DLCI = 17, DLCI USAGE = LOCAL, PVC STATUS = ACTIVE, INTERFACE = SERIAL0

```
INPUT PKTS 60               OUTPUT 57          IN BYTES 4848
OUT BYTES 4690              DROPPED PKTS 1     IN FECN PKTS 0
IN BECN PKTS 0              OUT FECN PKTS 0    OUT BECN PKTS 0
IN DE PKTS 0                OUT DE PKTS 0
PVC CREATE TIME 1:07:54     LAST TIME PVC STATUS CHANGED 1:05:24
```

SHOW FRAME LMI OUTPUT FOR ROUTER 2

```
INVALID UNNUMBERED INFO 0        INVALID PROT DISC 0
INVALID DUMMY CALL REF 0         INVALID MSG TYPE 0
INVALID STATUS MESSAGE 0         INVALID LOCK SHIFT 0
INVALID INFORMATION ID 0         INVALID REPORT IE LEN 0
INVALID REPORT REQUEST 0         INVALID KEEP IE LEN 0
NUM STATUS ENQ SENT 410          NUM STATUS MSGS RCVD 409
NUM UPDATE STATUS RCVD 0         NUM STATUS TIMEOUTS 1
```

SHO FRAME MAP OUTPUT FOR ROUTER 2

SERIAL0 (UP): IP 163.4.8.2 DLCI 17(0X11, 0X410), DYNAMIC, BROADCAST, STATUS DEFINED, ACTIVE problems. This command tells you which DLCIs are active and where they route from and to on the frame relay router interfaces. The other display for router 1 shows the output for the `show frame-relay pvc` command, which gives more detailed information on each DLCI operational in the switch. The number of dropped packets gives you an idea of how well the switch is performing its duties—clearly the fewer drops, the better.

If the number of drops is high, but you notice the FECN and BECN packets increasing more rapidly than usual, it could be an early sign that the network is running out of bandwidth. FECN and BECN packets indicate congestion on the network and tell switches to hold off sending traffic. As long as the packet buffers in switches can hold traffic peaks, packets do not have to be dropped. If too many packets for the available bandwidth or buffers are coming in, however, the switch will drop packets at some stage. The `show frame-relay pvc` command for router 2 has the same display as discussed above, but only for DLCI 17, the one associated with router 2 in this network.

The next two displays show, respectively, the LMI status and the frame relay maps for router 2. The frame relay map is as expected, i.e., router 2 knows that the DLCI presented to it by the switch (DLCI 17) will lead it to IP address 163.4.8.2, which is on router 3.

SMDS: Switched Multimegabit Data Service

SMDS, or *Switched Multimegabit Data Service*, has not yet gained significant market penetration, although it has begun to experience some growth. SMDS was viewed as a stepping stone to ATM, since some of the communications equipment and media are common to the two technologies. As SMDS is not available everywhere, and there is more interest in ATM, SMDS has had a hard time getting into the mainstream.

SMDS does, however, have some penetration; if your long-distance carrier is MCI, you may have cause to use this technology. The attraction of SMDS is that it has the potential to provide high-speed, link-level connections (initially in the 1 to 34 Mbps range) with the economy of a shared public network, and exhibits many of the qualities of a LAN.

In an SMDS network, each node has a unique 10-digit address. Each digit is in binary-coded decimal, with 4 bits used to represent values 0 through 9. Bellcore, the "keeper" of the SMDS standard, assigns a 64-bit address for SMDS, which has the following allocation:

- The most significant 4 bits are either 1100 to indicate an individual address, or 1110 to indicate a group address.
- The next 4 most significant bits are used for the country code, which is 0001 for the United States.
- The next 40 bits are the binary-coded decimal bits representing the 10-decimal digit station address.
- The final 16 bits are currently padded with ones.

To address a node on the SMDS network, all you need do is put the node's SMDS address in the destination field of the SMDS frame. In this way, SMDS behaves in a fashion similar to Ethernet or Token-Ring, which delivers frames according to MAC addresses. A key difference between SMDS and these LAN technologies, however, is the maximum frame size allowed. Ethernet allows just over 1500 bytes, and Token-Ring just over 4000 bytes, but SMDS allows up to 9188 bytes. These SMDS frames are segmented into ATM-sized 53-byte cells for transfer across the network. A large frame size gives SMDS the ability to encapsulate complete LAN frames, such as Ethernet, Token-Ring, and FDDI, for transportation over the SMDS network.

An SMDS network can accept full-bandwidth connections from DS0 (64 kbps) and DS1 (1.544 Mbps) circuits, or an *access class,* which is a bandwidth slice of a higher-speed link such as a DS3 (45 Mbps). These links terminate at what is known as the *Subscriber Network Interface* (SNI) and connect to the *Customer Premises Equipment* (CPE). The SNI typically is an SMDS CSU/DSU device and the CPE in this case will be a Cisco router. These elements are illustrated in Fig. 6-9.

SMDS is based on the 802.6 standard for *Metropolitan Area Networks* (MAN), which defines a *Distributed Queue Dual Bus,* and is a connectionless technology. The key difference between SMDS and 802.6 is that SMDS does not utilize a dual-bus architecture; instead, connections are centered on a hub and deployed in a star configuration.

SMDS Protocols

SMDS has its own layer 1 and layer 2 protocols that specify the physical connections and voltage levels used, along with the layer 2 addresses. These protocols are implemented in the *SMDS Interface Protocol* (SIP). SIP has three levels, with SIP levels 2 and 3 defining the Data Link layer functions.

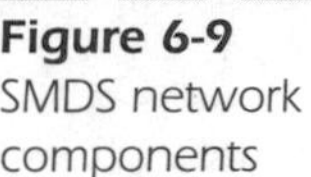

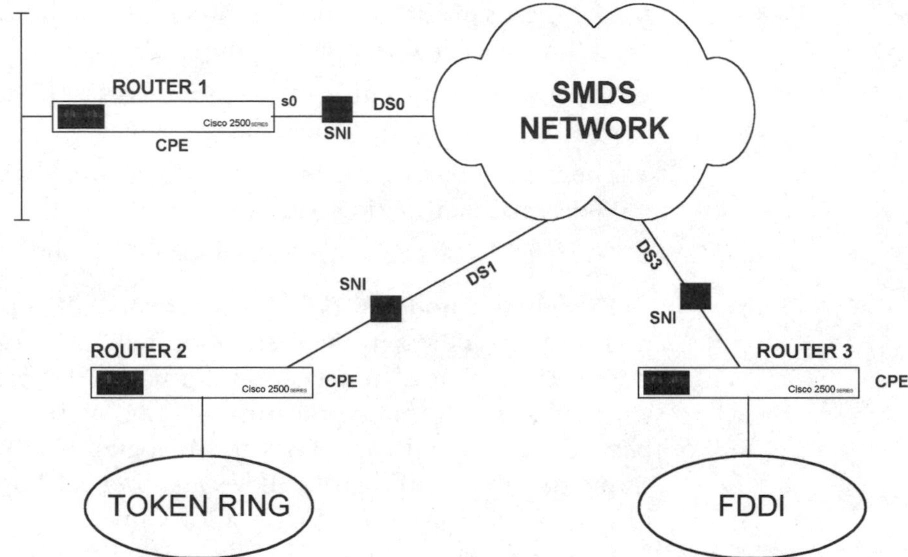

Figure 6-9
SMDS network components

SMDS carries IP information quite effectively. Let's say IP as a layer 3 (in OSI terms) protocol hands a frame down to the SIP level 3 protocol. SIP 3 will place a header and trailer on this frame to form a level 3 Protocol Data Unit. (This is "layer 3" in SMDS parlance, which is a part of the layer 2 protocol in OSI terms.) This expanded frame has SMDS source and destination addresses that include the aforementioned country codes and 10-digit decimal addresses.

The expanded frame is passed down to the SIP level 2 protocol, which cuts this expanded frame into 44-byte chunks, to which get added a header and trailer, enabling reassembly of the frame once the 44-byte chunks have been received by the destination. These 44-byte chunks are termed *level 2 Protocol Data Units.* The SIP level 1 protocol provides appropriate framing and timing for the transmission medium in use. The relationship between OSI and SIP layers is illustrated in Fig. 6-10.

In the example given above, SMDS is acting like a LAN as far as the IP level is concerned, with the only difference being that, instead of regular ARP and the ARP table, there must be a way of resolving IP addresses to SMDS 10-digit addresses.

In SMDS, IP ARP functionality is provided by *address groups,* which also are referred to as *Multiple Logical IP Subnetworks* by RFC 1209. Address groups are a group of predefined SMDS hosts that listen to a specific multicast address as well as to their SMDS node address. In this instance, if an IP host needs to find an SMDS address for an IP address in order to send a frame, an ARP query is sent to the address group and the SMDS host with the appropriate address responds with its SMDS address. Routing broadcast updates are distributed the same way across SMDS.

Typically, SIP levels 1 and 2 are implemented in the SMDS CSU/DSU, and SIP level 3 is implemented in the Cisco router.

Configuring SMDS

Because SMDS is not as widely deployed as the other network technologies presented in this chapter, we will examine only one simple configuration. The tasks to complete to configure an interface for connection to an SMDS service are as follows:

- Define an interface to have SMDS encapsulation.
- Associate an IP address with this interface to be mapped to the SMDS address supplied by the carrier company.
- Define the SMDS broadcast address to be associated with the interface, so that ARP and routing broadcasts are passed between SMDS nodes as needed.
- Enable ARP and routing on the interface.

Figure 6-11 shows the Cisco IOS configuration commands that could be appropriate for the serial 0 port of router 1 in Fig. 6-9.

SMDS COMMUNICATION LAYERS	OSI LAYERS
TCP/UDP	LAYER 4
IP	LAYER 3
SIP LEVEL 3 SIP LEVEL 2	LAYER 2
SIP LEVEL 1	LAYER 1

Figure 6-10 SMDS communication layers compared to OSI

Figure 6-11 Sample router configurations for SMDS

```
!
INTERFACE SERIAL 0
IP ADDRESS 164.4.4.3 255.255.255.0
ENCAPSULATION SMDS
SMDS ADDRESS C234.5678.9070.FFFF
SMDS MULTICAST IP E654.5678.333.FFF
SMDS ENABLE-ARP
```

The following discusses the SMDS-specific commands in the configuration for Serial 0:

- Command `encapsulation smds` sets the encapsulation to SMDS for the interface. Note that although the SMDS standard allows a maximum frame size of 9188, the Cisco serial port has buffer constraints that limit it to a frame size (MTU) of 4500. If the MTU size is set to a value greater than 4500 prior to the encapsulation SMDS command, performance problems may occur.
- Command `smds address c234.5678.9010.ffff` defines the SMDS address for this interface supplied by the SMDS network vendor. All addresses must be entered in this notation, with dots separating each four digits. Individual node addresses start with the letter "c" and multicast addresses start with the letter "e."
- Command `smds multicast ip e654.5678.3333.ffff` defines the multicast address for the access group to which this interface belongs. An optional argument can be used here to associate a secondary IP address with this port and a different SMDS multicast address, so that the same port can belong to two access groups simultaneously.
- Command `smds enable-arp` enables the ARP function for SMDS address resolution across the SMDS network. The only restriction on this command is that the SMDS address must already be defined.

X.25

X.25 has never been as widely deployed in the United States as it has in Europe, and particularly in the last few years its popularity has declined. It is still an important protocol, however, and we will discuss the basic operation of the protocol and simple X.25 configurations for Cisco routers.

X.25 is a packet-switched technology that supports PVCs, SVCs, and statistical multiplexing in the same way that frame relay does. The X.25 standards also define error correction, flow control procedures, and guaranteeing the correct sequencing for delivery of packets. The X.25 specifications only really covered DTE-to-DCE communication, leaving all X.25 routing functions to be defined by vendors of X.25 equipment.

The penalty to be paid for all this seemingly good stuff in terms of reliability is performance. The acknowledgments, buffering, and retransmission that happen within the X.25 protocols add latency (especially if there are many hops between source and destination), meaning this protocol provides poor performance for carrying TCP traffic that already handles these functions. If your main interest is in networking TCP/IP protocols and transporting legacy protocols such as IPX, SNA, or NetBIOS over a TCP/IP network, it is unlikely you will deploy X.25. In such situations, X.25 is really a competing technology to TCP/IP. Bearing this in mind, in the example configurations, we will only look at how two IP nodes can communicate across an X.25 network via encapsulation of IP data within an X.25 frame for transmission over an X.25 network (termed *tunneling*). We'll also examine how to translate X.25 traffic to IP, so that a host using TCP/IP communications can communicate with an X.25 host.

X.25 Basics

The physical layer of X.25 is described by the X.21 standard, which is a 15-pin connector. X.21 *bis* was defined to utilize the same functions within a 25-pin connector. This was done to leverage the large available pool of 25-pin connectors in the marketplace. The X.21 *bis* standard specifies support of line speeds up to 48 kbps. Just as the V.35 standard only specifies speeds up to 48 kbps but is commonly run at T-1 speeds (1.544 Mbps), the X.21 *bis* standard will also work at faster speeds as long as the cables used are not too long.

The X.25 second layer 2 is the *Link Access Procedure Balanced* (LAPB), which is in many ways similar to HDLC. This protocol is responsible for data transfer between a DTE and DCE, link status reporting and synchronization, and error recovery. The LAPB protocol handles all the reliability issues previously discussed. It is worth introducing the most common layer 2 header functions, and how they fit into establishing a DTE to DCE X.25 link.

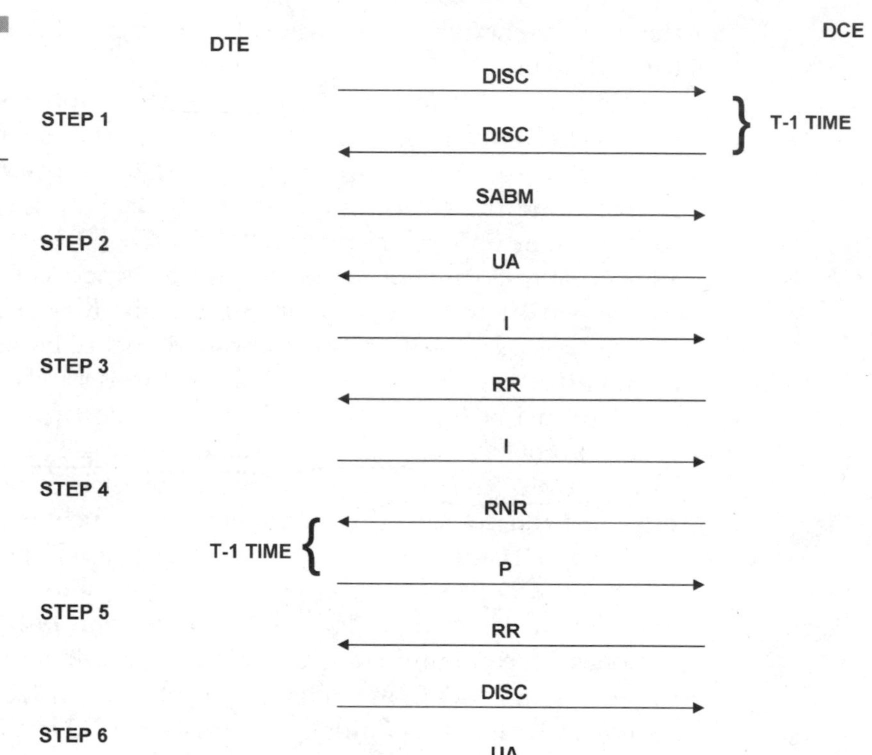

Figure 6-12 X.25 DTE-to-DCE flow control sequence

Link establishment uses unnumbered frames; numbered frames are used once the call is established and data is being transferred. The following step sequences, as shown in Fig. 6-12, can be viewed on a protocol analyzer that can decode X.25 frames. It is assumed that the link is using LAPB, rather than the older LAP protocol. LAP had more stages for establishing a call, and starts communication with a *Set Asynchronous Response Mode* (SARM) instead of a *Set Asynchronous Balanced Mode* (SABM). You need to make sure that both ends of the link are using the same protocol at this level.

1. The normal operation is for the DCE device to be sending out *DISC* (disconnect) frames at a time interval determined by its T-1 timer setting. This indicates that it is ready to receive a call.
2. The DTE device will initialize the link with one command, the SABM, which initiates the DCE sending back an Unnumbered Acknowledgment.

3. The DTE starts sending data using information frames, each of which is acknowledged by *RR frames*. RR frames are sent by the DCE and indicate that the receiver is ready for more information. If the DCE has information to send to the DTE, it can do this using the same RR frame that acknowledged receipt of DTE data. If the RR frame contains data, it is known as a *piggyback* acknowledgment.
4. If the DTE sends enough information to fill the buffers of the DCE, the DCE will send back a *Receiver Not Ready* (RNR) frame. Upon receipt of a RNR frame, the DTE will remain idle for the length of its T-1 timer, then poll the DCE to see if it is ready.
5. The DCE will respond to a poll with more RNR packets until it has space in its buffer to take more data, at which time it will send an RR frame to allow the DTE to start sending more Information frames.
6. The link is cleared by the DTE sending a DISC (disconnect frame), which is responded to by an Unnumbered Acknowledgment.

The third layer protocol in X.25 is called the *Packet Layer Procedure* (PLP) and provides the procedures for the control of virtual circuits within the X.25 network. The lower two layers have local significance, whereas the packet level has end-to-end significance, as illustrated in Fig. 6-13.

X.25 assigns *Logical Channel Numbers* (LCNs) to the multiple logical connections to a DTE that can exist over one physical link. In this respect, LCNs are similar to frame relay DLCI numbers when the frame relay interface is in point-to-point mode. LCNs do not have end-to-end significance; rather, they are only used between a specific DTE/DCE pair. This means that the same LCN number can exist in many places on an X.25 network without causing problems. In theory, an LCN can

Figure 6-13 X.25 level-three protocols have end-to-end significance

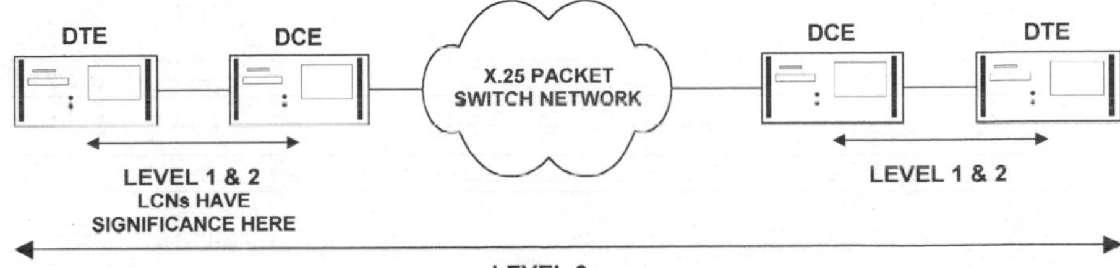

have a value between 0 and 4096; rarely, however, is there the ability or the need to configure more than 255 LCNs on one physical link. LCNs must be assigned to a DTE with some care, however. A call collision would result if both the DTE and DCE were trying to initiate calls on the same LCN. The LCN that most people refer to is actually made up of a Logical Channel Group Number and Logical Channel Number. If an X.25 network provider allocates you a 12-bit LCN, you have both LCGN and LCN. If the provider gives you a 4-bit LCGN and an 8-bit LCN, combine the two with the LCGN at the front to get a 12-digit LCN.

Figure 6-14 illustrates two hosts and a printer that have unique X.25 addresses having significance throughout the X.25 network. These addresses, known as *Network User Addresses* (NUAs), conform to the X.121 recommendation for public data networks, which specifies an address length of 14 digits, with 12 being mandatory and 2 being optional. The first four digits are known as the *data network identification number* (DNIC); the first three identify the country, while the fourth identifies the network within the country. The next eight digits are the national number, and the last two are optional subaddressing numbers allocated by the user, not the network provider.

Configuring an X.25 Network Connection

In this section we will use the three lab routers used in the frame relay example. One router will be configured as an X.25 router to emulate an X.25 network. The other two will connect as X.25 DTE devices, and will encapsulate IP traffic within X.25 to transport IP traffic over the X.25 network. This configuration is illustrated in Fig. 6-15.

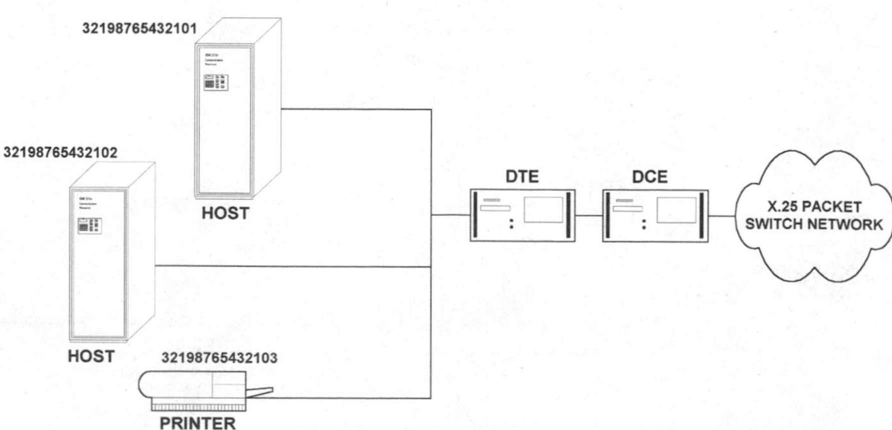

Figure 6-14 Two hosts and one printer connected to an X.25 WAN

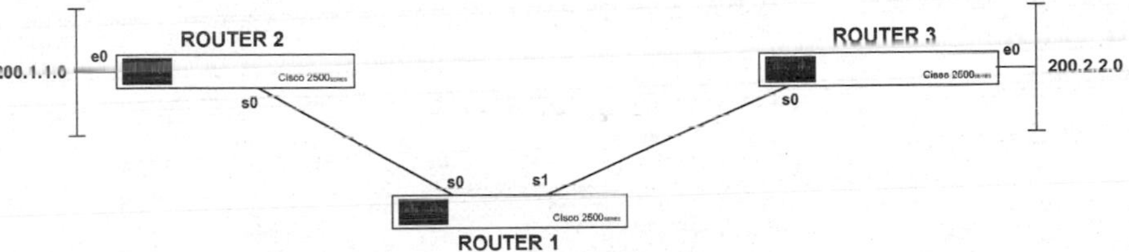

Figure 6-15 Configuration of a test X.25 network

The key configuration tasks are:

1. Enable X.25 routing on router 1 and configure it to route packets between router 2 and router 3 based on X.25 address.
2. Assign each serial interface connected via the X.25 network an IP address from the same IP network (or subnetwork) number.
3. Assign X.25 NUAs to the serial ports of router 2 and router 3.
4. Configure router 2 and router 3 for a routing protocol and enable routing protocol updates to traverse the X.25 network.

This configuration establishes between router 2 and router 3 a virtual circuit that allows IP traffic to be encapsulated within X.25, routed through the X.25 network, and delivered to the correct IP address. The configurations for these routers are shown in Fig. 6-16, and the outputs of the `show` commands to be examined are illustrated in Fig. 6-17.

Let's look at the configurations first. Router 3 and router 2 have similar configurations, so I will give a full explanation only of the configuration for the serial 0 port of router 3.

- Command `encapsulation x25` sets the frame encapsulation to X.25 in the default DTE mode. Modification to the X.25 encapsulation type can be specified with optional arguments to this command; for example, `ietf` could follow this command to specify the IETF type X.25 framing.
- Command `x25 address 21234554321` assigns this port the specified NUA. The NUA is used by the X.25 routers to route traffic from source to destination. This number normally will be assigned by the X.25 network provider.
- Command `x25 map ip 193.1.1.1 21234554321 broadcast` tells router 3 that whenever it needs to reach IP address 193.1.1.1, it will send packets across the X.25 network to NUA 2122344321. The broadcast argument enables forwarding of broadcast routing updates.

Figure 6-16
Router configurations for text X.25 network

```
Configuration for router 3
!
interface Ethernet0
ip address 200.2.2.1 255.255.255.0
!
interface Serial0
ip address 193.1.1.2 255.255.255.0
encapsulation  x25
x25 address 21234567894
x25 map ip 193.1.1.1 21234554321 broadcast
!
interface Serial1
ip address 160.4.5.1 255.255.255.0
shutdown
!
router igrp 12
network 200.2.2.0
network 193.1.1.0

!Configuration for router 2
!
interface Ethernet0
ip address 200.1.1.1 255.255.255.0
!
interface Serial0
ip address 193.1.1.1 255.255.255.0
encapsulation x25
x25 address 21234554321
x25 map ip 193.1.1.2 21234567894 broadcast
!
interface Serial1
ip address 160.4.5.2 255.255.255.0
shutdown
clockrate 64000
!
router igrp 12
network 200.1.1.0
network 193.1.1.0
!
Configuration for router 1
!
x25 routing
!
interface Ethernet0
ip address 200.1.1.1 255.255.255.0
shutdown
!
interface Serial0
no ip address
encapsulation x25 dce
clockrate 19200
!
interface Serial1
no ip address
encapsulation x25 dce
clockrate 19200
!
x25 route 21234554321 interface Serial0
x25 route 21234567894 interface Serial1
!
```

The rest of this configuration should be self-explanatory by now. Router 1 is emulating a public X.25 network by performing routing based on X.25 NUAs. The pertinent commands that configure X.25 on router 1 are explained below:

- Command `x25 routing` globally enables routing based on X.25 NUA on the router.
- Command `encapsulation x25 dce` configures the serial ports to be X.25 DCE devices. At the physical level, the cable end plugged into the serial port configures the serial port to be a Physical layer DCE, as shown by the `show controllers serial 0` command. X.25 requires an X.25 assignment of DTE and DCE also. Clearly, a DTE needs to connect to a DCE, because leaving both connected ports as the default DTE would not enable the line protocol to come up. You can view the X.25 DTE/DCE assignment with the `show interface serial 0` command, as shown in Fig. 6-17.
- Command `x25 route 21234554321 interface serial 0` tells the router to send traffic destined for this NUA (21234554321) out of port Serial 0. Configuration commands such as these are used to build the X.25 routing table, as shown by the `show x25 route` command in Fig. 6-17.

The result of this configuration is that from router 2, you can enter the command `ping 200.2.2.1` and successfully ping the Ethernet port of router 3 across the X.25 network. Note that IGRP updates the routing tables of all IP enabled routers in this network.

Cisco routers also can perform protocol translation, and in this case we will look at translating between IP and X.25. This feature is useful if a third party provides an X.25 connection and sends you X.25-encapsulated data, but you want to deliver it to a host that uses only the TCP/IP communications protocol suite. This can be achieved by connecting a cisco router between the TCP/IP and X.25 hosts. We configure one port to establish an X.25 connection with the X.25 network and a separate port to communicate using IP. The router is then enabled to route both IP and X.25 traffic. The key part to the configuration is to tell the router to translate between IP and X.25.

Let's say that an IP host needs to initiate communications with an X.25 host with an NUA of 1234567890. What we do is associate the IP address 195.1.1.1 with the X.25 address 1234567890 within the translation router. Then if the IP host needs to send data to a machine it thinks is at

Figure 6-17 The *show* commands for the test X.25 network

Show commands for router 1

```
router1#sho x25 route
Number     X.121          CUD  Forward To
 1    21234554321              Serial0, 1 uses
 2    21234567894              Serial1, 0 uses

router1#sho x25 vc
SVC 1024, State: D1, Interface: Serial1
  Started 1:13:09, last input 0:00:25, output 0:00:07
  Connects 21234567894  21234554321 to Serial0 VC 1
  Window size input: 2, output: 2
  Packet size input: 128, output: 128
  PS: 5 PR: 5 ACK: 5 Remote PR: 4 RCNT: 0 RNR: FALSE
  Retransmits: 0 Timer (secs): 0 Reassembly (bytes): 0
  Held Fragments/Packets: 0/0
  Bytes 3076/3076 Packets 61/61 Resets 0/0 RNRs 0/0 REJs 0/0 INTs 0/0

SVC 1, State: D1, Interface: Serial0
  Started 1:13:22, last input 0:00:20, output 0:00:38
  Connects 21234567894  21234554321 from Serial1 VC 1024
  Window size input: 2, output: 2
  Packet size input: 128, output: 128
  PS: 5 PR: 5 ACK: 4 Remote PR: 5 RCNT: 1 RNR: FALSE
  Retransmits: 0 Timer (secs): 0 Reassembly (bytes): 0
  Held Fragments/Packets: 0/0
  Bytes 3076/3076 Packets 61/61 Resets 0/0 RNRs 0/0 REJs 0/0 INTs 0/0
```

Show commands for router 2

```
router2>show x25 vc
SVC 1, State: D1, Interface: Serial0
  Started 1:17:03, last input 0:00:04, output 0:00:05
  Connects 21234567894
    ip 193.1.1.2
  cisco cud pid, no Tx data PID
  Window size input: 2, output: 2
  Packet size input: 128, output: 128
  PS: 0 PR: 0 ACK: 7 Remote PR: 0 RCNT: 1 RNR: FALSE
  Retransmits: 0 Timer (secs): 0 Reassembly (bytes): 0
  Held Fragments/Packets: 0/0
  Bytes 3214/3214 Packets 64/64 Resets 0/0 RNRs 0/0 REJs 0/0 INTs 0/0

router2>sho x25 map
Serial0: X.121 21234567894  ip 193.1.1.2
  PERMANENT, BROADCAST, 1 VC: 1*
```

Show command for router 3

```
router3#show x25 vc
SVC 1024, State: D1, Interface: Serial0
  Started 1:19:38, last input 0:00:08, output 0:01:16
  Connects 21234554321
    ip 193.1.1.1
```

Figure 6-17
Continued

```
  cisco cud pid, no Tx data PID
  Window size input: 2, output: 2
  Packet size input: 128, output: 128
  PS: 1 PR: 2 ACK: 1 Remote PR: 1 RCNT: 1 RNR: FALSE
  Retransmits: 0 Timer (secs): 0 Reassembly (bytes): 0
  Held Fragments/Packets: 0/0
  Bytes 3260/3306 Packets 65/66 Resets 0/0 RNRs 0/0 REJs 0/0 INTs 0/0

router3#show x25 map
Serial0: X.121 21234554321  ip 193.1.1.1
  PERMANENT, BROADCAST, 1 VC: 1024*

router3#sho int s0
Serial0 is up, line protocol is up
  Hardware is HD64570
  Internet address is 193.1.1.2 255.255.255.0
  MTU 1500 bytes, BW 1544 Kbit, DLY 20000 usec, rely 255/255, load 1/255
  Encapsulation X25, loopback not set
  LAPB DTE, modulo 8, k 7, N1 12056, N2 20
    T1 3000, interface outage (partial T3) 0, T4 0
    State CONNECT, VS 3, VR 3, Remote VR 3, Retransmissions 0
    Queues: U/S frames 0, I frames 0, unack. 0, retx 0
    IFRAMEs 91/91 RNRs 0/0 REJs 0/0 SABM/Es 179/1 FRMRs 0/0 DISCs 0/0
  X25 DTE, address 21234567894, state R1, modulo 8, timer 0
    Defaults: cisco encapsulation, idle 0, nvc 1
    input/output window sizes 2/2, packet sizes 128/128
    Timers: T20 180, T21 200, T22 180, T23 180, TH 0
    Channels: Incoming-only none, Two-way 1-1024, Outgoing-only none
    RESTARTs 1/1 CALLs 1+0/0+0/0+0 DIAGs 0/0
  Last input 0:00:54, output 0:00:54, output hang never
  Last clearing of "show interface" counters never
  Output queue 0/40, 0 drops; input queue 0/75, 0 drops
  5 minute input rate 0 bits/sec, 0 packets/sec
  5 minute output rate 0 bits/sec, 0 packets/sec
    2293 packets input, 45539 bytes, 0 no buffer
    Received 0 broadcasts, 0 runts, 0 giants
    208 input errors, 1 CRC, 0 frame, 3 overrun, 10 ignored, 1 abort
    2254 packets output, 43027 bytes, 0 underruns
    0 output errors, 0 collisions, 60 interface resets, 0 restarts
    0 output buffer failures, 0 output buffers swapped out
    156 carrier transitions
    DCD=up DSR=up DTR=up RTS=up CTS=up
```

IP address 195.1.1.1, the translation router will establish an IP connection to the IP host and pretend to be 195.1.1.1, then establish an X.25 session to the X.25 host and deliver the message to it in X.25 format. The configuration to do this is given in Fig. 6-18 and the X.25 command is explained fully as follows.

- Command `x25 routing` enables the router to perform routing based on X.25 address.
- Command `translate tcp 195.1.1.1 binary stream x25 1234567890` takes packets destined for IP address 195.1.1.1, takes the data out of them, repackages this data in X.25, and then sends the translated packets to host 1234567890.
- Command `x25 route 1234567890 serial0` tells the router which interface to use to get to the X.25 address 1234567890.

It is necessary to give the serial port of router 1 in Fig. 6-18 an IP address in the same network as the IP address that is being translated so that the router accepts the packet prior to it being translated.

Figure 6-18 Network configuration for X.25–IP translation

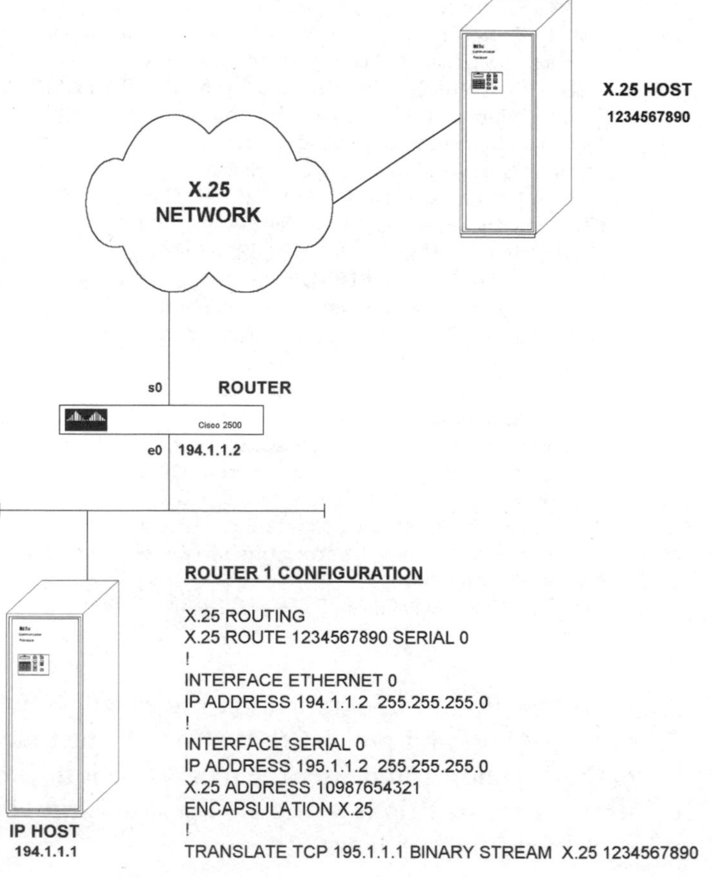
X.25 HOST
1234567890
X.25
NETWORK
s0
ROUTER
Cisco 2500
e0
194.1.1.2
ROUTER 1 CONFIGURATION
X.25 ROUTING
X.25 ROUTE 1234567890 SERIAL 0
!
INTERFACE ETHERNET 0
IP ADDRESS 194.1.1.2 255.255.255.0
!
INTERFACE SERIAL 0
IP ADDRESS 195.1.1.2 255.255.255.0
X.25 ADDRESS 10987654321
ENCAPSULATION X.25
!
TRANSLATE TCP 195.1.1.1 BINARY STREAM X.25 1234567890
IP HOST
194.1.1.1

Viewing X.25 Connection Status

We will now examine the `show` commands illustrated in Fig. 6-17. The first command, `show x25 route` shows the X.25 routing table for router 1. This display numbers each entry starting at 1 in the first column, then associates each X.121 address (otherwise referred to as the NUA) with the appropriate serial interface. This display states, for example, that the X.121 address 21234554321 can be reached via port Serial 0.

The `show x25 vc` command shows information about the active virtual circuits on this router. In this case, two SVCs have been established, one with ID 1024 and one with ID 1. The normal state for this type of connection is as shown, D1. This command is useful for seeing statistics on the general status of the virtual circuit, such as the number of Receiver Not Ready and *Frame Reject* (REJ) packets counted.

The `show x25 map` command shows any X.25 mappings defined for the router. In this case, router 2 has the Serial 0 port mapped for the X.121 address 212234567894, for IP address 193.1.1.2. This map is identified as a permanent mapping, meaning that it was configured with the X.25 `map interface` command and will forward broadcast datagrams destined for the IP host.

The `show interface serial 0` command shows useful summary information on the link. Primarily this command shows whether the port is up (physical connection is okay) and if the protocol is up (the line is synchronized). Beyond that, the key elements of the display are as follows:

- The `LAPB DTE` identifies this serial port as a DTE configuration, which will work only if the serial port of the corresponding device to which it is connected has a LAPB DCE configuration.
- The `modulo 8` indicates that this interface is not using extended addressing. If it were using extended addressing, this entry would show `modulo 128`. If needed, this parameter will be defined by the X.25 network provider.
- The `N1 12056` indicates the maximum layer 2 frame size. Under the X.25 DTE section, the packet size (at the X.25 layer three level) is given as 128.
- The `N2 20` indicates that the interface will allow 20 retries before timing out.

- The `T1 3000` indicates the T1 timer has a value of 3 seconds. When a command frame is sent, the sender will start this T1 timer. The transmitter will wait for the T1 timer to expire before it receives an acknowledgment of the command frame. If this timer expires without acknowledgment, the sender polls its destination to demand an immediate response. If a response is received, the unacknowledged packet is resent; if there is no response, the link is reset.
- The `X25 DTE` entry shows the X.121 address and normal operational state of the interface, which is R1.
- The `Input/Output window size` defines the number of packets that may be transmitted before an acknowledgment is received. This value can vary between 1 and 7, with a default of 2.

It is important that all these values match between the X.25 DTE and DCE devices. The following discusses how these values can be modified, if necessary.

Customizing X.25 Parameters

The first customization we will look at is assigning a range of numbers to be used by each type of virtual circuit. To recap, there are PVCs and SVCs, and communication between a DTE and DCE needs a unique virtual circuit number for each direction of communication. Between any DTE/DCE pair, the assignable values are from 1 to 4095. In the `show x25 vc` command output of Fig. 6-17, you can see that on router 1, two SVCs are active, one with LCN 1024 and one with LCN 1. SVC 1024 is associated with getting to router 3 and SVC 1 is associated with getting to router 2. These are two-way SVCs, taking the default values for the high and low LCN values. If two more SVCs were defined on this link, they would take the values 1023 and 2.

An X.25 network vendor may decide to allocate specific LCN ranges for different types of PVCs, and if this deviates from the default, you will have to alter your ranges. SVCs can be incoming, two-way, or outgoing, and a value can be assigned for the low and high value in each type's range by using the following commands in interface configuration mode:

- `x25 lic` *value* Defines the low incoming circuit number.
- `x25 hic` *value* Defines the high incoming circuit number.
- `x25 ltc` *value* Defines the low two-way circuit number.
- `x25 htc` *value* Defines the high two-way circuit number.

- `x25 loc` *value* Defines the low outgoing circuit number.
- `x25 hoc` *value* Defines the high outgoing circuit number.
- `x25 pvc` *value* Defines the PVC circuit number.

Note in the preceding commands that the word *value* is substituted with the desired circuit number for that command. If you have to specify circuit number ranges explicitly, you must adhere to the following numbering scheme:

- PVCs must have the lowest range.
- The next highest range is assigned to the incoming calls.
- The next highest range is assigned to the two-way calls.
- The highest range is assigned to the outgoing calls.

X.25 packet sizes also may be customized for both incoming and outgoing packets on an interface. The packet sizes may be changed with the following commands in interface configuration mode:

- `x25 ips` *bytes* To specify the input packet size in bytes.
- `x25 ops` *bytes* To specify the output packet size in bytes.

X.25 uses a windowing mechanism with a default window size of 2. With reliable links, this default value can be increased throughout the network to improve performance. This is achieved with the following commands:

- `x25 win` *value* The *value* defines the number of packets that can be received without an acknowledgment.
- `X25 wout` *value* The *value* defines the number of packets that can be sent without an acknowledgment.

Finally, as previously mentioned, the modulo can be regular (modulo 8), which allows virtual circuit window sizes up to 7, or enhanced (modulo 128), which allows window sizes up to 127 packets. This can be changed with the following command in interface configuration mode.

- `X25 modulo value` The *value* is either 8 or 128.

X.25 is rarely implemented in a private network these days; straight TCP/IP is far more popular. LAPB, however, does retain some popularity even when a TCP/IP network is implemented. Serial links typically use Cisco's default encapsulation of the Cisco proprietary HDLC. This is an efficient protocol but lacks error recovery. If a network link is experiencing noise interference and is carrying large amounts of UDP data, changing the encapsulation in the link from the default HDLC to LAPB will provide error recovery at the link layer, where before there was none.

Point-to-Point Protocols

In this section we look briefly at the older *Serial Line Interface Protocol* (SLIP), the newer *Point-to-Point Protocol* (PPP) that largely replaced it, and give an overview of HDLC. These protocols all provide connectivity in point-to-point connections; they do not provide multipoint communication, as does frame relay, or full routing functionality, as does X.25.

SLIP Communications

SLIP, as its name suggests, supports point-to-point communication for IP only. It was the first point-to-point protocol to do so for asynchronous connections and still has widespread support from many Unix vendors. The SLIP frame is very simple: There is no header, no error checking, and no option to define a protocol. (It is always assumed that IP is the higher-layer protocol.) SLIP is mainly used for asynchronous dial-up connections. Even for this limited application, SLIP is generally found wanting these days; there is no authentication process available, for example, which is a common requirement for security-minded organizations implementing a dial-up facility.

SLIP works only on asynchronous lines, and does not support address negotiation as part of the link startup procedure. The only time you are likely to need to use SLIP is when connecting to a third party's Unix machine via dial-up. Any new dial-up facilities being implemented should use PPP. In this instance, you will be provided with an IP address by the third-party administrator to use for the dial-up connection. The following is a simple configuration for an asynchronous port using SLIP:

```
Interface Async 1
encapsulation slip
ip address 193.1.1.1 255.255.255.0
```

This configuration may need to be enhanced with modifications to default hold queue lengths, buffers, and packet switching mode; we will address these issues in the discussion of PPP.

PPP Communications

PPP is the more modern point-to-point protocol; key features are that it supports the simultaneous running of multiple protocols over one link, synchronous as well as asynchronous communications, dynamic address assignment, and authentication. PPP is a layer 2 (Data Link) protocol; there is, however, a whole link negotiation process that must be completed before two nodes can exchange information at the Data Link level. Let's examine this negotiation process as a set of phases.

The first phase comprises exchange of Link Control Protocol packets. This is like an initial introduction. The two ends agree on the general characteristics of the communication that is about to take place, such as the use of compression or the maximum frame size. An optional phase checks the line quality to see if it can be used to bring up the Network layer protocols. Once the link configuration is agreed upon, an optional authentication process may take place, via either the PAP or CHAP protocol.

The *Password Authentication Protocol* (PAP) was the first authentication protocol deployed for PPP. To explain the way it works, imagine you have a remote PC using a dial connection to connect to a central router. In this setup, you configure a PAP username and password in the remote PC, which matches a username and password configured in the central router. When the remote PC dials the central router, it will start sending its PAP username and password repeatedly until it either is granted a connection, or the connection is terminated. This is a step up from having no authentication, but is open to a break-in method known as *modem playback*. Using this method, an intruder hooks into the telephone line, records the modem negotiation transmissions, and plays them back later. By doing this method, the intruder has recorded the username and password for future use.

The *Challenge Handshake Authentication Protocol* (CHAP) is a stronger authentication process. With CHAP, the remote PC will initiate a connection, negotiate the LCP parameters, and then be met with a "challenge" from the central router. The challenge comes in the form of an encryption key that is unique for every connection made. The remote PC then will use the encryption key to encode its username and password before submitting it to the central router. When the central router receives the encrypted username and password, it will decrypt them using the key sent for that connection and compare them against the valid usernames and passwords for which it is configured. The connection is either authenticated and progresses, or is terminated at this stage.

This method defeats modem playback because the encryption key is different each time; for every connection, it produces a different set of encrypted characters for exchange between remote PC and central router. Within CHAP, there are several different algorithms that may be used for encryption, the most popular being the *MD5 algorithm*. CHAP's authentication processes typically take place only at link startup time, but the specification allows for this challenge to be issued repeatedly during the lifetime of the connection. Implementation of this feature is up to individual vendors.

Once authentication is complete, the next stage involves defining the particular Network Control Protocols to be encapsulated within PPP. The only choices generally available in popular PC PPP stack implementations are *IPCP*, for encapsulating IP traffic, and *IPXCP* for encapsulating IPX traffic; however, a PPP session can support both simultaneously. Each NCP protocol will negotiate the specifics of communication for its Network layer protocol. Once the NCP negotiations are complete, the two endpoints can exchange data at the Data Link (layer 2) level for each of the Network (layer 3) protocols configured. Now that we know what PPP does, let's take a brief look at its frame format, as illustrated in Fig. 6-19.

This frame contains both useful and redundant fields. The redundant fields are the address and control fields, which always carry the same entries. The *address field* contains an all-ones byte, the layer 2 broadcast address. (Because PPP only connects two entities together, specific layer 2 addressing is not necessary and individual layer 2 addresses are not assigned.) The *control field* always contains the binary value 00000011, which defines the type of communication used. The useful fields are the *flag*, to indicate the start of a frame, the *protocol field*, which identifies the layer 3 protocol encapsulated in the frame, and the *Frame Check Sequence* to ensure no errors were introduced into the frame during transmission.

Asynchronous PPP Configurations. There is much to be said for the configuration of efficient asynchronous communications, some of which can be considered more art than science. We will examine the most common commands and then consider how these commands can be put together in a sample configuration.

FLAG	ADDRESS	CONTROL	PROTOCOL	DATA	FCS

Figure 6-19
The PPP frame format

The first command, as always when specifying a link layer protocol, is to define the encapsulation for the chosen interface. This is achieved with the following commands:

```
Router1(config)#interface async 1
Router1(config-int)#encapsulation ppp
```

If we are specifying PPP encapsulation, this implies that the asynchronous port will be used for a network connection. We therefore should place the port in dedicated mode. The mode choice for an async port is either dedicated or interactive. Placing the port in interactive mode presents the user with a command prompt and allows the user to manually input user name, passwords, and other connection-related information. For security reasons, I prefer to keep the async mode as dedicated, which is achieved with the following command:

```
Router1(config-int)#async mode dedicated
```

Next you will want to enable *Van Jacobsen header compression.* In reality, compressing headers makes comparatively little difference in link bandwidth consumed by the protocol, but with asynchronous communications you should do everything possible to improve throughput. Header compression is turned on by default, but it does not hurt to enable it in case it had been previously disabled. This is achieved in interface configuration mode:

```
Router1(config-int)#ip tcp header-compression on
```

The next issue is to assign IP addresses to the ports and to computers connecting to those ports. You have a choice, either to hard-code IP addresses into computers connecting to the async ports, or have the address assigned to the computer when it connects to the async port. If you choose the first option, you must ensure that the IP address assigned to the computer dialing in is in the same subnet as the address range assigned to the async ports themselves.

My preference is to have the IP address assigned to the computer by the async port upon connection. This makes life simpler and does not restrict a computer to being able to dial in to only one location. To have the async interface assign an IP address to a computer when it connects, three separate configurations need to take place. First the async port must be given an unnumbered address. (IP unnumbered is covered more fully in Chap. 7.) Next, the async port must be configured to deliver a specific IP address to the connecting computer. Finally, the connecting computer must have no IP address configured. The two entries in the router port configuration, to define IP unnumbered and 193.1.1.1 as the address assigned to a connecting computer, are as follows:

```
Router1(config)#interface async1
Router1(config-int)#ip unnumbered ethernet 0
Router1(config-int)#async default ip address 193.1.1.1
```

Next we discuss *Asynchronous Control Character Maps* (ACCMs). Flow control between asynchronous devices can either be of the hardware or the software variety. *Hardware flow control* relies on pin signaling, such as the state of the Data Set Ready (DSR) or Data Terminal Ready (DTR) pins to stop and start transmission. *Software flow control* uses special characters transmitted between asynchronous devices to stop and start transmission. When relying on characters transmitted between devices to signal modem actions, there is always a danger that strings within the data transmitted will match these special command strings and be inappropriately interpreted by the modems.

An ACCM can be configured to tell the port to ignore specified control characters within the data stream. The value of ACCM that tells an async port to ignore XON/XOFF (software flow control) characters in the data transmitted is A0000 in hexadecimal. This is the default value; if a TCP stack on the computer connecting to the async port does not support ACCM negotiation, however, the port will be forced to use an ACCM of FFFFFFFF. In this case, it is useful to manually set the ACCM with the following command:

```
Router1(config-int)#ppp accm match 000a0000
```

Next, we want to enable CHAP authentication on the link. This is done in two stages; first the CHAP user name and password are set in global configuration, then CHAP is enabled on the desired interface. This is achieved through the following commands:

```
Router1(config)#username chris password lewis
Router1(config)#interface async 1
Router1(config-int)#ppp authentication chap
```

If an asynchronous router is being used to route traffic from a LAN to a dial-up or other slow link, it can be desirable to slow down the speed at which packets are switched from one interface to another. If packets are switched from an Ethernet port running at 10 Mbps directly to an async port running at 19.2 kbps, the async port can quickly get overwhelmed. By entering the `no ip route-cache` command as shown below, the packets are switched at a slower speed. Effectively, this command, entered for each async interface in use, stops the router from caching destination addresses and forces a table lookup every time a packet needs to be routed.

```
Router1(config-int)#no ip route-cache
```

One aspect of asynchronous communication that causes endless confusion is the DTE rate configured for a port and its meaning in terms of data throughput on an async line. The receive and transmit DTE rate of async port 1 is set by the following commands, to 38,400 bits per second.

```
Router1(config)#line 1
Router1(config-line)#rxpseed 38400
Router1(config-line)#txspeed 38400
```

In asynchronous communications, the DTE rate as defined above dictates the speed at which each packet is sent from the router port to the modem. If the modem can only transfer data across a dial-up link at 14.4 kbps, it will use its flow control procedures to stop more packets from coming out of the router port than it can safely transfer across the link. Thus, over the course of 10 or 20 seconds, the amount of data transferred between the router port and the modem port will not be greater than an average of 14.4 kbps; however, each packet that the router does transmit will be received at a speed of 38.4 kbps from the device sending async characters.

These days most modems employ V.42*bis* compression, which will allow a modem to sustain effective throughputs that are higher than the modem-to-modem connection rate. V.42 compression is generally quoted at providing up to four times the data throughput that the connection rate would suggest. For example, with four-to-one compression, a 14.4 kbps link will support 57.6 kbps throughput. The effective compression ratio is determined by how compressible the data being transported is. Compressible data includes things such as ASCII text, although binary file transfers are not normally very compressible.

In brief, V.42*bis* compression looks for common sequences of bits and the modems agree to assign special characters to represent these often-repeated character sequences. By transmitting a special character, the modem may have to transfer only 1 byte of data, rather than the 4 bytes that both modems know it represents. Once a receiving modem receives a special character, it will send out the full associated character string on its DTE port.

Many newcomers to the world of asynchronous communications ask why, even if the DTE rate is set to 115,200 bps, communications across an async link are so slow, often slower than an ISDN link operating at 64 kbps. The answer is that you very rarely get sustained throughput of 115,200 on an async link. While each packet may be transferred between the router and modem at 115,200 bps, the modem flow control will stop the router port from transmitting continuously at that speed.

Chapter 8 gets into troubleshooting serial communication problems in more depth, but two configuration commands that help asynchronous communications are worth considering here. The first is the `hold-queue` command.

The hold queue of each interface has a specified size, which is the number of packets waiting to be transmitted that it can hold before the interface starts dropping packets. This value can be set for both incoming and outgoing packets. For asynchronous interfaces, it is worthwhile increasing the sizes of both the incoming and outgoing hold queues, which in the following example increases both values to 90.

```
Router1(config-int)#hold-queue 90 in
Router1(config-int)#hold-queue 90 out
```

If an interface (Async 1, for example) is exceeding its hold queue limits, an increased number of drops will be seen in the `show interface async 1` command. Drops also can increase if the router buffers for given packet sizes are overflowing. The second command we will overview here is the one that sets the number of packet buffers available in the router. To view the state of packet buffer use, enter the `show buffers` command. The output will show you the number of small, medium, large, very large, and huge buffers used and available, and the number of occasions on which buffers of a type were needed but a packet was dropped because none were available (shown as failures).

A point to note is that packets can be dropped even if the maximum number of buffers has not been exceeded. This phenomenon occurs if several packets of one particular size arrive at the router very quickly and the router cannot create buffers fast enough. If you suspect this may be happening, you can set the number of buffers of a given size to be permanently available. The following is an extract from a router configuration that has had its medium-size buffer allocation altered from the default.

```
!
buffers medium initial 40
buffers medium min-free 20
buffers medium permanent 50
buffers medium max-free 40
```

The first entry defines the number of temporary buffers that are to be available after a reload, which is useful for high-traffic environments. The second statement forces the router to try to always have 20 medium buffers free, and if a traffic surge reduces the number of free medium buffers to below 20, the router automatically will try to create more. The third entry defines 60 permanent buffers, which once created are not retrieved by the IOS for reuse of their memory allocation. Finally, the `max-free 40` entry ensures that memory is not wasted on unused buffers by returning memory used by more than 40 free medium buffers to the router's general memory pool.

Synchronous PPP Configurations. If a WAN is being built based on point-to-point links between router serial ports, the popular choices for the link-level encapsulation are the default Cisco version of HDLC and PPP operating in synchronous mode. PPP is a more modern protocol and offers better link-level authentication than Cisco's HDLC, but there is one compelling reason to build your network based on the Cisco HDLC. Consider Fig. 6-20.

Suppose the line protocol on the connected Serial 0 ports will not come up, but everything looks good with the interface configurations, so you want to test the line connecting the two CSU/DSU devices. A good way to start troubleshooting this situation is to first put CSU/DSU 1 in loopback and see if the line protocol on the Serial 0 interface of router 1 comes up, as shown by the `show interface serial 0` command. If this is okay, take CSU/DSU 1 out of loopback and put CSU/DSU 2 in loopback, then see if the Serial 0 interface comes up as a result. This is a simple yet powerful technique for locating a problem in a communication system, and works well if the encapsulation for both Serial 0 interfaces is set to default Cisco HDLC. With PPP encapsulation, an interface protocol will not reach an *up* state when connected to a

Figure 6-20 Router serial interfaces connected via CSU/DSU devices

CSU/DSU in loopback; you therefore do not have this type of troubleshooting as an option.

A situation in which you really do need to use synchronous PPP is one in which you decide to use the Cisco 1000 LAN Extender product. This product line was designed to link remote offices to a central location at low cost and with low maintenance. These LAN extenders are not real routers; they are layer 2 bridge devices. Figure 6-21 illustrates a typical configuration for a low-cost remote location installation. We will take some time now to explore configuring one of these devices.

In this configuration, the Cisco 1001 has two interfaces connected, a V.35 connector to the CSU/DSU and an Ethernet connection to the local PC. There is no configuration in the 1001; all configuration is kept in the central router, which makes installation and remote support of this device simple enough that even nontechnical staff can connect the device as needed. There are two parts to the configuration of the central router interface, one for the router 1 serial interface and one for the virtual LAN extender, which is configured as a LEX interface on router 1. The Serial 0 interface configuration for router 1 in Fig. 6-21 is given as follows:

```
!
interface serial 0
no ip address
encapsulation ppp
!
```

The configuration for the LEX port that also exists on router 1 is as follows:

```
!
interface lex 0
ip address 195.1.1.1 255.255.255.0
lex burned-in-address 0000.0c32.8165
!
```

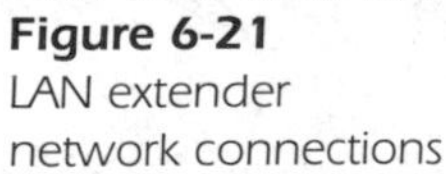

Figure 6-21
LAN extender network connections

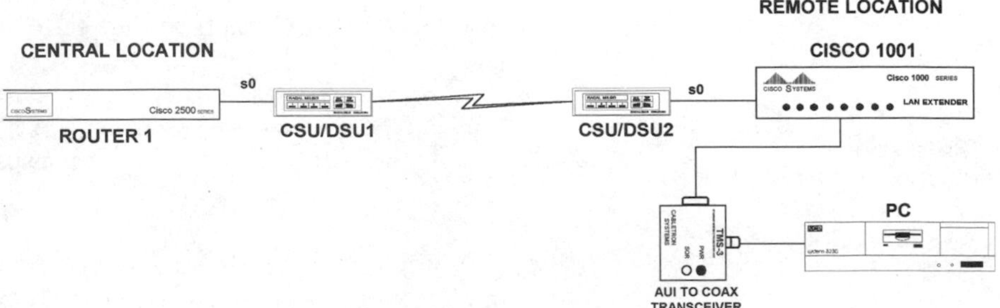

The `lex burned-in-address` is the MAC address of the Cisco 1001 being installed. When a LAN extender is installed, all the workstations connected to it are given addresses on the same subnet as the LEX port. With the configuration above, the PC in Fig. 6-21 would be addressed 195.1.1.2, while subsequent PCs connected to the 1001 device LAN would have addresses 195.1.1.3, 195.1.1.4, and so forth.

As you can see, all configuration that makes the connection unique is under the LEX configuration. This means that you can connect a remote LAN extender to any serial port that has no IP address and PPP encapsulation configuration. When a LEX first connects to the central router, it will try to bind to whatever port to which it is connected. To see the status of a LEX connection, issue the command `show interface LEX 0`, which will tell you what port the LEX is bound to, the LEX MAC address, its IP address, and the Ethernet encapsulation type. Once you know to what port the LEX is bound, you can use the `show interface serial 0` command (assuming the LEX is bound to Serial 0) to see the number of interface resets, carrier transitions, and CSU/DSU signals.

The price to pay for this relatively cheap and simple way of connecting remote devices is in the area of advanced troubleshooting information. To report problems, the LEX relies upon a set of front panel lights. Under normal conditions, these lights flicker to indicate traffic passing over the link. During error conditions, the lights blink solidly a number of times. The number of times the lights blink indicates the nature of the problem. It can be a challenge to get nontechnical users to notice the difference between a flicker and a solid blink and to correctly count the number of blinks generated by the LEX. The errors reported by the front panel lights are as follows:

- One blink — The serial link is down.
- Two blinks — No clock received from CSU/DSU.
- Three blinks — Excessive CRC errors on the line.
- Four blinks — Noisy line.
- Five blinks — CSU/DSU in loopback.
- Six blinks — PPP link negotiation failed.

SDLC

Many of the protocols we have discussed are based on the *High-level Data Link Control* protocol (HDLC) format, which is related to IBM's

Synchronous Data Link Control (SDLC). It is worth briefly looking at how these protocols work and at their interrelationships.

SDLC was designed for serial link communications in SNA networks in the 1970s and is in use for that purpose today. SDLC is a bit-oriented protocol; previously, protocols like IBM's BiSync and DEC's DDCMP were byte-oriented. Bit-oriented protocols offer more flexibility, are more efficient, and have now completely replaced byte-oriented protocols for new product development. Once IBM had written SDLC, it was used as a basis for further development by several standards bodies to produce SDLC variants, which are listed as follows:

- The ISO based its development of the HDLC protocol on SDLC.
- LAPB was created by the CCITT (now called the ITU, the International Telecommunications Union), which used HDLC as its starting point.
- The IEEE 802.2 used HDLC as a base for developing its link-level protocols for the LAN environment.

It is worth noting that the IBM *QLLC* protocol can be implemented at the Data Link layer when transporting SNA data over X.25 networks. In this scenario, QLLC and X.25 replace SDLC in the SNA protocol stack.

An IBM protocol, SDLC is geared toward everything being controlled by a central processor. SDLC defines a primary end and a secondary end for communications, with the primary end establishing and clearing links and polling the secondary ends to see if they want to communicate with the primary. An SDLC primary can communicate with one or more secondary devices via a point-to-point, multipoint (star), or loop (ring) topology. The SDLC frame format is shown in Fig. 6-22. The HDLC, LAPB, and 802.2 variants of SDLC do not define primary and secondary devices in communication.

SDLC frames are either *Information* frames for carrying user data and higher layer protocol information, *Supervisory* for status reporting, or *Unnumbered* for initializing an SDLC secondary.

HDLC is closely related to SDLC, but instead of one transfer mode, HDLC supports three. HDLC's *Normal Response Mode* is how SDLC oper-

Figure 6-22
SDLC frame format

FLAG	ADDRESS	CONTROL	DATA	FCS	FLAG

ates, wherein a secondary cannot communicate until the primary gives it permission. The HDLC *Asynchronous Response Mode* allows a secondary to initiate communication, which is the method used by the X.25 LAP protocol. HDLC also supports *Asynchronous Balanced Mode,* which is used by the X.25 LAPB protocol and allows any node to communicate with any other without permission from a primary.

LAPB operates only in Asynchronous Balanced Mode, allowing either the DTE or DCE device to initiate calls. The device that initiates calls becomes the primary for the duration of that call.

The IEEE 802.2 committee split the ISO Data Link layer in two, the upper half of which is the *Logical Link Control* (LLC) sublayer, and the lower half being the *Media Access Control* (MAC) sublayer. The 802.2 LLC layer interfaces with layer 3 protocols via *Service Access Points* (SAPs) and different LAN media, such as 802.3 and 802.5 implemented at the MAC layer. IEEE 802.2 has a similar frame format to SDLC.

ISDN

ISDN stands for *Integrated Services Digital Network;* it is a synchronous dial-up service offered by most local telephone companies these days. Unlike many of the other networking technologies we have examined, ISDN is not a packet switching technology; rather, it is a circuit-switched technology, similar to the plain old telephone service (POTS). My recommendation when implementing ISDN for a single PC is to not use one of the devices that connect to the serial COM*x* port on a PC. They may be easy to set up, but you will not get the full benefits of ISDN communications. These devices have to use asynchronous communications to exchange data with the PC serial port. You will get better performance if you connect ISDN synchronously all the way to your PC, as the serial port circuitry is not as efficient as a LAN card at getting data on and off your PC's bus.

Cisco offers a standard solution for this with the 1000-series LAN extenders. The 1004 LAN extender will take an ISDN BRI circuit in one side and an RJ-45 connector for Ethernet connectivity in the other side. If you then use a crossover RJ-45 cable, a twisted-pair Ethernet card in the PC can be connected directly to the Cisco 1004. This is shown in Fig. 6-23. In fact, the configuration shown in Fig. 6-23 could support an additional 22 remote PCs establishing ISDN connections simultaneously through ISDN to the one PRI connection.

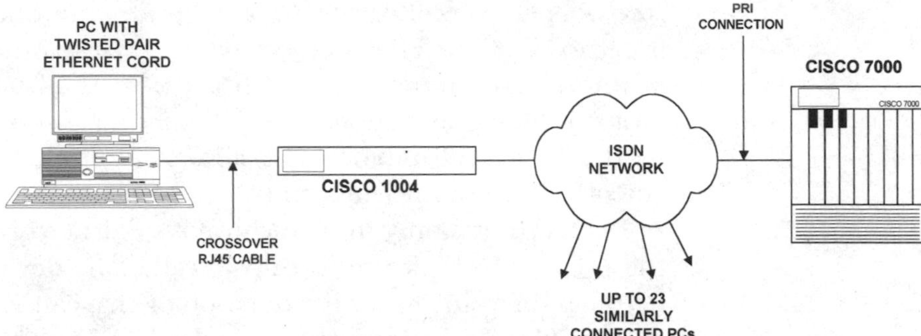

Figure 6-23 Communicating synchronously from a remote PC to a router via ISDN

ISDN Terminology. With ISDN there is a slew of new terms that might seem daunting at first; in reality they are quite simple, so let's define them first.

Basic Rate ISDN (BRI). A BRI consists of two B channels and one D channel. The B channels each have 64 kbps capacity, with the D channel being used for call signaling and having 16 kbps capacity. The two B (known as *bearer*) channels can be used for voice or data, and can be combined to provide 128 kbps throughput. BRI access is via the same copper telephone lines that now provide regular telephone service to homes. The attraction of this technology for telephone companies is that it allows higher-speed services to be delivered using the existing cabling. In many locations, however, the existing copper has had to be upgraded to support the encoding necessary to transmit this amount of data over a line.

Primary Rate ISDN (PRI). PRI services are delivered by a T-1 circuit (1.544 Mbps) in the United States and an E-1 (2.048 Mbps) in Europe. In the United States, a T-1 delivering PRI is split into 24 channels of 64 kbps, one of which is used as the D channel for signaling, leaving 23 for voice, data, or bonding together to form a connection of higher than 64 kbps. When a T-1 circuit provides channelized service, 8 kbps is lost to the channelization process, giving an available bandwidth of 1.536 kbps. A typical application for PRI would be to provide 23 central dial ports for remote branches to dial into on an as-needed basis. A PRI can be terminated in an RJ-45 type connector, which can be directly connected to a Cisco router device such as an AS-5200, or a PRI interface on a 7000-series router. This means that you can provide 23 dial connections on one physical interface without having to worry about individual modems and cabling.

Link Access Protocol D Channel. LAPD is a derivative of X.25's LAPB protocol and is used by the ISDN equipment at your site to communicate with the telephone company's central office switch all the while the connection is active.

Terminal Endpoint Identifier. TEI is a unique identifier for each of the up to eight devices that can hang off of an ISDN connection. Typically the TEI will be configured by the network via D channel exchanges, but it may be necessary to configure these identifiers by hand.

Q.931. The D channel uses control messages that conform to the ITU Q.931 specification to establish, terminate, and report on status of B channel connections. It is worth confirming that these control signals pass through a separate D channel (termed *out-of-band*); if a separate D channel network is not available, an extra 8 kbps is taken out of each B channel, leaving only 56 kbps available for data transmission.

SAPI. Frame relay or X.25 frames as well as control messages can traverse the D channel. It is the Service Access Point Identifier field in the LAPD frame that identifies which type of traffic is using the link.

SPIDs and DNs. A SAPI/TEI pair identifies a particular device on a given ISDN link, but has only local significance. For a call to traverse an ISDN network, network-wide parameters need to be defined. In concept, a SAPI/TEI pair are the same as an LCN in an X.25 network, in that the LCN is significant between a DTE and DCE, but an NUA is necessary to route traffic across an X.25 network. To establish an ISDN connection, you need a *directory number* (DN), which looks identical to a regular telephone number. With a DN, you know what number to use to call another ISDN user. That is not enough, however. We know that an ISDN connection may have many different types of devices attached, so to inform the ISDN switch in the telephone company's network what you have at your location, the telephone company will assign you one or more *service profile IDs* (SPIDs) that identify the equipment you are using on your ISDN connection.

Switch Types. You must know the Central Office switch type used by your ISDN provider and configure that in the device connecting to the ISDN circuit. In the United States, the switch type might be AT&T 5ess and 4ess, or Northern Telecom MS-100; in the United Kingdom, it might be Net3 and Net5; and in Germany, it is 1TR6.

Network Termination 1 (NT1). An NT1 is a device that converts ISDN digital line communications to the type used by the BRI interface. Outside of the United States, this is typically supplied by the telephone company, but inside the United States, subscribers generally have to supply their own NT1. In effect, it is the circuitry that interfaces your ISDN connection to the ISDN local loop network.

Terminal Endpoint Devices (TE1 and TE2). A TE1 is a native ISDN interface on a piece of communications equipment, such as a BRI interface on a Cisco router. A TE2 device is one that requires a *Terminal Adapter* (TA) to generate BRI signals for it. The TA converts RS-232 or V.35 signals in to BRI signals. A Cisco router serial interface needs to be connected to an NT1 via a TA device.

Let's see how a typical ISDN call is established by referring to Fig. 6-24, which shows how a TE1 is directly connected to the NT1 device, whereas a TE2 needs a TA device to connect to the ISDN network. Imagine we want to call a digital telephone that has an ISDN phone number of 123-4567. To do this, the originating equipment connects to the telephone company's Central Office switch. The CO switch knows what type of device the originating equipment is through its associated SPID. Next, the number 123-4567 is passed to the switch as the destination. The CO switch will then locate via SPID an appropriate device at the destination number that can accept the call. A D channel conversation takes place and a B channel is allocated from source to destination to transport data between the two ISDN devices.

Configuring ISDN BRI Services. ISDN connections generally are configured as a type of *Dial on Demand Routing* (DDR). This provides for a dial backup service to a leased line link, a dial connection for occasion-

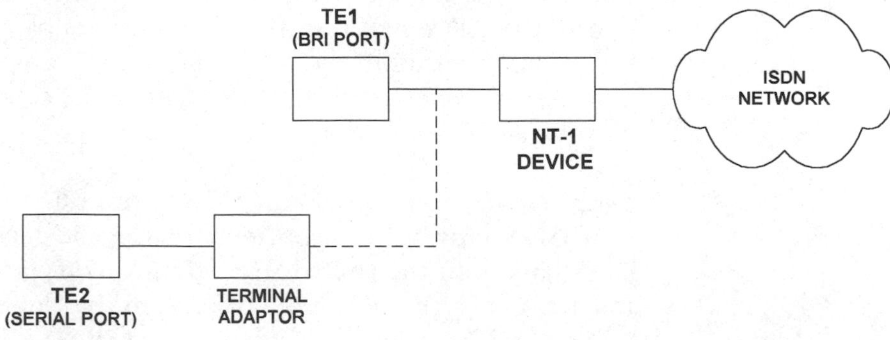

Figure 6-24 ISDN device interconnections

al Internet access, or a remote site dialing a central location for occasional server access.

The first example is for a Cisco 2501 that has its Serial 0 interface attached to a leased line connected to a central site. The Serial 1 port is connected to a Terminal Adapter device that dials back to the central site if the primary leased line on Serial 0 fails. In this application, some of the configuration commands need to be entered into the Terminal Adapter and some into the router.

For the Terminal Adapter configuration, we need to identify the ISDN provider's switch type, the number to dial, and the SPID assigned for the connection. In the router, we need to identify what will cause a dial connection to be made. Typically for this type of application, the router serial port connected to the Terminal Adapter will raise the DTR signal when a connection is needed; the TA will sense this and, having all the information necessary to make the desired connection, will initiate a call. This is the relevant configuration for the Serial 0 and Serial 1 ports:

```
interface serial 0
backup delay 10 45
backup interface serial 1
!
interface serial 1
ip unnumbered serial 0
```

The command `backup delay 10 45` for Serial 0 configures the router to attempt to establish a backup connection if the primary connection loses a carrier signal for more than 10 seconds, and will maintain that backup connection until the primary carrier signal has been constantly up for at least 45 seconds.

The command `backup serial interface 1` tells the router that Serial 1 is to be used as the backup interface. This command sets DTR low until the port is activated to establish a connection.

The only necessary command for the Serial 1 port is the one giving it an IP address, which in this case is an unnumbered IP address, linked to the address of Serial 0. (IP unnumbered will be covered in Chap. 7.) There typically will be an ISDN circuit ready at the central site to receive this call. Full connectivity is restored to the remote location when the ISDN circuit is established and the routing table on the central site router has adjusted so that it knows to get to the remote router via a new interface. (The routing protocol implemented, such as IGRP, will make these adjustments for you.)

The second example is for a router that has a BRI port and therefore does not need a TA device. The goal is to provide connectivity to a set of centrally located servers on an as-needed basis. The access needed from this router to the servers is sporadic, so the ISDN solution is implemented because a leased line connection is not cost-justified. This setup is illustrated in Fig. 6-25, along with pertinent extracts from the router configurations.

In this application, the ISDN link is made only when there is traffic that the DDR interface on router 1 deems "interesting." We have to tell the router what traffic is worth establishing a link for. For example, you probably will not want the ISDN link to be brought up every time a router wants to send a regular broadcast IGRP update. These types of links are usually set up with static routes to reduce ISDN utilization. You would therefore not enable a routing protocol process on router 1. The process to define a link can be summarized as follows:

- Configure global ISDN parameters.
- Identify the packet types that will initiate an ISDN connection.
- Define and configure the interface over which these identified packets will be sent out.
- Set the call parameters to be used for establishing the DDR link, such as the number to call.

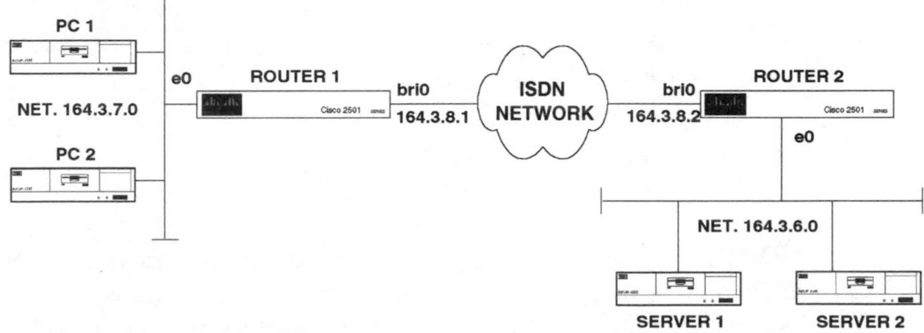

Figure 6-25 A dial-on-demand routing solution using a router BRI interface

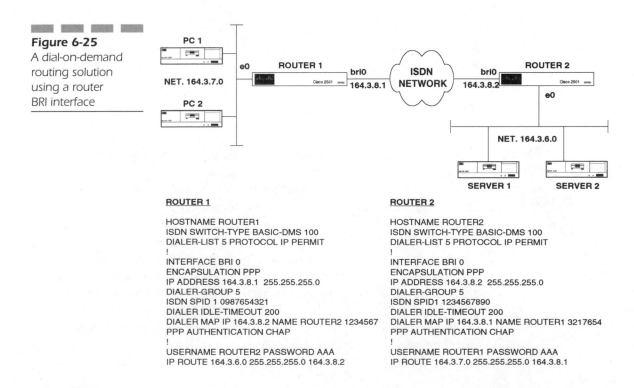

ROUTER 1

```
HOSTNAME ROUTER1
ISDN SWITCH-TYPE BASIC-DMS 100
DIALER-LIST 5 PROTOCOL IP PERMIT
!
INTERFACE BRI 0
ENCAPSULATION PPP
IP ADDRESS 164.3.8.1  255.255.255.0
DIALER-GROUP 5
ISDN SPID 1 0987654321
DIALER IDLE-TIMEOUT 200
DIALER MAP IP 164.3.8.2 NAME ROUTER2 1234567
PPP AUTHENTICATION CHAP
!
USERNAME ROUTER2 PASSWORD AAA
IP ROUTE 164.3.6.0 255.255.255.0 164.3.8.2
```

ROUTER 2

```
HOSTNAME ROUTER2
ISDN SWITCH-TYPE BASIC-DMS 100
DIALER-LIST 5 PROTOCOL IP PERMIT
!
INTERFACE BRI 0
ENCAPSULATION PPP
IP ADDRESS 164.3.8.2  255.255.255.0
DIALER-GROUP 5
ISDN SPID1 1234567890
DIALER IDLE-TIMEOUT 200
DIALER MAP IP 164.3.8.1 NAME ROUTER1 3217654
PPP AUTHENTICATION CHAP
!
USERNAME ROUTER1 PASSWORD AAA
IP ROUTE 164.3.7.0 255.255.255.0 164.3.8.1
```

The configurations illustrated in Fig. 6-25 are similar enough for the remote and central router BRI ports that we will explain only the remote router BRI port configuration in detail.

Global command `isdn switch-type basic-dms100` defines the switch type used by the ISDN provider company.

Global command `dialer-list 5 protocol ip permit` is paired with the `dialer-group 5` interface command. The `dialer-list` command here states that IP packets destined for, or routed through, the interface tagged as belonging to dialer-group 5 are "interesting" and will trigger a DDR connection. More complex permissions can be defined by the use of access lists. In order to use an access list, one must be defined in global configuration. If access list 101 is created, this access list can then be associated with a dial list with the following `dialer-list 5 list 101`. Appropriately specifying access list 101 will allow you to define specific IP addresses or protocols (such as Telnet or FTP) that may or may not cause a DDR connection to be made.

The commands `encapsulation ppp`, `ip address`, and `ip route` are as explained elsewhere.

Command `dialer-group 5` identifies the BRI 0 interface as belonging to this group, essentially marking BRI 0 as the port that will respond to the interesting packets defined by dialer-list 5.

Command `isdn spid1 0987654321` sets the SPID number for this ISDN connection as supplied by the ISDN connection provider.

Command `dialer idle-timeout 200` specifies that if there is no traffic on the connection for 200 seconds, the link will be dropped.

Command `dialer map ip 164.3.8.2 name router2 1234567` maps the telephone number 1234567 to the IP address 164.8.3.2. If router 1 wants to send a packet to the 164.3.6.0 subnet, its routing table will identify 164.3.8.2 as the address to which to forward the packet, setting off a DDR connection and causing router 1 to dial 1234567. This command can be modified if you know that the number you are dialing is a 56 kbps rather than 64 kbps ISDN connection. In this case, the command would be `dialer map ip 164.3.8.2 name router2 speed 56 1234567`. If we want to make router 2 a receive-only connection, we can input this command with no phone number argument. It is required to give the hostname of the router being called in this command, which must be the same as that defined in the `username` command (in this case, router 2).

Command `ppp authentication chap` identifies that CHAP authentication will be enforced prior to the granting of a connection.

Command `username router2 password aaa` generically identifies a username and password pair that is authenticated to connect to this router. If a workstation were connecting, it would have to use "router 2" and "aaa" to successfully negotiate CHAP. We now, however, have two routers that are connecting together and negotiating authentication. The username that each router will use is its hostname, and the password that it will use is the password set in this command. What all this means is that the username on router 1 must be the same as the hostname of router 2, and that both routers must have the same password set.

Command `ip route 164.3.6.0 255.255.255.0 164.3.8.2` defines a static route in the routing table that identifies that the BRI interface on router 2 is the next hop for subnet 164.3.6.0.

The third example is a user who wants to establish an ISDN connection from home to a central site when a network resource located at a central site is required. This type of requirement is well-suited to the Cisco 1004 configuration illustrated in Fig. 6-23. The 1004 is used in the United States because it has a built-in NT1, whereas the 1003 does not have an NT1 and is used elsewhere in the world; the NT1 in that case is usually supplied by the ISDN provider. The Cisco 1004 is very different from the 1001 discussed earlier. The 1004 has a PCMCIA slot for a memory card that holds the configuration. The 1004 is a router, running the full Cisco IOS, whereas the 1001 is a bridge.

The configuration for a 1004 is therefore the same as the remote router in the second example discussed above. A 1004 memory card can be configured at a central location and sent out to a remote site for a nontechnical person to insert in the PCMCIA slot.

Configuring ISDN PRI Services. In this section we will discuss how a PRI could be configured for multiple sites to dial into. A PRI is effectively 23 B channels and one D channel, each with 64 kbps bandwidth, all on one physical link. When setting up a central location with many interfaces available, it is more efficient to set up the interfaces so that a remote site can dial into any interface. This gives you more efficient use of the interfaces and you do not have to dedicate any to particular sites. Working on the theory that not all remote sites are connected at the same time, setting up the PRI to allow any site to dial any interface allows you to set up fewer interfaces than there are remote sites, yet provide service to all locations as they need it.

There are two methods for allowing remote sites to dial into any interface in a pool. With the first, the remote site gets its address from the interface it dials into at connection time. In the second method, the PRI is configured as some type of rotary group and has dynamic routing enabled so that all interfaces act as one pool of interfaces. The first option is best suited to single workstations dialing in, typically on asynchronous communications. The reason for this is that a single workstation does not need an IP address when it is operating in a standalone mode, and gets one when it needs one for networking. The second option is better suited for providing central backup for remote LANs. IP addresses will be assigned to the workstations on these LANs prior to establishment of the backup link, so some type of dynamic routing is necessary for the rotary to operate effectively.

Now we will examine the second option. There are some additional steps involved in setting up a PRI that are not necessary when setting up a BRI. A PRI is delivered on a T-1 in the United States and Japan, and on an E-1 elsewhere in the world. The settings shown here are for a T-1 circuit. To connect to a PRI, you need a CT1 Network processor Module for the 4*x*00-series router, or a Multichannel Interface Processor for the 7*x*00-series router. Let's assume we are using a 4700 router for the commands that follow.

Figure 6-26 illustrates a typical configuration for setting up a PRI to act as a rotary pool of interfaces for incoming connections that already have a configured IP address. The figure shows only one remote site (router1), but the configuration presented should support 50 or more

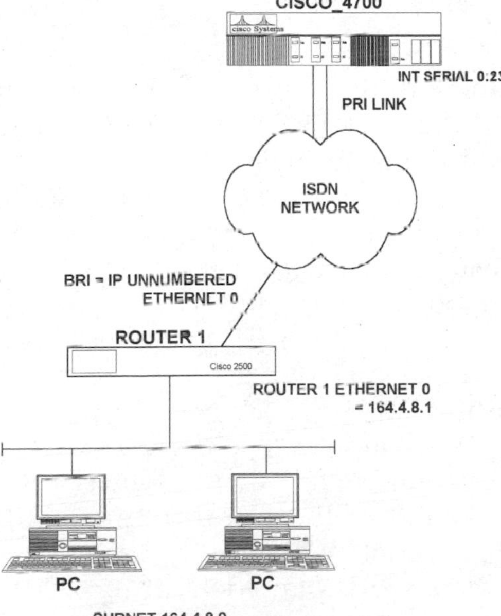

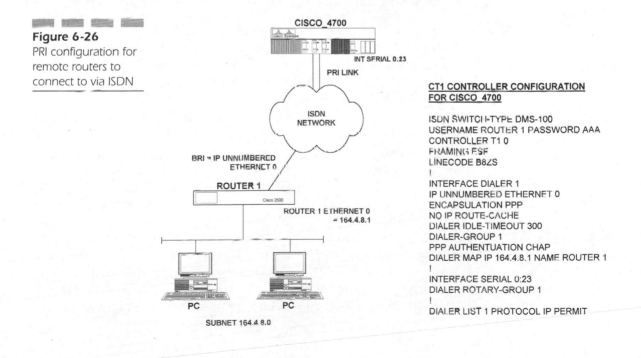

Figure 6-26 PRI configuration for remote routers to connect to via ISDN

<u>CT1 CONTROLLER CONFIGURATION FOR CISCO_4700</u>

```
ISDN SWITCH-TYPE DMS-100
USERNAME ROUTER 1 PASSWORD AAA
CONTROLLER T1 0
FRAMING ESF
LINECODE B8ZS
!
INTERFACE DIALER 1
IP UNNUMBERED ETHERNET 0
ENCAPSULATION PPP
NO IP ROUTE-CACHE
DIALER IDLE-TIMEOUT 300
DIALER-GROUP 1
PPP AUTHENTUATION CHAP
DIALER MAP IP 164.4.8.1 NAME ROUTER 1
!
INTERFACE SERIAL 0:23
DIALER ROTARY-GROUP 1
!
DIALER LIST 1 PROTOCOL IP PERMIT
```

remote sites occasionally dialing in. The key difference between the setup for a single dial connection and this multiconnection setup is that the username/password pair for each remote router must be configured on the central 4700. In addition, a `dialer map` statement must be present in the 4700 dialer1 interface section for each remote router. On subsequent versions of the Cisco IOS, `dialer map` statements are not necessary, and the router uses Inverse ARP in the same manner as it does in a frame relay network to map IP addresses to router names and telephone numbers. Let's examine each command in this configuration.

- Command `isdn switch-type dms-100` defines the switch type used by the telephone company as a Northern Telecom DMS-100.
- Command `username router1 password aaa` defines the valid username and password pairs for all remote routers dialing in.
- Command `controller t1 0` sets the necessary configuration for the T1 controller card in the 4700 slot 0.
- Command `framing esf` configures the T-1 controller slot 0 as the Extended Super Frame frame type, which is that used in the United States.
- Command `linecode b8zs` defines the line-code type as Binary 8 with Zero Substitute. This is the value required for T-1 PRIs in the United States.

Command `interface dialer1` is there to avoid having to enter the same thing into the router configuration multiple times. (There is no physical dialer interface.) This command enables you to specify a configuration that can be applied to multiple interfaces. To give a physical interface the configuration that is specified in the interface dialer section (in this case, dialer 1), put a single command in the physical interface to make it a member of the specific rotary group (in this case, dialer rotary group 1).

Command `ip unnumbered Ethernet0` is covered more fully in Chap. 7, but in this instance it lets the dialer 1 interface "borrow" an IP address from the Ethernet port. The BRI port at the remote end also will have an IP unnumbered configuration. IP unnumbered enables point-to-point connections to route packets between the networks at each end of the link, without dedicating a specific subnet number to the point-to-point link. Without this feature, it would not be possible to pool the central PRI connections. If each PRI channel had its own subnet, it could only directly communicate with other IP devices on that same subnet.

The remaining commands of interest are as follows:

- Command `encapsulation ppp` sets the encapsulation to PPP.
- Command `no ip route-cache` slows the speed of packets switched from a fast to a slow link.
- Command `dialer idle-timeout 300` drops the connection after an idle time of 300 seconds.
- Command `dialer-group 1` identifies the traffic that is to pass over the link as specified in the dialer list command.
- Command `ppp authentication chap` was discussed in the previous section on BRI.
- Command `dialer map ip 164.8.4.1 name router1` was discussed in the previous section.
- Command `dialer list 1 protocol ip permit` was discussed in the previous section.
- Command `interface serial 0:23` identifies the 24th channel, the D channel, because the channel numbers start at zero. The commands in this section configure all the B channel interface parameters
- Command `dialer rotary-group 1` applies all the configuration commands specified in the `interface dialer 1` section to the B channels.

Simple ISDN Monitoring. There are two basic commands for viewing the status of ISDN BRI connections: the `show controller bri` and `show interface bri` commands.

Command `show controller bri` displays status regarding the physical connection of the ISDN D and B channels. The most useful part of this display is that it states for each B and D channel whether the layer 1 (Physical layer) connection is activated. This is useful when performing remote diagnostics. If you can Telnet to the router, this command will tell you if a functioning ISDN line has been connected to the BRI port. The equivalent command for a PRI connection is the `show controller t1` command.

Command `show interface bri0 1 2` shows the connection status of the two B channels. If the numbers 1 and 2 are omitted, this command displays D channel information. The sort of information this command display gives you includes whether the PPP protocols such as LCP and IPCP successfully negotiated, the input and output data rate, the number of packets dropped, and the state of the hold queues.

Miscellaneous ISDN. There are a few ISDN commands that may prove useful in special situations and they are presented here in no particular order.

Use command `isdn caller 212654xxxx` if you want to accept calls only from a specified number. The format shown here is useful if you know that calls may be originating from several extensions in the one location. The calls accepted start with 212654, but may have any value for the last four digits. If you want to accept calls from only one number, you may specify the whole number, also. Care should be taken with this command, because if the ISDN switch to which you are connected does not support this feature, using this command will block all incoming calls.

Command `isdn not-end-to-end 56` sets the line speed for incoming calls to 56 kbps. This is useful if you know that the originating caller has a 56 kbps connection, but your receiver has a 64 kbps connection. If calls originate at one speed and are delivered at another, problems could occur with data corruption.

Command `dialer in-band`, if applied to an asynchronous interface, means that modem chat scripts will be used. If applied to a synchronous interface, it means that V.25*bis* commands will be used. Basically, this command configures the interface to use the bearer (B) channel for call setup and teardown on an ISDN connection, rather than the usual D channel.

Command `dialer load-threshold 191` configures the interface to start using the second B channel when the first has reached, in this case, 75 percent capacity. The figure 191 is 75 percent of 255; the valid numerical range for this command is 1–255.

Command `dialer string 1234567` is a simpler command to use than the `dialer map` command if the interface being configured is going to dial only one location. Essentially this command specifies the number that will be dialed whenever a connection is initiated.

Additional WAN Technologies

To finish this chapter, we'll discuss some general terms, technologies, and devices used in WAN implementations. First, let's take a closer look at the Cisco serial ports that interface to WAN connections.

Cisco Serial Interfaces

Cisco serial interfaces are either built in, as with the fixed-configuration routers such as the 2500-series, or installed, as with the *Fast Serial Interface Processor* (FSIP) card, for modular routers such as the 7500-series. Either way, the interface itself is basically the same device that will support speeds up to T-1 (1.544 Mbps) in the United States, and E-1 (2.048 Mbps) elsewhere. The only restriction here is that the FSIP card has two 4-port modules, with each module capable of supporting four T-1 connections; only three E-1 connections can be supported simultaneously because the aggregate throughput on this card cannot exceed 8 Mbps.

The Cisco serial port uses a proprietary 60-pin connector and configures itself according to the cable and equipment that are connected to it. As discussed in Chap. 3, a Cisco serial port will configure itself as DTE or DCE depending on the cable end connected to it. Cisco serial port cables will terminate in EIA-232, EIA-449, X.21, or V.35 connectors. These standards have differing capabilities regarding the distance over which they can transport communications at varying speeds. Table 6.1 shows the distances over which it is safe to deliver data at varying speeds for these interface standards. These are not necessarily hard-and-fast rules; it is possible to use longer cables—but if you do so, you start running the risk of frame errors being introduced by interference on the cable.

EIA-232 cannot transmit a given speed of data at the same rate as the other interface standards because it uses unbalanced signals. The terms *balanced* and *unbalanced* are often used in data communications, so we will explain the difference between these two types of communication here.

First we need to understand a little of what *voltage* is. Volts measure what is known as the *electrical potential difference* between two objects. Measuring a difference requires a common reference point for measurement against in order to make the number meaningful. It's like measuring the height of a mountain with reference to sea level rather than against the next closest mountain. It's the same with volts. They normally are quoted as so many volts above what is known as *ground,* which is taken as 0 volts, i.e., the electrical potential of the planet Earth.

TABLE 6-1 Serial Communications Distance Limitations

Rate	EIA-232 Distance (feet)	EIA-449, X.21, V.35 Distance (feet)
9600	50	1,025
56,000	8.5	102
1,536,000	N/A	50

Just as there is nothing inherently dangerous about standing on top of a tall building, there is nothing inherently dangerous about being at a certain voltage level. The danger comes if you fall off the building and come in to contact with the ground at high velocity. The same is true if you are at a given voltage level and come into contact with something at a different voltage level. When two objects at different voltage levels come into contact with each other, they will try to equalize their voltage by having current (amperes) flow between them.

In data communications, signals that represent data are measured in terms of a particular voltage level. In unbalanced communications, there is only one wire carrying the data signal, and its voltage level is measured against ground (i.e., the Earth's voltage level). With balanced communications, two wires are used to transmit the signal, and the signal voltage level is measured between these wires. Using two wires for data transmission significantly improves a cable's ability to deal with electrical interference.

The idea behind why two wires are better at dealing with electrical interference is simple. If a two-wire system is transferring data and is subject to electrical interference, both wires are similarly affected. Therefore, the interference should make no difference to the circuitry receiving the two-wire transmission, which determines the voltage level, and hence the signal, as the difference in electrical potential between the two wires. With unbalanced single-wire transmission, any electrical interference on the line directly affects the voltage potential of that wire with respect to ground. Therefore, unbalanced data transmission is less able than balanced transmission to deliver uncorrupted signals in the presence of electrical interference.

Serial Interface Configuration. If a serial interface is acting as a DCE and is generating a clock signal with the `clockrate` command, the normal operation is for the attached DTE device to return this clock signal to the serial port. If the attached DTE device does not return the clock signal to the serial port, you should configure the port with the `transmit-clock-internal` command.

Encoding of binary 1 and 0 is normally done according to the *Non-Return to Zero* (NRZ) standard. With EIA-232 connections in IBM environments, you may need to change the encoding to *Non-Return to Zero Inverted* (NRZI) standard as follows.

```
Router1(config)#interface serial 0
Router1(config-int)#nrzi-encoding
```

Cisco serial ports use a 16-bit *Cyclic Redundancy Check* (CRC) *Frame Check Sequence* (FCS). If a Cisco serial interface is communicating directly with another Cisco serial interface, better performance might be obtained by using a 32-bit CRC, as fewer retransmissions occur with a 32-bit CRC. To enable 32-bit CRCs, perform the following in interface configuration mode:

```
Router1(config-int)#crc32
```

High-Speed Serial Interface. I have mentioned technologies in this book that make use of speeds higher than T-1 speeds, for example, SMDS or frame relay delivered on a T-3 circuit. To accommodate these higher transmission rates, a modular Cisco router uses a *High-Speed Serial Interface* (HSSI). The HSSI, just one, is delivered on an *HSSI Interface Processor* (HIP) card. The HIP card is inserted in any slot on a 7*x*00-series router and interfaces directly to the router bus architecture, the Cisco eXtended bus, or *cxbus*.

The HSSI is now a recognized standard, known as the EIA612/613 standard and operating at speeds of up to 52 Mbps. This enables the interface to be used for SONET (51.82 Mbps), T-3 (45 Mbps), and E-3 (34 Mbps) services. The HSSI on the HIP is different from other Cisco serial ports in that it uses a 50-pin Centronics connector and requires a special cable to connect to the incoming line's DSU device. In other words, a regular SCSI cable will not do. Once installed and connected, the HSSI can be configured and monitored just as any other serial port. The following example applies an IP address of 193.1.1.1 to an HSSI on a HIP inserted in slot 2 in a 7*x*00 series router.

```
Router1(config)#interface hssi 2/0
Router1(config-int)#ip address 193.1.1.1 255.255.255.0
```

All Cisco serial ports are numbered starting at 0, and as there is only one HSSI on a HIP, it will always be port 0. Any other special encoding necessary, such as framing type or linecode, will be specified by the supplier of the high-speed line.

Line Types

For more than 25 years, telephone companies have been converting from analog to digital transmission their networks that carry voice transmission. Nearly all of the bulk communications between telephone company switching points is digital. It is only over the last mile or so from a CO to a home or small business that the communication is analog.

You may have wondered why so much of data communications is based upon 64 kbps circuits or multiples thereof. The reason is that, in digital terms, it used to take 64 kbps to cleanly transmit a voice signal. This single voice channel is referred to as a *DS0*. Data communications came along after the digitization of voice traffic, and therefore "piggy-backed" on the voice technology in place. Let's take a brief look at the basic unit of digital transmission lines, the 64 kbps circuit.

Dataphone Digital Service (DDS). *Dataphone Digital Service*, or DDS as it is commonly referred to, actually gives you only 56 kbps throughput. The additional 8 kbps is not available for data transfer and is used to ensure synchronization between the two ends of the DDS circuit. This is a function of the *Alternate Mark Inversion* (AMI) data encoding technique. DDS is essentially supplied over the same pairs of copper wires used for regular analog telephone connections, and two pairs, for a total of four wires, are needed for the service.

In the United States, the telephone company will install the line up to what is known as the "demarc," a point of demarcation with respect to troubleshooting responsibility. The demarc is a RJ-48 connector, to which you must connect a CSU/DSU device. In Europe and other parts of the world, the CSU/DSU is typically supplied with the circuit. The CSU/DSU is really two devices in one; the *Channel Service Unit* (CSU) interfaces to the telephone company's network for DDS and T-1 services, whereas the *Data Service Unit* (DSU), interfaces to your equipment, in this case a router.

In many locations, 64 kbps lines are now available through the use of B8ZS (*Bipolar with 8 Zero Substitution*) encoding that replaces AMI. This gives you back the full 64 kbps by use of a more intelligent line coding mechanism. This 64 kbps service is known as *Clear Channel Capability* or *Clear 64*. All you need to make sure of in your CSU configuration is that it has AMI encoding for 56 kbps services and B8ZS for 64 kbps service.

T-1, Fractional T-1, and T-3 Services. A T-1 is a collection of 24 DS0 circuits, and often is referred to as a *DS1*. T-1 service may be delivered as either channelized or unchannelized. The unchannelized option is the easiest to understand. In effect, the unchannelized T-1 acts as a 1.536 Mbps pipe that connects to one serial interface.

In its channelized form, the T-1 can be used to deliver 24 time slots, each having 64 kbps throughput, or the PRI service previously discussed in the section on ISDN. The channelized T-1 has two typical applications. The first is to supply 24 DS0 connections over one physical link. A T-1 configured this way can be directly connected to one of the two ports on a MIP card inserted in a 7*x*00-series router, or the one available port on the CT1 card inserted in a 4700-series router. Once connected, the T-1 can be addressed as 24 separate serial interfaces. The telephone company can "groom" each of the separate DS0 channels to any location on its network that is serviced by an individual DS0 circuit. This is done via a device termed the *Digital Access Cross Connect* (DACC).

Using a T-1 in this way simplifies central site equipment management considerably. Consider a head office that needs to be connected to (conveniently) 23 remote branches. All that is necessary in the head office is one T-1 connected to a MIP or CT1 card; no additional CSU/DSU or cabling requirements are necessary.

The following is an example of how to get into configuration mode for the 22nd DS0 channel on a channelized T-1 connected to port 0 in a MIP card that is inserted in slot 1 of a 7*x*00-series router.

```
Router1(config)#interface serial 1/0:22
Router1(config-int)#
```

From here, an IP address can be assigned, encapsulation defined, and any other configuration entered, just as for any other physical serial port.

A T-1 also can be used as an efficient way to deliver analog phone services, but to do this, an additional piece of equipment, a *channel bank*, is necessary to convert the digital T-1 signals to 24 analog telephone lines. This can be useful if you need to configure many centrally located dial-up ports, into which roving users will dial into with analog modems. The Cisco AS-5200 has a built-in channel bank and modems so that simply by connecting a single T-1 connector to it, you can have up to 24 modem calls answered simultaneously. In fact, the AS-5200 is even a little more clever than that. The AS-5200 also has a built-in T-1 multiplexer, giving it hybrid functionality for call answering. This means that if you connect a T-1 configured as a PRI to an AS-5200, the AS-5200 will autodetect if the incoming call is from a digital ISDN or analog caller and will answer the call with the appropriate equipment.

As we discussed previously for DS0 channels, a T-1 can use either AMI or B8ZS encoding and either the *Extended Super Frame* (ESF) or D4 framing format. As long as your T-1 equipment (I'm assuming it's a router) is configured to be the same as that used by the telephone company, you should be okay.

In Europe and elsewhere, multiple DS0 services are delivered on an E-1, which comprises 32 DS0 channels, giving 2.048 Mbps throughput. The E-1 uses *High Density Bipolar 3* (HDB3) encoding. If you order a 256 kbps or 384 kbps circuit from your carrier, you will get a T-1 installed and be allocated only the appropriate number of DS0 channels needed to give you the desired throughput. This service is known as *fractional T-1* and is a good idea. The one constant in data networking is the increased need for bandwidth, so it makes sense to install capacity that is easily upgraded, as it probably will be needed at a later stage anyway.

A T-3 or DS3 *connection* is a collection of 672 DS0 circuits of 64 kbps each, which gives a total throughput of 43,008 kbps. (DS3 is the term used for this speed communication over any medium, whereas T-3 is specific to transmission over copper wires.) The actual circuit speed is somewhat faster than that, but some effective bandwidth is lost to synchronization traffic. An HSSI is the only interface that a Cisco router can use to connect to a T-3.

The hierarchy of these circuits just discussed is as follows: a single DS3 comprises seven DS2 channels, which break out to 28 DS1 channels, generating a total of 672 DS0 channels.

All this potential for faster and faster throughput does not always materialize. Imagine that a company needs to perform a mission-critical file transfer across the Atlantic five times a day. The file transfer uses TCP as the layer 4 protocol to guarantee correct sequencing of packets and to guarantee delivery. The file that is being transferred is getting bigger and taking longer to transfer, so the company is prepared to spend money to upgrade the link to speed up the file transfer. The transatlantic link is currently running at 384 kbps, and the plan is to upgrade the link to 512 kbps. Will this speed up the transfer? It depends.

TCP works on the basis of requiring from the receiving device an acknowledgment confirming that the packets sent have arrived safely before it will send more packets. The number of packets TCP will send before it stops and waits for an acknowledgment is defined by the Window size.

Let's say the Window size is set initially at 7500 bytes. Now, if you measure the round-trip delay across the Atlantic, it normally will come to around 160 milliseconds (0.16 seconds). So we have to ask ourselves, "How long does it take to clock 7500 bytes onto the link?" If it takes less than 160 milliseconds, the sending device stops transmitting and waits for an acknowledgment from the receiver before it will send any more packets. If this occurs, clearly the full bandwidth is not being utilized. So let's work out what will happen.

Multiplying 7500 by 8 bits per byte yields 60,000 bits. A 384,000 bps link will take 0.156 seconds (60,000/384,000) to clock this number of bits onto the line. You can see that if the round-trip time is 0.16 seconds, the transmitter already will have been waiting for 0.04 second before it transfers any more data. Increasing the speed of the link to anything above 384 kbps means that the sending device will just spend more time idle, waiting for acknowledgments, and the speed of the file transfer will not improve.

The only way to improve the effective throughput if a higher-speed line is installed is to increase the Window size. If this value is changed on one machine, it must be changed on all other machines with which the machine communicates—which might be something of an implementation challenge.

Summary

This chapter examined the underlying technological operation of popular WAN protocols and discussed how to configure these protocols on Cisco router interfaces. The public data network technologies examined were frame relay, SMDS, and X.25. The point-to-point protocols illustrated were SLIP, asynchronous and synchronous PPP, SDLC, and ISDN. The chapter concluded with a brief discussion of additional WAN technologies, such as Cisco serial interfaces, and the different digital line types that are commonly available.

CHAPTER 7

Building a TCP/IP Router-Based Network

Objectives

In this chapter we will:

- Examine various options for building your internetwork in a scalable, robust, manageable, and cost-effective manner.
- Give some general guidelines and some options for each category, so you can choose which is most appropriate for your situation.
- Apply selected technology options to construct a sample internetwork.

The Base Internetwork

Here we will outline the sample internetwork we will build at the end of this chapter. This internetwork will form the basis for discussion of implementation, security, backup, and management issues as we progress through the chapter. First, let's define what we want to connect together.

We will assume a data center in Chicago, where the head office also is located, and approximately 100 branch offices clustered around major cities, such as New York, Atlanta, Dallas, San Francisco, and Los Angeles. A typical branch office has 20 PCs that need access to hosts located in the Chicago data center, local applications, e-mail, and the Internet. There also is a growing need to support staff working from home and roving users with dial access.

The issues that need to be resolved are as follows:

- Do I use InterNIC/IANA-assigned IP addresses, or make up my own?
- What topology will be used?
- What IP addressing scheme and routing protocol will I use?
- What options are available for providing backup links in the event of line failure?
- How do I minimize the manual-support burden for IP address and name resolution?
- What reasonable security measures should I enforce?
- How can I reduce support costs by making this internetwork easily manageable from one location?

These issues will form the basis of discussion for the following sections. With internetwork design, as with many other aspects of networked computing, many options are available, and each will be appropriate for one application and inappropriate for another. I hope to be fairly unbiased in my presentation of each option, but I will favor those solutions with which I have had the most success. The bulk of this chapter will discuss the options available to you for internetwork configuration. At the end of this chapter we will return to the aforementioned requirements and select appropriate configuration options to service them.

IANA or Not IANA?

IANA stands for the *Internet Assigned Numbers Authority*, which is essentially an independent body responsible for assigning Internet addresses, well-known port numbers, autonomous system numbers, and other centrally administered Internet resources. The people who actually assign IP addresses for use on the Internet in the United States are those at InterNIC. If you have to apply directly for Internet addresses (that is, if you do not want to go through an Internet service provider, or ISP), the documentation you have to fill out states that the InterNIC assigns Internet addresses under the authority of IANA. In Europe, address assignment is handled by the *Resaux IP Europeans* (RIPE), and the *Asia Pacific Network Information Center* (APNIC) assigns addresses in Asia.

The question is, do you use on your internetwork IP addresses that are globally valid on the Internet, or do you make up your own numbers to suit your particular internetwork's needs? Let's take a few moments to consider the benefits and pitfalls of each approach.

Assuming that a *firewall* of some kind is in place to separate your internetwork from the Internet (firewalls will be considered in more depth later in this chapter), the question boils down to: Should I use *network address translation* or a firewall's *proxy server* function to allow me the freedom of assigning my own addressing scheme, or do I want to get InterNIC addresses and be part of the global Internet addressing scheme?

We first should discuss the benefits of using a proxy server. If you have any concerns regarding security, it is appropriate to use a proxy server firewall machine as a single connection point from your internetwork to the Internet. A proxy server separates two networks from each other, but allows only prespecified communication between the two to occur. A proxy server has two sides, the inside (your Internetwork) and the outside (the Internet), and is configured to allow only certain types of communication to take place.

This means that if you decide to allow outgoing Telnet sessions, and if a client PC on the inside of a proxy server wants to establish a Telnet session with a host on the outside of the proxy server (the Internet side), a direct Telnet session between the two machines will not be made. What does happen is that the client PC will establish a Telnet session with the proxy server, the proxy server will establish a separate session with the host on the Internet, and the proxy server will pass information between the two. As far as the client PC and the Internet host are concerned, they are talking to each other directly; in reality, however, the client PC is talking to the client side of the proxy server, and the Internet host is talking to the Internet side of the proxy server. The proxy server passes any traffic that we have previously determined is allowable onto the other side, and, optionally, logs all communications that have taken place.

As a side benefit, this type of server shields the internal network numbering scheme from the external network. This means that an Internet proxy firewall server will have a set of InterNIC-assigned addresses on the Internet side and some user-defined addressing scheme on the internal side. To enable communication between the two, the proxy server maps internal to external addresses.

If you choose to implement your own addressing, this proxy server feature gives you a lot of freedom to design an appropriate networking scheme for the internal network. Addresses assigned by the InterNIC are typically Class C addresses, which might not fit the internal network's needs. Also, the application process to get addresses directly from the InterNIC is arduous, to say the least.

The same benefits of shielding the internal network numbering scheme can be delivered by a network address translation server. An address translation server changes the addresses in packet headers, as packets pass through it. This type of server does not run any application software and does not require hosts to run proxy-aware applications.

There are, however, some potential issues related to implementing your own IP addressing scheme that are avoided when addresses are obtained from the InterNIC. The most obvious is that if you assign to your internal network a network number that already is in use on the Internet, you will not be able to communicate with the Internet sites using that address. The problem is that the routing table on the proxy server directs all packets destined for that network number back to the internal network.

The *Internet Assigned Numbers Authority* (IANA) foresaw this problem and reserved some Class A, B, and C network numbers for use by internal networks that were isolated from the Internet by a proxy server. These reserved addresses are as follows:

Class A	10.0.0.0
Class B	172.16.0.0 to 172.31.0.0
Class C	192.168.*xxx*.0 (where *xxx* is any value 0—255)

This means that any number of organizations can use these addresses for their internal networks and still be assured of reaching all Internet sites. This solution creates another problem, however, because firewalls are not used only to connect to the Internet. Corporations in increasing numbers are connecting their networks to each other and need to secure communications between the two. This is particularly true for information service companies that deliver their information to a client's network. If two organizations use 172.16.0.0 as their internal network, they cannot connect their networks together unless one of them renumbers. The only alternative to renumbering would be for the two corporations to go through a double address translation stage, which would be difficult to manage. There are some benefits to having InterNIC-assigned addresses on your internal network. You have the peace of mind of knowing that your network can be safely hidden from the Internet, yet you still have the ability to access every Internet site out there. In addition, if you need to connect to another company's network, you should be okay. The chances of any given organization implementing network address translation and choosing your assigned address for their internal network are small.

On the downside, using InterNIC addresses can be restrictive and can necessitate implementation of a very complex network numbering scheme. If you have only 200 hosts that need addresses, you are likely to get only one Class C address. If you are particularly unlucky during the application process, you will not even be assigned Class C addresses. Some applicants now are expected to use only portions of a Class C network address, which requires a routing protocol that supports discontinuous subnets. This may cause restrictions to network design, or at the very least, a complex numbering scheme that will prove difficult to troubleshoot.

I recommend that unless you already have adequate addresses assigned by the InterNIC, you do not use InterNIC-assigned numbers for your internal internetwork. Most people who implement network address translation will use the IANA-reserved addresses, typically the Class A network number 10. If you are concerned that you might need to connect your internetwork to another company that has implemented network number 10 for its internal network, use network number 4 or 5. These class A numbers are reserved for the military and are not present on the Internet.

The rest of this chapter will assume that we have decided to hide the internal network numbering scheme and are free to assign a network numbering scheme that makes things easy to administer.

Internetwork Topology

In general, we can identify three classes of service within an internetwork: *backbone, distribution,* and *local* services. These three levels of service define a hierarchical design. The backbone services are at the center of the hierarchy, and handle routing of traffic between distribution centers. The distribution centers are responsible for interfacing the backbone to the local services, which are located in each site. At each site, the local services connect individual hosts (multiuser machines and PC workstations) to the distribution network.

In the requirement we have specified above, each major location, such as New York, Atlanta, and Los Angeles, becomes a distribution center, as illustrated in Fig. 7-1. The distribution center concept is a simple one in that it can be used to associate a specific range of IP addresses with one geographic location. This simplifies matters when troubleshooting, can reduce the size of routing tables, and hence can reduce the size of routing updates.

This topology gives you the flexibility to implement either a distance vector or link state routing protocol. We shall now look at alternatives for interconnecting sites on the backbone.

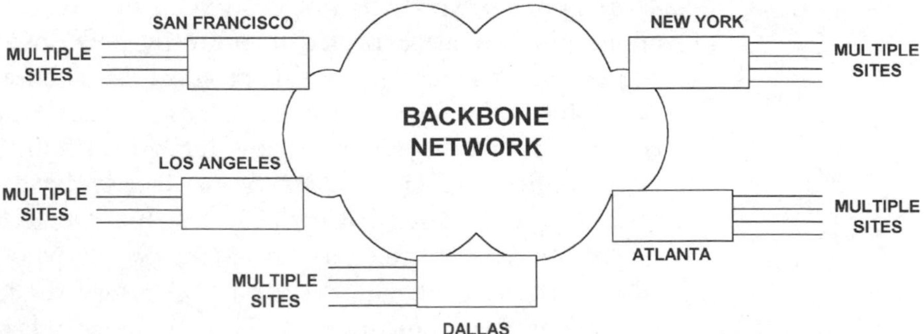

Figure 7-1 Distribution centers connected via a backbone network

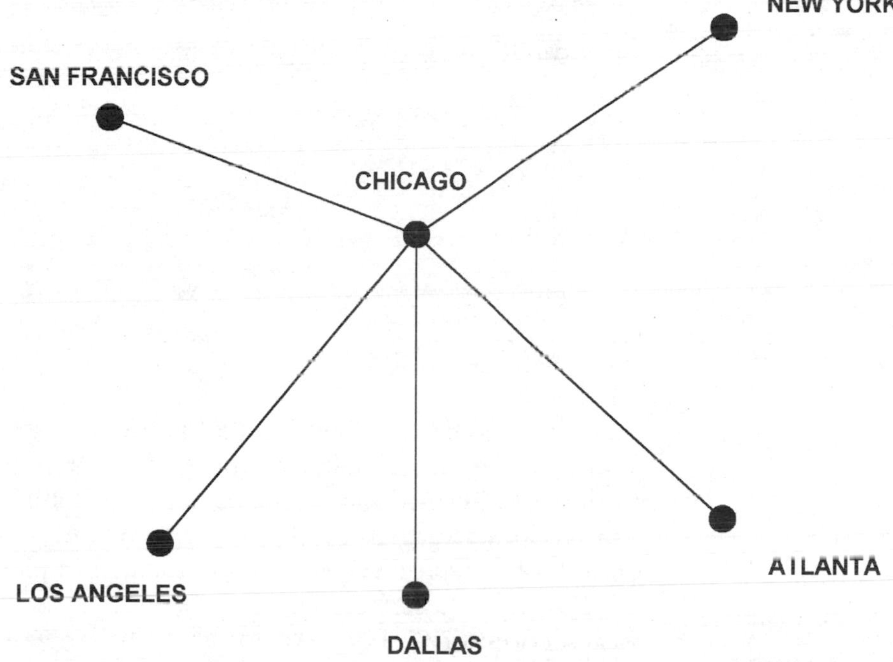

Figure 7-2 A backbone network utilizing a star topology

Backbone Topologies

The following discussions are based on connecting the main centers together. The goals for this part of the hierarchy are high availability, higher levels of throughput, and the ability to add new distribution centers with a minimum of disruption of service to the internetwork as a whole.

Star Topology. The *star network topology* is illustrated in Fig. 7-2, which shows Chicago in the center, with all lines emanating from there to the main locations. This topology is a simple one to understand and troubleshoot. It does, however, place a greater processing burden on the central router located in Chicago, because all traffic passing between distribution centers must pass through that router. In addition, only one full-time connection goes to each location. That means that if one of the main lines from a distribution center to the central site fails, all communication to or from that center stops until some dial backup mechanism reestablishes the link.

If the bandwidth necessary to provide full communications between a distribution center and the central site is greater than 128 kbps (what is achievable with a single ISDN connection), there are no simple and

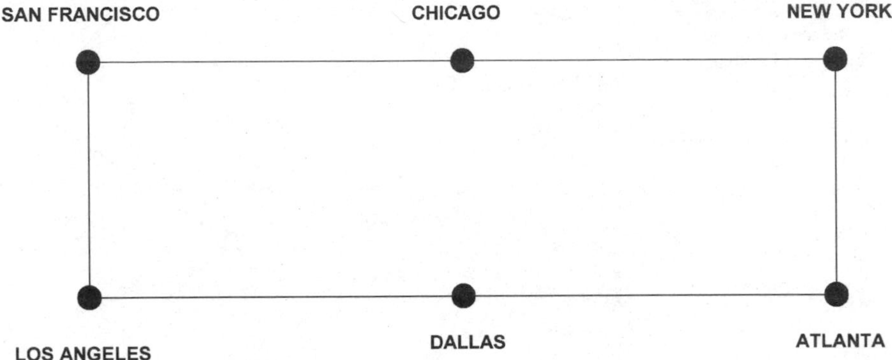

Figure 7-3 A backbone network utilizing a ring topology

inexpensive ways to establish a dial backup connection. Multilink PPP is just becoming available, and there are some proprietary ways to perform what is termed *inverse multiplexing*, the combining of several ISDN connections and making them appear as one line. This could be an option for the star topology if you decide to implement it.

Ring Topology. The ring topology, as its name suggests, forms a ring around all the main distribution centers (Fig. 7-3). The advantage is that each site has two permanent connections to it, so in the event of a single line failure, an alternate path is available to deliver traffic.

The downside is that traffic destined for Dallas from Chicago has to pass along the link from Chicago to New York, then to Atlanta, and finally to Dallas. This places a higher bandwidth utilization on the Chicago-to-New-York link than is necessary, because that link is carrying traffic destined for Dallas. Also, since it uses more lines than the star topology, there is less likely to be money for a dial backup system, which is okay since there are two lines feeding each location. If any two lines fail, however, the network is down hard until one of them comes back.

Fully Meshed Topology. This is the ultimate in resiliency, minimizing the number of intermediate routers through which traffic must pass, and reducing the amount of traffic on each link. The obvious drawback is the cost of all the leased lines. There are very few situations that justify a fully meshed network, because just adding one more distribution center to the backbone takes up significant resources in terms of router ports at each location. A fully meshed network is shown in Fig. 7-4.

Partially Meshed Topology. The concept behind the partially meshed network should be familiar to all those who have been involved in internetwork design, and that concept is compromise. The partially meshed network, as illustrated in Fig. 7-5, adds a few cross-connect lines to the ring topology, but not quite as many as would a fully meshed network. This is the most popular form of internetwork backbone because it can be adjusted to suit the requirements of the organization. Typically, the more important locations will receive the most connections feeding it. Also, network redundancy can be added as required, without the need to redesign the whole topology.

A backbone of this design does not rely on dial backup of its links; rather, it assumes that at least one of the main lines feeding each distribution center will be up at all times. Having alternate paths available in case of line failure complicates the process of deciding what size link to install between distribution centers. Let's say it is estimated that a 128 kbps line will adequately handle the traffic requirements between New York and Atlanta under normal conditions in the internetwork illustrated in Fig. 7-5.

Now suppose the link between Dallas and Atlanta fails. Assuming that a dynamic routing protocol of some kind is in operation, traffic between Dallas and Atlanta will be routed through Chicago, New

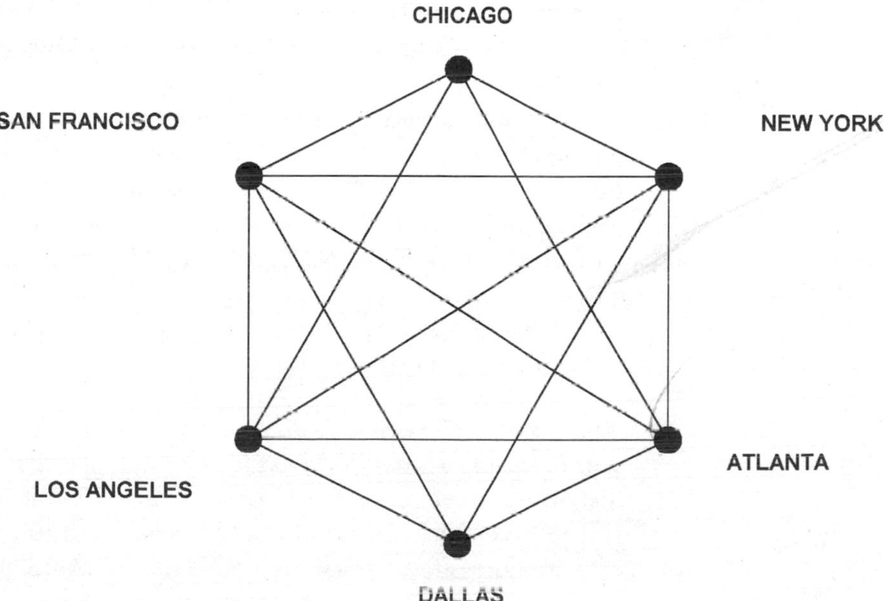

Figure 7-4 A backbone network utilizing a fully meshed topology

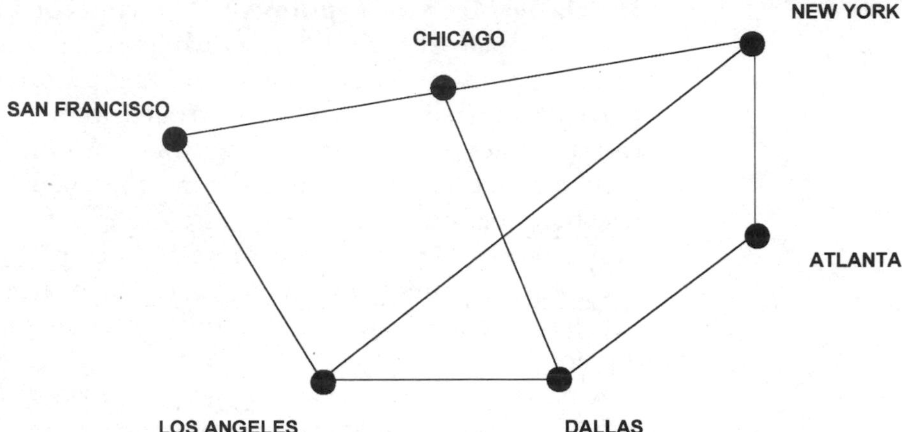

Figure 7-5
A backbone network utilizing a partially meshed topology

York, and on to Atlanta. The link between New York and Atlanta is now carrying its normal load, plus whatever normally flows between Dallas and Atlanta. If the combined level of this traffic is significantly above 128 kbps, the effects could be disastrous for the internetwork. If the combined traffic is, say, in the region of 160 kbps, backbone routers will begin to drop packets as soon as buffers start to overflow.

If this traffic is based on a connectionless protocol (like UDP), the data is merely missed, but if the traffic utilizes a connection-oriented protocol (such as TCP), even more traffic will be sent as retransmissions occur. This effect causes the New-York-to-Atlanta link to be overutilized and thus virtually unusable.

In this scenario, having an alternate path has made things even worse. Instead of the line failure affecting communication only between Dallas and Atlanta, it now adversely affects New-York-to-Atlanta traffic, and potentially Dallas-to-Chicago traffic, and Chicago-to-New-York traffic as well. As a general guideline, if you are going to rely on alternate paths to provide backup in the event of a link failure, backbone links should be no more than 50 percent utilized under normal conditions.

The Public Network Concept. The *public network concept* means that you delegate to a network vendor the management of the backbone and distribution center internetworking issues. Typically you will provide a single link (with optional dial backup, or duplicate leased line) from each remote site to the network vendor's cloud, and leave it up to the vendor to deliver the traffic to the main office location.

This type of approach has become popular with frame relay networks, as discussed more fully in Chap. 6. A frame relay solution even can be used to eliminate the need for distribution centers, as each office location could be linked directly to the frame relay service. Frame relay services became popular when frame relay vendors were trying to introduce the technology. Often a company could buy a very low CIR, and hence pay very little for the connectivity in relative terms, yet still get acceptable throughput. The reason for this was that the frame relay networks had surplus capacity.

This was not a frame relay vendor's idea of a good deal. From a vendor's perspective, the goal is to oversubscribe the shared network and thus lower costs, resulting in higher profits for the vendor and lowered prices for customers. This may seem a harsh judgment, but I know of many companies that bought a very cheap 4 kbps or so CIR and were very happy with its performance to begin with (often they were able to get burst rates of throughput of over 100 kbps), but became unhappy when the frame relay service became more popular and their allowable throughput diminished to much nearer 4 kbps, which made the network useless from their perspective.

The simple solution is to increase the CIR and pay the network vendor more money. I believe, however, that internetworks are there to provide users with reliable and responsive service to applications. If you need 64 kbps to do that, you need a 64 kbps CIR, which might start to approach the costs of having your own dedicated bandwidth. The bottom line is that with your own dedicated bandwidth, you are master of your own destiny and have a degree of certainty over how your internetwork will perform. It all depends on the nature of the traffic you have to transport; if all you need to get to users is Internet, e-mail, and occasional file transfer capabilities, frame relay or some other shared network solution might meet your needs. If you have to deliver mission-critical applications and therefore need guaranteed uptimes and response times, you need your own bandwidth.

Distribution Center Topologies

Conceptually, anything that was done with the backbone could be repeated for the distribution centers to interconnect individual sites to the internetwork. However, the distribution centers have a different function to perform than the backbone links and routers, which makes the star topology with dial backup by far the most common choice.

The link between a distribution center and a particular office where users are located has to carry traffic only for that office and therefore has a lower bandwidth requirement than does a backbone link. This makes dial backup utilizing technologies such as ISDN more attractive, as the dial-up link in this situation is more likely to be able to handle the traffic. The other network topologies are feasible, but the cost is rarely justified.

Assuming that at the distribution level we have individual links going from the distribution center to each site, we have a choice to make regarding dial backup. We can provide no dial backup if the network connection is not mission-critical, provide dial backup to the distribution center, or provide a central dial backup solution at the head office.

Deciding whether to provide one central pool of dial ports or distributed ports at each distribution point depends on what the users at each site ultimately need to access. Given that the remote sites need access to head office hosts, we have to consider where other servers, such as e-mail and office automation servers, will be located. The options for locations for these types of servers are the head office, the distribution center, and the remote site.

The most efficient design from the perspective of dial-up port utilization is to provide one central pool of ports. This enables you to provide the least number of ports and still provide sufficient backup capability for realistic network outages. If separate pools of ports are made available at each distribution center, more ports overall are necessary to provide adequate cover.

If all services to which users need access over the internetwork are located at the head office, it makes sense to go with one pool of ports located at the head office. If the user sites need access to servers located at the distribution centers as well as at the head office, it makes more sense to provide individual dial-up pools at the distribution centers.

There is one additional benefit to providing a central dial-up pool at the head office, and that is if a major outage that affects the whole internetwork, the dial-up pool can be used to bypass the internetwork. That option is not available with distributed dial-up pools in the distribution centers. There might be a slim chance that something will happen to bring down the entire internetwork, but it is not unheard of. More than one well-known long-distance telephone company has had problems on its network that have affected regional and even national data services.

All of this seems quite simple and is basically common sense; the decision of where to locate the dial-up ports, however, is inexorably linked to the IP addressing scheme used and the routing protocol implemented. Route summarization is a feature of IP networking using distance vector routing protocols such as IGRP. Let's discuss what this means with reference to Fig. 7-6.

This figure shows an internetwork utilizing the addresses reserved by the InterNIC for companies using network address translation to connect to the Internet. The backbone uses the Class B network number and the distribution centers use Class C addresses implemented with a 255.255.255.224 subnet mask. This gives six subnets, each supporting a maximum of 30 hosts. Assuming that a distance vector routing protocol is in use, route summarization means that the distribution center shown will only advertise each Class C network back to the backbone, as the backbone is a different network number. Under normal conditions this is okay, because traffic traveling from the head office network to a Class C subnet will take the same path through the backbone until it reaches the distribution center. If, however, site A in Fig. 7-6 loses its link to the distribution center and dials in to a central pool of dial-up ports, we have a problem. We now have two physical connections between the 172.16.0.0 network and the 192.168.1.0 network.

In this situation, routers at the head office will have to choose between a route to the 192.168.1.0 network via the dial-up port, or through the backbone. This is because the routing tables in the head office routers will accept only whole network number for networks that are not directly connected. What ends up happening is that whichever of the two routes to 193.168.1.0 has the lowest metric is the one that gets entered in the head office routing tables, and the other route to the 193.168.1.0 network will never get traffic.

If this network numbering scheme is chosen, distributed dial-up port pools are the only option. If the whole internetwork was based on the

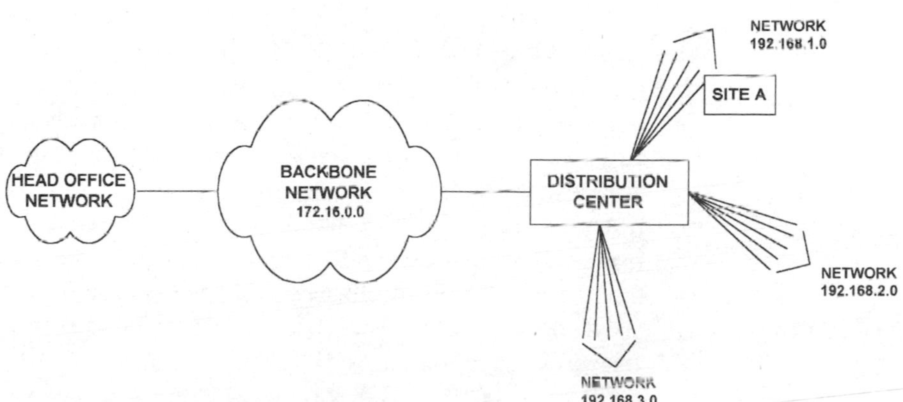

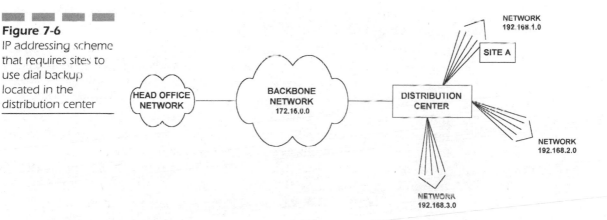

Figure 7-6
IP addressing scheme that requires sites to use dial backup located in the distribution center

one Class A or Class B network, appropriately subnetted, either central or distributed dial-up port pools would work. This is because all sites are on the same major network number and subnet mask information is utilized throughout the internetwork to identify where individual subnets are physically attached.

Head Office and Remote Site Topologies

At a user site, such as site A in Fig. 7-6, the on-site router connects the site LAN to the distribution center and initiates dial backup when needed. A host machine such as a user PC typically will be configured for one router address as the default router, sometimes referred to as the *default gateway*. This means that if the PC has to send traffic to a network address that is not on the directly connected segment, it will send the traffic to the default router, which will be expected to handle routing of traffic through the distribution and backbone networks. This becomes a problem only if the site router fails, but this is a rare occurrence and should be easily and quickly fixed by a hardware swap-out.

This type of routing is fine for a user site that services up to 20 or so single-user PCs, but it might not serve the needs of the central site with multiuser hosts that are accessed by more than 100 remote offices. To eliminate the central router as a single point of failure, Cisco has developed the *Hot Standby Router Protocol* (HSRP), a proprietary mechanism for providing the functionality of the IETF's *Router Discovery Protocol* (IRDP).

The functionality these protocols provide can best be explained with reference to Fig. 7-7, which shows how the WAN interconnections illustrated in Fig. 7-5 may be implemented with physical hardware for the Chicago head office.

If hosts 1 through 3 are configured using default gateways, each host will send all traffic destined for remote network numbers to its default gateway. What happens if this router fails? All the router devices on the network (assuming that a routing protocol such as IGRP is in use) will adjust their routing tables to reflect this change in network topology and will recalculate new paths to route around the failure. The hosts, however, do not run IGRP and cannot participate in this process. The hosts will continue sending traffic destined for remote networks to the failed router and remote access to the hosts will not be restored.

IRDP is a mechanism that requires a host TCP/IP stack that is IRDP-aware. A host that uses IRDP to get around this problem listens for hello packets from the router it is using to get to remote networks. If

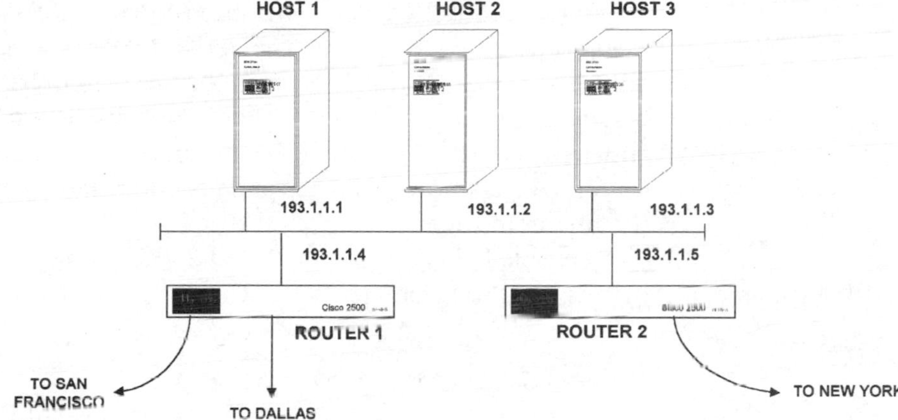

Figure 7-7
A potential network configuration for the Chicago head office

the hello packets stop arriving, the host will start using another router to get to remote networks. Unfortunately not all hosts support IRDP, and to support these non-IRDP hosts, Cisco developed HSRP.

To implement HSRP, you manually configure each host to use a default gateway IP address of a router that does not physically exist, in essence a "ghost" router, which is referred to in the Cisco documentation as a *phantom.* In Fig. 7-7, router 1 and router 2 will be configured to provide HSRP functionality to hosts 1 through 3. To achieve this, we enable HSRP on router 1 and router 2 and configure them to respond to hosts sending traffic to the phantom router MAC address. Note that you do not configure the phantom's MAC address anywhere; you just assign an IP address for the phantom in the configuration of routers 1 and 2 that matches the default gateway IP address configured in the hosts. Whichever of router 1 or router 2 gets elected as the active router will respond to ARP requests for the phantom's MAC address with a MAC address allocated from a pool of Cisco MAC addresses reserved for phantoms.

Using the addressing scheme of Fig. 7-7, we could define the default gateway for all hosts as 193.1.1.6. The process by which one of these hosts delivers a packet to a remote client PC, e.g., 200.1.1.1, would be like this:

- The destination network is not 193.1.1.0, therefore the host will send the packet to the default gateway.
- The ARP table will be referenced to determine the MAC address of the default gateway.
- A packet will be formed with the destination IP address of 200.1.1.1 and with destination MAC address as that of the default gateway.

Routers 1 and 2 will be configured to run HSRP, which at boot time elects one of the routers as the active HSRP router. This active router will respond to all traffic sent to the MAC address of the device numbered 193.1.1.6. Routers 1 and 2 will continually exchange hello packets and in the event the active router becomes unavailable, the standby router will take over routing packets addressed to the MAC address of the phantom router.

To enable HSRP on routers 1 and 2, the following configuration commands need to be entered for both routers:

```
Router(config)#interface Ethernet 0
Router(config-int)#standby ip 193.1.1.6
```

Any host ARP requests for the MAC address of 193.1.1.6 will be answered by the active router. As long as the active router is up, it will handle all packets sent to the phantom router, and if the active router fails, the standby router takes over routing responsibility for the phantom router with no change in configuration or ARP tables of the hosts.

Designing Physical Network Layout

Each networking technology has its own physical restrictions and requirements within its own specifications. There are, however, some generic guidelines that are useful when designing an internetwork that has to provide a high degree of availability.

Communication Vendor Issues. The first thing to consider if you are going to install ISDN links as dial backups to the main communication lines is that the leased lines and ISDN lines likely will be provided by different vendors and delivered to a site by separate networks. If the ISDN and main link are provided by one vendor service to one of your remote locations which, then experiences a lack of service due to problems at one of your communication vendor's central offices, going to dial backup is unlikely to help, as the ISDN connection most likely will be routed through the same central office that is experiencing problems.

There are additional issues to consider for a central site. Typically at a central site that is housing the multiuser hosts accessed by the remote branches, you should seek to have two points of access to your communication vendor's facilities. In most major metropolitan areas, high-speed communication links are being delivered on fiber optic SONET (can also be referred to as SDH) rings. The idea behind this is that placing a central site on a SONET ring enables the communication vendor to have two physical routes to your central site, and if one side of the ring is broken, the vendor can always get traffic to you by using the other side.

This works only if the two fiber cables being used to deliver the service to your central site never use the same physical path. This means there must be two points of access to your building so that the fibers can be diversely routed into your premises. I have seen several organizations that had hoped to reap the reliability benefits of being on a SONET ring but were unable to do so because both fibers were pulled through the same access point to the building. In this case, if one fiber gets broken, for example, if road workers break all cables going into one side of your building, both fibers will be broken, thus taking away part of the benefit of being on a SONET ring.

In metropolitan areas, many sites will be serviced with fiber links directly to the building. In less densely populated areas, communication vendors typically have to extend service to a building using a direct copper link of some kind. Typically it is not cost-justified for a communication vendor to extend a SONET ring to a remote area. In the main, this is something you just have to live with. The issue you face is that copper connections are more susceptible to interference than fiber cables, and you should expect more problems getting a copper-connected site operating at full throughput than you would with a fiber-connected site.

Reducing Manual Configuration

So far we have discussed issues related to internetwork design and configuration that have assumed all devices have an IP address configured. Manually configuring IP addresses for each host router and PC implemented on a large internetwork can be a time-consuming task. There are, however, some mechanisms such as RARP, BOOTP, and DHCP that can reduce this burden.

RARP: Reverse Address Resolution Protocol

Reverse Address Resolution Protocol (RARP) converts MAC addresses into IP addresses, which is the reverse of what the regular ARP protocol does. RARP originally was designed for supplying IP addresses to diskless workstations in an Ethernet environment. A diskless workstation has no hard drive on which to locate its IP address; it does, however, have a unique MAC address on its network card. When the diskless workstation boots up, it sends out a layer 2 broadcast (all 1s in the destination MAC address). When a server running RARP receives one of these broadcasts, it looks up a table (in a Unix machine, this table is usually located in the */etc/ethers* file) and supplies the IP address that the table associates with the MAC address back to the machine originating the broadcast.

The functionality of RARP was enhanced by the bootstrap protocol BOOTP, and later the *Dynamic Host Configuration Protocol.* DHCP is a superset of what BOOTP does. BOOTP and DHCP are implemented with both client and server software, the former to request IP configuration information, and the latter to assign it. Because DHCP was developed after BOOTP, DHCP servers will service IP configuration information to BOOTP clients.

DHCP: Dynamic Host Configuration Protocol

Assuming that a DHCP server exists on the same local segment as a client machine needing to find its IP configuration via DHCP, the client machine will issue a broadcast on startup of the IP protocol stack. This broadcast will contain the source MAC address of the workstation, which will be examined by the DHCP server.

A DHCP server can operate in one of three modes, the first of which is *automatic assignment,* which permanently assigns the one IP address to a given workstation. This is appropriate for environments with plenty of available addresses for the number of hosts on the network, typically one that is connecting to the Internet via a Network Address Translation machine of some kind.

The second mode, *dynamic addressing*, allocates IP addresses to hosts for a predetermined amount of time. In this configuration, IP addresses are returned to a pool of addresses that can be reassigned as new hosts become available and old hosts are retired. Dynamic addressing is most appropriate for sites that have a limited address space and need to reallocate addresses as soon as a host is retired. Typically, these sites are using InterNIC-assigned addresses and are connected directly to the Internet.

The third mode for DHCP, *manual mode,* uses DHCP merely as a transport mechanism for a network administrator to manually assign IP configuration information to a workstation. Manual mode is rarely used for DHCP implementations.

DHCP is the most popular method of automatically assigning IP addresses, and is the default method used by Microsoft products. DHCP has been put forward by many as a method to simplify renumbering of an internetwork, should that become necessary for any reason. It would be much simpler to change the IP information on a few dozen DHCP servers than on hundreds or thousands of hosts. The downside is that there is no built-in cooperation between DHCP and DNS (discussed in the next section). Obviously the DNS information will become useless if a host is using an IP address different from the one listed in the DNS database.

Cisco will be providing a product that will coordinate DHCP and DNS for you, such that if DHCP assigns a new IP address to a host, the change in that host address will be reflected in the DNS database.

Centrally Managing Host Names

So far, we have only discussed translation of host names to IP addresses via reference to a host table. On a large internetwork, distributed host files on numerous hosts become burdensome to manage. Imagine moving a host from one subnet to another and having to manually alter hundreds of host files located around the internetwork to reflect that change.

Fortunately, there is a service called *Domain Name Service* (DNS) that enables you to centrally manage the mapping of host names to IP addresses. DNS does not rely on one large table, but is a distributed database that guarantees new host information will be disseminated across the internetwork as needed. The major drawback of DNS is that there is no way for a new host to advertise itself to DNS when it comes online. Although DNS will distribute information throughout an internetwork, a host initially must be manually configured into a central DNS machine when the host first comes online.

You have to configure each host to use DNS in preference to a host file for name resolution, and supply the IP address of the DNS server that must be referenced. When a DNS server receives a request for information regarding a host it does not currently know about, the request is passed on to what is known as an *authoritative server*. Typically each domain has an authoritative server that supplies answers to several DNS servers that each have a manageable number of hosts to service. A previous version of DNS was called *nameservice*. Nameservice and DNS are differentiated by the port numbers they use; nameservice uses port number 42 and DNS uses 53.

If your internetwork is going to accommodate more than a dozen or so hosts, it is worth implementing DNS. In the following discussion, we will examine in overview how DNS is implemented on the Internet. It is a good model for illustrating how DNS can be scaled to very large internetworks.

A DNS hierarchy is similar to the hierarchy of a computer's file system. At the top is the *root domain* consisting of a group of *root servers,* which service the *top-level domains.* These top-level domains are broken into organizational and geographic domains. For example, geographic domains include *.uk* for the United Kingdom, *.de* for Germany, and *.jp* for Japan. Normally no country-specific domain is associated with the United States. The U.S. top-level domain is split into organizational groups, such as *.com* for commercial enterprises, *.gov* for government agencies, and so forth. Some of the top-level domains for the United States are shown in Fig. 7-8.

Just as you can locate files in a file system by following a path from the root, you can locate hosts or particular DNS servers by following their paths through the DNS hierarchy. For example, a host called *elvis* in the domain *stars* within the commercial organization *oldies* is locatable by the name *elvis.stars.oldies.com.*

In some ways the operation of DNS can be thought of as similar to the way routing tables work for routing packets through an internetwork. No single DNS server has a complete picture of the whole hierarchy; it just knows what is the next DNS server in the chain to which it is to pass the request. A particular domain is reachable when pointers for that domain exist in the domain above it. Computers in the *.edu* domain cannot access computers in the *.work.com* domain until a pointer to the DNS server of the *.work* subdomain is placed in the servers of the *.com* domain. A DNS database in the *.com* DNS servers contains name server records that identify the names of the DNS servers for each domain directly under the *.com* domain.

Figure 7-8
Top-level domains for the Internet

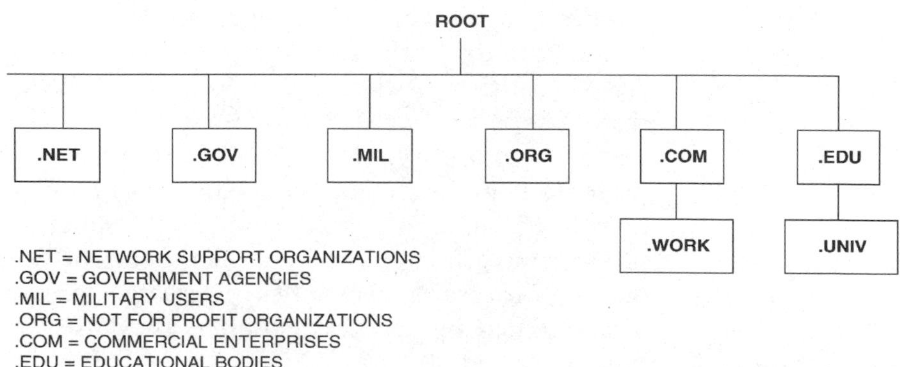

Let's clarify this by considering an example. Supposing a domain under *.edu* has been created called *.univ* and a domain under *.com* has been created called *.work* (illustrated in Fig. 7-8). Now, a computer in the *.univ* domain (let's say it is named *vax*) needs to contact a machine in the *.work.com* domain (which is called *sun*). The task to accomplish here is to provide to the machine *vax.univ.edu,* the IP address of *sun.work.com.* The process to complete this task is as follows:

- The *vax.univ.edu* host is configured to have its DNS server as the machine with IP address 201.1.2.3, so it sends a DNS request to that IP address. This computer must be reachable by *vax.univ.edu.*
- Host *vax.univ.edu* receives a reply stating that a machine named *overtime.work.com* has all DNS information for the *.work.com* domain, and the IP address of *overtime.work.com* is included in the reply.
- Host *vax.univ.edu* will then send a query to the IP address of *overtime.work.com* for the IP address of *sun.work.com.*
- The computer *overtime.work.com* replies with the requested IP address, so *vax.univ.edu* can now contact *sun.work.com.*

DNS is normally implemented on a Unix machine via the *Berkeley Internet Name Domain* (BIND) programs. *BIND* has two elements, the *Name Server* and the *Resolver.* The Resolver forms queries that are sent to DNS servers. Under BIND, all computers run the Resolver code (accessed through libraries). The Name Server answers queries, but only computers supplying DNS information need to run the Name Server.

On a Unix machine running BIND, the *named.hosts* file contains most of the domain information, converting host names to IP addresses and also containing information about the mail servers for that particular domain. DNS and BIND are subjects that justify a complete book in their own right. The preceding discussion is intended to give a very brief overview of how DNS can simplify administration of a large TCP/IP-based internetwork. If you want to set up DNS on your network (I recommend that you do), refer to the publication *DNS and BIND* by Cricket Liu and Paul Albitz, published by O'Reilly and Associates.

If you can configure DNS and either BOOTP or DHCP, your life as administrator of a large TCP/IP-based internetwork will be much simpler.

Securing a TCP/IP Internetwork

Security is a concern to all network mangers and administrators, but the level of security that is appropriate for any given internetwork can be determined only by those responsible for that internetwork. Obviously, an internetwork servicing financial transactions between banks justifies more security measures than an internetwork providing access to public-domain technical articles. When implementing security measures, there often is a tradeoff between security and user-friendliness. The risk of a security breach, along with its likely occurrence and its impact on the internetwork owner, must be judged on a case-by-case basis.

Broadly, there are three areas to be considered when security is designed into an internetwork: physical, network, and application layer issues.

Application Layer Measures

At the Application layer, features such as Application level usernames and passwords can be implemented, and parameters such as the number of concurrent logins for each username, frequency at which a password will be forced to change, and minimum length of passwords can be enforced. Typically, all traditional multiuser systems (such as mini- or mainframe hosts, and PC servers like Novell or Windows NT) support these type of features as standard. For further information on the Application-level security features of any network operating system, refer to the supplier's documentation.

As more and more information is made available via the World Wide Web technologies such as *HyperText Markup Language* (HTML) and *Hyper-Text Transport Protocol* (HTTP), new Application layer security issues have arisen. We will highlight some of the issues associated with implementing security measures at the Application level for the newer Web-based technologies that utilize browsers and Web servers. These issues are relevant to securing communications on either an internal intranet or the public Internet. It should be noted that the following discussion is intended only to introduce the concepts of Application level security, because the focus of this book is on the Network and lower layers and how Cisco implements the features of these layers.

Traditional servers (NetWare, NT, etc.) authenticate users based on the use of *stateful* protocols. This means that a user establishes a connection to the server and that connection is maintained for the duration of the user's session. At any one time, the server will know who is logged on and from where. HTTP servers were designed for the rapid and efficient delivery of hypertext documents and therefore use a *stateless* protocol. An HTTP connection has four distinct stages:

1. The client contacts the server at the Internet address specified in the URL.
2. The client requests service, and delivers information about what it can and cannot support.
3. The server sends the state of the transaction and, if successful, the data requested; if unsuccessful, it transmits a failure code.
4. Ultimately the connection is closed and the server does not maintain any memory of the transaction that just took place.

Because the server does not maintain a connection, it does not know if multiple people are using the same username and password, or from what protocol address they are connecting. This is a concern, as users could share usernames and passwords with unauthorized individuals without any loss of service to themselves. What is needed is a mechanism that restores the functionality of allowing only one username and password to be used from one location at a time.

Cookies can help in this situation. In HTTP terms, a *cookie* is a type of license with a unique ID number. Cookies give you the ability to force a user to log in again if he or she uses the same username and password from a different workstation. Cookies work like this:

- A user logs in for the first time, in this case his/her browser has no cookie to present. The server either issues a cookie associated with this user if the user has logged in before, or issues a new cookie number if the user has not.
- If a request from another workstation using the same username and password comes along, the server issues a new cookie to that connection, making the original cookie invalid.
- The user at the original workstation makes another request, with the cookie number originally received. The server sees that a new cookie number already has been issued and returns an "unauthorized" header, prompting the user for the username/password pair.

This mechanism ensures that each username and password pair can be used only from one location at a time. Cookies don't answer all security issues, but they are a piece of the puzzle for providing security features in an environment using Web-based technologies.

Overview of Cryptography. Having illustrated the conceptual difference between the traditional stateful protocols and the Web-based stateless protocols, we will discuss what technologies can address the following concerns:

1. How do I authenticate users so that I can be assured users are who they claim to be?
2. How can I authorize users for some network services and not others?
3. How can I ensure that store-and-forward (e-mail) applications, as well as direct browser-to-server communications, are conducted privately?
4. How do I ensure that messages have not been altered during transmission?

The foundation for supplying answers to these questions is based on *cryptography,* which is a set of technologies that provides the following capabilities:

- Authentication to identify a user, particular computer, or organization on the internetwork.
- Digital signatures and signature verification to associate a verified signature with a particular user.
- Encryption and decryption to ensure that unauthorized users cannot intercept and read a message before it reaches its destination.
- Authorization, using access control lists to restrict users to accessing specified resources.

There are two types of cryptography that use a key system to encrypt and decrypt messages, *symmetric-key* and *public-key.* The following explanations are simplifications of what actually takes place; the implementations use sophisticated mathematical techniques to ensure their integrity. Symmetric-key cryptography uses the same key to encrypt and decrypt a message. The problem with this method is the need to securely coordinate the same key to be in use at both ends of the communication. If it is transmitted between sender and receiver, it is open to being captured and used by a malicious third party.

Public-key cryptography uses a different approach, wherein each user has a public key and a private key. When user 1 wants to send a message to user 2, user 1 uses the public key of user 2 to encrypt the message before it is sent. The public key of user 2 is freely available to any other user. When user 2 receives the message, it is decrypted using the private key of user 2. Sophisticated mathematical techniques ensure that a message encrypted using the public key can be decrypted only by using the proper private key. This enables messages to be securely exchanged without the sender and receiver having to share secret information before they communicate.

In addition to public-key cryptography, *public-key certificates,* which are also called *digital IDs,* can be used to authenticate users to ensure they are who they claim to be. Certificates are small files containing user-specific information. Defined in an ITU standard (X.509), certificates include the following information:

- A name uniquely identifying the owner of the certificate. This name includes the username, company, or organization with which the user is associated, and the user's country of residence.
- The name and digital signature of the device that issued the certificate to the user.
- The owner's public key.
- The period during which the certificate is valid.

Public-Key Technologies. Public-key technology is implemented in industry-standard protocols such as the *Secure Sockets Layer* (SSL) and the *Secure Multipurpose Internet Mail Extensions* (S/MIME) protocols. These protocols address the issues raised at the beginning of the section as follows:

- Authentication of users is by digital certificates.
- Authorization, to grant users access to specific resources, is provided by binding users listed in access control lists to certificates and checking of digital signatures.
- Ensuring privacy of communication between two computers is enabled by the use of public-key technologies.
- Ensuring that messages have not been altered during transmission is covered by the implementation of Digest algorithms, such as Message Digest 5 (MD5) as used by Cisco's implementation of CHAP. CHAP will be discussed more fully in the section on Network layer security.

Typically, browser-to-Webserver communications are based on HTTP, which uses a default port number of 80 for communications. SSL uses port 443, so you can force all connections to use SSL and therefore be subject to SSL security features by allowing connections to a Web server only using port 443. This is easily achieved by using Cisco access lists, as shown in Fig. 7-9.

Packet-Level Security

In this section we cover issues related to Cisco router configuration that affect the overall security of your internetwork. This comprises Data Link (encryption) as well as Network layer (routing restriction) functions. As with Application layer security, there is a trade-off between providing a user-friendly system and one that is highly secure. A balance must be struck that provides reasonable ease of access to authorized users and restricts access to unauthorized persons.

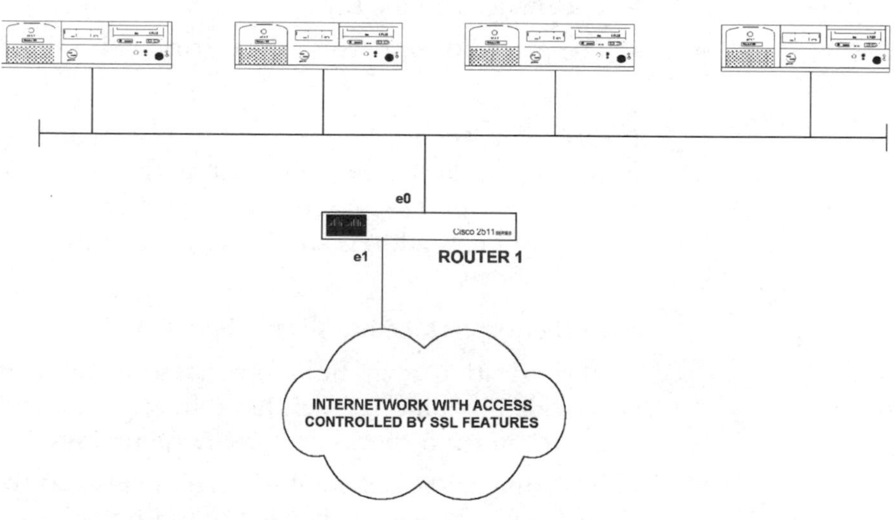

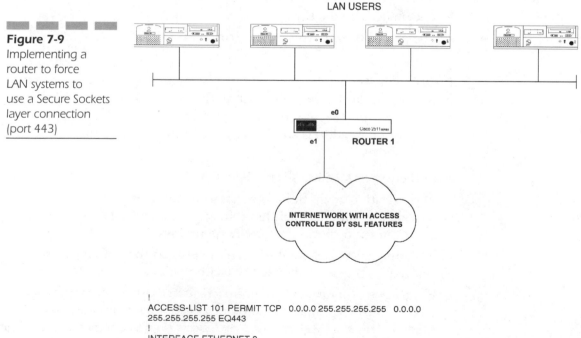

Figure 7-9 Implementing a router to force LAN systems to use a Secure Sockets layer connection (port 443)

```
!
ACCESS-LIST 101 PERMIT TCP  0.0.0.0 255.255.255.255  0.0.0.0
255.255.255.255 EQ443
!
INTERFACE ETHERNET 0
IP ACCESS-GROUP 101 IN
```

It must be understood that users can undermine security measures if these measures do not fit with work practices. Many times I have seen usernames and passwords written on pieces of paper that have been stuck to a screen. Users resorted to this kind of behavior because the passwords were changed too frequently and were obscure. To implement security measures fully, you must have the backing of senior management, must educate users about security issues, and must have agreed-upon procedures known to everyone in the organization.

Having said this, there are many security measures a network administrator can implement without user knowledge that will significantly improve the security of the internetwork. Let's talk first about controlling access to Cisco routers.

Password Access to Cisco Routers. First let's see what can be done to restrict unauthorized users from attaching an ASCII terminal to the console port and determining information about the internetwork by using well-known `show` commands. There is no default password assigned to the console port; simply by attaching the appropriately configured terminal and pressing the Enter key, you get the router prompt echoed to the screen. You can add a console password with the following commands:

```
Router1(config)#line console 0
Router1(config-line)#login
Router1(config-line)#password gr8scot
```

Now each time a terminal is connected to the console port, a password prompt rather than the router prompt is presented to the user trying to get access. On Cisco 2500-series routers, the auxiliary port can be used the same way as a console port to attach an ASCII terminal for displaying the router prompt. It is a good idea to password-protect the auxiliary port by using the following commands:

```
Router1(config)#line aux 0
Router1(config-line)#login
Router1(config-line)#password gr8scot
```

It is always best to make the nonprivileged-mode password a relatively easy-to-remember combination of alphanumeric characters. The password shown here is an abbreviation of the statement, "Great Scott!"

A similar situation is true for Telnet access, and it is a good idea to prompt users with Telnet access to the router for a nonprivileged-mode password before allowing them to see the router prompt. Each Telnet session is identified by the router as a virtual terminal. Many simultaneous virtual terminal accesses can be supported, but a typical configuration puts a five-session limit on Telnet access. It does this by identifying terminals 0 through 4, which is implemented with the following commands:

```
Router1(config)#line vty 0 4
Router1(config)#login
Router1(config)#password you8it
```

This discussion covers what can be done to secure access to nonprivileged mode on a Cisco router. Restricting access to privileged mode is even more crucial than restricting access to nonprivileged mode. Once nonprivileged mode has been gained to the router, only the security of the Enable password or secret stops an unauthorized user from getting full control of the router. Only the network administration staff needs to know the Enable password or secret that allows a user into privileged mode, and it therefore should be obscure and changed frequently. It is part of a network administrator's job to keep track of such things.

The Enable secret is always encrypted in the router configuration. If privileged mode access to a router is given through an Enable password, it should be encrypted in the configuration as follows:

```
Router1(config)#service password-encryption
```

This command is followed by no arguments and encrypts all password displays.

Centralizing Router Access. It generally is good practice to limit any type of remote access to routers on your internetwork to a limited set of network numbers. It's typical for one network number to be dedicated for use by network administrative staff only. It is then possible to configure a router to accept network connections that can be used for router management functions only if they originate with this particular network.

It is possible to restrict this type of access to just one service, such as Telnet, from a central location. Ping, SNMP, and TFTP are useful utilities when managing remote devices; however, so restricting access to just one network number usually is sufficient. This can be achieved by implementing a simple access list on all routers. Access list 13, shown next, (defined in global configuration mode) identifies the network used by administration staff to get to the routers, which is the 200.1.1.0 network.

```
Router1(config)#Access-list 13 permit 200.1.1.0 0.0.0.255
```

Once this list has been defined, it must be applied to an interface. If this list is applied to the virtual terminal lines, because the only connections coming into these ports are Telnet sessions, the only Telnet sessions accepted will be those that originate from the 200.1.1.0 network. Applying this access list to the virtual terminal lines is done via the `access-class` command as shown:

```
Router1(config)#line vty 0 4
Router1(config-line)#access-class 13 in
```

The TACACS Security System. The discussion so far has centered around defining access configurations on each individual router. It is possible to centralize password administration for a large number of remote routers by using the *TACACS* system. TACACS stands for the *Terminal Access Controller Access Control System.* Though TACACS usually is deployed to centralize management of CHAP usernames and passwords, which are defined on a per-interface basis, it also can be used to authenticate users seeking Telnet (and hence Enable) access to a router. TACACS provides the freedom to authenticate individual users and log their activity, whereas an Enable password defined on a router is a global configuration and its use cannot be traced to a specific user.

To configure this type of access checking, you need to set up the TACACS daemon on a Unix machine, configure all routers to reference that Unix machine for TACACS authorization, and configure the virtual terminals to use TACACS to check login requests. Assuming that a Unix machine is appropriately configured for TACACS, with the address 210.1.1.1, the configuration for each remote router to will be as follows:

```
tacacs-server host 200.1.1.1
tacacs-server last-resort password
!
line vty 0 4
login tacacs
```

The first line identifies as a global configuration the IP address of the TACACS host machine. The next entry configures the router to prompt the user trying to get access to use the standard login password defined with the `Enable password` command. This command comes into play if the router cannot gain access to the TACACS server defined in the first configuration entry. The entry `login tacacs` refers all requests for connections coming in over the virtual terminals to the TACACS server for authentication.

With this configuration, access to the nonprivileged mode is authenticated by the TACACS server. Access to Enable mode can be similarly checked by TACACS if the following configuration commands are added:

```
!
tacacs-server extended
enable use-tacacs
tacacs-server authenticate enable
enable last-resort password
!
```

Here's what these commands do:

- Command `tacacs-server extended` initializes the router to use extended TACACS mode.
- Command `enable use-tacacs` tells the router to use TACACS to decide whether a user should be allowed to enter privileged mode.
- Command `tacacs-server authenticate enable` is necessary, and if it is not in the configuration, you will be locked out of the router. In this example, it may appear redundant, as this command defines the Enable form of authentication, but it can be used to authenticate protocol connections and more sophisticated options using access lists.
- Command `enable last-resort password` allows use of the Enable password in the router's configuration if the TACACS server is unavailable.

The TACACS server authenticates users against those listed in its configuration. Usernames and passwords are simply listed in the TACACS server as shown here:

```
username user1 password aaa12
username user2 password bbb34
```

Extensions to the Cisco-supplied TACACS system allow for the use of a token card that is synchronized with the TACACS server software, which changes the password for users every three minutes. To successfully log in to such a system, the user must carry a token card that displays the new password every three minutes. This makes a system very secure; however, the user must keep the token card in a safe place, separate from the computer where the login takes place. Leaving the token card next to the computer being used for login is as ineffective in terms of providing the intended level of security as posting the password on the screen.

Securing Intercomputer Communication. In the previous section we looked at using passwords and TACACS to restrict access to privileged and nonprivileged mode on the router. Here we will look at using CHAP and TACACS for the authenticating, authorizing, and accounting of computers attempting to make connections to the internetwork and participate in the routing of packets. CHAP is preferred over PAP as a method for authenticating users because it is not susceptible to the modem playback issues discussed in Chap. 6. CHAP is available only on a point-to-point link; in Cisco router terms, this means serial interfaces, async interfaces, or ISDN interfaces. You cannot implement CHAP on a LAN interface.

The basic idea behind the operation of CHAP is that the router receiving a request for a connection will have a list of usernames and associated passwords. The computer wanting to connect will have to supply one of these valid username and password pairs in order to gain access. Implementing CHAP on serial interfaces connecting routers together uses the same configuration as defined for the ISDN connections using CHAP as illustrated in Chap. 6. Here we will discuss how TACACS, can enhance the security features of CHAP.

Many of the configuration commands for using TACACS to provide security on network connections begin with the letters *AAA*, which stand for Authentication, Authorization, and Accounting. Authentication is used to identify valid users and allow them access, and to disallow access for intruders. Authorization determines what services on the internetwork the user can access. Accounting tracks which user did what and when, which can be used for audit-trail purposes.

We now will examine the commands that you put into a router or access server to enable TACACS when using AAA security on network connections. Let's list a typical configuration that would be input on a router to configure it for centralized TACACS+ management, and then discuss each command in turn. Figure 7-10 shows the configuration, command explanations follow.

Figure 7-10 Typical router configuration for centralized TACACS+ management

```
!
AAA NEW-MODEL
TACACS-SERVER HOST 210.5.5.0
TACACS-SERVER HOST 205.7.7.3
!
AAA AUTHENTICATION LOGIN DEFAULT TACACS +
AAA AUTHENTICATION ENABLE DEFAULT TACACS +  ENABLE
AAA AUTHENTICATION PPP DEFAULT TACACS + ENABLE
AAA AUTHENTICATION NETWORK TACACS +
AAA ACCOUNTING CONNECTION START-STOP TACACS +
!
LINE 1 16
LOGIN AUTHENTICATION DEFAULT
!
INTERFACE SERIAL 0
PPP AUTHENTICATION CHAP DEFAULT
```

Command `aaa new-model` enables TACACS+, as the Cisco implementation of TACACS is known. This can be done either by the `tacacs-server extended` command shown earlier, or by the `aaa new-model command`, which enables the AAA access control mechanism and TACACS+.

Command `tacacs-server host 210.5.5.1` identifies the IP address of the TACACS+ host that should be referenced. This command appears twice in the configuration, allowing the router to search for more than one TACACS+ server on the internetwork in case one is unavailable.

Command `aaa authentication login default tacacs+ line` sets AAA authentication at login, which in the case of a serial line connection is when both ends of the point-to-point connection are physically connected and the routers attempt to bring up the line protocol.

The preceding command is used to create an authentication list called `default`, which specifies up to four methods of authentication that may be used. At this stage, we have just created the list, but it has not yet been applied to a line or connection. Further down in this configuration, these access methods have been applied to lines 1 to 16 and the Serial 0 interface. In this command, we have specified a single option for authenticating any computer that belongs to the default group for authentication. Authentication for this group can be achieved only by using TACACS+ authentication. This command covers authenticating users for nonprivileged mode access.

Command `aaa authentication enable default tacacs+ enable` defines how privileged mode (Enable mode) access is authenticated. In the same way that the previous command defined `tacacs+` as the method of authenticating access to nonprivileged mode for the default group, this command defines `tacacs+` and the Enable password as methods for authenticating users belonging to the list `default` for privileged-mode access.

In the command `aaa authorization network tacacs+`, the word `network` specifies that authorization is required for all network functions, including all PPP connections, and that TACACS+ authentication will be used to verify service provision. The stem of this command is `aaa authorization`, which can be followed by one of the words `network`, `connection`, or `exec` to specify which function will be subject to the authorization methods that follow (in this case `tacacs+`).

Command `aaa authentication ppp default tacacs+ enable` defines TACACS+ followed by the Enable password as the authentication methods available for serial interfaces that belong to the default list. This command specifies a list name `default` that is used for the interface command `ppp authentication chap default`.

In this configuration we have looked at three configuration options for the `aaa authentication` command; AAA authentication will invoke authorization for nonprivileged (login), privileged (Enable), and PPP access.

Command `aaa accounting connection start-stop tacacs+` sets up the accounting function, now that authentication and authorization configurations have been defined. Within this command we specify what events will trigger accounting, which in this case is the starting or stopping of any outbound Telnet or Rlogin session as defined by the argument `connection`. Logging of the specified events is sent only to the TACACS+ server.

Command `line 1 16` specifies the line range number we are about to configure.

Command `login authentication default` sets the methods to be used to authenticate connections on lines 1 through 16 as those specified by the default list. These methods for the default list are specified in the `aaa authentication login default` command.

Command `interface serial 0` identifies the serial interface we are going to configure for authentication.

Command `ppp authentication chap default` uses the default list specified in the `aaa authentication ppp default` command to authorize PPP connections on this interface.

In summary, there are global authorization commands for login, enable, and PPP access, with each command defining a list name and the authorization methods that will be used on the line or interface the list name is applied to. The configuration shown uses the default list (as defined in the global `aaa authentication login` command) to authenticate login requests on line 1 through 16, and the default list (as defined in the `aaa authentication ppp` command) for authenticating PPP connections on interface Serial 0.

SNMP Security Issues. We will discuss the *Simple Network Management Protocol* (SNMP) as a way of simplifying the management of a large internetwork of routers later in this chapter. If you enable SNMP on your routers, you are opening the door for potential security loopholes. SNMP can be used to gather statistics, obtain configuration information, or change the configuration of the router.

An SNMP command issued to an SNMP-enabled router is accompanied by what is known as a *community string*, which has either read-only or read/write access to the router. The community string is used to identify an SNMP server station to the SNMP agent enabled on the router. Only when the correct community string is supplied will the router agent act upon the SNMP command. With SNMP version 1, this community string is passed over the network in clear text, so anyone who is capable of capturing a packet on the network can obtain the community strings. With SNMP version 2, which is supported on Cisco IOS version 10.3 and later, communication between an SNMP agent and server uses the MD5 algorithm for authentication to prevent unauthorized users from gaining the SNMP community strings.

If you are using SNMP version 2, there is a further precaution to take to ensure that unauthorized individuals cannot obtain the SNMP community strings, and that is to change the read/write community string to something known only to authorized personnel. If SNMP is enabled without a specified community string, the default of *public* is assumed. With this knowledge, unauthorized personnel can gain full SNMP access to any router with an SNMP agent enabled that does not specify an R/W community string.

Before we look at the commands to enable the SNMP agent on a router, we need to explore one further concept. Access lists are useful for defining which IP addresses can be used by stations issuing SNMP commands to routers. This feature restricts those workstations eligible to issue SNMP commands to the one or two management stations you have on the internetwork.

The following router configuration defines station 200.1.1.1 as able to issue read-only commands, and station 200.1.1.2 as able to issue read and write commands.

```
!
access-list 1 permit 200.1.1.1
access-list 2 permit 200.1.1.2
snmp-server community 1view RO 1
snmp-server community power1 RW 2
```

The router will grant read-only access to the station with source address 200.1.1.1 only if it supplies the community string `1view`, and the station with source address 200.1.1.2 will have read/write access if it supplies the community string `power1`.

Once a workstation is authenticated to issue SNMP commands, the router's *Management Information Base*, or *MIB*, can be queried and manipulated. The MIB contains configuration, statistical, and status information about the router. SNMP commands can issue "get" strings to obtain information from the MIB about the status of interfaces, passwords, and so forth, and then can set new values with "set" strings.

The Router As a Basic Firewall. Many computer configurations could be considered a firewall of some description. The role of a firewall is to keep unwanted traffic out of our internetwork, typically to prevent an unauthorized user from accessing computers on our internetwork, or finding out information about the internetwork.

The simplest form of firewall is a router configured with appropriate access lists that restrict traffic based on source, destination, or service type. Beyond this, features such as *application wrappers* and *proxies* should be evaluated, depending on the connectivity and security needs of your internetwork.

A *wrapper* is a Unix host application that takes the place of regular host daemons such as Telnet and FTP, and provides extra functionality beyond the regular daemon. When an inbound request for one of the wrapper services arrives at the host, the source requesting the service is checked by the wrapper to see if it is authorized to make the request. If the wrapper decides the request is from an approved source, the request is granted.

A *proxy* provides tighter security features. Proxy servers completely separate the internal and external traffic, passing information between the two in a controlled fashion. There are two types of proxy, *circuit-level* and *application-level*. A circuit-level proxy works on a low level, forwarding traffic without regard to the data content of a packet. An application-level proxy unbundles, repackages, and forwards packets, understanding the nature of the communication taking place. For in-depth discussion of constructing application-level firewalls, refer to *Firewalls and Internet Security*, by Cheswick and Bellovin, published by Addison-Wesley.

We will discuss in more depth here the use of a Cisco router to provide some firewall capability when connecting to an external network. A typical setup for using a Cisco router as the most basic type of firewall is illustrated in Fig. 7-11.

The Information Server provides DNS, Webserver, or e-mail services that both the internal and external networks need to utilize. The external network generally is the Internet (which is what I will assume throughout the rest of this discussion), but the same considerations apply when you are connecting your internetwork to any external network.

The goals of implementing restrictions on the traffic passing through this router are as follows:

1. Allow the hosts on the internal network to contact the computers they need to contact in the external network.

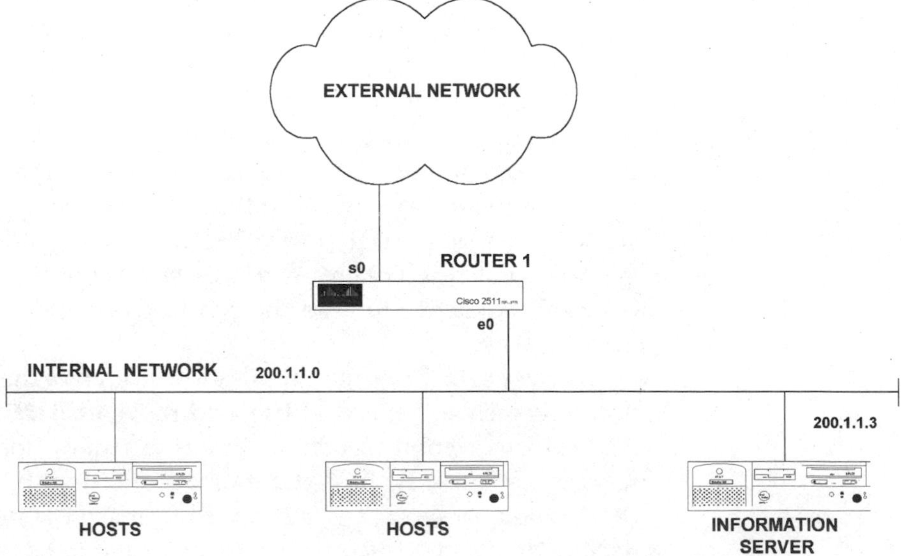

Figure 7-11 Connections for a basic firewall implementation

2. Allow users on the external network access only to the information server, and to use only the services we want them to use.

We achieve these goals by implementing an access list on the router. Since a router can read source address, destination address, protocol type, and port number, it is possible to tell the router what it should or should not allow, with a high degree of customization.

Before we examine access list construction, let's review TCP and UDP communications. With TCP connections, it is easy to identify which machine is initiating communication because there is a specific call setup sequence starting with a SYN packet. This enables a router to allow TCP connections that originate from one interface but not those from another. This enables you to configure the router to do things such as allowing Telnet sessions to the external network, but deny any sessions originating from the external network.

It's a different story with UDP connections. UDP conversations have no discernible beginning, end, or acknowledgment, making it impossible for a router that uses only protocol information to determine whether a UDP packet is originating a conversation, or part of an existing conversation. What we can do is restrict traffic on the basis of its source and destination. For example, we can restrict all traffic coming into our network from the external network, allowing it only to connect to the information server.

Securing a Router by Access Lists. Before we start building the configuration for this elementary firewall router, let's review the construction of a Cisco access list. IP access lists are either *regular* if numbered between 1 and 99, or *extended* if numbered between 100 and 199. A regular access list enables you to permit or deny traffic based on the source node or network address. An extended list is much more sophisticated, and enables you to restrict traffic based on protocol, source, and destination, and to allow established connections.

Allowing established connections is useful, for example, if you want hosts on the internal side of the router to be able to establish a Telnet session to a host on the external side, but do not want an external host to have the ability to establish a Telnet session with an internal host. When configured for established connections, a router will allow a TCP connection into the internal network only if it is part of a conversation initiated by a host on the internal network.

An access list will execute each line in order, until either a match for the packet type is found, or the end of a list is reached and the packet is discarded. With this type of processing, the sequence of access list entries is important. To keep things simple, all `permit` statements should be entered first, followed by `deny` statements. At the end of every access list is an unseen, implicit `deny` statement that denies everything. This makes sense, as typically you will want to allow a certain type of access through an interface and deny all others. The implicit `deny` saves you the bother of having to end all your access lists with a deny-everything statement.

Let's consider what we want to do with the access list for the router in Fig. 7-11. Assuming that the external network is the Internet, we want to allow external users to establish TCP connections to the information server for HTTP access to Web pages, Telnet, and SMTP sessions for mail, and allow UDP packets to pass for DNS traffic. Let's look at how each connection is established and how we will code these restrictions into the router's access list.

HTTP, Telnet, and SMTP all use TCP as the Transport layer protocol, with port numbers 80, 23, and 25, respectively. The port numbers listed are the port numbers that the host daemon program listens to for requests. When a client PC wants to establish an HTTP session with a Web server, for example, it will send a TCP request destined for port 80 addressed to the IP number of the Web server. The source port number used by the client PC is a random number in the range of 1024 to 65,535. Each end of the communication will be identified with an IP address/port pair. In this configuration, we are not concerned with restricting packets going out onto the Internet; we are interested only in restricting what comes in. To do that, we create an accesslist that permits connections using TCP ports 80, 23, and 25 to the IP address of the information server only, and apply that access list to packets inbound on the Serial 0 port of router 1. The access list is created in global configuration mode as follows:

```
access-list 101 permit tcp 0.0.0.0 255.255.255.255 200.1.1.3 0.0.0.0 eq 80
access-list 101 permit tcp 0.0.0.0 255.255.255.255 200.1.1.3 0.0.0.0 eq 23
access-list 101 permit tcp 0.0.0.0 255.255.255.255 200.1.1.3 0.0.0.0 eq 25
```

The 0.0.0.0 255.255.255.255 in each line allows any source address. The 200.1.1.3 0.0.0.0 allows only packets destined for IP address 200.1.1.3. Had the mask been set to 0.0.0.255, that would have allowed through any packets destined for the 200.1.1.0 Class C network.

All access lists are created in the same manner, and it is when they are applied in the router configuration that the syntax changes. When applied to an interface, the access list is applied as an *access group,* and when applied to a line, the access list is applied as an *access class*. When applied to routing updates, an access list is applied as a *distribute list*.

Access list 101 is applied to interface Serial 0 as follows:

```
Router1(config)#interface serial 0
Router1(config-int)#ip access-group 101 in
```

Next we allow remote machines to issue DNS queries to our information server. To enable hosts on the Internet to query our information server, we must allow in packets destined for UDP port 53. In addition, we need to allow TCP port 53 packets into our network for Zone Transfers (this will be from a machine specified by the ISP). We can let Zone Transfers and DNS queries through by specifying the following additions to our access list:

```
access-list 101 permit tcp 210.7.6.5 0.0.0.0 200.1.1.3 0.0.0.0 eq 53
access-list 101 permit udp 0.0.0.0 255.255.255.255 200.1.1.3 0.0.0.0 eq 53
```

The 210.7.6.5 is the server address specified by the ISP. We can finally add the entry to allow incoming packets addressed to high-numbered ports, for replies to connections originated from within our network, by the following:

```
access-list 101 permit tcp 0.0.0.0 255.255.255.255 200.1.1.3 0.0.0.0 gt 1023
access-list 101 permit udp 0.0.0.0 255.255.255.255 200.1.1.3 0.0.0.0 gt 1023
```

We now have entries in the router configuration that allow packets destined for TCP ports 80, 23, 25, 53, and those greater than 1023, as well as UDP port 53 and those greater than 1023. There are two more restrictions on the access list that we should implement to improve the security on this system. The first is to deny packets using the loopback source address (127.0.0.1). It is possible for a malicious intruder to fool our information server into thinking that the loopback address can be reached via the firewall router, and thus the intruder can capture packets not meant for the outside world. This can be restricted by the following access list entry:

```
access-list 101 deny ip 127.0.0.1 0.0.0.0 0.0.0.0 255.255.255.255
```

The same situation arises if an intruder uses the local network number as a source address, enabling him or her to get packets destined for local hosts sent out the firewall. This can be negated by another entry in the access list as follows:

```
access-list 101 ip deny 200.1.1.0 0.0.0.255 0.0.0.0 255.255.255.255
```

Global and Interface Security Commands. In addition to the access list restrictions already implemented, there are other configuration changes that we can make to improve the security of the firewall. The first is to deny any ICMP redirect messages from the external network. Intruders can use ICMP redirects to tell routers to redirect traffic to them instead of sending it to its legitimate destination, and thus gain access to information they should not have. ICMP redirects are useful for an internal internetwork, but are a security problem when you allow them through from external or untrusted networks. ICMP redirects can be denied on a per-interface basis. In this example, we want to prevent ICMP redirects from entering the router on interface Serial 0, which is implemented as follows:

```
Router1(config)#interface serial 0
Router1(config)#no ip redirects
```

The next potential security risk we want to eliminate is the use of source routing. Source routing, as described in Chap. 5, uses layer 2 (Data Link layer) information to route a packet through the internetwork. This technique overrides the layer 3 routing information; by doing so, it could allow an intruder to specify incorrect route selections for packets on the local network. The intruder could instruct packets that would be delivered locally to be delivered to his or her workstation on the external network. Source routing can be disabled with the following global command:

```
Router1(config)#no ip source-route
```

Problems with a One-Router Firewall. Although it might seem that we have tied things up pretty tight, this solution has a number of areas that many will find unacceptable for most business environments. The main two issues are that internal network topology can be determined from the outside, and that you are allowing external users direct access to an information server that has complete information on your network.

Although we have restricted access to the information server to well-known applications such as Telnet and SMTP, obscure security loopholes do surface from time to time. The greatest risk is that by allowing anyone on the Internet direct access to your information server, an intruder will be able to place a program on the information server and launch an attack on your network from your own information server. There is an organization that lists the applications that you should deny because they are known to have security loopholes in them. This organization, the *Computer Emergency Response Team* (CERT), recommends that you do not allow the services listed in Table 7.1.

TABLE 7.1

CERT Advisory Service Listing

Service	Port Type	Port Number
DNS Zone Transfers	TCP	53
TFTP daemon	UDP	69
link	TCP	87
Sun RPC	TCP and UDP	111
NFS	UDP	2049
BSD Unix r commands	TCP	512—514
line print daemon	TCP	515
UUCP daemon	TCP	540
Open Windows	TCP and UDP	2000
X Window	TCP and UDP	6000

CERT recommends that DNS zone transfers not be allowed, yet we have configured them. The relationship you have with the external network vendor (in this case an ISP) determines whether you are going to allow this service or not.

A Better Router Firewall. The previous router configuration allowed incoming queries only to the information server. The problem, as previously mentioned, is that a competent intruder could get access to the information server from somewhere on the Internet and launch an attack on other computers in our network from the information server. We have made openings in our firewall configuration to allow the intruder to get in—on port numbers 80, 21, 25, 53, or any port higher than 1023.

To improve security, we can implement a router that has three configured interfaces, allowing us to reduce the traffic permitted into our internal network. The one interface that is connected to our internal network only allows outgoing connections for TCP. Of course, for any communication to take place, packets must travel in both directions. By specifying that an interface will support only outgoing connections, we mean that incoming packets are allowed, if they are in response to a request initiated by a computer on our internal network. The connections to support this type of configuration are shown in Fig. 7-12.

With this configuration, there is no harm in leaving the previously constructed access list for the Serial 0 interface intact and implementing

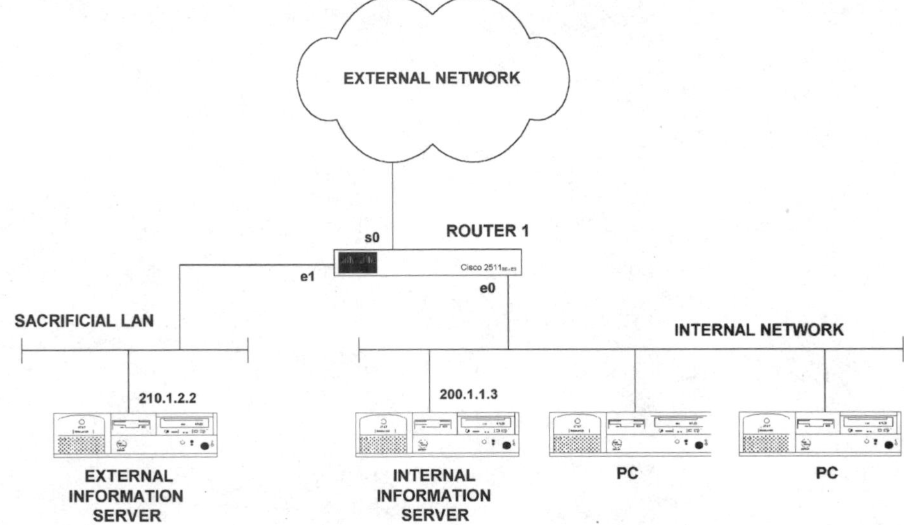

Figure 7-12 Connections for a three-interface router firewall

another access list for the Ethernet 0 interface. The access list for this interface is simple and is given as follows:

```
access list 102 permit tcp any any established
```

This access list is applied as follows to the Ethernet 0 interface:

```
Router1(config)#interface ethernet 0
Router1(config-int)#access-group 102 out
```

The problem with this configuration is that we still have to allow responses to DNS queries back in. Let's say a host on the internal LAN wants to retrieve a document from the Web, for example, address *http://www.intel.com.* The first thing that needs to happen is for that name to be resolved to an IP address. The information server on the internal network (which is providing local DNS service) needs to get information from the an external DNS server to obtain the IP address for *intel.com.* The reply with the required information will come back on UDP, aimed at the port number on which the information server initiated the request (a port greater than 1023).

To minimize our exposure, we probably will have DNS on the internal LAN set with a pointer to the information server on the sacrificial LAN. So when a host needs to resolve the IP address of *intel.com,* it will request the information from the local DNS server, which will request the information of the server on the sacrificial LAN. The sacrificial LAN server will get the information from the Internet root servers and pass it back to the internal DNS server, which finally gives the IP address to the host. We can get the information we need to the internal DNS server with the following addition to access list 102.

```
access-list 102 permit udp 210.1.2.2 255.255.255.255 200.1.1.3 255.255.255.255 gt 1023
```

We must be clear about why we are applying this access list out, rather than in, for this situation. As access list 102 stands, there are no restrictions on packets into the Ethernet interface. This means our internal LAN can send anything it likes into the router for forwarding onto the external network. The only restriction applies if a machine on the external network or the sacrificial LAN wants to send a packet to our internal network. In this case, the packet comes into the router and attempts to go out from the router onto our internal network. These are the packets we want to stop, so the access list is applied on the Ethernet 0 port for packets outbound from the router.

The only exception to this is if a computer on the external network tries to respond to a TCP connection request that originated from a computer on our internal network. In that case, the ACK bit will be set on the packet coming from the external network, indicating that it is a reply, and the router will pass it on to the internal LAN.

You might think that a devious attacker could set the ACK bit on a packet to get it through our firewall. An attacker might do this, but it will not help establish a connection to anything on our internal LAN, for a connection can be established only with a SYN packet, rather than an ACK. To break this security, the attacker would have to inject packets in to an existing TCP stream, which is a complex procedure. (There are programs of this type available on the Internet.) Of course, we still have the issue of an intruder launching an attack from the server on the sacrificial LAN using UDP port numbers greater than 1023.

At this stage, the only packets that can originate from outside our internal network and be passed through the router to our internal network are packets from the sacrificial LAN server to a UDP port greater than 1023. Given that SMTP uses TCP port 25, you may wonder how mail gets from the external network to the internal LAN. Mail systems use the concept of the post office, which is used as a distribution center for mail messages. Messages are stored in the post office and forwarded to their destination when new messages are requested by a user, typically at user login time.

The server on the sacrificial LAN is set up to accept mail messages from the Internet, and a post office machine on the internal LAN can be set up to retrieve mail messages on a regular basis. This maintains security by allowing TCP packets into our internal network only if they are a response to a TCP request that originated from within our internal network, and allows us to retrieve mail messages from the Internet. By using a three-interface router, we have reduced the number of potential security loopholes through which an intruder could gain access to our internal network. We can, however, further improve the situation.

Cisco's PIX Firewall

To provide the type of security that most organizations require these days requires implementation of a dedicated firewall computer. Router firewalls are only filters at best, and they do not hide the structure of your internal network from an inquisitive intruder. As long as you allow a machine on an external network (in our example, either the Internet or the sacrificial LAN) direct access to a machine on your internal network, the possibility exists that an attacker will compromise the security of the machine on your internal LAN and be able to host attacks onto other machines from there.

Most dedicated firewall machines that offer proxy services are based on Unix systems, which have their own security flaws. Cisco offers the *PIX* (*Private Internet eXchange*) firewall that runs its own custom operating system and so far has proved to be resilient to attacks aimed at compromising its security. Let's have a quick review of how a proxy system works, before we discuss in more detail the stateful network address translation operation of the PIX firewall.

Overview of Proxy Server Operation. Proxy servers are a popular form of Application level firewall technology. In concept, one side of the proxy is connected to the external network, and one side of the proxy is connected to the internal network. So far, this is no different from our firewall router. Let's consider an example of establishing a Telnet session through a proxy server to illustrate how it provides additional levels of security.

If a machine on the external network seeks to establish a Telnet session with a machine on the internal LAN, the proxy will run two instances of Telnet, one to communicate with the external LAN, and another to communicate with the internal LAN. The job of the proxy is to pass information between the two Telnet connections. The benefit is that nothing from the external network can establish a direct session with a machine on the internal network.

A malicious user from the external network is prevented from gaining direct access to the internal LAN information server and cannot launch an attack from that server to other machines on the internal LAN. The attacker will never know the real IP address of the information server, because only the IP address used by the proxy server to communicate with the outside world will be available. A significant benefit to this type of operation is that the addressing scheme of the internal LAN is completely hidden from users on the outside of the proxy server.

Because a proxy server has a pool of external addresses to map to internal addresses, when internal computers request external connections, no computer on the outside can establish a connection with a machine on the inside. That's so because an external machine will never know which external address maps to computers on the inside of the proxy.

With this setup, you still have to worry about how a client PC on the internal LAN resolves hostnames to addresses for hosts out on the Internet.

Most configurations of this type run DNS on the proxy machine. DNS on the proxy machine will then know about computers on both the internal and external networks and can service locally generated DNS queries directly. The drawback is that an external user is able to find out some information regarding the internal topology through the proxy server. The proxy does, however, stop a malicious external user from actually getting to those computers.

All the good stuff a proxy gives you is dependent on the security of the operating system on which it runs. In most cases this is Unix, a complex system to set up securely. Additionally, running two instances of Telnet, FTP, WWW services, etc., requires an expensive and powerful processor. The PIX firewall provides the same benefits without these two drawbacks. The PIX runs its own secure operating system and delivers proxy-type benefits by directly manipulating the header information of packets without the need to run two versions of service programs.

Implementation of PIX poses one significant problem. To enable hosts on an internal LAN to access the network numbers on the Internet, the PIX must advertise a default route through itself to internal LAN routers. This means that all internal LAN hosts will send all packets destined for networks not listed in their routing tables to the

PIX. This is fine for normal operation. If a network failure eliminates an internal network number from host routing tables, however, traffic destined for that network number will now be sent to the PIX. This may overwhelm the PIX connection to the Internet and take it out of service.

PIX Operation. The *Private Internet eXchange* (PIX) machine requires a router to connect to an external network. However, Cisco is planning to deliver PIX functionality within the Cisco IOS in the near future. A typical configuration to connect an internal LAN to the Internet via a PIX is given in Fig. 7-13.

The PIX has two Ethernet interfaces, one for connection to the internal LAN, and one for connection to the router that interfaces to the Internet or other external network. The external interface has a range of

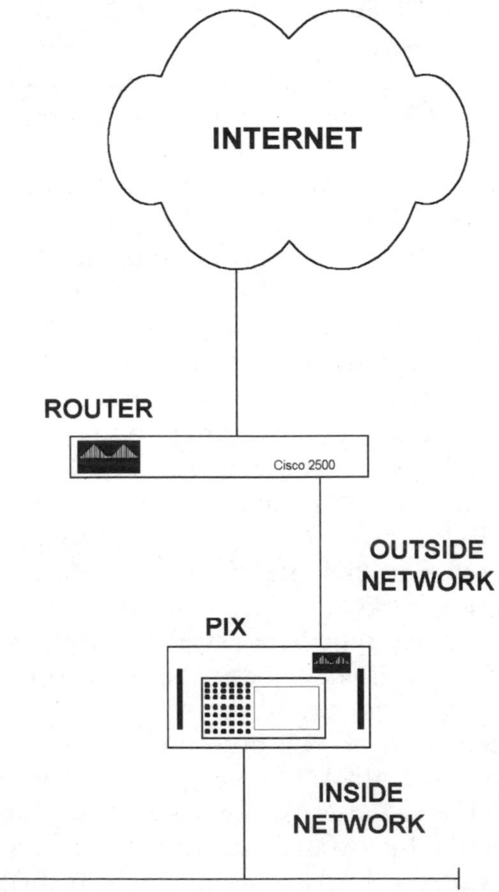

Figure 7-13 Using a PIX for securely connecting an internal LAN to the Internet

addresses that it can use to communicate with the external network. The internal interface is configured with an IP address appropriate for the internal network numbering scheme. The main job of the PIX is to map internal to external addresses whenever internal computers need to communicate with the external network.

This makes internal computers appear to the external world as if they are directly connected to the external interface of the PIX. Because the external interface of the PIX is Ethernet, MAC addresses are needed to deliver packets to hosts. To make the internal hosts appear as if they are on the external interface at the Data Link as well as the Network layer, the PIX runs Proxy ARP. Proxy ARP assigns Data Link MAC addresses to the external Network layer IP addresses, making internal computers look as if they are on the external interface to the Data Link layer protocols.

In most cases, the communication with the external network originates from within the internal network. As the PIX operates on the packet rather than application level (the way proxy servers do), the PIX can keep track of UDP conversations as well as TCP connections. When an internal computer wants to communicate with an external computer, the PIX logs the internal source address and dynamically allocates an address from the external pool of addresses and logs the translation. This is known as *stateful NAT*, as the PIX remembers to whom it is talking, and which computer originated the conversation. Packets coming into the internal network from the external network are permitted only if they belong to an already identified conversation.

The source address of the internal computer is compared to a table of existing translations, and if an existing translation exists, the external address already assigned is used. If an existing entry is not present, a new external address is allocated. Entries in this translation time out with a preconfigured timeout value.

This mechanism is efficient for most normal implementations. In this fashion, a small number of assigned Internet numbers can service a large community of internal computers, as not all internal computers will want to connect to the Internet at the same time.

There are instances, however, when you need to allow external computers to initiate a conversation with selected internal computers. Typically these include services such as e-mail, WWW servers, and FTP hosts. The PIX allows you to hard-code an external address to an internal address that does not time out. In this case, the usual filtering on destination address and port numbers can be applied. An external user still cannot gain any knowledge of the internal network without cracking into the PIX itself. Without knowledge of the internal network, a malicious user cannot stage attacks on the internal network from internal hosts.

With the PIX protecting your internal LAN, you might want to locate e-mail, WWW servers, and FTP hosts on the outside network. The PIX then can give secure access to these machines for internal users, and external users have access to these services without having to traverse the internal LAN.

Another key security feature of the PIX is that it randomizes the sequence numbers of TCP packets. Since IP address spoofing was documented in 1985, it has been possible for intruders to take control of an existing TCP connection and, using that, send their own data to computers on an internal LAN. To do this, the intruder has to guess the correct sequence number. With normal TCP/IP implementations this is easy, because most start a conversation with the same number each time a connection is initiated. The PIX, however, uses an algorithm to randomize the generation of sequence numbers, making it virtually impossible for an attacker to guess the sequence numbers in use for existing connections.

A Simple PIX Configuration. Configuring the PIX is a relatively straightforward task. It is much simpler than setting up a proxy server and multiple DNS machines to provide an equivalent level of security. In concept, what you need to do is assign an IP address and pool of addresses to use for access on the outside, and an IP address and netmask for the internal connection, RIP, timeout, and additional security information. Figure 7-14 shows a sample configuration.

- Command `ifconfig outside 200.119.33.70 netmask 255.255.255.240 link rj up` assigns the IP address and netmask to the outside LAN card, specifies the link type as RJ-45 for twisted-pair cabling, and enables the interface with the `up` keyword.

Figure 7-14
A simple PIX configuration

```
IFCONFIG OUTSIDE 200.119.33.170  NETMASK 255.255.255.240 LINK RJ UP
IFCONFIG INSIDE 1.1.1.2 NETMASK 255.255.255.0 LINK RJ UP
GLOBAL -A 200.119.33.171 - 200.119.33.174
ROUTE OUTSIDE 200.119.33.161
ROUTE INSIDE 1.1.1.1
TIMEOUT XLATE 24:00:00 CONN 12:00:00
RIP INSIDE DEFAULT NOPASSIVE
RIP OUTSIDE NOPASSIVE
LOGHOST 0.0.0.0
TELNET 200.119.38.51
ARP -T 600
```

- Command `ifconfig inside 1.1.1.2 netmask 255.255.255.0 link rj up` performs the same configuration options for the inside LAN card.
- Command `global -a 200.119.33.171-200.119.33.174` configures the pool of global Internet addresses that will be used to communicate with computers on the Internet. At least two addresses must be assigned with this command.
- Command `route outside 200.119.33.161` specifies the machine with this IP address as the default gateway for the network on the outside.
- Command `route inside 1.1.1.1` specifies the machine with this IP address as the default gateway for the internal network.
- Command `timeout xlate 24:00:00 conn 12:00:00` sets the translate and connection idle timeout values. The values shown here are the defaults of 24 and 12 hours, respectively.
- Command `rip inside nodefault nopassive` modifies RIP behavior for the inside interface. The `nodefault` means that a default route is not advertised to the internal network, and `nopassive` disables passive RIP on the inside interface.
- Command `rip outside nopassive` configures the PIX to not listen to RIP updates coming from the outside network.
- Command `loghost 0.0.0.0` disables logging. If you want to log events to a Unix syslog machine, you must specify its IP address with this command.
- Command `telnet 200.119.33.161` allows Telnet session to be established with the PIX only from the machine using this source address.
- Command `arp -t 600` changes the ARP persistence timer to 600 seconds. With this command entered, the PIX will keep entries in its ARP table for 600 seconds after the last packet was received from a given computer.

This simple configuration is appropriate for connecting to the Internet an internal LAN that does not have any WWW or FTP hosts that external computers need in order to initiate connections. You can add a static translation that makes an inside host contactable from the outside by using the `static` and `conduit` commands. An example of this addition is given as follows:

```
static -a 200.119.33.175 1.1.1.5 secure
conduit 200.119.33.175 tcp:11.1.1.5/32-25
```

The first command adds a *static map* and defines that the external address 200.119.33.175 will be mapped permanently to the internal address 1.1.1.5 in a secure fashion. This means that very few services will be allowed through on this static map, e.g., no SMTP or DNS.

If we want to receive mail on the internal machine, for example, we need to create an exception to this security for the specified service. The `conduit` command creates the exception for us. The `conduit` command specifies that the external host with address 11.1.1.5 will be able to connect on TCP port 25 to the external address 200.119.33.175 (which is statically mapped to the internal machine 1.1.1.5). The 32 near the end of the `conduit` command specifies that all 32 bits of the source address will be used for comparison to decide if the connection is allowed. A value of 24 would allow any host from the 11.1.1.0 subnet to establish a connection.

Once you have the PIX up and running, you have delivered a secure Internet connection for your internal LAN. Outside hosts typically will be able to ping only the external interface, and internal hosts ping only the internal interface. An attacker on the outside of the PIX will not be able to find open ports on the outside connection to which to attach, or to determine the IP addresses of any of the machines on the inside. Even if told the IP address of machines on the inside, pinging or attaching to them directly will be impossible.

One other application for which the PIX is useful is the connection of two sites via an untrusted network such as the Internet. The PIX has a private link feature that encrypts data sent between two PIX machines. This could be a cost-effective solution for connecting two remote sites together via the Internet, while being assured that an intruder could neither gain unauthorized access, nor passively read the data sent between the two sites.

Physical Layer Security

Physical layer security is concerned with securing physical access to internetwork devices. A subsequent section in this chapter will show you how to determine the Enable password, or see the router's entire configuration, if physical access can be gained to the device. The simple rule is that all live routers on an internetwork should be kept in a safe place, with only authorized individuals able to gain access to the rooms in which they are located. Once data is routed out of one of your routers and onto a telephone company's network, you no longer can guarantee the physical security of the data you are transporting. Although rare, it is possible for intruders to passively listen to the traffic transmitted on selected cables in the phone company system. This is a minimal risk, as there are generally more fruitful ways to get physical access to interesting data.

Generally the greatest security risks come from Internet and dial-in connections. If you follow the PIX guidelines for Internet connections and the CHAP and TACACS guidelines for dial-in connections, you will be protected.

IP Unnumbered and Data Compression

This section illustrates the use of two configuration options for Cisco routers that do not fall neatly in to any other section. Both IP unnumbered and data compression, useful when building an internetwork, are explained fully here.

IP Unnumbered

IP unnumbered has been explained in overview previously. The first benefit of IP unnumbered is that it allows you to save on IP address space. This is particularly important if you are using InterNIC-assigned addresses on your internetwork. The second benefit is that any interface configured as IP unnumbered can communicate with any other interface configured as IP unnumbered, and we need not worry about either interface being on the same subnet as the interface to which it is connected. This will be important when we design a dial backup solution.

The concept behind IP unnumbered is that you do not have to assign a whole subnet to a point-to-point connection. Serial ports on a router can "borrow" an IP address from another interface for communication over point-to-point links. This concept is best explored by using the three-router lab we put together earlier. The only change to the router setup is that router 1 and router 2 now are connected via their serial ports, as shown in Fig. 7-15.

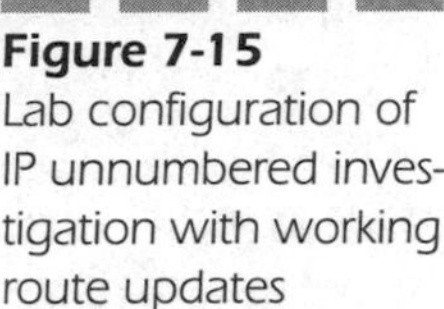

Figure 7-15 Lab configuration of IP unnumbered investigation with working route updates

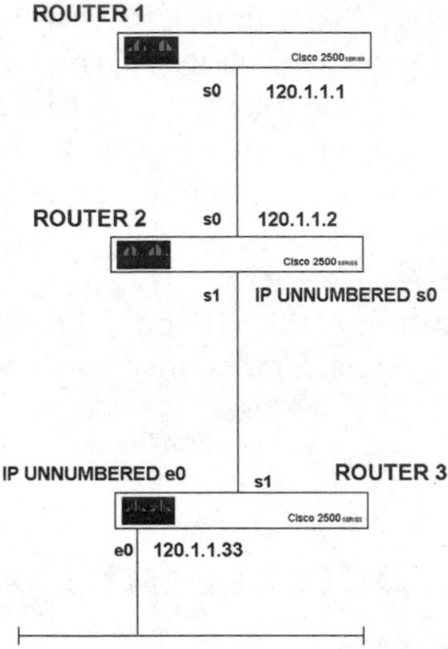

CONFIGURATION FOR ROUTER 2

```
INTERFACE SERIAL 0
IP ADDRESS 120.1.1.2  255.255.255.224
INTERFACE SERIAL 1
IP UNNUMBERED SERIAL 0
ROUTER IGRP11
NETWORK 120.0.0.0
```

CONFIGURATION FOR ROUTER 3

```
INTERFACE SERIAL 1
IP UNNUMBERED ETHERNET 0
INTERFACE ETHERNET 0
IP ADDRESS 120.1.1.33  255.255.255.224
ROUTER  IGRP 11
NETWORK 120.0.0.0
```

With the IP addressing scheme shown in Fig. 7-15, effectively one major network number with two subnets, the route information about subnets is maintained, as we can see by looking at the routing table on router 2 and router 3.

```
Router2>show ip route
   120.0.0.0 255.255.255.224 is subnetted, 2 subnets
I  120.1.1.32 [100/8576] via 120.1.1.33, 00:00:42, serial1
C  120.1.1.0 is directly connected, serial 0
```

```
Router3>show ip route
   120.0.0.0 255.255.255.224 is subnetted, 2 subnets
C  120.1.1.32 is directly connected, ethernet 0
I  120.1.1.0 [100/10476] via 120.1.1.2 00:00:19, serial1
```

This routing table shows us that router 3 has successfully learned about the 120.1.1.0 subnet from Serial 1, which is being announced from router 2 with the source address 120.1.1.2. This is as we would expect, as the Serial 1 interface on router 2 is borrowing the address from its Serial 0 interface. If the Serial 1 interfaces on both routers had their own addressing, we would expect the routing table in router 3 to indicate that it had learned of the 120.1.1.0 subnet from the address of the Serial 1 interface on router 2, not the borrowed one.

IP unnumbered is easy to break: Just change the address of the Ethernet interface on router 3 to 193.1.1.33 and see what happens, as illustrated in Fig. 7-16.

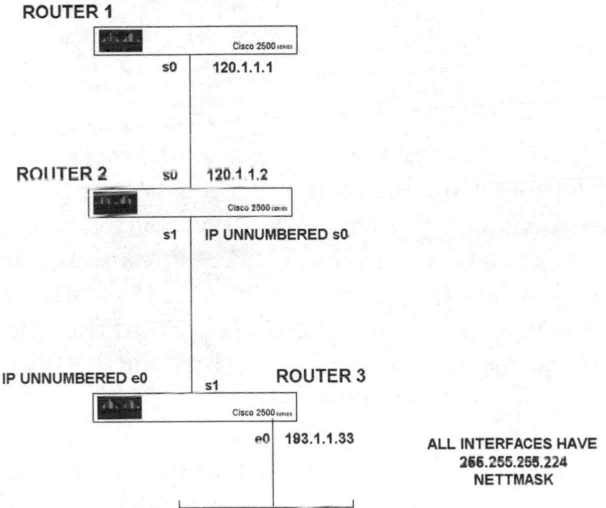

Figure 7-16 Lab configuration for IP unnumbered investigation with nonworking route updates

CONFIGURATION FOR ROUTER 2

```
INTERFACE SERIAL 0
IP ADDRESS 120.1.1.2  255.255.255.224
INTERFACE SERIAL 1
IP UNNUMBERED SERIAL 0
ROUTER IGRP 11
NETWORK 120.0.0.0
```

CONFIGURATION FOR ROUTER 3

```
INTERFACE SERIAL 1
IP UNNUMBERED ETHERNET 0
INTERFACE ETHERNET 0
IP ADDRESS 193.1.1.33  255.255.255.224
ROUTER IGRP 11
NETWORK 193.1.1.0
```

To speed the process of the routing table in router 2 adapting to the change in topology, issue the `reload` command when in privileged mode. After router 2 has completed its reload, try to ping 120.1.1.2 from router 3. The ping fails, so let's look at the routing table of router 3.

```
Router3>show ip route
   120.0.0.0 255.255.255.224 is subnetted, 1 subnets
I  120.1.1.0 [100/10476] via 120.1.1.2, 00:00:18, serial 1
   193.1.1.0 255.255.255.224 is subnetted, 1 subnets
C  193.1.1.32 is directly connected, Ethernet 0
```

Everything here appears to be fine, so let's examine the routing table of router 2 to see if we can determine the problem.

```
Router2>show ip route
   120.0.0.0 255.255.255.224 is subnetted, 1 subnets
C  120.1.1.0 is directly connected, serial 0
   193.1.1.0 is variably subnetted, 2 subnets, 2 masks
I  193.1.1.0 255.255.255.0 [100/8576] via 193.1.1.33 00:01:15, serial 1
I  193.1.1.32 255.255.255.255 [100/8576] via 193.1.1.33 00:01:15, serial 1
```

Straight away, the words *variably subnetted* should make you aware that something is wrong. From the discussion on IGRP in Chap. 4, we know that IGRP does not handle variable-length subnet masks properly, so any variable-length subnetting is likely to cause us problems. Looking more closely, we see that router 2 is treating 193.1.1.32 as a host address, because it assigned a netmask of 255.255.255.255 to that address. Treating 193.1.1.32 this way means that there is no entry for the 193.1.1.32 subnet, and therefore no way to reach 193.1.1.33.

The reason behind all this is that subnet information is not transported across major network number boundaries and an IP unnumbered link is treated in a similar way to a boundary between two major network numbers. So router 3 will advertise the 193.1.1.32 subnet to router 2, which is not expecting subnet information; it is expecting only major network information, so it treats 193.1.1.32 as a host.

A simple rule by which to remember this is that the network numbers on either side of an IP unnumbered link can use netmasks only if they belong to the same major network number.

Data Compression

Once you have optimized the traffic over your internetwork by applying access lists to all appropriate types of traffic and periodic updates, you can further improve the efficiency of WAN links by *data compression*, a cost-effective way to improve the throughput available on a given link. If you have a 64 kbps link that is approaching saturation point, your choices are to upgrade to a 128 kbps link or to see if you can get more out of the existing link by data compression.

All data compression schemes work on the basis of two devices connected on one link, both running the same algorithm that compresses the data on the transmitting device and decompresses the data on the receiving device. Conceptually, two types of data compression can be applied, depending on the type of data being transported. These two types of data are *lossy* and *lossless*.

At first, a method called "lossy"—a name that implies it will lose data—might not seem particularly attractive. There are types of data, however, such as voice or video transmission, that are still usable despite a certain amount of lost data. Allowing some lost data significantly increases the factor by which data can be compressed. *JPEG* and *MPEG* are examples of lossy data compression. In our case, though, we are building networks that need to deliver data to computers that typically do not accept any significant data loss. Lossless data compression comes either as *statistical* or *dictionary form*. The statistical method is not particularly applicable here, as it relies on the traffic that is being compressed to be consistent and predictable, when internetwork traffic tends to be neither. Cisco's data compression methods, *STAC* and *Predictor*, are based on the dictionary style of compression. These methods rely on the two communicating devices sharing a common dictionary that maps special codes to actual traffic patterns. STAC is based on the *Lempel-Ziv algorithm* that identifies commonly transmitted sequences and replaces those sequences in the data stream with a smaller code. This code is then recognized at the receiving end, extracted from the data stream, and the original sequence inserted in the data stream. In this manner, less data is sent over the WAN link even as transmission of the same raw data is permitted.

Predictor tries to predict the next sequence of characters, based upon a statistical analysis of what was transmitted previously. My experience has led me to use the STAC algorithm, which, although it is more CPU-intensive than Predictor, requires less memory to operate. No matter which method you choose, you can expect an increase in latency. Compression algorithms delay the passage of data through an internetwork. While typically this is not very significant, some client/server applications that are sensitive to timing issues may be disrupted by the operation of data compression algorithms.

One of the great marketing hypes of the networking world has been the advertisement of impressive compression rates from vendors offering data compression technology. To its credit, Cisco has always advertised the limitations of compression technology as well as its potential benefits. First of all, there is no such thing as a definitive value for the compression rate you will get on your internetwork. Compression rates are totally dependent on the type of traffic being transmitted. If your traffic is mainly ASCII text with 70 to 80 percent data redundancy, you may get a compression ratio near 4:1. A typical target for internetworks that carry a mix of traffic is more realistically 2:1. When you implement data compression, you must keep a close eye on the processor and memory utilization. The commands to monitor these statistics are `show proc` and `show proc mem`, respectively.

Implementing Data Compression. The first data compression technique to which most people are introduced is *header compression,* as implemented by the Van Jacobson algorithm. This type of compression can deliver benefits when the traffic transported consists of many small packets, such as Telnet traffic. The processing requirements for this type of compression are high, and it is therefore rarely implemented on links with greater throughput than 64 kbps. The most popular implementation of Van Jacobson header compression is for asynchronous links, where it is implemented on a per-interface basis. Many popular PC PPP stacks that drive asynchronous communication implement this type of header compression as default.

The following enables Van Jacobson header compression on interface Async 1, where the `passive` keyword suppresses compression until a compressed header has been received from the computer connecting to this port.

```
Router1(config)#interface async 1
Router1(config-int)#ip tcp header-compression passive
```

Clearly, Van Jacobson header compression works only for IP traffic. Better overall compression ratios can be achieved by compressing the whole data stream coming out of an interface by using *per-interface compression,* which is protocol-independent. You can use STAC or Predictor to compress the entire data stream, which then is encapsulated again in another Data Link level protocol such as PPP or LAPB to ensure error correction and packet sequencing. It is necessary to re-encapsulate the compressed data, as the original header will have been compressed along with the actual user data and therefore will not be readable by the router receiving the compressed data stream.

A clear disadvantage to this type of compression is that, if traffic has to traverse many routers from source to destination, potentially significant increases in latency may occur. That can happen because traffic is compressed and decompressed at every router through which the traffic passes. This is necessary for the receiving router to read the uncompressed header information and decide where to forward the packet.

Per-interface compression delivers typical compression rates of 2:1 and is therefore worth serious consideration for internetworks with fewer than 10 routers between any source and destination. This type of compression can be implemented for point- to-point protocols such as PPP or the default Cisco HDLC. The following example shows implementation for PPP on the Serial 0 interface. For this method to work, both serial ports connected on the point-to-point link must be similarly configured for compression.

```
Router1(config)#interface serial 0
Router1(config-int)#encapsulation ppp
Router1(config-int)#compress stac
```

The per-interface type of compression that requires each router to decompress the received packet before it can be forwarded is not applicable for use on a public network such as frame relay or X.25. The devices within the public network probably will not be configured to decompress the packets in order to determine the header information needed to forward packets within the public network. For connection to public networks, Cisco supports compression on a per-virtual-circuit basis. This type of compression leaves the header information intact and compresses only the user data being sent. An example of implementing this type of configuration for an X.25 network is shown as follows. As with per-interface compression, both serial ports that are connected (this time via a public network), must be similarly configured.

```
Router1(config)#interface serial 0
Router1(config-int)#x25 map compressedtcp 193.1.1.1 1234567879 compress
```

This command implements TCP header compression with the `compressedtcp` keyword. Per-virtual-circuit compression is implemented via the `compress` keyword at the end of the command. Great care should be taken when you are considering implementing compression on a per-virtual-circuit basis. Each virtual circuit needs its own dictionary, which quickly uses up most of the available memory in a router. My happiest experiences with compression have been with per-interface compression on networks with a maximum hop count of around 6 or 7 from any source to any destination.

Overview of Managing an Internetwork

Network management is one of the hot topics of the internetworking world. The idea of being able to control, optimize, and fix anything on a large, geographically dispersed internetwork from one central location is very appealing. Applications that enabled a network manager to monitor, troubleshoot, and reconfigure remote network devices tended to be vendor-specific until the *Simple Network Management Protocol* (SNMP) came along.

We should not forget that many of the functions of network management can be accomplished without SNMP. For example, we can use TFTP for configuration management, and Telnet for `show` and `debug` commands. (Common commands of this type are covered in the Chap. 8 section on "Troubleshooting.") The fact that documentation of a particular device states that it supports SNMP does not mean that it will fit nicely into the network management system you are putting together. We'll examine why in the next section on the components of an SNMP system.

SNMP System Components

SNMP version 1 is the most widely implemented version today. Network management applications that fully support SNMP version 2 features are only now becoming available. The basic subsystems of an SNMP v1 system are shown in Fig. 7-17.

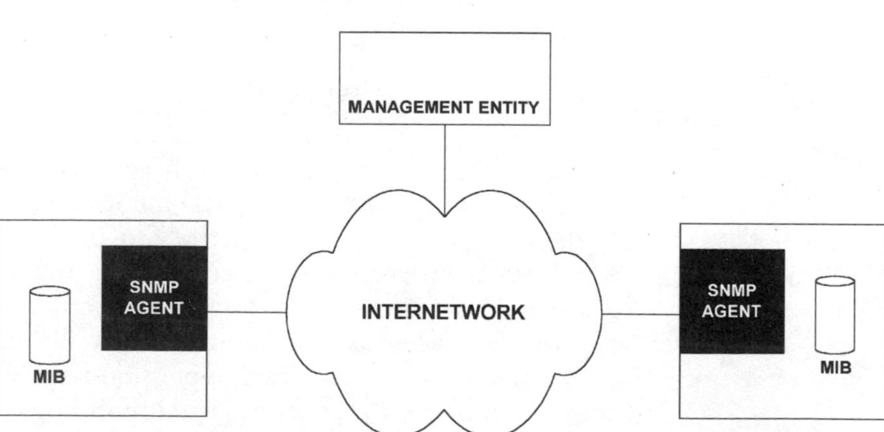

Figure 7-17 SNMP system components

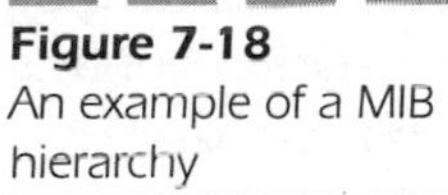

Figure 7-18
An example of a MIB hierarchy

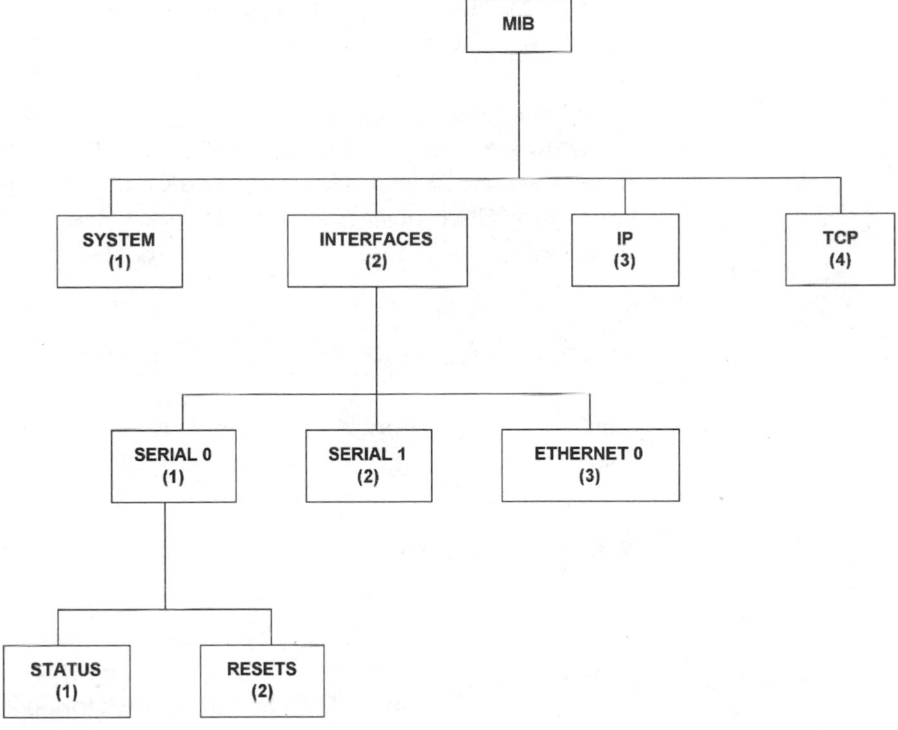

Let's start our discussion with the *Management Information Base*. The *MIB* is a database of objects arranged in hierarchical form, similar to that shown in Fig. 7-18. The exact numbering of leaves in the MIB tree shown in Fig. 7-18 is not important, because it is a fictitious tree; the issue is how the database stores, retrieves, and modifies values. Each level in the hierarchy has containers numbered from 1 onward. SNMP messages coming from a management station are of either the `get` type or `set` type. If a management station needs to determine the status of the device's Serial 0 port, it will issue a `get` command followed by the string 1.2.1.1. This period-separated value identifies the value in the MIB hierarchy to be retrieved. A management station can be used to set certain variables, such as setting a port from being administratively shut down to up by a similar mechanism of identifying the correct period-separated string for the variable that needs to be changed in the MIB hierarchy.

If the documentation for a device tells you that it can be managed by SNMP, it may well mean that it has a MIB and a device agent (shown as the SNMP agent in Fig. 7-17) to interpret SNMP strings. Unless you want to spend hours writing programs to generate appropriate `set`, `get`, and other commands with the appropriate strings to follow the commands, you should check on whether the network management station application you intend to use has a *management entity* for the device in question. A management entity is software that resides on the management station and provides a friendly interface for the user to request information or set variables on the remote device. Cisco provides management entities for Cisco devices as part of CiscoWorks, its SNMP-based network management system.

Systems Management Objectives

There are many models for network management, and here I'll present the short list of what you can reasonably be expected to achieve with current network management tools.

- Centralized distribution of Cisco operating system software.
- Centralized configuration management.
- Event management for notifying an operator or other network administrator of the following: faults, attempted security breaches, performance failures (such as buffer overflow, overutilization of available bandwidth, excessive dropped packets, etc.).
- Log generation for audit and review purposes.

The big question when you're setting up a systems management system is: Do you collect information from remote devices by traps or by polling them? A *trap* is generated when a device agent becomes aware that a monitored event, such as an interface going down, has occurred. Collecting data via traps is risky, since it relies on the device and its line of communication to you being up and operational. Polls, on the other hand, are initiated by the network management station and proactively request information from remote devices. If the device does not respond, you have a pretty clear indication that something is wrong. The problem with polling every device on the network for status of all its monitored variables is that the traffic generated can become too high for the internetwork to support. This is a bigger problem the larger the network becomes.

Deciding how to split what you monitor via traps and what you monitor via polls is more of an art than a science, and it depends on the size of your internetwork, the interconnections in place, and the criticality of the various variables you wish to monitor. A reasonable starting point might be to poll key devices on a fairly infrequent basis, say once every 10 minutes, to check that they are functioning and accessible, then set traps for more detailed alerts, such as individual links to remote sites going up or down. If you really need to monitor specific MIB variables, such as dropped packets or bandwidth utilization, you have to poll the remote device for those particular values. This can place an unacceptable burden on the bandwidth available for user traffic on a large and growing internetwork.

We'll revisit these issues in the section on the CiscoWorks management station. For now, let's look at what we need to do on each router out in the field to bring it under the control of a centralized management system.

Sample Router Configuration for SNMP Management

The following commands taken from a router configuration file define the basics for enabling a router to be monitored from an SNMP management station.

```
access-list 2 permit 193.1.1.0 0.0.0.255
snmp-server community hagar RW 2
snmp-server packetsize 4096
snmp-server trap-authentication
snmp-server host 193.1.1.1 public
```

Let's explore these commands one by one, then look at some additional SNMP commands.

Command `snmp-server community hagar RW 2` allows read and write access to hosts presenting the SNMP community string `hagar` if access list 2 permits it. The community string is like a password; a device wanting SNMP read and write access to the router will need to supply the correct community string. Access list 2 only permits packets from the 193.1.1.0 network. (It is assumed that your network management station is on this network number.) It is a good security measure to restrict SNMP access to hosts on your network management LAN.

Command `snmp-server packetsize 4096` raises the maximum packet size, which for SNMP communications defaults to 484 bytes—very small. It is more efficient in terms of network resource utilization to send a smaller number of larger packets than to send many small packets.

Command `snmp-server trap-authentication` works hand-in-hand with the `snmp-server host` command. By enabling trap authentication, you are telling the router to send an SNMP trap to the host address specified in the `snmp-server host` command. The trap is sent when the router becomes aware of any entity sending SNMP commands with an incorrect community string (i.e., one that is failing authentication).

Command `snmp-server host 193.1.1.1 public` identifies the host address to send traps back to. If you want to send traps to multiple hosts, they must each have their own `snmp-server host` entries. The community string sent along with the trap is `public`, a default community string name. As it stands, this command sends traps of all types; optional keywords can limit the traps sent to specific types, such as `tty` (for when a TCP connection closes) or `snmp` (for traps defined in RFC 1157).

Some additional `snmp` commands you may wish to consider to expand the functionality of an SNMP monitoring system are as follows:

Command `snmp-server queue-length` can help handle situations where a router does not have an entry in its routing table to reach the management station, or is in a state where traps are being constantly generated, and a queue of messages to be sent out is building up. This command specifies the maximum number of messages that will be outstanding at one time; the default is 10.

Command `snmp-server trap-source` specifies the interface, and by implication the IP address, to use for the source address when sending traps back to the management station. This could be useful if you know that all the serial ports on your internetwork routers belong to one major network number. You then can accept only those traps coming from this major network number and add some security to the process of trap collection.

The use of SNMP generally has been a good thing for people charged with managing internetworks. I recommend you use caution, however, when deciding which management station software to use, and be careful about deciding what you monitor via polling devices. Ideally, what you should look for in implementing a network management system is a minimum amount of traffic overhead placed on the internetwork, combined with operators being notified of monitored events on the internetwork as they happen. A network management station generally utilizes a graphical display of some kind, and uses visual prompts to notify operators of events on the internetwork. In most cases these events can trigger such things as e-mail and beeper notification.

I stated earlier that the optimal way to monitor an internetwork was to poll the most significant devices and set traps for all the ancillary devices and variable thresholds in which you are interested. With the management systems available today, achieving this is not always straightforward. Some management stations will not allow the status of a monitored device to be set when a trap is received. These management stations accept the trap, then poll the device to determine the exact nature of the trap sent. In other cases, the SNMP-managed device is a problem because some device agents do not allow traps to be generated for all the MIB variables that you want to monitor. In this situation, the only way to determine if a MIB variable that you have interest in has exceeded a given value is to poll the device and retrieve the MIB variable directly.

All this makes optimal management of an internetwork via SNMP a significant challenge. The key points to consider when purchasing a management system are summarized as follows:

1. Will the management station respond appropriately to traps sent by monitored devices and not require a separate poll to be sent to the monitored device?
2. Can you obtain device agents that will send traps for all the variables you wish to monitor?
3. Can you set traps and threshold limits for all the variables you want to monitor simply by using a graphical user interface, without having to resort to programming arcane strings?
4. If the management system suffers a catastrophic failure, can you use a text interface to manage device operation over modem lines?

Overview of Managing an Internetwork with CiscoWorks

CiscoWorks is Cisco's network management station software, which is supported on Sun Net Manager, IBM's NetView for AIX, and HP Openview platforms. CiscoWorks provides facilities for managing router configurations, notifying operators when specific events occur, and writing logs for audit purposes. CiscoWorks also has functions to help with performance and fault management. We will focus on the performance and fault management functions provided within the IOS user interface when we cover troubleshooting in Chap. 8.

The goal of this book is to introduce Cisco router technology to those with responsibility for, or interest in, internetworked environments. It is possible to effectively run and manage a Cisco router internetwork without a system such as CiscoWorks. When your internetwork grows to more than 60 or 70 routers, however, simple administrative tasks like changing the Enable password, or implementing a new configuration command on all routers, become onerous. This section provides a brief overview of CiscoWorks and how it can help monitor events and manage router configurations. The next section will cover loading IOS software on remote routers.

CiscoWorks Concepts. CiscoWorks (CW) is installed as an add-in to existing network management platforms such as HP Openview or Sun Net Manager. CW runs as separate applications under these management platforms. The means of accessing these applications is different for each platform, so we'll look at the functionality these applications provide, rather than focusing on how to access them from all platforms.

The foundation of the CW system is a Sybase database that keeps track of your internetwork's IP devices, their configuration, and selected status data. This database is presented graphically as maps on the management station display. Figure 7-19 shows a top-level map display for a sample internetwork. Typically, this top-level display will allow you to select a *Point Of Presence* (POP) location and display the detail of connections in that area via another map display.

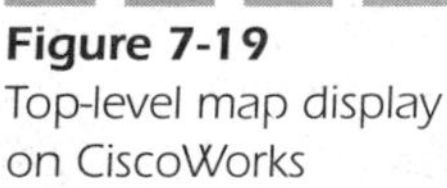

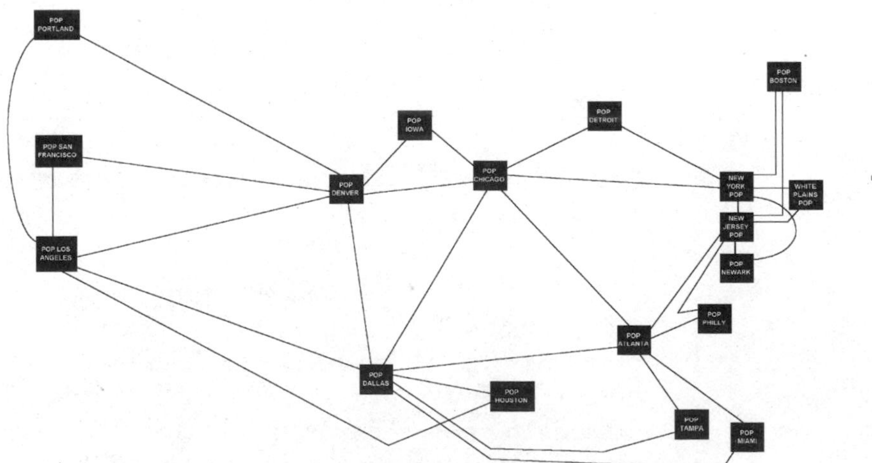

Figure 7-19 Top-level map display on CiscoWorks

Usually there will be several users of the CW system, which allows different usernames to be assigned their own passwords and appropriate user privileges. To set up the CW system, the internetwork either is searched automatically or devices are added manually. If devices are found automatically, it is done by IP address and you will want to modify the device type to be the specific Cisco router in use. Once you are satisfied that you have collected all the information, you will synchronize the CW Sybase database with the management system's database that you have installed.

The main benefits of CW are the ability to poll devices and receive traps to generate alerts for operators, and to simplify configuration changes through the *Snap-In Manager* tool, which allows you to set configuration changes for multiple routers on your network. The CW station can be used as the TFTP server for auto-install procedures and to retrieve remote router configurations on a regular basis for backup purposes.

CW notifies an operator of a network event—such as a polled device becoming unreachable, or an interface going down on a router enabled to send traps—by the color of the device's display changing from green to red. An alert box appears on the screen and, optionally, audio alarms can be set off.

It must be noted that running a CW system efficiently is not a trivial task; it requires substantial knowledge of the underlying management platform and the operating system on which it is running.

Router Software Management with CiscoWorks. We have discussed using a TFTP server to store and download router configuration files, particularly for the auto-install procedure. Using plain TFTP will simplify things for you; some CiscoWorks applications will assist you even further. CW comes as a set of applications, the most useful of which we will overview here.

The CW *Configuration Management* application allows you to edit, upload, and download Cisco router configuration files. In general, the process involves creating a file by using a text editor, then executing the `file to database` command in the configuration management window, followed by the `database to device` command. This ensures that the Sybase database on the CW computer holds the most recent copy of the device's configuration.

The Configuration Management application has another feature that is sometimes useful in troubleshooting because it allows you to compare two configuration files and identify differences between the two. This can help in determining whether configuration changes made to a router have caused an internetwork problem. This is of value only if you have configurations for both before and after the internetwork problem started. Some users of CW systems perform an overnight backup of all router configurations, just for this purpose.

The *Device Software Manager* application simplifies the procedure for upgrading IOS or microcode remotely. This application actually consists of three applications: the *Software Library Manager*, to maintain and list the sources of software available; the *Software Inventory Manager*, to list current software status and sort device information according to platform and software image; and the *Device Software Manager*, to automatically upgrade the system software on a selected router. This software automatically performs all the tasks detailed in the section on remotely upgrading IOS from a TFTP server, which is covered in detail in the next section.

Global Command Manager allows you to automate the running CW applications such as upgrading devices or sending common configuration changes to routers. The application's concept is the same as that of the Unix *cron* utility. Any Unix or CW command that you can specify manually can be automated to execute at a specified time. The Global Command Manager can be used to schedule database tasks such as backups and purge of log files, device polling to retrieve MIB variable information, and use of the Configuration Snap-In Manager. For a command to be executed by this application, it must be created as a global command, which will add it to a log file of commands to be executed at the specified time.

The *Configuration Snap-In Manager* allows a common set of configuration commands to be sent to a set of devices. To use this application, define a set of commands as a snap-in, which can be applied to a defined set of devices. Snap-in commands must be of the same type; for example, you can send three `snmp-server` commands in one set, but you can't send an `snmp-server` and a `logging buffered` command in one set. The most useful things you can do with this application are to globally change the Enable password on your router configuration, and change security management station configurations such as access lists or source addresses.

Remotely Upgrading Router IOS from a TFTP Server

Different routers in the Cisco product line have different capabilities regarding the loading of IOS from a remote location. Some of the higher-end routers, such as the 7000- and 7500-series, have enough memory facilities to allow a new version of IOS to be loaded remotely, and the new IOS to take effect when the router is next booted or when a reload is issued. These routers also allow you to keep more than one version of IOS held in memory, in case you need to fall back to a prior version because of a problem with the new version.

In all probability, the most common router implemented in a Cisco internetwork is the 2500-series, because it is the cheapest and provides the functionality needed to bring a small remote office online to the corporate internetwork. One of the compromises in delivering a product like the 2500 is that it is limited in available memory. A 2500 router runs its IOS from flash memory rather than ROM. To upgrade the IOS in this type of router, the flash memory must first be erased, so that the new version of IOS can become the first file in flash memory and hence be the one from which the router is running.

To safely erase the contents of flash memory, you must be running at least a small operating system from somewhere other than flash; otherwise the router will stop running. This is where the Cisco *Rxboot* image comes into play. This boot image is a small operating system that runs from ROM chips on the router motherboard, and provides just enough functionality to boot the router with empty flash memory and load a new version of the IOS into flash.

Because the 2500 series is the most complex to upgrade remotely, and probably the most common device we need to upgrade remotely, we will examine its upgrade process in detail here.

The Rxboot ROM Program. Rxboot supports Telnet and TFTP operations, but does not support routing, SNMP, routers with more than one interface enabled, TACACS, or IP unnumbered. These limitations have implications when you want to remotely upgrade router configuration.

The first step is to shut down all interfaces except for the serial port on which the router is to receive the new version of IOS. In addition, if the serial port normally uses IP unnumbered, it must be given a specific IP address prior to the upgrade process. Finally, the `ip default-gateway` command must be entered into the configuration of the router in global configuration mode, prior to the upgrade.

To execute an upgrade process, you must have a computer to use for Telnet access to the remote 2500, and a TFTP server somewhere on the internetwork that has loaded onto it a copy of the new version of the IOS. We covered TFTP server configuration in Chap. 3 when we discussed loading configuration files over a LAN. The same TFTP server configuration can be used for this purpose.

Preview of the Upgrade Process. We will discuss each step in detail, but it is useful here to check a summary view of what we are about to do.

1. Check that the TFTP server can ping the remote router to be upgraded, and configure the remote router to use a default gateway once its routing functionality has been disabled.
2. Load the new version of IOS on to the TFTP server, ready for loading onto the remote router.
3. Play it safe by completing a backup of the remote router's IOS and configuration file, should things go wrong.
4. Reboot the router to use the Rxboot image, by loading its operating system from the ROM chips.
5. Copy the new version of IOS to the remote router's flash memory and check that the checksum is the same as the file on the TFTP server, to ensure that nothing happened to the new version of IOS in transit.
6. Boot the router from flash memory and check to make sure everything is functional before moving on to the next router.

Executing a Remote Upgrade. Let's consider a situation in which a remote 2501 needs to have its IOS upgraded, as shown in Fig. 7-20.

First, Telnet to the 2501 router and issue the following command:

```
2501>ping 193.1.1.1
```

Unless you get success at the ping level, you are not going to get very far, so it's worth checking this before we go any further.

Next, all serial ports other than the one we will use for the upgrade must be shut down and the `ip default-gateway` command entered, as follows:

```
2501(config)#interface serial 1
2501(config-int)#shutdown
2501(config-int)#exit
2501(config)#ip default-gateway 210.18.1.5
2501(config)#<Ctrl-Z>
2501#write memory
```

No change will be seen to the routing table of the 2501 router at this stage. The `ip default-gateway` command does not take effect until the routing process is disabled.

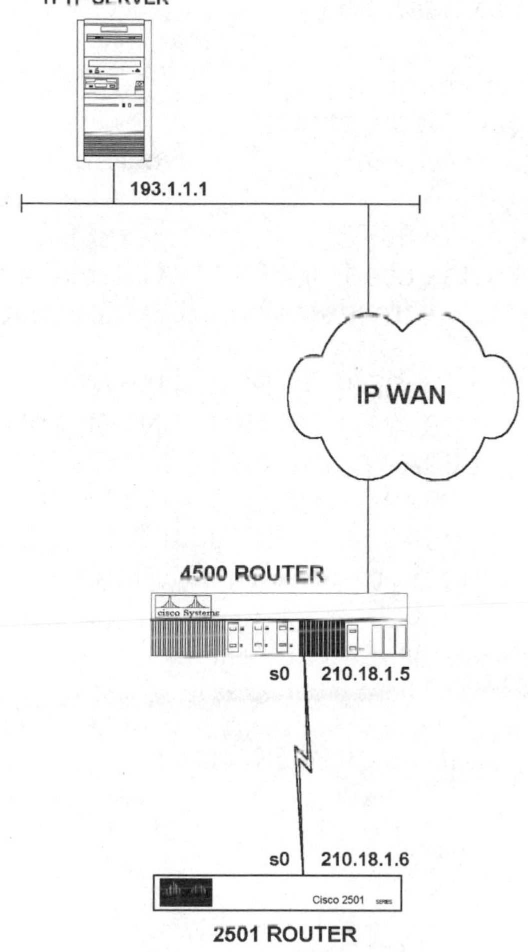

Figure 7-20 Internetwork configuration for remotely upgrading a 2500 router

Loading the new version of IOS onto the TFTP server can be done many ways, from a software distribution disk, from Cisco's Internet site, or loading onto the TFTP server from a router already running the new IOS version. Whichever method you choose, you need to know the filename used. Let's look at saving the existing IOS to the TFTP server as a fallback consideration.

To save the IOS image file to the TFTP server, you must know the image filename, which can be determined by issuing the `show flash all` command. A sample screen output shown in Fig. 7-21 displays the router's IOS image filename, which in is *10_3_7.ip* in this case.

The commands, subsequent router prompts, and responses to save this filename to the TFTP server are seen in Fig. 7-22.

```
router1>sho flash all

System flash directory:
File  Length   Name/status
      addr     fcksum                  ccksum
  1   3126004         10_3_7.ip
      0x40     0x86EC                  0x86EC
[3126068 bytes used, 1068236 available, 4194304 total]
4096K bytes of processor board System flash (Read ONLY)

  Chip   Bank   Code    Size    Name
   1      1     89A2   1024KB   INTEL 28F008SA
   2      1     89A2   1024KB   INTEL 28F008SA
   3      1     89A2   1024KB   INTEL 28F008SA
   4      1     89A2   1024KB   INTEL 28F008SA
Executing current image from System flash
```

Figure 7-21 Screen output of the *show flash all* command

Now we start the real work. The 2501 router must be booted from ROM to use the Rxboot program as its operating system. To achieve this, the configuration register on the 2501 must be changed from 102 in hex, to 101 in hex, which is achieved as follows:

```
2501#conf t
2501(config)#config-reg 0x101
2501(config)#<Ctrl-Z>
2501#reload
```

At this stage, the Telnet session you have established to the router will be terminated while it reloads its operating system from boot ROM. For many, this is nerve-wracking the first time they attempt the process. Don't worry. Everybody has to do this for the first time once, and the process does work well.

After you give the router a few minutes to reload, you should be able to Telnet back in to it, and instead of the familiar login prompt, you will see the following prompt:

```
2501(boot)>.
```

To get into Enable mode, you will have to type the Enable password, and not the Enable secret. The Rxboot program does not recognize the Enable secret.

Next we want to load the new IOS from the TFTP server. Let's again play it safe by checking that the 2501 router can ping the TFTP server. Assuming that all is okay, we can proceed. If something has happened on the internetwork to prevent IP connectivity from the 2501 to the TFTP server, that must be resolved before we can continue. The new IOS is downloaded with the `copy tftp flash` command as shown next.

```
2501(boot)#copy tftp flash
IP address or name of remote host [255.255.255.255]?193.1.1.1
Name of file to copy? "New IOS filename"
Copy "new IOS filename" from 193.1.1.1 into flash address space? [confirm]
<Enter>
Erase flash address space before writing? [confirm] <Enter>
loading from 193.1.1.1    !!!!!!!!!!!!!!!!!!!!!!!!!!!!!!!!!!!!!!!!!!!!!!!!!!!
```

The exclamation points indicate that a data transfer is in progress. The next stage is to verify that the file was transmitted successfully without alteration from the source. You can check this by verifying that the checksum shown at the end of the display from the `copy tftp flash` command matches that of the new IOS image as reported on the software distribution materials (either a disk, or as stated on the Cisco Internet site). If the checksum values don't match, again execute the `copy tftp flash` command. If after several attempts the checksums still don't match, try to reload the original file before executing yet again. If noisy line is introducing errors into the new IOS image as it is downloaded (remember TFTP uses UDP and not TCP, so there is no error correction), you should not boot the router from flash until the noise problem has been fixed and a good IOS version has been loaded into flash.

Assuming that the new IOS image is loaded successfully, you can return the router to normal operation as follows:

Figure 7-22
Screen output of the *copy flash TFTP* command to save a router's IOS to a TFTP server

```
router1#copy flash tftp

System flash directory:
File Length Name/status
 1  3126004 10_3_7.ip
[3126068 bytes used, 1068236 available, 4194304 total]
Address or name of remote host [255.255.255.255]?193.1.1.1
Source file name?10_3_7.ip
Destination file name[10_3_7.ip]?press enter
Verifying checksum for'10_3_7.ip'(file#1)...OK
Copy'10_3_7.ip'from Flash to server
 as'10_3_7.ip'?[yes/no]
```

```
2501(boot)#conf t
2501(config)#config-reg 0x102
2501(config)#no ip default-gateway 210.18.1.5
2501(config)#<Ctrl-Z>
2501#reload
```

Once the reload has executed and you can Telnet back in to the router, you can remove the shutdown command from the Serial 1 port and the 2501 should be functioning with a new version of IOS.

Overview of Cisco Router Password Recovery Procedures

It should never happen, but it is possible that the router Enable password or secret may get lost, thus denying configuration or many troubleshooting options. There is a way to break into the router if you can operate an ASCII terminal directly connected to the console port. The process in overview is as follows.

- Power cycle the router and break out of the bootstrap program.
- Change the configuration register, to allow you either to get into Enable mode without a password (if the flash image is intact), or to view the current configuration. Then initialize the router so that the router will boot from the ROM system image.
- Either enter the `show configuration` command to display the router configuration file and read the Enable password, or change the Enable password directly.
- Change the configuration register back to its initial setting, and power cycle the router.

A few words of caution are in order here. Suppose that the image of IOS in flash memory is not intact and you elect to change the configuration register so that you can read only the configuration. As you saw in the original configuration file, knowing the Enable password will not help you if there is an Enable secret set. The Enable secret always appears encrypted in the configuration file. If an Enable secret is set, all this process will allow you to do is write down the configuration, or save it to a TFTP server, so that you can issue the `write erase` command and then recreate the router configuration with a password you know. If an Enable secret is not set, but the Enable password is encrypted, you are in the same situation.

The exact process for each of the routers in Cisco's product line varies slightly. Here is a step-by-step guide of what to do for all the Cisco 2500, 680*x*0-based 4000- and 7000-series routers. The 4700-series routers are based on a different processor and have a different procedure, which can be obtained directly from Cisco.

First, type the `show version` command and note the configuration register setting. If the console port has had a login password set that you do not know, you can assume that the configuration register is 0*x*2102 or 0*x*102.

With an ASCII terminal or PC running a terminal emulator attached to the console port, turn on the router and enter the break sequence during the first 60 seconds of the router bootup. The most difficult part of the procedure often is determining the break sequence. For Microsoft terminal products, such as Windows Terminal and Windows 95 Hyperterminal, the break sequence is the Control and Pause keys pressed simultaneously. For Procomm it is the Alt and B keys pressed simultaneously. When the correct break sequence is entered, the router will present a ">" prompt with no router name.

Next you must decide if you are going to enter the mode that allows you only to view and erase the configuration, or if you are going to restart the router so that you can get directly into Enable mode and change the configuration. Assuming that the flash memory is okay, enter `o/r0x42`, which configures the router to boot from flash. Entering `o/r0x41` has the router boot from the boot ROMs next time the IOS is reloaded. As we know, the boot ROMs of a 2500 only contain a stripped-down version of IOS. Note the first character is the letter "o" and the fourth character is the numeral "0".

Next type the letter "I" at the > prompt and hit enter, which will initialize the router.

The router will now attempt to go through the setup procedure, and you will just answer no to all the prompts, which will leave you with a `Router>` prompt.

From here, you can get into privileged mode by entering the word Enable, from which you can view or change the configuration. You should proceed with some caution at this stage if you do not want to lose your existing configuration file. If you used the `o/r0x42` command and want to change the configuration, issue the `conf mem` command to copy the configuration file from NVRAM into working memory; otherwise all the changes you make will be to the configuration file in RAM, which prior to the `conf mem` command was blank. If you did not realize this, made configuration changes to the blank file, and saved it prior to reloading the router software, you would overwrite the original configuration file that you want to keep. Once you have issued the `conf mem` command, you can enter configuration mode and alter the original configuration file, as it is now in RAM. Enter configuration mode with the `conf t` command.

Once you have changed the Enable password, or completed whatever configuration changes you want, enter `config-reg 0x102` at the configure prompt, then press <Ctrl-Z> to exit from configuration mode. Type `reload` at the `Router#` prompt and select Yes to save the configuration.

Putting Together the Sample Internetwork

In this section, I will pull together the various sections of this chapter to illustrate how the concepts presented can be integrated to build an internetwork. The requirements of each and every individual internetwork vary considerably. It is unlikely that the design I present here will be the optimal one for your internetwork; however, it does present a reasonable base from which to start. Unlike in other chapters, where I have tried to be objective, in this section I have to be opinionated, because without a specific problem to solve with documented evidence, there are only opinions.

Where applicable, I will highlight tradeoffs made and areas where the design presented will run into problems under certain types of traffic loads. Additionally, most of what I say is based on my practical experience and therefore cannot be taken as statistically significant, as I am only one engineer among thousands. Having suitably qualified the statements I am about to make, in an attempt to save my home and family from those who hold views different from mine, I shall press on.

Defining the Problem

As mentioned at the outset of this chapter, we have an organization headquartered in Chicago, with concentrations of branches around New York, Atlanta, Dallas, Los Angeles, and San Francisco. All hosts are located in

Chicago, with local Windows NT servers in each remote site for delivering file and print services. The internetwork must deliver host access, Internet, e-mail, and remote dial access to all users. Here are the design decisions I have made:

1. The Windows NT servers in each branch will use TCP/IP for WAN communications, utilizing a centralized WINS server located in Chicago for name resolution.
2. Dial-up services for users operating outside their branch will be provided centrally via a pool of asynchronous interfaces located in Chicago. Users then access their branch-based NT servers over the WAN. To dial the asynchronous interfaces in Chicago, the users dial an 800 number.
3. The backbone will rely on multiple links between distribution centers rather than on dial backups for redundancy.
4. Branch routers will use ISDN to establish a dial backup connection in the event that their link to their distribution center (New York, Atlanta, Los Angeles, etc.) goes down. The ISDN link will be made back to the central location in Chicago.
5. The whole internetwork will be based on one of the IANA-reserved Class B addresses and connected to the Internet via a PIX firewall located in Chicago.
6. HSRP will not be used at the Chicago location, so we will have to think about how to protect host access from being lost by one router failing.
7. I will use individual leased lines rather than a commercial frame relay service.
8. I will use Cisco HDLC rather than PPP for the encapsulation on the point-to-point WAN links.

Let's see if I can justify my reasons for setting things up this way. First of all, let's tackle the idea of distributed rather than centralized Windows NT servers. Some high-level managers I know like the idea of centralizing servers for ease of administration and point out that workstation-to-server communications can be achieved over a WAN link as easily as over a LAN link. This is true, and I can set up a workstation to access a server over a WAN link and it will work well. The issue I take with this scheme is with how well it scales as the network grows. Basically, it does not. The more workstations you add, the more traffic the WAN link has to support—not only requests for file services, but announcements, advertisements, and other overhead generated by network operating systems grow as the number of workstations grow.

Next, let's discuss providing Internet services from the central location. This is enough to give a network administrator a heart attack on the spot. Just think: All those graphics, audio files, searches, and so forth taking up valuable WAN bandwidth. I agree that providing Internet services over your own WAN bandwidth when the Internet already has bandwidth available in the branch office locations may seem like a waste. I believe, however, that connecting your internetwork to the Internet is one of the prime security risks you run.

My opinion is that allocating lower priority to Internet traffic over the WAN and feeling good about secure centralized Internet access is a good tradeoff. Additionally, there are technical problems involved in providing one router to a remote site to access the corporate WAN and another to access the Internet. PCs can define only one router as the default, either the WAN or the Internet router. Therefore, providing Internet access at remote locations requires a more complex router, one that probably has a proxy server to connect to the Internet. This becomes costly.

So what about the backbone having multiple routes between distribution centers, and no dial backup for these links? This is easy: As the backbone links grow in capacity, they become more and more difficult to back up with dial links. With a sensible backbone configuration, you can design in enough redundancy for your needs. T-1 and fractional T-1 services are reliable these days, and if you experience specific problems, additional links can be added piecemeal to improve redundancy.

A big point of contention for many business managers is justifying the potential additional costs of individual leased lines compared to subscription to a public frame relay network. The arguments I gave in the frame relay section still hold. Frame relay networks were good when first put together, when utilization was low, because you could subscribe to a low CIR and get substantially more throughput on average. Now that vendors' frame relay networks are more fully subscribed, that "free" bandwidth is not available and performance over these networks is not what it was. In some cases, the need to specify a CIR approaching what you would need on a leased-line basis approaches the cost of having your own dedicated bandwidth. I also like having control of how my network traffic gets from source to destination, not to mention that since these frame relay networks are public, you face additional security risks that you don't encounter with your own leased lines.

Next, why have dial-up users dial the central location and access local files over the WAN instead of having them dial the branch location? In this case, the argument to provide a central rather than distributed resource wins out. With a central dial-up pool, you can set up an 800 number service and get a lower rate for users calling long-distance to access their data. While users will be using WAN bandwidth to access NT server files, they will not be using WAN bandwidth to access host applications or the Internet, so I think it's a wash. (I would not allow any application to be downloaded over a dial-up link, however; all applications need to be loaded on the hard drives of the computers being used for dial-up connections.)

I feel confident that I will have full backing in this judgment from anyone who has tried to remotely support an asynchronous communications server, modem, and telephone line. A central pool of ports that can be tested, one in which bad ports can be busied out and components easily replaced, is a significantly smaller headache than distributed facilities. Some branch managers argue that when they go home and want to dial in, it is a local call to the office, so why do they have to dial an 800 number and incur expense for the company? This may be true, but I believe that most calls will be made by users traveling on business and would be long-distance phone calls anyway. I'll stick with a central dial pool on both technical and cost grounds.

Next, let's talk about using Cisco HDLC rather than PPP for the point-to-point links on the internetwork. PPP offers the opportunity for CHAP authentication, which HDLC does not, and is a more modern protocol with generally more configuration options. The deciding factor for me, though, is that with Cisco HDLC, you can put a CSU/DSU device in loopback, and if the connection between the router port and the CSU/DSU is good, the line protocol will come up. With PPP it will not. This is a good starting point to have when you are trying to troubleshoot, particularly an initial line installation. If, however, you choose to utilize any LAN extender devices, you will have to use PPP. I will choose PPP for the asynchronous links, as the improved security features of this protocol make it the obvious choice for a potential security loophole such as dial-up connections.

Now we will discuss having the remote site routers use ISDN to dial the central location in Chicago, rather than their distribution center, in the event of a line failure. This has many implications, not the least of which is how you choose to implement your IP addressing scheme. The first point to consider is what IP address the interface on the branch router will have for dialing in to a central pool. It's not feasible for these interfaces to have their own IP addresses.

Think about what happens when the ISDN connection to the backup pool is made. Normally a router interface will expect the directly connected devices to be addressed on the same subnet as itself. In addition, a subnet on a properly designed internetwork will appear at only one location. So what subnet does the backup pool use? This cannot be resolved if you assign specific addresses to the backup pool, as you will never know which subnet from the field will be trying to dial in. So both the serial interface used for ISDN dial backup and the interfaces in the central location dial backup pool must use IP unnumbered.

Next, should we implement one Class B network number with subnets, or allocate one network number for the backbone and different network numbers for the distribution and branch connections? The latter option reduces the size of the routing tables in the backbone routers, and hence reduces the size of routing updates. The reason is that network numbers are summarized into one route at the boundary between major network numbers. This means that a network number that is broken up into multiple subnets in the distribution center will only have one entry in the routing table of the backbone router. As we have chosen to have branch routers connect to the central location in Chicago, however, we cannot implement an addressing scheme with one network number for the backbone and separate network numbers for the distribution centers.

Figure 7-23 illustrates one way to interconnect sites in our sample WAN.

With just one network number and multiple subnets, the routing tables (and hence the size of routing updates) grow as the number of branches grows. This can be a problem for branches connected on dial backup, as large routing updates can consume significant bandwidth. If the internetwork grows to the point that it's servicing more than 1000 branches, you might be forced to implement a distributed dial backup scheme. An option we will consider is using access lists applied as distribution lists to restrict the size of routing advertisements sent on low bandwidth links.

With a central dial backup pool of ports, we will implement one network number for the entire internetwork and choose an appropriate netmask for all interfaces. I could choose a netmask of 255.255.255.224. This gives 30 usable addresses for each location and 2046 subnets. If a location has more workstations than that, a secondary address can be used to give another 30 usable addresses from a different subnet. If, in our sample internetwork, most of the sites have more than 30 workstations, we can

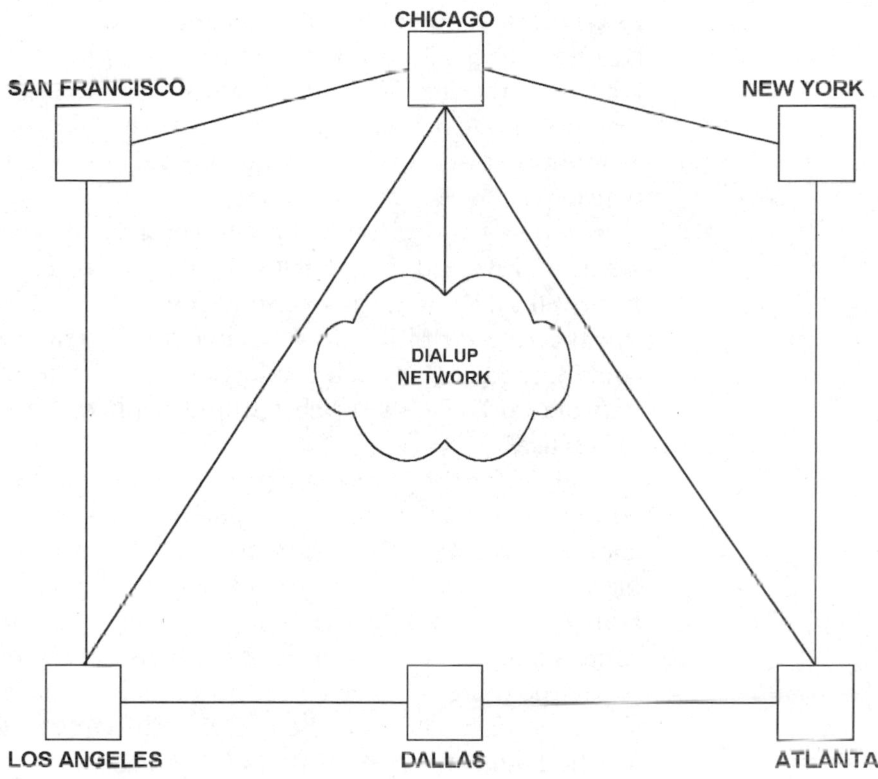

Figure 7-23 Illustration of how the sample network could be connected and addressed

assign a netmask of 255.255.255.192 for all interfaces, which gives us 62 usable addresses for each subnet, with 1022 subnets. Let's use 255.255.255.192, as this company cannot imagine having more than 1000 locations, and having more usable addresses in the subnet makes it easier if a few branches are larger than 30 workstations.

The Central Site Configuration

This is where all the hosts and access points for the Internet, as well as the pool of ISDN ports used for dial backup connections, are located. When putting together an internetwork of this type, I would go to great pains to ensure that access to the hosts is via the TCP/IP protocols. Most hosts support TCP/IP directly and allow remote client computers to connect via Telnet, and even IBM hosts have capabilities for this through TN3270 and TN5250. An emerging technology—software loaded on the host that allows hosts to be accessed via HTTP and display host information in a WWW format—also is a possibility. As long as we restrict our WAN to using TCP/IP, however, we are in good shape whichever way we go.

The next big decision is how to connect the central site LAN to the WAN. We have said that HSRP will not be used in this instance, and why not? Well, HSRP is a really good idea if both of the routers that are sharing the responsibility of servicing traffic sent to the phantom have equally good routes to all destinations. This is not the case in our internetwork, so let's look at what would happen if we were to implement HSRP here.

An HSRP configuration has two routers, one of which will be elected to service traffic sent to the phantom. In our internetwork, we may choose to connect San Francisco and Los Angeles to one router, and New York and Atlanta to the other. This configuration would enable traffic to get to all distribution centers even if one of the HSRP routers failed. Let's look at what happens during normal operation.

Say the router connected to San Francisco and Los Angeles is elected as the primary and will then service all requests sent to the phantom. Traffic bound for New York and Atlanta, therefore, will be sent to Los Angeles first and the direct links to New York and Atlanta will not be used. The only time they would be used is if the router connected to San Francisco and Los Angeles failed. Clearly this is far from an optimal situation. In this case I recommend a low-tech solution: Have an identically configured standby WAN 4700 router in the same cabinet as the live one, and manually swap over connections if it fails.

If you need the resilience that HSRP offers, then you need to put together a more complex set of WAN interconnections, something like that shown in Fig. 7-24. This configuration has each router in the HSRP pair with the same WAN connections; it does not matter so much which router gets elected as the master and routes all the traffic bound for the HSRP phantom. As you can see, HSRP gets expensive on WAN bandwidth and the lines connected to the inactive HSRP router do not carry any traffic. Given that Cisco hardware really is reliable, in this situation I would stick with the manual swap-over option.

Finally, for the central site, we should mention that a separate LAN has been set aside for the network management station. This is so we can tell all the routers out in the field to accept SNMP commands only

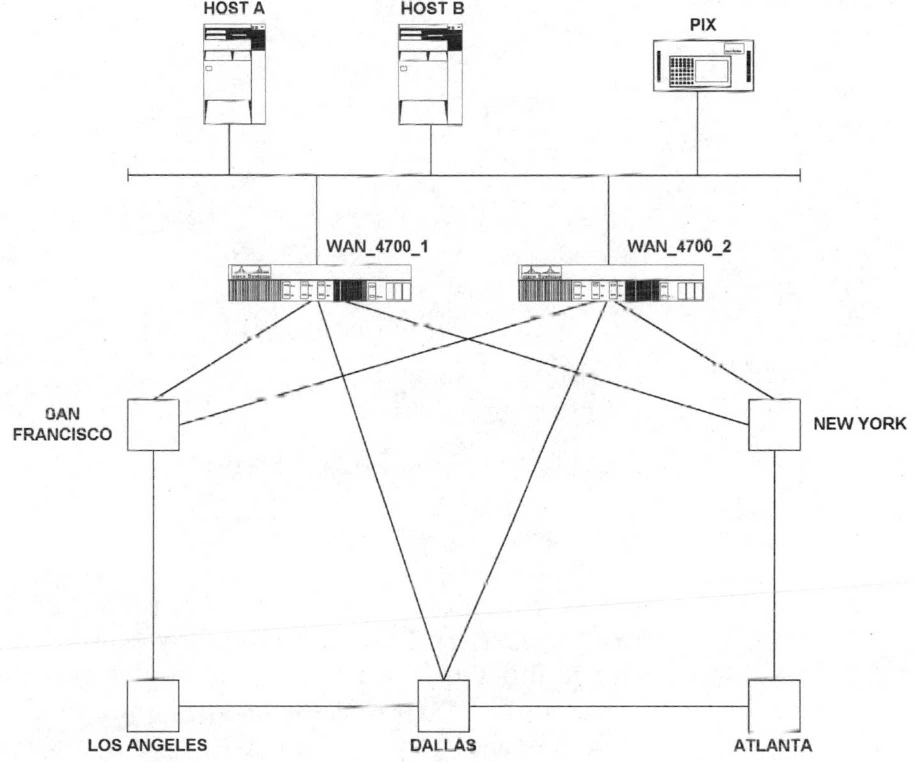

Figure 7-24 WAN interconnectivity of HSRP implementation

from this LAN. The final configuration for the central location in Chicago is given in Fig. 7-25.

Distribution Center Configuration

The distribution center configuration is fairly simple. Each distribution center router will have serial port connections to the backbone and serial port connections to the individual branches. There are no Ethernet connections because no servers are located at the distribution center in this design, and no ISDN connections because the branches dial back to the central location if a local loop fails.

The issues related to managing the distribution routers are more procedural than technical. First, will the distribution center router be located in a branch, or in a communication vendor's facility? The advantage to it being located with other communications equipment in a vendor's facility is that it will be in a secured room, probably one

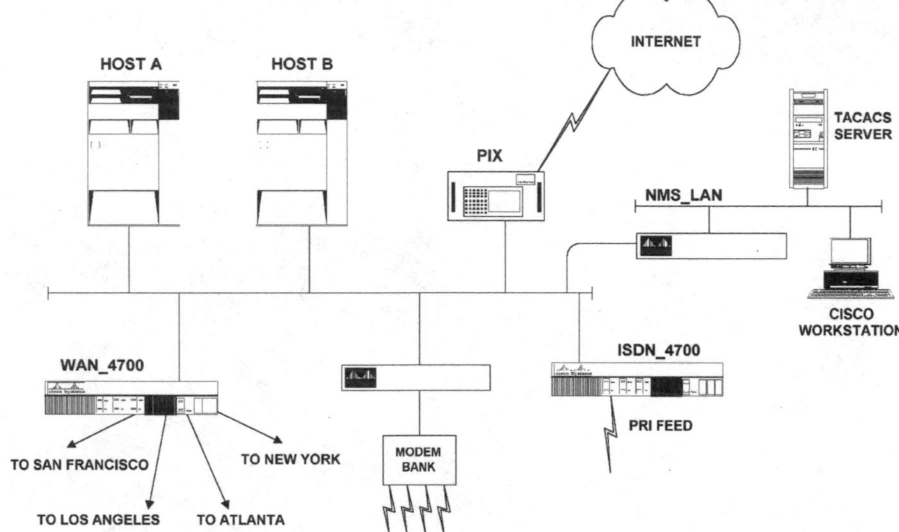

Figure 7-25 Central location network configuration

with air-conditioning, uninterruptible power supply, and maybe even a backup generator. This might be costly, however, and most of the vendor's facilities are not staffed; if the router needs rebooting, or it fails and needs to be replaced, the distribution center will be out of action until someone can make the trip there to do the necessary work.

Remote Site Configuration

Here I choose to give the Serial 0 port a fixed IP address and use IP unnumbered for the ISDN backup. I have covered why we use IP unnumbered for the ISDN backup port, but why don't we use it for the primary connection? The section on upgrading IOS for 2500-series routers gives us the answer. Operating from the Rxboot program, IP unnumbered is not supported. It is simpler to assign an IP address for the port that will be used during the upgrade process than to change the IP configuration just for the upgrade.

The next question is why use an ISDN terminal adapter instead of a built-in BRI? In the internetwork as it stands, using a built-in BRI probably makes more sense. Let's look to the future, however. Many businesses, as they grow and their dependency on technology gets more significant, look to developing a disaster recovery plan. Typically a disaster recovery site will be built. Let's consider what happens if the central site burns down and operations need to be run from the disaster recovery site.

All the distribution centers are hard-wired to the primary location, so what we need to achieve is the ability for all branches to dial into the disaster recovery site. Under normal conditions, the ISDN dial port is configured to dial the original central location. If that location has burned down, there is no way to Telnet to the branch routers and change the dial string so that they dial to the backup site. If you have a terminal adapter, however, you can instruct branch personnel to change the ISDN numbers dialed through the front panel of the terminal adapter and pull out the primary connection in the branch router's Serial 0 port. You now have a means of connecting branches to your disaster recovery site fairly quickly, albeit with some manual intervention. The remote site configuration discussed here is illustrated in Fig. 7-26.

ISDN Backup and Asynchronous Dial-Up Service Configuration

Chapter 6 gives detailed configuration for the router that is to provide the ISDN backup pool and we will not repeat that discussion

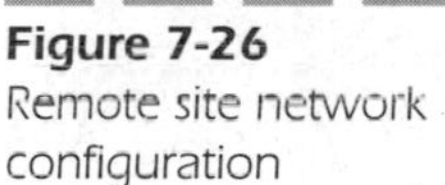

Figure 7-26 Remote site network configuration

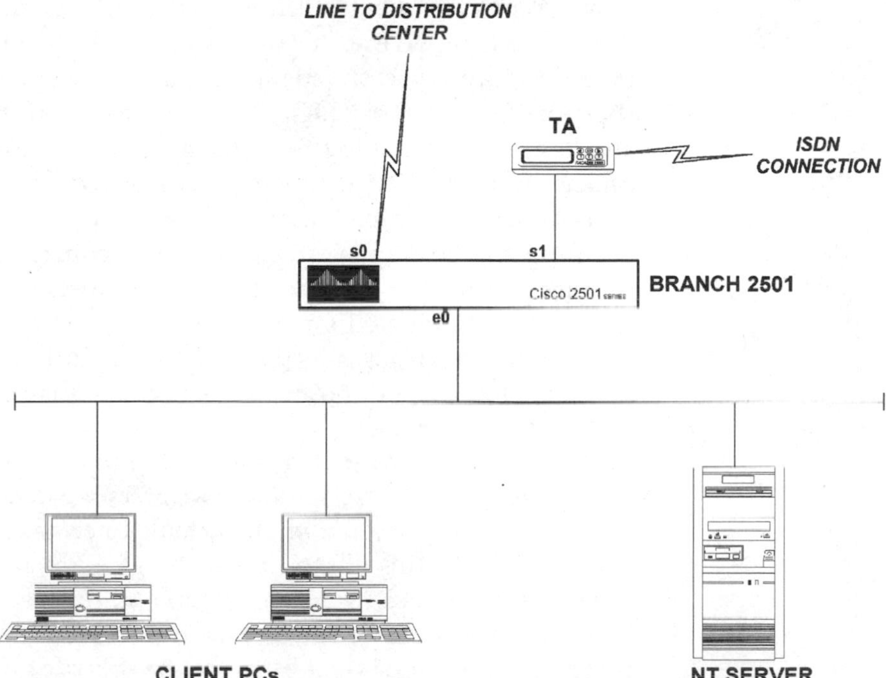

here. Configuration of asynchronous communications also has been discussed in Chap. 6, under the section on PPP communications. The key points for configuring an asynchronous routed interface are:

- IP addresses are assigned to a computer at connect time, a step that simplifies providing the ability for any computer to connect to any port.
- CHAP authentication is in place and managed by a TACACS server that logs what user logged in, when, and for how long.

Miscellaneous Issues

There are many miscellaneous issues to consider when assembling an internetwork of this kind. The first, and probably most important, is the type of routing protocol to implement. My choice is among a distance vector protocol such as IGRP, a link state protocol such as OSPF, or a hybrid like EIGRP. Link state protocols scale well and have many attractive features, but I think they are overly complex to optimize and deploy. If you choose to devote your life to becoming expert in link state routing protocol implementation, you will always have work; however, I seem to find better things to do with my time.

For the type of internetwork we are talking about here, Fast IGRP or EIGRP are perfectly adequate. IGRP has been around longer and therefore is very stable. EIGRP has become more stable in recent times and is ready for deployment in large internetworks. I have a slight preference for EIGRP at this stage. An important part of taking advantage of the enhanced facilities of modern routing protocols is defining the correct bandwidth in the configuration of each serial interface used. This is imperative, as it ensures that the most appropriate metric is calculated for each route. If a bandwidth command is not implemented on each interface, the default of T-1 bandwidth is assumed for the purposes of metric calculations, and suboptimal route selection results.

With the design presented, it is possible to have only one LAN interface on each host and NT server and have everyone delegate routing responsibilities to a router, by use of the default gateway command in each host and server. I like this way of doing things. Cisco routers are much better routers than any host or server. Servers and hosts should do what they do best: serve applications, file, and print services to users, and authenticate usernames. Routing should be left to the specialist router devices.

The next issue to consider is how to get to know your internetwork once it is operational. Despite advances in network management in recent years, there is still no real substitute for a network administrator knowing how the internetwork operates under normal conditions and being able to spot trends and abnormal activity. "Abnormal activity" might mean an intruder or a new application behaving inefficiently. In many cases, the only way to know what is at fault is to know in some detail how the internetwork performs when all is well. So what should be monitored? Here is a short list of generic criteria, which you probably will add to for your specific situation, but this list is a good start. We will cover these measurements again in Chap. 8, from a troubleshooting perspective.

The `show interface` command (discussed in more detail in Chap. 8) should become a good friend. It will give you the following information very easily for each interface you want to examine:

- *Current throughput, presented as a 5-minute average:* There may be times when you want to know the throughput over a shorter time span. Unfortunately, you cannot do this with a Cisco router; you need a network analyzer of some type to get this information.
- *Number of packets dropped by the router:* Typically a router will drop a packet if its buffers are full, or the hold-queue value (which is the number of packets allowed to be outstanding for a particular interface) is exceeded.

It is also worth knowing how many carrier transitions are normal for the lines used on your internetwork. This normally should be a low number, as it represents how many times the leased line supplied by the telephone company went down and came back up again.

In addition, the `show buffers` command presents useful information. This display (again, discussed in more detail in Chap. 8) shows the different sizes of buffers, their utilization, and whether you are running out of buffers of a specific size on a regular basis.

The `show proc` and `show proc mem` commands help you keep track of processor and memory utilization, which should not be subject to large changes. You can collect these values either manually or regularly via SNMP from a management station. If you can keep track of all these variables, you should be in a good position to determine what has caused a problem when it arrives—and problems always come along for an internetwork. It's part of life.

Summary

This chapter discussed the technologies you might wish to deploy when building your own Cisco router TCP/IP-based internetwork. After this discussion, a sample network was presented that would service a fairly generic set of requirements. The issues covered were network topology selection, reducing manual management tasks, and securing the internetwork.

CHAPTER 

Troubleshooting

Objectives

Troubleshooting is rather a nebulous thing to discuss. Until a specific problem crops up, we're just hypothesizing. The art of troubleshooting—and I do consider it as much of an art as a science—is in knowing where to look for the source of the problem. This comes through an analytical thought process. It is possible to learn all the facts available about communications systems and not be effective at resolving problems. Hands-on experience is the best teacher on the subject of troubleshooting; still I will:

- Outline a simple process that will get you on the right track to solve most problems.
- Focus mainly on specific examples.

A General Troubleshooting Blueprint

One of the best math tutors I ever had gave me some simple but effective advice. He said that before I try to solve a problem, I should write down what I have to find out and what information I have to work with. This advice carries over to troubleshooting internetwork problems as well, i.e., if you can get a clear definition of what you are trying to do and gather appropriate information on the problem, you are well on the way to solving the problem.

When solving mathematics problems, all the information needed generally is presented to you, but when solving internetwork problems you have to get the information yourself. Cisco makes this as straightforward as it can be by extensive `show` and `debug` commands. You, however, must know which of these commands to use in a given situation in order to get the information you need. Therein lies the art.

Internetwork problems generally fall into one of the following categories:

1. A Physical layer issue with device interconnection, hardware, or line failure.
2. A Data Link layer issue involving configuration of internetwork device interfaces.

3. A Network layer issue with network protocol configuration or operation.
4. Performance or traffic congestion problems causing Transport layer timeouts.
5. A software bug either in the application using the internetwork, or within the Cisco IOS itself.

The first four points follow the first four layers of the ISO data communications model, starting at layer 1, the Physical level. The fifth point covers all issues that arise in the top three layers of the ISO model. This is generally the way I recommend people start to troubleshoot internetwork problems. Start from the Physical layer and work upward. It may not always work out so neatly that you can pinpoint an internetwork problem as being sourced within one layer's operation, but checking the operation of protocols on a layer-by-layer basis will give you a good view of how the problem manifests itself.

Before reviewing the simple troubleshooting scenario explored in Chap. 3, there is one more point to consider before you rush in to fix things. In many cases, it is very simple to make the situation drastically worse. By rushing in and changing the configuration of devices on an internetwork, problems can occur that make the original situation seem like Nirvana. The next two points always should be at the forefront of your mind when you're troubleshooting.

1. Only change one variable at a time and observe the effect this has on the problem.
2. Always but always, and without exception, have a means of backing out of the change you are about to make.

There are a few other subtleties to consider, such as the effect on the processing power that issuing a given debugging command will have, but we will cover these on a case-by-case basis when we examine examples. If you adhere to the aforementioned two guidelines, you should be in good shape, and will probably not turn a problem into a crisis.

I will not examine the use of third-party devices such as LAN or WAN analyzers, although there are many excellent products on the market that will help you. In the main, the tools provided by Cisco are adequate to troubleshoot the vast majority of problems encountered. If you master all that Cisco offers you, however, by all means explore third-party devices.

Troubleshooting the First Three ISO Layers

In this section, we'll review the process of troubleshooting internetwork problems that was first introduced at the end of Chap. 3. This will not prepare us to do much real troubleshooting work, but does get the thought process started off in the right direction. The real troubleshooting work starts when we consider the individual cases that follow.

The hypothetical problem we have to solve in the review taken in this section is that router 1 cannot ping router 3 via router 2 on the simple internetwork shown in Fig. 8-1.

We will consider simple troubleshooting techniques at each of the first three layers of the ISO data communications model. In practice, you would troubleshoot a connectivity problem such as this one link at a time from source to destination, testing the Physical, Data Link, and Network layer operations in turn, attempting to identify the point where the communication is failing. We consider each layer separately here as an introduction to troubleshooting techniques and to highlight that similar commands display different information for different interface types.

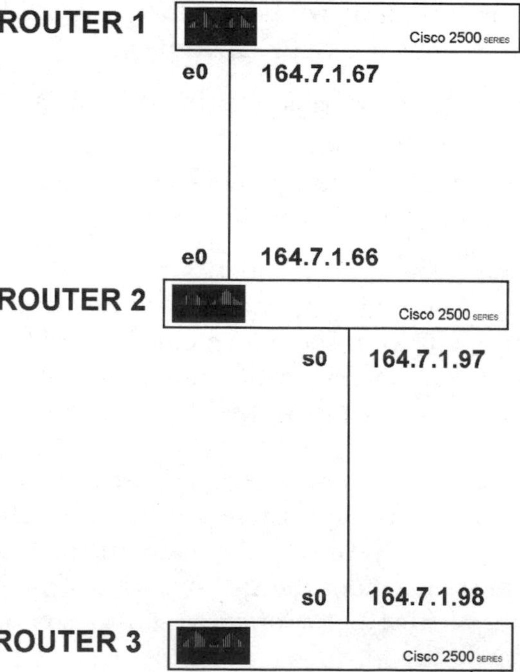

Figure 8-1 Three router setups for basic troubleshooting review

Simple Troubleshooting at the Physical Layer

Troubleshooting the Physical layer deals with issues such as:

1. Are the devices physically connected in an appropriate way?
2. Are interconnecting cables correct?
3. Are the CSU/DSU devices configured and operating properly?

So the problem we have to solve is that router 1 cannot ping router 3. Having stated the problem, we need to gather information, which we will do beginning with the Physical layer issues. The first thing we can do at the Physical level is check to determine whether the devices are physically connected. This is okay if the routers are all in one location, since we can just take a look, but if they are geographically dispersed, we need to use displays generated by the Cisco IOS to tell us the state of physical connections. Imagine router 1 and router 2 are local in New York, and router 3 is in Atlanta.

Seeing whether the Ethernet interfaces are connected for router 1 and router 2 should be straightforward. Cisco routers typically have an AUI connector for an Ethernet interface, and as most cabling these days is based around twisted-pair cables, a transceiver is used to convert media from the AUI 10Base5 to 10Base-T. A transceiver has an LED display to tell you if it is connected to the router interface and whether it is receiving traffic from a hub.

So let's think about what could happen on a physical connection level to stop things from working, and then see how Cisco IOS can or cannot report the condition, which is necessary if we want to troubleshoot a remote connection such as the Ethernet 0 interface on router 3.

1. Transceiver disconnected from Ethernet interface.
2. Transceiver connected to Ethernet interface, but disconnected from hub.
3. Ethernet interface connected to hub on which it is the only device.

We generally can gather pertinent information by using one or more of the following: a `show` command, a `debug` command, or a `ping/trace` command. We know that our problem is that router 3 is not reachable from router 1 by using the `ping` command, so let's start the troubleshooting process with the `show` command on the Ethernet interface of router 1, as illustrated in Fig. 8-2.

Figure 8-2 Output of the *show interface ethernet 0* command

```
router1 #show int eO
Ethernet0 is up, line protocol is up
  Hardware is Lance, address is 0000.0c47.42dd (bia 0000.0c47.42dd)
  Internet address is 164.7.1.67 255.255.255.224
  MTU 1500 bytes, BW 10000 Kbit, DLY 1000 usec, rely 255/255, load 1/255
  Encapsulation ARPA, loopback not set, keepalive set (10 sec)
  ARP type: ARPA, ARP Timeout 4:00:00
  Last input 0:00:01, output 0:00:00, output hang never
  Last clearing of "show interface" counters never
  Output queue 0/40, 0 drops; input queue 0/75, 0 drops
  5 minute input rate 8000 bits/sec, 4 packets/sec
  5 minute output rate 8000 bits/sec, 4 packets/sec
    717 packets input, 297281 bytes, 0 no buffer
    Received 567 broadcasts, 0 runts, 0 giants
    0 input errors, 0 CRC, 0 frame, 0 overrun, 0 ignored, 0 abort
    0 input packets with dribble condition detected
    3756 packets output, 475281 bytes, 0 underruns
    0 output errors, 0 collisions, 1 interface resets, 0 restarts
    0 output buffer failures, 0 output buffers swapped out
```

The first place to look on this display is at the status of the interface and the line protocol. Generically, a `show` command will display the interface as up, down, or administratively down; the line protocol will either be up or down. "Administratively down" means that the `shutdown` command has been entered into the configuration of the interface and needs to be removed with the `no shutdown` command. With LAN interfaces, the interface will never show a down condition unless something is seriously wrong with the router hardware. We will consider the case in which an asynchronous interface can report a down condition due to a misconfigured interface in the section on troubleshooting asynchronous communications.

For LAN interfaces, we are left with using the status of the line protocol to tell us if the physical connections are made. With the transceiver disconnected from the AUI interface, the line protocol is down. With the transceiver connected to the AUI interface, but disconnected from the hub, the line protocol report is still down. With the router the only device connected to the hub, the line protocol reports up.

At this stage, the only other command to look at is the `media-type` command if you are using a 4000-series router. This command can configure an interface for either 10Base-T or AUI operation; this command, set in interface configuration mode, must match the type of connection physically made to the router interface.

As you can see, we have limited remote monitoring capabilities to tell whether the physical connections are made for LAN connections. The best we can do remotely is see if the line protocol is up or down. If it is down, we have to get someone local to check the physical connections, because the only way to bring it up is to connect the interface to a working hub.

Before we move on to checking the status of the physical connections for the serial interfaces, we should try to determine if the router is connected to the correct hub to reach the devices it must reach. We do this by pinging the IP addresses of the other devices that we expect to be on the same segment. If we are operating in a Cisco IPX network environment, we can also issue IPX ping commands. Not all Novell servers support this functionality, so it cannot be used as a general troubleshooting tool such as the IP ping utility.

Now let's look at using Cisco IOS to check physical connectivity of the serial interfaces in use. In practice, I would now move on to checking the Data Link and Network layer issues with the Ethernet interfaces before moving on to the serial interfaces. For this introduction, however, it is useful to contrast the function of the `show interface` command for Ethernet and serial interfaces.

The `show interface serial 0` command issued on router 2 produces the display shown in Fig. 8-3.

The main points of interest regarding the physical connections are the status of the interface, the line protocol, and the status of the EIA signals given at the bottom of the display. Let's first consider what might be wrong at the Physical level and consider how we might use this display to detect these problems. At the Physical level, we will want to detect the following:

Figure 8-3 Output of the *show interface serial 0* command on router 2

```
router2#show int serial 0
Serial0 is up, line protocol is up
  Hardware is HD64570
  Internet address is 164.7.1.97 255.255.255.224
  MTU 1500 bytes, BW 1544 Kbit, DLY 20000 usec, rely 255/255, load 1/255
  Encapsulation HDLC, loopback not set, keepalive set (10 sec)
  Last input 0:00:01, output 0:00:00, output hang never
  Last clearing of "show interface" counters never
  Output queue 0/40, 0 drops; input queue 0/75, 0 drops
  5 minute input rate 4000 bits/sec, 3 packets/sec
  5 minute output rate 4000 bds/sec, 3 packets/sec
    336 packets input, 226009 bytes, 0 no buffer
    Received 95 broadcasts, 0 runts, 0 giants
    0 input errors, 0 CRC, 0 ftame, 0 overrun, 0 ignored, 0 abort
    3372 packets output, 293703 bytes, 0 underruns
    0 output errors, 0 collisions, 1007 interface resets, 0 restarts
    0 output buffer failures, 0 output buffers swapped out
    12 carrier transitions
    DCD=up DSR=up DTR=up RTS=up CTS=up
```

1. Is the serial interface connected to a working CSU/DSU device?
2. Is the local CSU/DSU communicating properly with the remote CSU/DSU?
3. Is the remote CSU/DSU connected to the remote router serial port?

Again we want to see the `show interface serial 0` command report that the interface is up and the line protocol is up. First, what will happen if the serial interface on router 3 is disconnected from the local CSU/DSU? The interface reports down and the line protocol also reports a down state. We also see that the EIA signals DCD, DSR, and CTS disappear. EIA signals are either generated from the router interface or the CSU/DSU device. In this case, the CSU/DSU generates DCD (carrier detect), DSR (data set ready), and CTS (clear to send). If these signals are not present, we know that the cable between the interface and the CSU/DSU is disconnected, or that the CSU/DSU is powered off.

We should also check the `show controllers serial 0` command at this stage to check whether the correct cable is connected to the serial interface. Remember from Chap. 3 that the serial interface will configure itself as a DTE or DCE depending on the configuration of the cable connected to it. A CSU/DSU device is always a DCE, so the router interface must be configured as a DTE.

Assuming that the correct cable is in use and that the CSU/DSU is powered on and connected to the router serial interface, how do we tell if the connection between the local and remote CSU/DSU is good? In a case in which the line between local and remote CSU/DSU has failed, we look at the `show interface serial 0` output again, and see that all the EIA signals are present except the DCD signal. This tells us that the router-to-local-CSU/DSU connection is made, but there is no carrier signal between the CSU/DSU devices. This is the way that a router typically reports that a leased-line connection has gone down.

If we can get to the stage at which the `show interface serial 0` command shows all signals present, the last thing to check on the Physical level is the remote CSU/DSU-to-remote-router interface connection. If you have a way of logging into the remote router 3, such as a dial-up connection to the console port, you can issue the `show interface serial 0` command to see if the EIA signals are present, thus confirming the remote CSU/DSU-to-router interface connectivity. Without a way to log into router 3, you have to rely on local personnel to confirm connections and that devices are powered up.

As you can see, at the Physical layer we can get useful information from Cisco IOS for serial connections, but limited information for Ethernet connections.

Simple Data Link Layer Troubleshooting

Again, we will look at the Data Link layer issues for both Ethernet and serial interfaces to contrast the information that similar commands present for different interface types. At the Data Link layer, the protocols are concerned with forming frames and synchronizing devices prior to the exchange of data.

For Ethernet interfaces, we are mainly concerned about confirming that the interface has the same encapsulation as the other devices with which it must communicate. We can see the encapsulation used either by examining the router configuration, or by looking at the `show interface ethernet 0` command and reading the fifth line of the output. There are four options for Ethernet encapsulation; other networking systems, unfortunately, know them by different names. A comparison of Cisco and Novell terminology is given as follows:

- ARPA is known to Novell systems as the `ethernet_ii` frame type. This is a common frame type for implementing IP on NetWare-based networks.
- SNAP is known to Novell systems as frame type `ethernet_snap`. The SNAP encapsulation is more common in Token-Ring environments.
- SAP is known as `ethernet_802.2` and is the default frame type for NetWare 3.12, 4.*x*, and later servers.
- Cisco's term for Novell's 802.3 is `novell-ether`. Novell implemented its own frame type, 802.3, when NetWare was designed. This caused some confusion in the world of support personnel. IEEE 802.3 can support many layer 3 protocols; Novell 802.3, however, supports only IPX at the Network layer. Cisco avoids this confusion by referring to Novell's 802.3 as `novell-ether`.

Before you can proceed any further, the encapsulation on the interfaces must match that of the other devices with which it is to communicate. For Ethernet devices, that is all we need to check for this problem. In the section on troubleshooting Ethernet, we will look at other Data Link layer issues such as undersized or oversized packets and collisions.

For serial interfaces, the encapsulation must be the same on the communicating interfaces. The best way to check this is by looking at the configuration of each connected interface. Encapsulation on serial interfaces can be one of the following:

- ATM-DXI
- Frame relay
- HDLC
- LAPB
- PPP
- SMDS
- X.25

For serial interfaces, we can check to make sure the clock signal is operating correctly by issuing the `show controllers serial 0` command. This display will show the speed of the clock signal received from the CSU/DSU device, if present. This is important, because if the clock signal is not there, the serial interface and CSU/DSU cannot communicate.

The clock signal is one area in which Ethernet and serial interfaces differ considerably. With serial interfaces, a constant clock signal synchronizes router interface to CSU/DSU communications. On an Ethernet interface, there is no such synchronization signal. Each packet sent on Ethernet uses the preamble at the front of the Ethernet frame to synchronize all devices on the Ethernet network as the frame is transmitted.

Simple Troubleshooting at the Network Layer

An Ethernet interface will show the line protocol as up, even if there are no other devices on its network segment; it does not need to see another IP device. It's different with serial interfaces. Before the line protocol comes up, serial interfaces need to see a device on the other end of the serial link that has an IP address in the same network number or subnet for which its serial interface is configured.

This is an important point. In order for the network or subnet number for which a serial interface is configured to appear in the router's routing table, the serial interface's line protocol must be up. So even if everything is correct at the Physical and Data Link layers, the routing table will not have the necessary entries to allow router 1 to ping router 3 if the router 1 and router 2 Serial 0 interfaces are not addressed for the same subnet.

Network layer troubleshooting is based around viewing the routing table on the routers along the path from source to destination, along with examining the IP addresses (or other protocol IDs) of those router interfaces. Typically, if routes do not appear in a routing table, you will check to see that appropriate static, default, or dynamic routes have been entered and then either configure any missing routes manually, or troubleshoot any dynamic routing process, such as RIP or IGRP, to get the routing tables updated.

As we have just shown, if a router's line protocol is down, all the routes that were accessible through that interface will be eliminated from the routing table. This is a good justification for following the process of Physical and Data Link troubleshooting before beginning Network layer troubleshooting. If you jump straight into Network layer troubleshooting, you could start to investigate a routing protocol issue, whereas the real problem might be, for example, with a line protocol down due to a missing CSU/DSU clock signal.

Summary of a Simple Troubleshooting Process

Let's try to summarize what we would do to troubleshoot if router 1 were not able to ping router 3. When following this process, you must rectify any unexpected results from the `show` commands before proceeding to the next stage, such as reconnecting disconnected cables, and correcting incompatible encapsulation types, IP addresses, and routing processes.

1. Issue the `show interface ethernet 0` command on router 1, to make sure that the interface and line protocol are up.
2. Ping the address of the Ethernet 0 interface on router 2 from router 1.
3. Telnet into router 2 and issue the `show interface serial 0` command and check that the interface and line protocol are up.
4. Ping router 3 from router 2.
5. Issue the `show ip route` command on all three routers to check that a route at the IP level exists between source and destination.
6. Ping router 3 from router 1.

This process is simplified greatly if you have more than one way to remotely log into a remote router. If your only means to log onto a router located in another city is via the serial interface connection, and that connection is not functioning, troubleshooting options are limited. Having some dial-up facility to a console port, even if it requires local personnel to power on the modem before you can get in, greatly improves your abilities to troubleshoot.

As with dial access, the importance of documentation cannot be overstressed. My recommendation is that you try to automate documentation by regularly downloading router configurations to a central management station, so that you do not have to rely on manual procedures. In my experience, manual procedures are never maintained for long in the fast-moving world of internetwork management.

Having taken an overview of troubleshooting, we will examine specific problems and specific troubleshooting commands in more depth. The next section will examine troubleshooting specific interface types. The techniques used to analyze problems in this section will be useful when troubleshooting connectivity for individual segments from source to destination. A subsequent section will examine troubleshooting protocol-specific issues and problems with multilink end-to-end connectivity.

If you can get access to a Cisco router while you read this section, I recommend that you familiarize yourself with the use of the "?" character. While in privileged mode, you can use the "?" character after the `show` or `debug` keywords to inform you of what displays are available to give you information on the status of interfaces, protocols, and router processes. An example of using the `show ?` command is given in Fig. 8-4, and it should be noted that each of the options displayed as a result of the `show ?` command have sub-options under them. For example, typing `show ip ?` would display just the `show` commands for IP.

Figure 8-4 The *show ?* screen output to list all *show* options

```
router3#sho ?
  access-expression     List access expression
  access-lists          List access lists
  aliases               Display alias commands
  arp                   ARP table
  async                 Information on terminal lines used as router interfaces
  bridge                Bridge Forwarding/Filtering Database [verbose]
  buffers               Buffer pool statistics
  cdp                   CDP information clock     Display the system clock
  cmns                  Connection-Mode networking services (CMNS) information
  compress              Show compression statistics.
  configuration         Contents of Non-Volatile memory
  controllers           Interface controller status
  debugging             State of each debugging option
```

Figure 8-4
Continued

dhcp	Dynamic Host Configuration Protocol status
dialer	Dialer parameters and statistics
dnsix	Shows Dnsix/DMDP information
dxi	atm-dxi information
entry	Queued terminal entries
flash	System Flash information flh-log Flash Load Helper log buffer
frame-relay	Frame-Relay information
history	Display the session command history
hosts	IP domain-name, lookup style, nameservers, and host table
interfaces	Interface status and configuration
ip	IP information
line	TTY line information
llc2	IBM LLC2 circuit information
logging	Show the contents of logging buffers
memory	Memory statistics
ntp	Network time protocol
printers	Show LPD printer information
privilege	Show current privilege level
processes	Active process statistics
protocols	Active network routing protocols
queue	Show queue contents
queueing	Show queueing configuration
registry	Function registration information
reload	Scheduled reload information
rhosts	Remote-host+user equivalences
rif	RIF cache entries
route-map	route-map information
running-config	Current operating configuration
sessions	Information about Telnet connections
sands	SMDS information
snapshot	Snapshot parameters and statistics
snap	snap statistics
spanning-tree	Spanning tree topology
stacks	Process stack utilization
standby	Hot standby protocol information
startup-config	Contents of startup configuration
subsystem	List subsystems
tcp	Status of TCP connections
terminal	Display terminal configuration parameters
users	Display information about terminal lines
version	System hardware and software status
whoami	Info on current tty line
x25	X.25 information

Troubleshooting Interface Problems

In this section, we'll examine serial, asynchronous, Ethernet, and Token Ring interfaces, the most commonly implemented types of interface.

Troubleshooting Serial Interfaces

Serial interfaces are used with many different types of encapsulation: Cisco HDLC, PPP, frame relay, X.25, etc. In this section, we'll examine serial interface troubleshooting in some depth, assuming the default Cisco HDLC encapsulation. Most of what is done here is applicable no matter what the interface encapsulation is. Troubleshooting activities that are specific to one type of encapsulation will be examined in the section on troubleshooting protocol problems.

Show Interface Serial Revisited. When connectivity problems arise on a specific serial interface, the first place to start is always with the `show interface serial X` command, to analyze its screen display. Figure 8-3 showed a typical screen display generated by the `show interface serial` command, and Table 8.1 explains each entry of interest to us in this display.

TABLE 8.1 Explanation of Show Interface Serial Command Display

Screen Output	Explanation
Serial 0	Displays whether the interface is up, down, administratively down, or disabled.
line protocol	Displays an up down or looped condition.
Hardware is	Identifies the hardware type with a code.
MTU	Maximum Transmission Unit, the maximum message size that will be sent out this interface before it is fragmented.
Bandwidth	The value used by certain routing protocols (such as IGRP) for calculating a metric to associate with this interface's link.
DLY	The value for delay that the IOS assigns to a link of this bandwidth for metric calculation purposes.
Rely	The reliability of the link measured as a fraction of 255. This value is used in metric calculations for which it is usually taken to be 1.
Load	The load on the interface bandwidth, as a fraction of 255, which is used by some routing protocols for metric calculation.
Encapsulation	This reports which Data Link layer protocol is used for encapsulating packets sent on this interface.
loopback	Displays whether a software loopback condition has been set.

TABLE 8.1 Continued

Screen Output	Explanation
Keepalive	Indicates whether keep-alive packets have been explicitly defined for this interface.
last input, last output	Length of time since last packet input or output on this interface.
Last clearing of show interface	Reports when the last time the interface statistics, such as drops, were cleared.
output queue	Reports the size of the output queue and the number of packets dropped on this interface since the last clearing of statistics.
input queue	Reports the size of the input queue and number of packets dropped on this interface since the last clearing of statistics.
input rate	The rate of traffic inbound on this interface, measured as an average over 5 minutes and quoted in bits per second and packets per second.
Output rate	The rate of traffic inbound on this interface, measured as an average over 5 minutes and quoted in bits per second and packets per second.
Packets and byte input	The number of packets and bytes input since the last clearing of counters.
Received	A breakdown of the type of traffic received, as broadcasts, runts (packets shorter than allowed by the encapsulation method used), giants (long packets), and input errors such as CRC, frame, and overrun errors.
output	Number of packets and bytes output since the last clearing of counters, along with appropriate output error statistics.
interface resets	The number of times the line protocol has had to restart due to an interruption in end-to-end connectivity
carrier transitions	The number of times the DCD signal has been lost and returned.
EIA signals	The status of DCD, RTS, CTS, DTR, and DSR.

Interface and Line Protocol Status in Detail. Let's look at the possible combinations of interface and line protocol status that can be reported in the `show interface serial` command.

- Serial 0 up, line protocol up
- Serial 0 up, line protocol down

- Serial 0 down, line protocol down
- Serial 0 up, line protocol up (looped)
- Serial 0 up, line protocol down (disabled)
- Serial 0 administratively down, line protocol down

The Serial 0 interface up and the line protocol up is the fully working condition. Both the interface and line protocol have initialized and protocol keep-alives are being exchanged.

The most common fault condition, Serial 0 up but line protocol down, can be due to a variety of conditions. This display tells you that the router is connected to a device that is providing a DCD signal, indicating that a carrier signal is present between the local and remote CSU/DSU. Due to a problem with router configuration or CSU/DSU operation, however, protocol keep-alives are not being exchanged properly between the two ends of the connection. This condition is reported if there are problems with clocking on the CSU/DSU, if the two serial interfaces connected via the link are not on the same subnet, when there is a noisy leased line or a remote router failure of some kind.

The best way to troubleshoot this condition is to follow the loopback tests outlined in a later section in this chapter. If these procedures do not identify the problem, and you are sure both routers are configured correctly, use the `debug serial interface` command (also covered in a later section in this chapter) to identify clocking problems. If all else fails, start to replace pieces of hardware until the faulty device has been located.

If both the Serial 0 interface and the line protocol are down, it means that the serial interface is not sensing a carrier detect (DCD) signal from its attached CSU/DSU. This can be due to a telephone company line problem, a cabling issue or a CSU/DSU failure. The most frequent cause of this display is a problem with the telephone company's leased line. Following loopback tests, outlined later in this chapter, will identify which link in the chain is causing the problem.

When you put a CSU/DSU in loopback mode, the condition of Serial 0 up and the line protocol up (looped) is displayed. The router interface recognizes that it is receiving the same keep-alive messages it is sending. If you see the condition reported when the local CSU/DSU is in loopback, you know all is good with the router and CSU/DSU interface and connecting cable. If this condition is displayed when just the remote CSU/DSU is in loopback, you know all is good up to the line interface of the remote CSU/DSU. If the line protocol will not come up when the loopback is removed from the remote CSU/DSU, there is something wrong with the remote CSU/DSU DTE interface, the cable between the remote CSU/DSU and the remote router, or the remote router itself (including its configuration).

The condition of Serial 0 up and line protocol down (disabled) is seen if the router interface has received more than 5000 errors during one keep-alive period (which is 10 seconds by default). The most likely cause of this condition is either a faulty CSU/DSU device at either end of the link, or a faulty telephone company line.

Finally, the condition of Serial 0 administratively down and line protocol down is reported when the `shutdown` command has been entered into the configuration of the interface. The condition is removed by taking the entry out of the interface configuration by entering the `no shutdown` command.

Troubleshooting Packet Drops and Errors. Once we have an up condition for both the interface and line protocol, the basic communications across a serial link are established. There are, however, plenty of potential problems that can arise, and in this section we'll examine problems reported with packet drops and errors.

Packet drops, whatever the cause, are generally a bad thing. If the packet dropped by the router is part of a TCP stream, the packet will be retransmitted, adding to network load; if it is part of a UDP broadcast and there are no other Application or Data Link layer retransmission mechanisms in place, the packet and its associated information will be lost forever. The goal for drops either input to, or output from, an interface is for them to be zero (or some very low number with infrequent increments in their value).

If packet drops are increasing regularly, it typically means there is more traffic passing through the interface than the interface can handle. If this is due to attempts to send more packets through the interface than the physical bandwidth of the line will allow, the only solution is to increase the capacity of the line in use. This is the expensive solution (in terms of dollars to the telephone company), but simple; in many, if not most cases, however, drops occur for reasons other than lack of available bandwidth.

The first place to look is the status of the input and output hold queues in the `show interface serial` command output. Hold queues are specific to an interface and are set while in interface configuration mode. If you see that the number of packets in the hold queue (the hold queue defines the number of packets that can be held awaiting hand-off to a transmit buffer) is reaching the maximum allowed, it is worth trying to increase the size of the hold queue. It is possible that by doing this, more misses appear at the stage at which packets are buffered as reported by the `show buffers` command. We will examine router buffers and how they can be optimized later in this section.

The way to think about a packet passing through a router is that it comes into an interface hold queue, gets passed off to a system buffer of an appropriate size, and is switched to the desired interface to be sent to its next hop destination.

The nature of LAN traffic means that it is bursty, i.e., lots of packets arrive at one time instead of in a constant predictable stream. This makes it difficult to issue the `show interface serial` command at the right moment and catch overutilization of hold queues. The `show serial interface` command is a static display, a snapshot at the moment you issue the command. If you see drops reported after the input or output queue usage statistics, however, it costs little to increase the size of these queues and see if that improves matters. An example of increasing an output hold queue from its default of 40 to 100 packets is given as follows:

```
Router1(config)#interface serial 0
Router1(config-int)#output hold-queue 100
```

The other configuration change that should be made as a matter of course when experiencing packet drops on an interface is for the `no ip route-cache` command to be entered into the configuration of the interface experiencing drops. This command stops any packets from being *fast-switched*, which means that every packet to be switched from one interface to another must be processed by the router processor, which slows down the passage of packets through a router.

The next place to look for problems if packets are being dropped is the `show buffers` command, a sample output of which is illustrated in Fig. 8-5.

A router has buffers of five different sizes, and will place an incoming packet in the smallest buffer size possible. With reference to Fig. 8-5, you can see that on an Ethernet network with a maximum packet size of just over 1500 bytes, no "verybig," large, or huge buffers will be utilized. On networks that use Token-Ring, on which the maximum packet size is more than 4 kilobytes, some verybig or large buffers may be used. Let's examine what each entry in this display means.

Buffer Elements. These are nothing that you should be directly concerned with; they are markers used by the IOS to keep track of buffers and where they reside in memory.

Figure 8-5
Output of the *show buffers* command

```
router3#show buffers
Buffer elements:
    406 in free list (500 max allowed)
    114 hits, 0 misses, 0 created

Public buffer pools:
Small buffers, 104 bytes (total 50, permanent 50):
    50 in free list (20 min, 150 max allowed)
    5 hits, 0 misses, 0 trims, 0 created
Middle buffers, 600 bytes (total 25, permanent 25):
    25 in free list (1 0 min, 150 max allowed)
    12 hits, 0 misses, 0 trims, 0 created
Big buffers, 1524 bytes (total 50, permanent 50):
    50 in free list (5 min, 150 max allowed)
    5 hits, 0 misses, 0 trims, 0 created
VeryBig buffers, 4520 bytes (total 10, permanent 10):
    10 in free list (O min, 100 max allowed)
    10 in free list (O min, 1 00 max allowed)
Large buffers, 5024 bytes (total 0, permanent 0):
    0 in free list (0 min, 10 max allowed)
    0 hits, 0 misses, 0 trims, 0 created
Huge buffers, 18024 bytes (total 0, permanent 0):
    0 in free list (0 min, 4 max allowed)
    0 hits, 0 misses, 0 trims, 0 created

Interface buffer pools:
Ethernet0 buffers, 1524 bytes (total 32, permanent 32):
    8 in free list (0 min, 32 max allowed)
    24 hits, 0 fallbacks
    8 max cache size, 8 in cache
Serial0 buffers, 1524 bytes (total 32, permanent 32):
    7 in free list (0 min, 32 max allowed)
    25 hits, 0 fallbacks
    8 max cache size, 8 in cache
Serial1 buffers, 1524 bytes (total 32, permanent 32):
    7 in free list (0 min, 32 max allowed)
    25 hits, 0 fallbacks
    8 max cache size, 8 in cache

0 failures (0 no memory)
```

Hits, Misses, Trims, and Created. A *hit* occurs when an attempt to allocate a buffer is successful, and indicates the desired state of affairs regarding the operation of available buffer resources. A *miss* is not necessarily a bad thing, although its name can give rise to some concern. The number of misses is the number of times the buffer pool needed to grow because a buffer was required, but no buffer of the appropriate size was available. *Trims* and *created* reflect the number of buffers deleted and added for a given buffer size and illustrate the dynamic nature of system buffer allocation in Cisco routers.

Small, Middle, Big, Verybig, Large, and Huge Buffers. These names represent blocks of main memory used to hold network packets.

Total, Permanent, Free List, Min, and Max Allowed. These values are quoted for each size of buffer. The total number of buffers of this size is quoted, along with an indication of how many of these are permanent and will not be trimmed by the operating system if they are unused. The *min* and *max allowed* display the minimum number and maximum number of this size of packet that the operating system will allow to be free at any given time.

Interface Buffer Pools, Fallbacks, and Failures. The interface buffer pools are small amounts of fixed memory allocated to packets passing through an interface. These buffers cannot be directly manipulated by router configuration commands. The display for the interface buffer pool contains many entries that are the same as for the public buffer pools. The exceptions are fallbacks and failures. *Fallbacks* occur when a buffer cannot be allocated from the interface pool and needs to be allocated from the public pool, which is a normal occurrence and does not warrant any particular action. *Failures* are a bad thing, since the failures are the number of times a buffer allocation failed because a buffer was not available, which results in a lost packet. The display additionally tells you how many of these failures were a result of no memory being available to create a new buffer.

Once you have optimized hold queues and buffers as much as possible, and potentially increased the amount of physical memory available for main RAM, the only option left for reducing persistent drops is to increase the bandwidth on the link.

In practice, trial and error is generally the only way to optimize the size of hold queue and buffer pool. The statistic with which you should be most concerned is the number of drops reported by the `show interface` command. If you are experiencing drops, first try increasing the size of the hold queue. If this does not help, it might be that there are not enough buffers of a certain size. The system will create more buffers as they are needed, but this takes time.

While the system is creating more buffers, it is possible for the hold queue to be overrun and to start dropping packets. If you suspect this might be the case, you will need to increase the number of buffers of the size that is reporting misses. A similar situation can occur if you see a lot of trims and created for a given size of buffer, since it takes time for the router to add or delete a buffer. If you see lots of trims or created, you should increase the max-free and min-free amounts for the buffer size in question. The effect of increasing the min-free and max-free value should ensure that there always will be enough buffers available to take incoming packets, without the need for the system to create more buffers.

Although it is nice to be able to have a system with few or no drops, the steps taken to minimize drops (increasing hold queues and buffers) add latency to the link, which can cause problems for protocols such as DEC's LAT, which does not tolerate delays.

In addition to reporting drops experienced on a given interface, the `show interface serial` command also gives useful information on many of the different types of errors that can be encountered on a line. The errors are grouped under input and output errors as follows:

- *Input errors:* CRC, frame, overrun, abort
- *Output errors:* collisions, interface resets, carrier transitions

Input errors generally come from a faulty leased line, CSU/DSU hardware, or out-of-spec cable. *CRC errors* mean that the packet received is not the same as the packet sent, indicating that there is interference on the transmission path. All cables, telephone company lines, and CSU/DSU services should be checked if this value is 1 percent or more of total traffic.

A *framing error* means that the packet received does not end on an 8-bit byte boundary. Errors of this type can come from interference of the kind that results in a CRC error. Additionally, framing errors can occur whenever CSU/DSU setups (framing and line coding values) on either end of the link are incompatible with the framing of the line in use. All internetwork devices should be configured to use a clock from one source, because if devices on the one link are using disparate clock sources, framing errors can occur.

Overruns are rare; they occur if packets arrive too quickly for the router to handle. This typically is a problem only if the router CPU utilization is very high and all you can do is upgrade to a router with a faster processor, or try to offload some of the work of the router to another device.

Abort packets occur when an illegal sequence of bits has been received. Typically, to maintain synchronization, a sequence of seven or more 1s is not allowed by line coding schemes. If seven or more 1s appear in a data stream, 0s are inserted to transmit the packet over the line, and are removed at the receiving end. Therefore, a packet containing seven 1s is a code violation and results in an abort.

Output errors generally have a lesser impact on internetwork performance than input errors. The `show interface serial` command lists *collisions*, which are only really applicable to Ethernet media, so rarely will this number be anything other than 0.

If *interface reset* errors are reported, it is because keep-alive packets are being missed. This could be caused by constant carrier transitions (which will be covered next), or significant output drops, or increasing numbers of input errors. Generally, one of these other reported problems must be resolved to resolve interface reset problems.

Carrier transitions are counted whenever the carrier signal changes state. This typically is due to a faulty line, or, on a less regular basis, CSU/DSU failure or faulty cabling.

Resolving Problems with Clock Sources. A single reliable clock source is essential for synchronous communications over a telephone company data line. The speed of the clock source determines the bandwidth of the line that is available for data transmission. For example, a 128 kbps line will have a clock source running at 128,000 cycles per second. This means that the clock source will "clock" 128 kilobits of data onto the line in 1 second.

A string of data being transmitted down a line consists of 1s and 0s, represented by electrical signals at a given voltage level. The clock tells all devices that are communicating what length of time is used to represent a 1 or a 0. Let's say for argument's sake that the clock states that a constant voltage level for 8 μs represents 1 bit (roughly what our 128 kbps clock does). If a constant voltage level is transmitted for 16 μs, that means that 2 bits of the same value have been sent. You can see that if the communicating devices do not agree precisely on the clock signal, they will not be able to interpret data sent between them properly.

When you look at the connectors between a CSU/DSU and a router interface, you see many pins, some of which are dedicated to producing a clock signal. Between CSU/DSU devices, there is a telephone company line of some type that has far fewer connectors, typically two or four wires. Due to the lack of individual wires on a line, the clock signal is embedded in the data stream sent over the line. This means that the CSU/DSU must derive a clock signal from the data that passes through it.

To achieve this, the CSU/DSU must receive at least one 1-bit value every 8-bit byte. If the data stream contains eight or more 0s, the CSU/DSU encoding mechanism must insert a 1-bit value for transmission over the line and remove it from the data stream at the other end. This technique is referred to as *maintaining one's density*. The line supplied to you by the telephone company and your CSU/DSU must agree on the method of maintaining one's density, or the clock source will be lost and errors will occur. For example, T-1 lines now use *Extended Superframe Format* (ESF) framing with Binary 8-Zero Substitution (B8ZS). Previously, T-1 lines used *Superframe Format* framing with *Alternate Mark Inversion* (AMI) encoding.

If there are significant input errors (between 0.5 percent and 1.5 percent of traffic), you should check that all clock sources are set to the same source and that all use the same framing and encoding schemes.

So far we have talked about the clock source that is used to transmit data between CSU/DSU devices. A clock also is used to transmit data between the CSU/DSU and the router interface. The CSU/DSU retrieves a clock signal from the data it receives over the line to use for transmitting data to the router interface. On this link, no encoding schemes are necessary, as a separate wire carries the clock signal. When it comes time for the router interface to send data back to the CSU/DSU, the router generates its own clock and transmits it on a pin known as the *serial clock transmit external* (SCTE) pin. When the CSU/DSU device uses this clock rather than the one it derived over the line from data stream received, it is better able to decipher the data from the router without error. You should check that your CSU/DSU devices support and are configured for SCTE timing, especially if data rates above 64 kbps are used.

If an interface reports increasing input errors, leading you to suspect problems with the clock source, the best means of tracking down the problem are by using loopback and ping tests to identify which link in the chain from source to destination is causing a problem; these tests are covered in the next section. The following points summarize what we have discussed so far regarding the resolution of clocking problems:

1. Check that both CSU/DSU devices take their clock source from the line.
2. Check that the CSU/DSU device has a configuration that matches the line supplied by the telephone company; this includes framing, encoding, and other line characteristics, such as impedance level.
3. Check that SCTE is in use by both CSU/DSU devices.
4. Check that cable lengths are within specification and are of the shielded type if problems with interference on cables persist.

CSU/DSU Loopback Tests. Loopback tests are useful for identifying where in the chain of links from source to destination either communications are failing, or errors are being introduced. Most CSU/DSU devices have an option to go into what is referred to as *digital loopback*. Digital loopback provides two loops, one from the CSU/DSU to the router interface and the other from the CSU/DSU to the telco leased line. By putting first the local CSU/DSU in loopback, as shown in Fig. 8-6, we can see if the connection from router 1 to CSU/DSU1 is okay by looking at the `show interface serial 0` output on router 1. We also can view the state of the connection from router 2 all the way through the telco network to CSU/DSU1.

I have stated that loopback tests do not work for synchronous PPP connections, and neither do they work for X.25 or frame relay connections. If, however, the type of communications you're using allows loopbacks (such as the Cisco HDLC encapsulation), they are a useful troubleshooting tool. On more complex internetworks, where connections pass through many router devices, ping tests help you identify where connectivity fails and, potentially, which link is introducing errors in communication. To check connectivity, the `ping` command issued in nonprivileged mode sends 5 ICMP ping packets, each of 100 bytes. This is good for checking physical connectivity and ensuring that routing tables have all the necessary entries. To use the `ping` command to check the integrity of connections, you must be in privileged mode, which gives you options to set the size, number, and data pattern of ping packets sent. A typical screen display for pinging in privileged mode is given in Fig. 8-7.

The extra functionality of the extended ping allows you to generate traffic on a serial link in order to test how the link operates under full-load conditions. Also, by specifying an all 1s or all 0s data pattern, the coding and framing configurations can be tested.

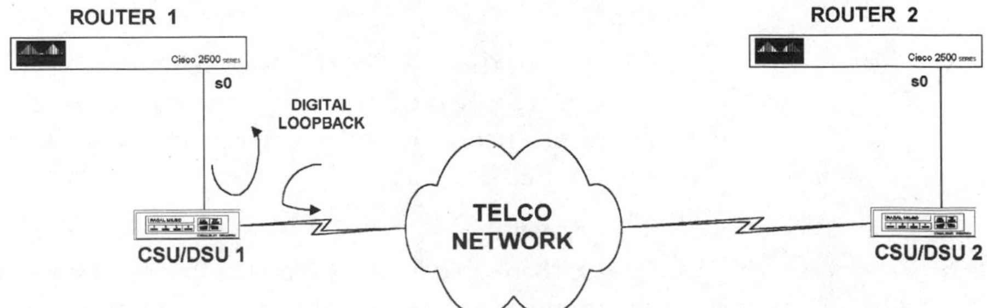

Figure 8-6 Putting a CSU/DSU in digital loopback

Figure 8-7
Use of ping in privileged mode

```
router2#ping
Protocol [ip]:
Target IP address: 164.7.1.67
Repeat count [5]: 100
Datagram size [100]: 1000
Timeout in seconds [2]:
Extended commands [n]: y
Source address: 164.7.1.97
Type of service [0]:
Set DF bit in IP header? [no]:
Data pattern [0xABCD]: 0xFFF
Loose, Strict, Record, Timestamp, Verbose[V]:
Sweep range of sizes [n]:
Type escape sequence to abort.
Sending 100, 1000 byte ICMP Echos to 164.7.1.67, timeout is 2 seconds:
Packet has data pattern 0x0FFF
Reply to request 0 (8 ms)
Reply to request 1 (4 ms)
Reply to request 2 (4 ms)
Reply to request 3 (8 ms)
Reply to request 4 (4 ms)
Reply to request 5 (4 ms)
Reply to request 6 (8 ms)
Reply to request 7 (4 ms)
Reply to request 8 (4 ms)
Reply to request 9 (4 ms)
Reply to request 10 (4 ms)
```

Debug Serial Interface Command. There are many debug commands that can be used when troubleshooting serial communications, which are specific to the encapsulation used on the interface. We will examine some of these encapsulation-specific debug displays when we consider troubleshooting the specific protocol in question. At this stage, we will consider the `debug serial` command screen output generated when the interface is using the default Cisco HDLC encapsulation.

Before we look at this display, let's review how best to use debug mode on Cisco routers.

Debug mode potentially can use a lot of processor power and cause the router to drop a high percentage of packets. In fact, one sure way to make a router stop functioning until it is powered off, then on, is to issue the `debug all` command. This will debug all packets passing through the router and, if there is even a modest amount of network traffic, will bring the router to its knees.

The most efficient way to have the router report debug information is to use the `logging buffered` global command to have the `debug` command output written to a log file. The output then can be viewed with the `show log` command. At times you may elect to see debug messages appear on the terminal display as they are generated. This can be achieved either by attaching a terminal directly to the console port of the router, or, if accessing the router via Telnet, issuing the `term mon` command. This command copies the output going to the console to your Telnet session.

Debug information usually is checked once all other standard troubleshooting procedures have failed. If the line protocol continually reports a down condition when all configurations and connections appear to be good, you can use the `debug serial interface` command to see if a timing issue at either end of the communication link is interfering with the exchange of keep-alive messages. A typical screen output for the `debug serial interface` command is illustrated in Fig. 8-8.

The `myseq` (my sequence), `mineseen`, and `yourseen` are the interesting parts of this display. During normal operation, the `myseq` and `mineseen` values are equal and increment after each keep-alive is sent by this router. The `myseq` is the sequence number of the keep-alive sent, and the `mineseen` is the sequence number last acknowledged by the remote router. The `yourseen` value is the last sequence number received from the remote router. It is normal for a keep-alive message to be lost once in a while, but three consecutive missed keep-alives causes the link to be reset. When the link is reset, the sequence numbers revert back to the last acknowledged sequence number values.

If everything else on the link looks good, but you are consistently missing keep-alives, you should report this condition to the telephone company that supplies your lines.

Troubleshooting Asynchronous Communications

Asynchronous communications are one of the most problematic areas in providing comprehensive internetwork services to an organization. We covered the security aspects of dial-up networking in Chap. 7 with CHAP and use of a TACACS server. The main challenge of asynchronous communications, however, is providing reliable service to users. The chief issue is minimizing drops while transporting what is typically LAN-based traffic over an asynchronous link. A LAN operates at 10 Mbps or above, whereas modems at best connect at 28.8 kbps, but very often, due to line conditions, only at 26.4 or 21.6 kbps. With V.42*bis* compression, throughput rates can exceed 50 kbps temporarily, but this can pose problems for many applications.

```
Serial0: HDLC myseq 129, mineseen 129, yourseen 129, line up
Serial0: HDLC myseq 130, mineseen 130, yourseen 130, line up
Serial0: HDLC myseq 131, mineseen 131, yourseen 131, line up
Serial0: HDLC myseq 132, mineseen 132, yourseen 132, line up
Serial0: HDLC myseq 133, mineseen 133, yourseen 133, line up
Serial0: HDLC myseq 134, mineseen 134, yourseen 134, line up
Serial0: HDLC myseq 135, mineseen 135, yourseen 135, line up
Serial0: HDLC myseq 136, mineseen 136, yourseen 136, line up
Serial0: HDLC myseq 137, mineseen 137, yourseen 137, line up
Serial0: HDLC myseq 138, mineseen 138, yourseen 138, line up
Serial0: HDLC myseq 139, mineseen 139, yourseen 139, line up
```

Figure 8-8
Log output for the *debug serial interface* command

Assuming that you have minimized all service and route advertisements with the use of access lists for the protocols in use over the asynchronous link, the discussion in the previous section on dealing with input and output drops via manipulation of the hold queues and buffer pools applies. Exact settings for hold queues and buffers can be determined only on a case-by-case basis and may require the installation of more main RAM in the router.

Before we examine router-based troubleshooting of asynchronous communications, let's review external factors that can contribute to poor or nonperformance of a dial-up link. The first is the configuration of the PC hardware at the remote end. A remote PC must be using a 16550 UART (Universal Asynchronous Receive Transmit) chip in the circuitry of the serial port used to connect to the remote modem. Previous UART chips were inadequate; for example, the 8250 operated only at up to 9600 kbps and, although the 16450 operated at higher speeds, its buffer capabilities were too limited for it to be useful. If the remote PC does not use a 16550, throughput will be severely limited, which will increase the number of packets dropped by the router.

The next external factor is the quality of the connection made between the local and remote modem by the telephone company switch. Even in a perfect system, you should expect around 3 percent of connections to fail because of poor connections provided by the telephone company switch. Significantly more failures can be experienced if one of the local loops from the telephone company central office to either the local or remote modem is of poor quality.

Some higher-end modems provide a front panel display that reports the dBm receive and transmit levels, the signal quality, and the error rate of the attached line. A poor signal quality or high error rate means you should contact the telephone company and have them check that local loop. In many cases, telephone companies will check only to determine that a dial tone is delivered by the local loop and will look no further. If this happens, it is useful to be able to quote the receive and transmit dBm levels. The receive dbm level should be around −9 to −15 dBm; if it is out of that range, the telephone company should be able to get the line back in specification.

We have appropriate router access lists, hold queues, buffer settings, V.34 modems for both the router interface and remote PC (which uses a 16550 UART), and good local loop dial connections at both ends. What else do we need to check?

The next thing to check is the setup of the modems used at both ends of the link. The setup for the modem attached to the remote PC is not so much of a problem, because it normally is initiated every time you make a new dial connection. Most PC communication programs have you identify the modem you are using and send an appropriate setup string prior to issuing the dial command. The modem connected to the router interface is, however, a different story. That modem normally sits there waiting for a connection to arrive from a remote modem and does not receive a setup string prior to that connection being made. This means that the modem should receive its setup prior to it having to answer any calls, and should have that setup saved to memory. It also means that you should have a way to initiate a modem remotely, if one loses its configuration or needs to be replaced.

A simple way to do this is to use modems that allow configuration via a front panel. An alternative is to connect the modem to a router asynchronous interface and initiate a reverse Telnet session to the interface to send setup commands to the modem. Let's say you are logged on to router 1 and want to initiate a reverse Telnet session to the first asynchronous port. You would accomplish this by entering the following:

```
Router1>telnet 193.1.1.1 2001
```

This assumes that 193.1.1.1 is an interface on the router that has its line protocol up. The number 20 has to precede the number of the asynchronous interface to which you wish to connect. If router 1 is an access server, such as the 2511 (which has 16 asynchronous ports), the 01 interface will be the first asynchronous interface. If router 1 is a 2501, the 01 interface is the auxiliary interface. On a 2511, the auxiliary interface is number 17. A Telnet session to an asynchronous interface will be refused only if a user already is connected on the interface, or the `modem inout` line command has not been executed. (We will review the configurations necessary for the line section later in this section.)

Once the Telnet session has been established, you can verify connectivity by typing the letters `AT` followed by the Enter key, to get an `OK` echoed back from the modem. You then can send the setup string appropriate for your modem and set it up the way you want. A typical setup string will have the modem answer after one ring, lock in the DTE rate to a given value, hang up the connection if the DTR signal is not present, set the DCD signal to high only on carrier detect, enable compression, utilize hardware flow control, and write this configuration to memory.

The item in the modem configuration just given that needs further explanation is locking of the *DTE rate*, which is the speed of communications from the modem to the router interface. Generally, modems set the DTE rate to automatic, meaning that the modem will set its DTE rate according to the speed of the communication sent from the device connected to it. In the case of a modem connected to a router interface used for dial-in connections, this does not work. For a dial-in connection, the modem initiates communication with the router interface. This means that nothing is being sent from the router to the modem to set the modem DTE rate. Therefore, the modem DTE rate must be preset in the modem to equal the DTE rate of the router async interface for the modem to initiate communications. If you are using V.34 modems, setting the router interface and modem DTE rate for 115,200 bps will give you the best potential for the highest throughput.

For serial interfaces, the `show` commands we made use of were the `show interface` and `show controllers` commands. For asynchronous interfaces, the `show interface` and `show line` commands provide the most useful information.

Taking the first asynchronous interface as an example, the `show interface async 1` command produces a screen display similar to that illustrated in Fig. 8-9.

The status reported for the interface still is given as up, even if carrier detect is not high, which is unlike the `show serial interface` display. The only time the interface will report a down condition is if the encapsulation type is not set for the interface. The line protocol display behaves the same as the line protocol for the serial interface. Other than the interface and line protocol status, the `show interface async 1` command is as useful for monitoring throughput, drops, and resets as it is for serial interfaces.

One additional set of information that the `show interface` command provides is related to the fact it uses PPP encapsulation. With this configuration, the `show` command reports the status of the PPP, LCP, and NCP protocols. These reports are the most valuable when multiple protocols are being used on the one link. For example,

Figure 8-9 Output of *show interface async 1* command

```
router2#show int async 1
Async1 is up, line protocol is down
  Hardware is Async Serial
  Interface is unnumbered. Using address of Ethernet0 (164.7.1.66)
  MTU 1500 bytes, BW 9 Kbit, DLY 100000 usec, rely 255/255, load 1/255
  Encapsulation PPP, loopback not set, keepalive set (10 sec)
  DTR is pulsed for 5 seconds on reset
  lcp state = REQSENT
  ncp ccp state = NOT NEGOTIATED ncp ipcp state = NOT NEGOTIATED
  ncp osicp state NOT NEGOTIATED ncp ipxcp state = NOT NEGOTIATED
  ncp xnscp state = NOT NEGOTIATED ncp vinescp state = NOT NEGOTIATED
  ncp deccp state = NOT NEGOTIATED ncp bridgecp state = NOT NEGOTIATED
  ncp atalkcp state = NOT NEGOTIATED ncp lex state = NOT NEGOTIATED
  ncp cdp state = NOT NEGOTIATED
  Last input never, oldput 0:00:00, output hang never
  Last clearing of "show interface" counters never
  Output queue 0/100, 0 drops; input queue 1/100, 0 drops
  5 minute input rate 0 bits/sec, 0 packets/sec
  5 minute output rate 0 bits/sec, 0 packets/sec
    0 packets input, 0 bytes, 0 no buffer
    Received 0 broadcasts, 0 runts, 0 giants
    0 input errors, 0 CRC, 0 frame, 0 overrun, 0 ignored, 0 abort
    36 packets output, 864 bytes, 0 underruns
    0 output errors, 0 collisions, 0 interface resets, 0 restarts
    0 output buff er failures, 0 output buffers swapped out
    0 carrier transitions
```

if IP and IPX are being used on this interface, you would expect to see the `ipcp` and `ipxcp` state as `negotiated` when a user has dialed in. If the user is experiencing difficulty in accessing some applications and not others over the dial link, it might be because one of the protocols has not successfully negotiated. In this situation, the interface and line protocol will report up, and the only indication that one of the protocols in use over the link has failed is the state of the NCP negotiations.

The major omission for the `show interface async 1` display is in reporting the status of EIA signals. This is given in the `show line 1` command, which is illustrated in Fig. 8-10.

The `show line` command displays the receive and transmit speeds set for that interface, whether hardware flow control has been set, and the status of the EIA signals CTS, DSR, DTR, and RTS. Unlike serial interfaces, in which all configuration is entered under the serial interface section, asynchronous interfaces have some things (such as encapsulation and hold queues) set on the interface, and DTE rate and modem control set under the line configuration. A typical line configuration that would appear in a router configuration file and be applied to asynchronous interfaces 1 through 16 is given as follows.

```
Line 1 16
modem inout
rxspeed 115200
txspeed 115200
```

All configuration changes made on line 1 will apply to asynchronous interface 1, and it is easiest just to think of the line commands as extensions to the interface configuration commands. The `rxspeed` and `txspeed` commands set the receive and transmit DTE rates to 115,200 (which has to match the setting for the DTE rate on the attached modem), and the `modem inout` command enables modem control for the interface.

The reporting of the EIA signals on the `show line 1` display is interesting. If no modem is connected to asynchronous interface 1, the EIA signals report:

noCTS noDSR DTR RTS

If a modem is attached that has CTS high, the EIA signals are reported as:

CTS noDSR DTR RTS

which is the normal display for an interface connected to a modem on which no remote modems currently are connected. (Your modem

Figure 8-10 Output of *show line* command

router2#**show line 1**
Tty Typ TxtRx A Modem Roty AccO Acci Uses Noise Overruns
A 1 TTY 9600/9600 - - - - - 0 0 0/0

Line 1, Location: "", Type: ""
Length: 24 lines, Width: 80 columns
Baud rate (TX/RX) is 9600/9600, no parity, 2 stopbits, 8 databits
Status: Ready, Active, Async interface active
Capabilities: Line is permanent async interface
Modem state: Ready
Special Chars: Escape Hold Stop Start Disconnect Activation
^^X none - none
Timeouts: Idle EXEC Idle Session Modem Answer Session Dispatch
0:10:00 never none not set
Session limit is not set.
Time since activation: never
Editing is enabled.
History is enabled, history size is 10.
Full user help is disabled
Allowed transports are pad telnet riogin. Preferred is telnet.
No output characters are padded
No special data dispatching characters
Modem hardware state: noCTS noDSR DTR RTS
Line is running PPP routing.
0 output packets queued, 1 input packets.
Async Escape map is 11111111111111111111111111111111

should be configured to have CTS high by default, lowering the signal only to throttle traffic.) When a remote modem calls in and establishes a connection, carrier detect will be raised on the modem and the EIA signals will be reported as:

CTS DSR DTR RTS

The connection from a 2511 router to a modem on an asynchronous interface is via an RJ-45 cable, which has eight wires. To improve the cable's ability to deal with interference, Cisco uses balanced wiring, which means that two wires rather than one wire are dedicated to transporting a signal, and therefore only four EIA signals can be reported. The interesting thing about this implementation is that the reported status of DSR on the screen display actually reports the status of the DCD signal coming out of the modem. This might be confusing the first time you monitor it, but as long as you are aware of this condition, the display works well.

Debug Commands for Asynchronous Connections. The most usual encapsulation for an asynchronous interface is the PPP encapsulation. If you're troubleshooting the interface and line configuration on the router and the modem connections, setup, and telephone line do not resolve problems, you can get additional information from the `debug ppp` commands.

The `debug ppp` command can be followed by one of four keywords: `packet`, `negotiation`, `errors`, or `chap`. The screen outputs from these commands are hard to understand and it's difficult to derive useful information from them. If this command does generate screen output, however, at least you know that everything on the Physical layer is working. If you have to resort to using these commands, start with the `debug ppp errors` and report these to Cisco technical support. The type of problems that are resolved by the debug commands are usually related to improper PPP commands being sent by a faulty PPP driver on the remote PC, which these days is a rare occurrence.

Asynchronous Troubleshooting Summary. If you have a correctly configured remote PC and modem that can successfully dial in to one interface, but not to another, the steps outlined next will help identify where the problem lies.

1. Use the `show line` command and check that the CTS signal is present, to prove that the modem is connected to the correct interface and powered up.

2. Check that the line `rxspeed` and `txspeed` match that of the modem.
3. Check all the modem settings and the operation of the telephone line attached to the modem. (Connecting the line to an analog telephone handset lets you hear if the line is okay.)
4. Check encapsulation and CHAP setting for the interface.
5. Use the `debug ppp` command to see if PPP errors are being reported and seek help from Cisco technical support if necessary.

If communication over the asynchronous link is poor, do the following:

1. Check the number of drops and buffer pool misses and increase the size of hold queues or buffer pools that are experiencing problems.
2. Check your modem for reports on the telephone line quality and dBm levels.
3. Check the speed of modem connection; it should be at or above 21.6 kbps. If it is not, try to change telephone lines on either or both ends.
4. Make sure that the DTE rate for all device interfaces is 115,200 bps and compression is enabled on both modems.
5. Check that the remote PC has a 16550 UART chip in use in its serial port.

Troubleshooting Ethernet

Compared to the problems encountered with serial and asynchronous interfaces, troubleshooting the setup of Cisco Ethernet interfaces is simple. The most common problems on Ethernet interfaces have nothing to do with how the router is set up; rather, the problems typically involve overutilization of bandwidth, a high number of collisions, or systems using incompatible frame types.

Collisions, drops, utilization (as reported by throughput), and frame type are reported on the `show interface ethernet 0` command as illustrated in Fig. 8-2. Other problems, such as LAN card drivers incorrectly forming frames that are either too long (giants) or too short (runts), are rare these days. The major challenges of implementing Ethernet networks are in the areas of physical design and management of cabling systems. We will review how Cisco IOS screen displays report typical Ethernet problems.

Once the Ethernet interface and line protocol report an up condition, which is achieved by connecting the Ethernet interface to a hub, little optimization can be achieved through interface configuration. The most significant factor in serial line performance problems we examined was with packet drops. You rarely see drops on an Ethernet interface, even on a heavily utilized segment. The only time drops are likely to become a factor is when you have a router connecting a heavily utilized FDDI ring and an Ethernet segment. The FDDI ring operates at a much higher rate than the Ethernet and may overwhelm the Ethernet interface with packets that need to be switched onto the Ethernet segment. If this happens in your internetwork, the same steps used in optimizing a serial interface, i.e., of disabling fast switching by use of the `no ip route-cache` command on the Ethernet interface, and adjusting buffers and hold queues, might help.

In most cases, drops on an Ethernet interface are rare. This is due in part to the way Ethernet operates. Any node at any time can transmit on the LAN cable as long as no other node is using the cable. Therefore packets are stored in a router for a relatively short period of time before being switched out an Ethernet interface and do not get held in buffers or hold queues. On an Ethernet interface, congestion normally displays itself through packet collisions after the packets have been transmitted out of an interface.

Collisions occur when two interfaces try to transmit a packet onto the network cable at the same time. A small number of collisions is expected in an Ethernet network, but the obvious question is what constitutes "a small number." That is different for each network; if you see a collision more than once every 3 to 5 seconds, you should investigate the source.

The source of collisions usually is the result of cabling that is too long, overly high utilization, or what is commonly referred to as a *deaf node,* one that has faulty circuitry that keeps it from hearing other nodes using the network cable.

Again, we have the question of what utilization is too high. Again the answer is that it is different for every network. If your network has a high percentage of broadcast packets, the utilization at which performance starts to degrade will be lower than for a network with few broadcasts. Typically, if the network utilization reaches 40 percent, you can expect problems. The way you detect utilization on a Cisco router is by the throughput on the interface. This statistic as reported by the 5-minute average is not particularly useful, as short peaks in utilization are not reported. If your router is reporting excessive collisions for any reason, you are better off using a LAN analyzer to determine if utilization is the cause of the problem.

Out-of-specification cabling causes more collisions because a node will listen to the network cable for a set period of time before determining that no other node is using it. The further away another node is, the greater the propagation delay of the signal from that node to the listening node. If a node is further away than the specification states, there will be more instances when a listening node determines that the network cable is free, when in fact the cable is carrying a packet that has not yet reached the listening node. Under such conditions, a collision will result when the listening node transmits a packet.

The only time you should have to look closely at the router Ethernet interface configuration is when the interface and line protocol report an up state and all physical connections to another node are good, but they still cannot communicate. The probable cause of this problem is that the two nodes are using incompatible frame types. The frame type is displayed on the output of the `show interface ethernet 0` command. If you know the frame type used by the other node, it should be a simple mater to match them up.

If you need to communicate with two devices on the same network that use different frame types, you can use sub-interfaces on the router interface and assign different encapsulation frame types for each sub-interface. A sample configuration for assigning both the `ethernet_ii` and `novell-ether` (802.3) frame types to different sub-interfaces on the Ethernet 0 physical interface for a Novell network is given here.

```
Interface ethernet 0.1
ipx network 1234 encapsulation arpa
Interface ethernet 0.2
ipx network 5678 encapsulation novell-ether
```

As you see, each sub-interface is considered a different network, since it is not possible to assign different frame types to the same interface for the same network number.

Troubleshooting Token-Ring

Token-Ring and Ethernet both handle communication between computer nodes on a local area network. That is where the similarity between these two technologies ends, however. Token-Ring is a deterministic system, which means that its performance is always predictable (in theory) and that only one node on the network has the choice of using the network at any given time. This is achieved by having a special packet, called the `token`, that constantly circulates the ring. The only node that can transmit is the one with the token. This method eliminates the possibility of collisions, but does potentially waste transmission time by always asking all nodes if they have anything to send on the network, even if they have nothing to send.

Because Token-Ring interfaces have to hold packets for transmission until the router receives the token, you sometimes need to adjust hold queue sizes from the default to eliminate packet drops. Drops are reported in the `show interface tokenring` command, as illustrated in Fig. 8-11.

When a Token-Ring network is initialized, one node on the ring is elected the *Active Monitor*. This node is responsible for monitoring the passage of the token around the ring, deleting duplicate tokens if they occur, and generally making sure that everything runs smoothly. The process of electing an Active Monitor is transparent to network users and to network administrators. The `show interface tokenring` command will display the ring status as "initializing" if the router has just been connected to the ring. This is because the router interface will need to be added into the sequence of computers to receive the token.

Figure 8-11 Output of the *show interface tokenring 0* command

```
Router1>show int to0
Tokenring0 is up, line protocol is up
Hardware is TMS380, address is 0000.3Oe2.c44d
Internet address is 194.3.3.2 255.255.255.0
MTU 4464 bytes, BW 16000 Kbit, DLY 630 usec, rely, 255/255, load 1/255 Encapsulation
SNAP, loopback not set, keepalive set (10 sec)
ARP type: SNAP, ARP timeout 4:00j0
Ring speed: 16Mbps
Single ring node, Transparent Bridge Capable
Group address: 0x00000000, Functional Address: 0x08800000
Ethernet Transit OUI: 0x0000F8
Last input0:00:00, output 0:00:00, output hang never
Last clearing of "show interface" counters never
Output queue 0/40, 0 drops: input queue 0/100, 0 drops
5 minute input rate 9000 bits/sec, 9 packets/sec
5 minute output rate 1000 bhs/sec, 3 packets/sec
   7471015 packets input, 1593087959 bytes, 0 no buffer
   Received 8888699 broadcasts, 0 runts, 0 giants
   0 input errors, 0 CRC, 0 frame, 0 overrun, 0 ignored, 0 abort
   2902191 packets output, 253383249 bytes, 0 underruns
   0 output errors, 0 collisions, 1 interface resets, 0 restarts
   0 output buffer failures, 0 output buffers swapped out
   4 transitions
```

This process is referred to as the router interface "being inserted into the ring." If a hardware error has occurred, the `show interface tokenring` command will report an interface status of Reset.

The most common problems reported on token rings are incompatible ring speeds, ring beaconing conditions, source routing not enabled, or a large number of transitions. Ring speeds can be set either to 4 Mbps or to 16 Mbps with the commands shown as follows.

```
Router1(config)#interface tokenring 0
Router1(config-int)#ring-speed 4
```

The default is 16 Mbps, and if the interface is changed to 4 Mbps with the command above, the interface speed can be changed back again with the `ring-speed 16` configuration command. The current ring speed setting is given in the screen display of the `show interface tokenring` command.

Ring beaconing occurs when a serious problem with a network component, such as the cabling, Multistation Access Unit (MSAU), or a node interface is detected. As a token gets passed around a ring, each node receives the token from its *Nearest Active Upstream Neighbor* (NAUN). Should a node not receive a valid token from its NAUN, the node will report a beacon condition to all other stations on the network. In theory, this should initiate an auto-reconfiguration process, whereby the suspect NAUN and node reporting the beacon are taken out of the ring and normal operation is restored for the rest of the ring. I have rarely seen this work in practice. If a serious problem exists and a node sends out beacon frames, the problem generally has to be fixed by manual intervention before the ring is operational again.

Source routing was discussed in detail in Chap. 5. The `show interface tokenring` command display tells you whether the interface is configured for source routing. The display will either indicate the interface is a `single ring node` or `multi-ring node`. Multi-ring nodes are enabled to collect and utilize RIF field information and therefore can participate in source routing. This line also tells you the type of bridging for which the interface is enabled. The interface whose `show interface tokenring` command is displayed in Fig. 8-11 is enabled only for transparent bridging and not for source route bridging. For the commands needed to enable source route bridging on an interface, refer to the section on Chap. 5 on source route bridging.

If transitions are reported on an interface, it indicates that the ring made a transition from an up to a down state, or vice versa. A continually increasing count of transitions means that either the ring or the router interface are experiencing problems and you need to investigate cabling and hardware problems.

There are other commands that will give you information on Token-Ring packets, but little additional information is presented that will assist in the resolution of common problems. When working with Cisco technical support, you may be required to note the displays given by the `show controllers tokenring` command, which gives information on the hardware interface and summary packet statistics. The other command that sometimes is used is the `debug tokenring` command that identifies the MAC source and destination addresses for every packet that passes through the interface.

Troubleshooting Protocol Problems

In this section we'll cover two main areas. First, we will look at troubleshooting general IP connectivity related to routing protocol issues. Second, we'll examine basic troubleshooting for popular WAN protocols. In both of these sections we will consider troubleshooting lost connectivity and poor performance.

Troubleshooting IP Connectivity

The usual way to determine if a device is reachable via the IP protocol on an internetwork is by using the ping utility. Ping sends an ICMP packet from the source to the specified destination. If successful, the returned ping packet proves that all Physical, Data Link, and Network layer functions are operating correctly from the source to the destination. For the purposes of this discussion, failed IP connectivity will mean that a ping packet does not get a reply. It will be assumed that all physical connections are in place and all interfaces and line protocols are up along the path from source to destination. Initially, the discussion focuses on distance vector protocols; a section on OSPF follows.

Troubleshooting Distance Vector Protocols. If a ping is failing in an internetwork with good Physical and Data Link connections, the first place to look are the routing tables of all routing devices between the source and destination. Each one in turn should have an entry that states the next hop for the ultimate destination network number. For example, if you are trying to ping a device with an IP address of 164.7.8.33 and the netmask in use on your internetwork is 255.255.255.224, then you would expect to see an entry for the subnet 164.7.8.32 in all the routing tables between the ping source and its destination.

This simple statement, although neat, might not be always true. Suppose the device from which you are sending the ping is on the 170.5.0.0 network and, as routes are summarized at the boundary between major network numbers, each of the devices on this network will have only one entry in its routing table for the 164.7.0.0 network. Once the path from source to destination takes you from the 170.5.0.0 network into the 164.7.0.0 network, you expect to see entries for the 164.7.32.0 subnet. In addition, you expect to see entries in the routing table of all the devices from the destination to the source, for the source's subnet number, so that the ping reply can find its way back to the source.

So what do we do if one of the devices is missing a routing table entry? The first thing is to check that each device has a routing protocol appropriately enabled. This means that all devices need a routing protocol enabled for the same autonomous system number, and network entries need to be configured for each network that is directly attached to a router.

By viewing the configuration of all the routing devices from source to destination, you confirm that all devices are in fact correctly configured for a routing protocol. What next? You probably want to use some debug commands, starting with `debug ip igrp events`, which tells you which hosts sent IGRP information and to which hosts IGRP information was sent. The `debug ip igrp transactions` command details the content of the IGRP updates received and sent in terms of the network numbers and their associated metrics. In a network using RIP, `debug ip rip` tells you the content of routing updates and which routers they are sent to and received from. Figure 8-12 provides sample outputs from these commands.

If the Physical and Data Link layer connections between the source and destination are good and the routing protocols are correctly configured but appropriate routes still do not appear in all the routing tables necessary, the output from these commands should give a clue as to where the route information is being dropped. The route information might be dropped because of passive interfaces, incorrectly configured redistribution, access lists, or distribute lists.

Assuming the output of the debug commands identifies where in the chain of routers from source to destination the required routing information is being dropped, you can examine the configuration of the suspect

Figure 8-12
Control statements and the number of paths they generate

LOG OUTPUT OF DEBUG IP IGRP EVENTS COMMAND

```
IGRP: received update from invalid source 193.1.1.1 on Ethernet0
IGRP: received update from 164.7.1.98 on Serial0
IGRP: Update contains 0 interior, 1 system, and 0 exterior routes.
IGRP: Total routes in update: 1
IGRP: sending update to 255.255.255.255 via Ethernet0 (164.7.1.66)
IGRP: Update contains 1 interior, 1 system, and 0 exterior routes.
IGRP: Total routes in update: 2
IGRP: sending update to 255.255.255.255 via Serial0 (164.7.1.97)
IGRP: Update contains 1 interior, 0 system, and 0 exterior routes.
IGRP: Total routes in update: 1
```

The first line is interesting as it identifies an IGRP update that appeared on this interface from a source on a different network number and is therefore not accepted on this interface. The rest of the display identifies valid updates received and sent via broadcast.

LOG OUTPUT OF DEBUG IP IGRP TRANSACTIONS COMMAND

```
IGRP: sending update to 255.255.255.255 via Ethernet0 (164.7.1.66)
    subnet 164.7.1.96, metric=8476
    network 193.1.1.0, metric=8576
IGRP: sending update to 255.255.255.255 via Serial0 (164.7.1.97)
    subnet 164.7.1.64, metric=1100
IGRP: received update from invalid source 193.1.1.1 on Ethernet0
IGRP: received update from 164.7.1.98 on Serial0
    network 193.1.1.0, metric 8576 (neighbor 1100)
```

This command logs more detailed information on each routing update received and sent.

LOG OUTPUT OF DEBUG IP RIP COMMAND

```
RIP: sending update to 255.255.255.255 via Serial0 (164.7.1.97)
RIP: Update contains 1 routes
RIP: received update from invalid source 193.1.1.1 on Ethernet0
RIP: received update from 164.7.1.98 on Serial0
    193.1.1.0 in 1 hops
RIP: sending update to 255.255.255.255 via Ethernet0 (164.7.1.66)
    subnet 164.7.1.96, metric 1
    network 193.1.1.0, metric 2
```

This log output shows the detail of RIP updates sent and received, including the interface received on and route metrics.

router to check for any passive interfaces that will not send out any routing updates, or those that have a distribute list applied. Distribute lists are useful if you want to reduce the size of routing updates sent. A distribute list works with a defined access list to identify the routes that will be advertised and the routes that will not. An example configuration of this combination is given here, allowing updates only from the 164.7.0.0 network number for the IGRP protocol.

```
access-list 1 permit 164.7.0.0
router igrp 11
network 164.7.0.0
distribute-list 1 out
```

If there are no impediments to routing information by passive interfaces or distribution lists, incorrectly configured redistribution could be causing route update problems. If you suspect redistribution, the first thing to check is the default metric configured for redistributed routes. If this is missing or using a value that makes subsequent routers discard the route information, an adjustment in its value is necessary.

Having covered typical problems with Network layer configuration that result in lost connectivity, what can we do if two nodes can communicate, but there is a severe performance problem? We first would look at Physical and Data Link issues, such as performance of leased lines, framing or line errors, buffers, and hold queues. If checking these areas fails to cover any problems, we can examine what is happening at the Network layer to cause slow performance. The best tool for diagnosing performance problems that are suspected to being due to Network layer operation is the Cisco `trace` command. An example of the use of trace is given in Fig. 8-13.

In the first part of the display, we see how `trace` reports a successful ping from router 1 to router 3 through router 2 in the lab setup of three routers we have used throughout the book. The trace reports the path that is taken from source to destination. The second part of Fig. 8-13 shows an unsuccessful trace. Here, the `trace` command reports that the router can find the subnet where the destination IP address should be located, but it cannot find the host on the subnet, so it queries all devices it knows about on this subnet to see if they know about the target address. This display will continue indefinitely until it is stopped by the break sequence (pressing the Ctrl and 6 keys simultaneously).

With internetworks that are either poorly designed, or which are experiencing a fault condition, the paths selected for routes can become suboptimal, leading to poor performance. A typical example of this is if

Figure 8-13
Use of the *trace* command

```
Router1>trace ip 164.7.1.97

Type escape sequence to abort.
Tracing the route to 164.7.1.97

  1 164.7.1.66 4 msec 4 msec*

Router1>trace ip 164.7.1.98

Type escape sequence to abort.
Tracing the route to 164.7.1.98

  1 164.7.1.66 4 msec 4 msec 4 msec
  2 164.7.1.98 20 msec 20 msec*

Router1>trace ip 164.7.1.99

Type escape sequence to abort.
Tracing the route to 164.7.1.99

  1 164.7.1.66 4 msec 4 msec 4 msec
  2 164.7.1.98 16 msec 20 msec 16 msec
  3 164.7.1.97 16 msec 16 msec 16 msec
  4 164.7.1.98 32 msec 32 msec 32 msec
  5 164.7.1.97 32 msec
Router1 >
```

a bridge or repeater is connected through the internetwork to two interfaces on a router. This will lead to a router receiving duplicate routing updates—effectively receiving the same updates on two interfaces. This is a condition that a router cannot deal with effectively, and unpredictable routing decisions result. The `trace` command output can identify these types of problems by reporting the path packets take from source to destination. If a suboptimal path is taken, the interconnections made on the internetwork need to be examined to resolve any conditions that the routing protocols cannot handle.

Overview of OSPF Troubleshooting. OSPF and other link state protocols are more complex to troubleshoot than distance vector protocols. The problem we will consider initially is that of a ping packet that is not returned successfully from a remote host. Assuming that the Physical and Data Link layers have checked out and that all devices have OSPF enabled for the same autonomous system number, troubleshooting an OSPF internetwork starts off in the same way as for an IGRP internetwork. The first task is to review the routing table entries, because each routing device from source to destination must have routing table entries that enable a packet to be routed in both directions for a ping request to be successful.

Assuming that the ping fails because of a lack of routing table entries, we would look first for any passive interfaces or distribute lists stopping the route information from being disseminated. If none exists, the OSPF configuration for each router device must be reviewed. All interfaces that are to participate in OSPF routing need to have the network numbers to which they belong listed in the network commands that are entered as subcommands under the OSPF major command.

You can check whether OSPF is running on all expected interfaces by issuing the `show ip ospf interface` command for each interface. (A sample display was illustrated in Fig. 4-17.) Obviously, any interface that is not reporting OSPF information for this command is incorrectly configured and needs to be investigated.

Another useful command for troubleshooting at this level is the `show ip ospf neighbor` command, illustrated in Fig. 8-14, which identifies all the neighbors the router knows about via the OSPF protocol. If a router that you expect to see on this list does not show up, further investigation into the missing router's configuration is required.

If all the routers appear in the `show ip ospf neighbor` and all interfaces are enabled for OSPF, but you still cannot ping the desired host, check to make sure that each OSPF area has at least one border

Figure 8-14 Output of the *show IP OSPF neighbor* command

```
Router1#show ip ospf neighbor
ID                 Pri    State                      Dead Time      Address
        Interface
193.1.1.137    1    FULL/DR                  0:00:31      160.8.8.3       Ethernet0
193.3.4.1      1    FULL/DROTHER             0:00:33      160.3.48.1      Serial0
192.1.8.2      1    FULL/DROTHER             0:00:33      160.3.48.20     Serial0
193.1.1.1      5    5                  FULL/DR      0:00:33         160.3.48.18
        Serial0

Router1#show ip ospf neighbor 193.1.1.37
 Neighbor 193.1.1.37, interface address 160.8.8.3
   In the area 0.0.0.0 via interface Ethernet0
   Neighbor priority is 1, State is FULL
   Options 2
   Dead timer due in 0:00:32
   Link State retransmission due in 0:00:04
Neighbor 193.1.1.37, interface address 192.31.48.189
   In the area 0.0.0.0 via interface Seriali0
   Neighbor priority is 5, State is FULL
   Options 2
   Dead timer due in 0:00:32
   Link State retransmission due in 0:00:03
```

The ID is the router ID of the OSPF neighbor, Pri is the priority of this router that affects it being chosen as a designated router, Address is the source address of the interface that advertised this router, which was received through the interface listed.

router and that border router is connected to area 0. The only way to check this is by viewing the configuration of the border router. This is an important configuration requirement for OSPF internetworks, as all interarea communication has to go through area 0.

The last consideration is that of mismatched hello and dead timers. These timers can be viewed in the `show ip ospf interface` display. The value for these timers should be the same for all interfaces. If mismatched values are found, they can be altered in interface configuration mode by the `ip ospf dead-interval` and `ip ospf hello-interval` commands.

Troubleshooting Packet-Oriented WAN Protocols

This section will provide the essential information for initial troubleshooting of the packet-oriented WAN protocols, frame relay and X.25. The focus of this section is to explore why nodes might not be communicating for each of the protocols considered. Typically, there is more in the router configuration of an X.25 connection that can cause intermittent or poor performance than in a frame relay connection.

A frame relay connection is normally configured for connection to a public network, and performance issues with this type of connection are generally linked to the public network itself, or to Physical layer issues such as noisy lines or router buffer problems. Troubleshooting noisy lines and router buffer problems for frame relay follow the same process as described previously. We shall therefore look mainly at what can cause connectivity to fail in a frame relay environment. With X.25, we will look at router issues that can contribute to poor performance as well as to no connectivity.

Troubleshooting Lack of Connectivity over Frame Relay. The most usual configuration for connecting a router to a public frame relay network is for the public frame relay network to send *data link connection identifier* (DLCI) information to the router via an agreed LMI interface type. Again assuming that everything at the Physical and Data Link layers are working and that the `show interface serial` command reports an up condition for both interface and line protocol status, we will first want to see if LMI information is being received and sent.

The place to start is with the `show frame-relay map` command, as shown in Fig. 6-8, which will tell you if the router has successfully learned of the remote device protocol IDs. If this process has failed, there will be no entries in the display of this command. The process that should take place is that the *local management interface* (LMI) informs the router of the available DLCI numbers and the router uses inverse ARP to determine the protocol address of the devices at the other end of the PVCs identified by the DLCIs.

If a router is not registering the available DLCIs on its frame relay connection (which can be determined by issuing the `show frame-relay PVC` command as illustrated in Fig. 6-8), you should determine whether the switch is sending the information via the LMI. In this situation, the `debug frame-relay lmi` command should be used. If the frame relay switch is sending DLCI numbers via the LMI, they will be listed in the output of this command. If this debug command lists DLCI numbers being sent by the frame relay switch that are not shown in the `show frame relay map` command, the LMI type used by the router should be confirmed as correct. If no DLCI numbers are listed, you need to contact the company supplying the frame relay connection to have the frame relay switch send the correct data.

This covers LMI operation; checking whether Inverse ARP worked is a little more tricky. If the router learns about its DLCI numbers, but does not establish entries in its `show frame-relay map` command output, there are two possibilities. Either the two nodes communicating over the frame relay network are not configured to send broadcast routing updates, or the frame relay network is improperly configured. Chapter 6 covered setup of broadcast IGRP updates over frame relay links, and I will not repeat that here. If you find a situation in which the router knows of its DLCI numbers, and you are sure that all connected devices are set up for broadcast, and that IGRP, or some other appropriate routing protocol, is properly enabled on the connected devices, you have to inform the frame relay provider that Inverse ARP is not working over the network and seek help. In the meantime, static maps can be entered into the router with the `frame-relay map` command.

Troubleshooting Lack of Connectivity over X.25. There are many similarities between a frame relay link and an X.25 link, such as the use of packet switching, PVC and SVC allocation, and support for multiple logical connections being established over a single physical connection. The differences between the two technologies are significant enough, however, to justify different troubleshooting procedures.

In frame relay, the DLCI number provides the key to delivering traffic on a frame relay connection. In X.25, the X.121 address is the key addressing element. A DLCI and an X.121 address are very different things. The DLCI has only local significance, so the same DLCI number can be assigned at both ends of the link and it will still work. The X.121 address, by contrast, has significance throughout the X.25 network and is an address that can be used to identify a single host on the network. Also, X.25 does not have the same Inverse ARP capabilities, so the router's configuration must be filled with all the necessary X.25 map statements to map IP to X.25 addresses.

Having established that X.25 is a very different type of packet switching technology to frame relay, let's consider how to resolve X.25 issues that can result in no connectivity across a network, then those that result in poor connectivity.

The case that we will use for this discussion is of two IP networks interconnected via an X.25 network, which is similar to the configuration used in the discussion on configuring X.25 interfaces in Chap. 6.

Assuming that all the Physical layer issues having to do with leased lines and cables are operational but connectivity across the X.25 network is still not available, we need consider what at the X.25 level can stop communication. The first thing to do is determine that the X.121 addresses are correct, both for the address assigned to your X.25 interface and those used to address remote hosts in the X.25 `map` statements.

Next, check that one of the devices is configured as an X.25 DTE and the other as an X.25 DCE. This has nothing to do with the DTE and DCE that we talk about at the Data Link level, where we are concerned with the DCE supplying a clock signal for synchronization. In X.25, there is a DTE and DCE specification at the Network layer as well as at the Data Link layer. The default condition is for the interface to be configured as an X.25 DTE. To change it to DCE, the encapsulation configuration command must be entered as `encapsulation x25 dce`.

Next, check whether routing updates are getting from and to the remote locations. To do this, you must view the configuration of the routers and make sure that all the X.25 `map` statements include the keyword `broadcast`. This keyword ensures that IGRP or other routing protocol updates are transported over the X.25 network to all remote locations defined in the X.25 `map` statements.

The remaining issues that we shall consider can degrade performance, or in severe cases, deny connectivity altogether over an X.25 network.

The `show interface serial` command output for an interface with X.25 encapsulation (as illustrated in Chap. 6), lists *frame reject* (REJ), *Receiver Not Ready* (RNR), *Frame Error* (FRMR), *line disconnects* (DISC) and *protocol restart* (RESTART) values that should all be low, by which I mean less than 0.5 percent of the number of information frames (IFRAME). If any of these values is greater than this 0.5 percent number, there is a problem either at the Physical level with the hardware and leased lines, or there is a configuration mismatch. With X.25 connections, you need to be concerned about matching the configuration of many variables for the connected devices at both the LAPB and X.25 level to ensure optimum communication. Table 8.2 lists the ID of the variable as reported in `show interface serial` and `show x25 vc` commands, a description of this variable, and the configuration command to change the variable.

If you can verify cabling, hardware, and leased-line operation; have appropriate addresses and X.25 DTE/DCE configuration; and can verify that all of the variables listed in Table 8.1 are compatible between the two communication devices, there should be no reason to stop communication. If problems still exist, the last resort is to connect a serial line analyzer and see if one end is sending the SABM initialization sequence and the other is responding with UA frames. If all the troubleshooting activities listed here check out okay (i.e., that everything is functioning as it should), you should contact the X.25 network vendor and ask for assistance in resolving any other issues.

The outputs of the `debug lapb` and `debug x25` commands provide extensive and in-depth analysis of the communication between X.25-connected devices. If you are going to spend considerable amounts of time with LAPB and X.25 communication problems, it is worth referring to the Cisco documentation or talking to a Cisco Systems engineer.

Summary

In this chapter, we presented a troubleshooting blueprint that recommends that you start troubleshooting from the Physical layer, then move up the OSI layers through the Data Link and Network layers to the network application. The basic troubleshooting scenario presented in Chap. 3 was reviewed, followed by troubleshooting for serial interfaces, asynchronous communications, Ethernet, Token-Ring, frame relay, and X.25 protocols.

TABLE 8.2 LAPB and X.25 Configuration Variables

ID of the Variable	Description	Configuration Command
LAPB T1	Retransmission timer, or how long the router will wait for an acknowledgment before polling for a response	lapb t1 (value in milliseconds)
LAPB N1	Maximum bits per frame	lapb n1 (no. of bits)
LAPB N2	Number of retransmit attempts allowed before the link is declared down	lapb n2 (no. of tries)
LAPB k	LAPB window size, the maximum number of frames that can be transmitted before an acknowledgment is required	lapb k (number)
LAPB modulo	Frame numbering scheme, the maximum window size is the modulo less 1	lapb modulo (8 or 128)
channels: incoming, two-way, outgoing	The lowest and highest permissible incoming, outgoing, and two-way X.25 logical channel numbers	x25 lic, hic, ltc, htc, loc, hoc
x25 modulo	The packet sequence numbering scheme	x25 modulo (8 or 128)
window size input, output	The window size configured for X.25 inbound and outbound packets	x25 win, wout
packet size input, output	The maximum X.25 packet size	x25 ips, ops
x25 timers	T10—13 for a DCE and T20—23 for DTE, set the restart, call, reset, and clear timers	x25 t10 t11, t12, t13, t20, t21, t22, t23

S. Swan

INDEX

E

F

G

H

I

L

M

N

S

T

U

V

W

X